PUBLIC POLICY

Continuity and Change

Carter A. Wilson
University of Toledo

WAVELAND
PRESS, INC.
Long Grove, Illinois

For information about this book, contact:
Waveland Press, Inc.
4180 IL Route 83, Suite 101
Long Grove, IL 60047-9580
(847) 634-0081
info@waveland.com
www.waveland.com

For Letta, Karim, Mustafah, and Sayedah,
my children and grandchildren—
the future belongs to you.

Brief Contents

Contents

PART III

Protective and Competitive Regulatory Policy

PART V
Distributive Policy

Preface

There are several goals of this text. The first goal is to provide students with a broad survey of public policy theory in a language that is clear and comfortable for undergraduate students and useful for graduate students. The second goal is to offer brief historical sketches of the evolution of select public policies. These sketches are designed to build a foundation for understanding contemporary public policies and for ascertaining why policies exist, how they develop, and why they take the shape they do. The third goal is to use policy theory to explain continuity and change in public policies. Several public policy theories are examined: pluralist, elitist, state centered, and social movement theories. These theories attempt to explain long-term patterns of public policy stability and period of massive policy change. Although the text provides a heavy dosage of policy theory, it is mostly about specific public policies. The fourth goal is to provide an instructive examination of a wide range of different types of public policies. The text focuses on distributive (economic and educational policies), redistributive (social welfare), competitive regulatory (communications and antitrust policies), protective regulatory (environmental protection), and morality policies (abortion policies). Finally, the intent of the text is to contribute to some insights into policy controversies and debates, to assist in building a balanced perspective, to help avoid the mistakes of the past, and to nurture thoughtful students of policy analysis.

↠ Acknowledgments

I am grateful to the many reviewers who read several drafts of this book, provided helpful and constructive comments, and helped it grow and improve: Robert Bilodeau, South Plains College; Gerald Blasi, University of Missouri, St. Louis; William Cunion, Ohio University; Brian Fife, Indiana University–Purdue University, Fort Wayne; John L. Foster, Southern Illinois University; James A. Gazell, San Diego State University; Doug Goodman, Mississippi State University; Eugene R. Goss, Long Beach City College; Martin Gruber, University of Wisconsin, Oshkosh; Linda Gugin, Indiana University Southeast; Glen S. Krutz, University of Oklahoma; Robert Kulisheck, Northern Michigan University; Matthew J. Lindstrom, Siena College; Barbara Coyle McCabe, Arizona State University; Eric Monkkonen, University of California, Los Angeles; Barbara Neuby, Kennesaw State University; Scott E. Robinson, University of Texas at Dallas; Richard T. Saeger, Valdosta State University; Charles Shipan, University of Iowa; Jonathan West, University of Miami; and Denis J. Woods, Shepherd College.

I am thankful for the support, encouragement, and feedback from my colleagues and graduate students at The University of Toledo. I owe special thanks to my brother David Wilson for reading early drafts of the first few chapters and two of the policy chapters, to Cary Kart for reading the chapter on health care policy, to Ronald Randall for reading the chapter on social welfare policy, to Renee Heberle for reading the fertility control policy chapter, to Ed Bollinger for advice with the chapter on criminal justice, and to David Davis for his insights on environmental policy. I owe thanks to James Hogan of Seattle University who also read the first draft of the first four chapters and provided constructive comments and words of encouragement. I give credit to my colleagues whose comments helped make a better book, but I take full responsibility for the faults that remain.

Carter A. Wilson
The University of Toledo

About the Author

Carter A. Wilson is a professor and director of the Master of Public Administration program in the Department of Political Science and Public Administration at The University of Toledo. He earned his PhD in political science from Wayne State University in 1982. He has published several articles in scholarly journals including *Administration and Society*, the *Journal of Public Policy*, *Urban Affairs Quarterly*, the *Urban Education Review*, and many others. He is the author of *Racism from Slavery to Advanced Capitalism* and a contributing author to Bryan Jones and Lynn Bachelor's book, *The Sustaining Hand*.

Introduction

Public policy issues are everywhere. They are visible in the news: on television and radio, in newspapers and magazines. Examples of public policy issues include abortion, gun control, affirmative action, school prayer, school vouchers, capital punishment, and many more. Debates over these issues are sometimes intense. Some issues, such as abortion, are so intense that people fight over them. Pro-choice and pro-life groups have engaged in shouting matches against each other in public and in the streets. There have been cases of violence against abortion clinics.

This textbook is about public policy. It examines many different contemporary public policy issues. It covers the debates and fights over these issues, such as the pros and cons over abortion. It takes somewhat of a historical and theoretical approach.

The historical approach helps explain why we have government and public policies. It helps to develop a greater respect and appreciation for the policies and government programs that exist today. The theoretical approach provides the tools needed to understand the issues, to explain how they developed, and to predict how they will evolve in the future. Theory presents ideas that help explain the world. It focuses attention on specific aspects of policy, consists of models useful for analyzing contemporary problems and issues, and offers a broader understanding of public policy debates.

The study of policy history and theory helps answer these critical public policy questions: What are public policies? Why do we have them? What are different types of public policies? What are some of the more controversial policy issues today? What are the different positions on the issues? Why do we have government? Why does the government attempt to solve certain types of problems and ignore others? What is and has been the government's response to the different public policy issues?

→ *Explaining Continuity and Change in Public Policy*

The central question in this text is why are public policies stable and why do they change—that is, what explains continuity and change in public policies? Public policies tend to be stable over time. They change slowly and in tiny steps. Periodically, however, they change profoundly. Public policy making over time is characterized by a pattern of long-term stability, interrupted by a short period of substantial change. Consider four examples of public policies that follow this pattern of continuity and change: clean air, abortion/birth control, civil rights, and homeland security.

Clean air policy is one example. From 1900 to 1970 the federal government did nothing to regulate air pollution, although there was a dirty air problem in cities like Chicago, Detroit, Gary, and Pittsburgh, especially with the rapid expansion and concentration of the steel and automobile industries. Air pollution had been a serious problem wherever industries were concentrated. In the 1950s the federal government allocated some money to study the dirty air problem. Congress enacted a few clean air bills in the early 1960s, encouraging states to develop plans for addressing the problem. However, there were no real federal clean air regulations throughout much of the 20th century. Then, all of a sudden, Congress passed the Clean Air Act of 1970, created the Environmental Protection Agency, and mandated the reduction of polluting gases such as carbon monoxide and carbon dioxide. The passage of the Clean Air Act of 1970 marked a profound change from past policies.

Consider, for another example, sexual reproduction policies. Initially, these policies were liberal in the United States; abortions and contraceptives were permitted with few restrictions until the last quarter of the 19th century. However, these policies changed abruptly and substantially in the 1870s. During this period the American Medical Association (AMA) opposed abortions because mortality rates were high among abortion patients and because most abortions were not performed by physicians. A number of civic and religious organizations joined the AMA and successfully campaigned for the enactment of laws prohibiting abortions and contraceptives. State governments then passed laws prohibiting abortions and forbidding the sale and distribution of contraceptives. In 1873 Congress enacted the Comstock Act, which prohibited the distribution of obscene materials and contraceptives across state lines. Once enacted, these laws remained in effect throughout most of the 20th century. There were a few minor changes. The Supreme Court struck down the Comstock Act in 1937, and some states allowed physicians to dispense contraceptives. In 1960 the Food and Drug Administration approved the birth control pill to be dispensed by a doctor's prescription. A profound change occurred in sexual reproduction policies the mid-1960s and early 1970s. In the *Griswold v. Connecticut* decision of 1965, the Supreme Court acknowledged the right to privacy and invalidated state laws prohibiting the sale and distribution of contraceptives. In the 1973 *Roe v. Wade* decision, the Court struck down state laws forbidding abortions. A number of states, such as New York, had liberalized their abortion laws as early as 1970. The point is that abortion and contraceptive policies changed abruptly and profoundly.

Consider also civil rights policies. These policies had been stagnant throughout the first half of the 20th century. The South remained segregated from 1900 to the mid-1960s. State laws in the South mandated segregation and outlawed integration. These laws made it illegal for blacks to go to the same schools as whites, to meet in the same meeting halls as whites, to eat at the same dining tables in the same restaurants as whites, to play together at the same amusement park, or to swim in the same public swimming pools or beaches. Southern states even made it illegal for black and white couples to get married.

There were small, gradual changes from 1900 to 1950 in civil rights policies. In the first quarter of the century, the Supreme Court invalidated state laws that denied individuals the right to vote exclusively on account of race. Such laws blatantly violated the Fifteenth Amendment, which prohibits states from denying individuals the right to vote on account of race, color, or previous condition of servitude. At the same time, the Court allowed state poll taxes, literacy tests, and character tests to deny the right to vote to almost all blacks and many whites, especially those whites who supported the Republican Party. In 1941 President Franklin D. Roosevelt created the Fair Employment Practices Committee to investigate racial discrimination in employment. Not until the end of World War II did President Harry Truman integrate the armed forces. It was not until 1954 that the Supreme Court invalidated state laws that mandated segregation in public schools. Nevertheless, segregation continued and there was severe resistance to even a few blacks going to an all-white school. Profound changes occurred in the mid-1960s with a series of civil rights laws and Supreme Court decisions. With the Civil Rights Act of 1964, the federal government prohibited racial segregation in public accommodations and facilities. The act also prohibited discrimination on the basis of race, gender, religion, and nationality in employment. The Voting Rights Act of 1965 restored the right to vote. The civil rights laws of the 1960s changed the entire racial social system of the South. These earthshaking changes came abruptly.

Homeland security provides another example. Homeland security has to do with protecting American citizens from violent attacks from politically motivated groups, domestic or foreign, who target large numbers of people to provoke terror. One example of this type of attack is the 1995 bombing of the federal building in Oklahoma City. Another example is the September 11, 2001, destruction of the twin towers of the World Trade Center in New York City by two hijacked jet aircraft. The first involved a domestic group; the second a foreign group. The two terrorist attacks precipitated profound public changes. Congress passed the Antiterrorism and Effective Death Penalty Act in 1996, which brought about incremental changes. In reaction to the September 11 attacks, Congress passed the USA PATRIOT Act of 2001 and the next year the president established the Department of Homeland Security.

Public policies are remarkably stable. They evolve over time with only small changes. Big changes occur in spurts or in rare bursts of policy change energy. These bursts of change are generally precipitated by a major historical event: a catastrophe, social movement, technological change, economic dislocation, or some other type of extraordinary event. Examples include the Progressive Era of the first decade of the 20th century, the New Deal of the 1930s, and the Great Society of the 1960s. In the face of these periods of massive policy change, the central question is: What explains these episodes of earthshaking changes in public policies?

❖ Using Policy Theory to Explain Policy Change

To answer the central question, the text explores several different strands of policy theory: state centered, decision making, pluralist, elitist, cyclical, eclectic, and policy typology. Each theory differs in terms of its focus on agents of public policy change.

State centered theory focuses on the role of government organization or leaders in maintaining policy stability or producing policy change. For example, state centered theory underscores the role of the national government's system of checks and balances in maintaining long-term policy stability and the role of key government officials—the president, members of Congress, or Supreme Court justices—in facilitating policy change. This strand of policy theory also includes decision-making models, such as incrementalism or cost-benefit analysis. Recent state centered theories have focused on the role of political parties in Congress in changing policies. State centered theories locate the center of power and policy change inside government, within elected or bureaucratic officials.

Pluralist theory emphasizes the role of organized interest groups in preserving the status quo or bringing about policy change. Pluralists assume that government responds to organized interest groups rather than the majority of its citizens and that these groups play a primary role in sustaining or changing public policies. Elitist theory focuses on the role of business elites or corporate leaders in the policy-making process.

The text includes two cyclical models: liberal-conservative cycles and the policy cycle. The liberal-conservative cycle theory suggests that a decade of liberal policy expansion would be followed by a decade of conservative policies. For example, the 1960s was a period characterized by the expansion of liberal antipoverty programs. It was followed by the 1980s, which was characterized by the contraction of antipoverty programs and the expansion of conservative anticrime and antidrug programs. The policy cycle model assumes that policy making is an ongoing and continuous process. The life cycle model presumes that government agencies have life cycles, like a living organism: youth, maturity, and old age.

Finally, the text presents eclectic theory, that is, theories that combine different theories into a larger or broader theory. In some cases, policy changes are the result of the decisions made by a few key public officials who are isolated from interest groups or structural or cultural changes in society. Hence, a state centered theory may best explain policy change. In other cases, policy change is the result of a combination of factors such as structural or cultural changes precipitating the emergence of new organized interest groups that attract the attention of key policy makers. In these cases, an eclectic theory or a combination of several theories best explains policy change. The text examines three eclectic theories: social movements, punctuated equilibrium, and policy regimes.

Social movement theory examines how structural changes precipitate the rapid growth of organized interest groups and how these groups affect changes in public opinion and public policies. Punctuated equilibrium comes from the biological theory of evolution. It suggests that policies, like living organisms, are remarkably stable over long periods of time, interrupted or punctuated by short periods of profound change.

Policy regime model draws from the other theories to explain periods of long-term stability and episodes of abrupt and substantial policy change. A policy regime consists of several dimensions, not including the policy itself: (1) power arrangements, (2) organizational arrangements, and (3) the dominant policy paradigm. These three dimensions of the policy regime operate to maintain long-term policy stability. Major changes in public policies are generally preceded by stressors. Policy stressors—catastrophic events, new technology, massive economic dislocation, social movements, demographic shifts, or modes of production changes—impact policy regimes and make substantial regime change possible.

The text is designed to examine specific public policies over time and to apply select theories to explain patterns of continuity and change. Although the text favors policy regime theory, it is open to the application of other theories that offer the best explanation of policy change. These theories are discussed in Chapter 2.

→ Policy Types

There are many different types of public policies. Journalists talk about educational policies, health care policies, transportation policies, and others; that is, they classify policies according to topic. Policy literature groups topics into several policy categories such as redistributive, distributive, protective regulatory, competitive regulatory, and morality. Redistributive policies appear to shift resources, privileges, or values from advantaged groups to disadvantaged groups. Welfare policies fall in this category. Distributive policies allocate resources or services broadly or in ways that benefit most people. Interstate highways are examples of distributive policies. Protective regulatory policies protect the public from harm. Environmental protection policies fit this category. Competitive regulatory policies control entry into a market, prices, and practices in the market. The role of the Federal Communications Commission in licensing broadcasting stations is a good example of this type of policy. Morality policies tend to be the most contentious, as they entail conflicts over principles of right and wrong, values, or religious issues. Examples of morality policies include abortion, prayer in school, or pornography. Morality policies have also been referred to as social policies. This text, however, uses the term *morality* to prevent confusion with social welfare policies. Policy types are discussed in the first chapter.

→ Organization of the Text

This text is divided into five parts. Each part consists of two or more chapters. Part I covers policy definition, theory, and process. Chapter 1 answers questions about public policies. It explains why there is government, defines public policies, and explains why governments exist. It identifies many different types of policy.

Chapter 2 considers policy theory. It provides explanations for the patterns of policy change outlined in the first chapter and surveys the major theories and models of public policy. It covers in more detail pluralist, elitist, and social movement theories. It elaborates on the policy cycle and the various stages of this model: problem definition, agenda setting, policy adoption, implementation, and evaluation. It discusses the punctuated equilibrium and policy regime theories.

Chapter 3 provides a brief history of the evolution of public policies in the 20th century with the purpose of illustrating long-term patterns of public policy development. It underscores three periods of substantial policy change: the Progressive Era at the beginning of the century, the New Deal period of the 1930s, and the liberal policy expansion of the Great Society in the 1960s. The chapter also discusses major policy changes of the 1980s and beyond. It applies two theories to explain long-term policy change: punctuated equilibrium and liberal-conservative cyclical theory.

Chapter 4 examines the institutions of government: the organization and role of Congress, the presidency, the bureaucracy, and the courts in making public policy. It identifies several patterns of policy making involving the interaction of these institutions and organized interest groups. It also covers the role of state and local governments in the making and execution of public policies.

The next parts of the text examine the four policy types: redistributive, protective and competitive regulatory, morality, and distributive. Table I.1 summarizes this organization, specific policies examined, and the defining legislation and the major stressor that produced the policy change.

Part II focuses on redistributive policies. Chapter 5 examines social welfare programs including Social Security; the Temporary Assistance to Needy Families program (TANF), formerly Aid to Families with Dependent Children; food stamps; school nutrition; and job training policies. Chapter 6 investigates the development of health care policy, paying close attention to Medicare and Medicaid.

Chapter 7 covers civil rights policy, tracing the development of civil rights policies throughout the 19th and 20th centuries. Although these policies can be classified as protective regulatory because they protect everyone from harm, it is classified here as redistributive because of the level of conflict in the 1960s and the ideological disputes over civil rights. Moreover, civil rights conflicts continue, especially over affirmative action and gay rights issues. This chapter also reviews affirmative action policies.

Part III covers protective and competitive regulatory policy. Chapter 8 looks at the evolution of environmental protection policies in the 20th century. It examines clean air, clean water, hazardous waste disposal, and pesticide policies. It pays careful attention to the Clean Air Acts of 1970, 1977, and 1990. Chapter 9 deals with labor policy, tracing the development of labor policies throughout the 20th century, with special emphasis on the National Labor Relations Board (NLRB) and the Occupational Safety and Health Administration (OSHA). Chapter 10 analyzes competitive regulatory policies. It focuses on the now defunct Interstate Commerce Commission, the active Federal Communications Commission (FCC), and the Antitrust Division of the Justice Department. It looks at issues pertaining to the FCC and the regulation of radio, television, and cable, and the emergence of computers and the Internet. Competitive regulatory policies also involve regulating competition, and one of the most controversial cases, the antitrust suit against Microsoft, is examined in this chapter.

Part IV covers morality policy, the most controversial policy area and probably the most interesting to new students of public policy. Morality policies are about sex, birth control, abortion, drugs, and pornography. Chapter 11 deals with fertility control policies or reproduction issues: contraceptives and abortion. It examines the changing social position of women and the women's liberation movement. It analyzes abortion cases, particularly *Roe v. Wade*. Chapter 12 is about criminal justice policy. It covers issues such as drugs, violence, gun control, and capital punishment. It looks at efforts to reduce violence in society and examines the controversial issues of incarceration and capital punishment as solutions.

TABLE I.1

Summary of Key Public Policies Covered in Text

Policy Type	Substantive Policy	Defining Legislation (Recent Issues)	Major Stressors
Redistributive	Social welfare	Social Security Act of 1935 (Personal Responsibility and Work Opportunity Act of 1996)	The Great Depression
	Health care	Title XVIII and Title XIX of the Social Security Act of 1965 (Medicaid/Medicare; 2003 drug bill)	Antipoverty social movement, new technology, and demographic change
	Civil rights	Civil Rights Act of 1964 (2003 University of Michigan affirmative action case; same-sex marriage)	Civil rights movement
Protective and Competitive Regulatory	Environmental protection	Clean Air Act of 1970 (acid rain regulations)	Environmental social movement; catastrophic event
	Labor	Wagner Act of 1935 and Fair Labor Standards Act of 1938; Occupational Safety and Health Act of 1970 (overtime regulations)	The Great Depression and the labor movement; social movements
	Antitrust	Sherman Antitrust Act 1890 (2002 Microsoft case)	Progressive movement
	FCC regulations	Federal Communications Act 1934 (Janet Jackson/Howard Stern cases)	Technological change (invention and popular use of radio/TV)
Morality	Fertility control	*Roe v. Wade* (partial-birth abortion)	Women's movement
	Criminal justice	USA PATRIOT Act of 2001 (civil liberties: death penalty)	9/11 attacks
Distributive	Education	States establishing public schools (state legislation establishing charter schools)	Industrial Revolution
	Economic	Federal Reserve Board Act of 1913 (tax cuts and budget deficits)	Progressive movement

Part V discusses distributive policies. Chapter 13 reviews the evolution of educational policies, charter schools, school vouchers, and equalized school funding. Chapter 14 deals with economic policies, particularly fiscal and monetary efforts to regulate the economy. Fiscal efforts involve the use of the national budget to fine-tune the economy through federal taxing and spending. Monetary policies entail the regulation of the money supply.

Each chapter in Parts II through V examines the development of policies over time, periods of abrupt and profound change, and episodes of policy regime changes.

Chapter 15 concludes the text. It sums everything up. It comments on continuity and change in our five policy areas. It asserts how well the policy regime model explains patterns of stability and change in the policies examined. It also references other theories of public policy making and change. It underscores the role of interest group organizations, power alignments, and policy paradigms in sustaining or changing policies.

PART I

Policy Definition, Theory, and Process

CHAPTER 1

The Meaning of Public Policy

In the 1980s movie *Ghostbusters,* a government bureaucrat entered ghostbuster headquarters with a police escort. The ghost busters had captured numerous ghosts and demons and imprisoned them in a contraption powered by nuclear energy. The bureaucrat ordered the shutdown of the contraption. By turning off the energy, the bureaucrat unwittingly released the ghosts and demons to terrorize the citizens and wreak havoc throughout New York City.

This scene from *Ghostbusters* illustrates how bureaucrats and government bureaucracies are portrayed in popular American culture. Bureaucrats are often depicted as arrogant, inflexible, closed-minded, rigid, and thoughtless officials who do more harm than good. In everyday speech, the term *bureaucracy* often has negative connotations. The government bureaucracy is generally portrayed as a large, inefficient organization top heavy with administrators, entangled in archaic rules and unnecessary paperwork, that waste taxpayers' money and impose costly and burdensome regulations.

Americans are ambivalent about government and public policies. On the one hand, we don't like government. We tend to believe the critics who say that government is too big, too wasteful, and too intrusive. We doubt the ability of government bureaucracies to accomplish anything. We support limiting the size of government and view its expansion as a threat to our freedom. For example, Ronald Reagan said:

> I hope we have once again reminded people that man is not free unless government is
> limited. There's a clear cause and effect here that is as neat and predictable as a law of
> physics: as government expands, liberty contracts. (*New York Times,* January 12, 1989)

We Americans have always valued individualism and limited government and have had some distrust of government. By the mid-1990s, in some sectors of American society, trust and confidence had deteriorated into anger against government. For example, in 1995 the executive vice president of the National Rifle Association wrote, "It doesn't matter to them [members of Congress] that the semi-auto ban gives jackbooted government thugs more power to take away our constitutional rights, break in our doors, seize our guns, destroy our property, and even injure or kill us . . ." (quoted in Tolchin 1996, 117). Barbara Roberts, former governor of Oregon, summarized this anger against government:

> Citizens don't trust government. The anti-government attitude is of proportions that
> threaten our democracy. Citizens are bombarded with stories of government failure. That
> means they are believing nobody. We're painting all politicians with the same broad brush.
> (quoted in Tolchin 1996, 108)

Extremists groups such as the Michigan Militia have defined the government as the enemy of the people.

On the other hand, Americans accept and support specific public policies. A national opinion poll indicated that while 68 percent of the respondents believed that taxes were too high, well over 60 percent believed that spending was too low for education (73 percent), health (66 percent), and environmental (62 percent) policies (Patterson 2001, 159). Clearly, Americans are ambivalent about government and public policies. We generally don't like government and believe it is wasteful and taxes are too high, yet we support specific public policies. Moreover, trust in government has declined substantially since the mid-1960s but has increased since 9/11. Using an index based on several survey questions related to trust in government, Figure 1.1 illustrates the long-term trend of trust in government. In 1966 this index indicated a peak level of trust at 61 percent. By 1974 trust levels had declined to 29 percent and to 27 percent by the end of the decade. Trust increased somewhat during Reagan's first

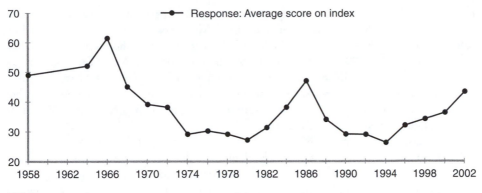

NOTE:

Index constructed using data from the following questions:

"How much of the time do you think you can trust the government in Washington to do what is right?"
"Would you say the government is pretty much run by a few big interests looking out for themselves or that it is run for the benefit of all the people?"
"Do you think that people in the government waste a lot of money we pay in taxes, waste some of it, or don't waste very much of it?"
"Do you think that quite a few of the people running the government are crooked, not very many are, or do you think hardly any of them are crooked?"

FIGURE 1.1   *Trust in Government Index 1958–2002*

SOURCE: The National Election Studies, Center for Political Studies, University of Michigan. The NES Guide to Public Opinion and Electoral Behavior (http://www.umich.edu/~nes/nesguide/nesguide.htm). Graph 5A.5, 16SEO03. Ann Arbor, MI: University of Michigan, Center for Political Studies [producer and distributor], 1995–2000.

These materials are based on work supported by the National Sciences Foundation, under grant numbers SBR-9707741, SBR-9317631, SES-9209410, SES-9009379, SES-8808361, SES-8341310, SES-8207580, and SOC77-08885, as well as the Russell Sage Foundation under grant number 82-00-01, and the University of Michigan.

Any opinions, findings and conclusions or recommendations expressed in these materials are those of the author(s) and do not necessarily reflect those of the funding agencies.

term but declined by the end of the 1980s and had dropped to an all time low by 1994. Trust in government gradually increased in the late 1990s and 2000. By 2002, the trust index was at 43 percent. No doubt government response to the 9/11 tragedy boosted trust and confidence in government. The images of firefighters and police officers going into the World Trade Center to rescue people inspired respect and pride for government officials.

This chapter explores the meaning of public policy, arguing that there is much about government and public policies that we take for granted. It defines public policy and elaborates on the different types of public policies. It shows how different political ideologies have different perspectives on public policies. It answers the question of why we have government and public policies, a critical question in a period of ambivalence over them. Finally, it explains why we are so ambivalent about government and public policies and how we became so cynical and distrustful.

⤳ *Why Government and Public Policies Are Essential*

Government and public policies are much more essential than we realize. Public policies enhance our lives in many ways and make modern conveniences possible. For example, when we go to the store to buy groceries, we drive down a street made possible by local government. We navigate safely through traffic regulated by government. We purchase meat inspected by the U.S. Department of Agriculture. We choose the best breakfast cereal by reading nutrition labels required by the federal government under the *Nutritional Labeling and Education Act of 1990*. We enjoy a wide selection of food transported to the grocery on interstate highways built by federal money. We listen to the weather report, news, and music on the car radio, broadcast by a single station on a single frequency, uninterrupted by other stations, because of the Federal Communications Commission, a government agency that regulates radio and television broadcasts.

Government does many things to enhance the quality of our lives. It offers money for research for the advancement of new technologies, for the arts and humanities, and for the cure of diseases. State and federal moneys for colleges and universities have made higher education more accessible and affordable to more Americans. Federal, state, and local governments maintain parks and recreational areas and facilities. Local governments provide libraries and museums. Government attempts to protect the health and safety of workers. It operates to safeguard children from labor exploitation and physical and sexual abuse. It eases the hardships of unemployment and poverty by providing unemployment insurance, Social Security, and food stamps. It provides health insurance (Medicare) for the elderly and for poor single women with dependent children (Medicaid).

Government plays a role in stabilizing the economy by regulating the money supply and maintaining fair business practices. When we put money in the bank, government insures our deposits and provides security in the banking industry. Government stimulates purchasing in the housing market by guaranteeing loans for new homeowners.

While many people are cynical about government and distrustful of public officials, most support these various roles and activities of government.

↛ *Definition of Public Policy*

Public policies are the authoritative statements or actions of government which reflect the decisions, values, or goals of policy makers.

Although there are many variations, scholars offer similar definitions of **public policies.** Thomas Dye (1998, 2) referred to public policies as "whatever governments choose to do or not to do." James Anderson defined a policy as "a purposive course of action followed by an actor or set of actors in dealing with a problem or matter of concern." A public policy consists of courses or patterns of goal-oriented actions developed and executed by governmental officials (Anderson 1994, 5). James Lester and Joseph Stewart concluded (1996, 5) that the common element in these definitions is "a process or a series or pattern of governmental activities or decisions that are designed to remedy some public problem, either real or imagined."

Public **policy statements** express the intentions, goals, and values of government. The *Clean Air Act of 1970* expressed clear goals, as it called for a 90 percent reduction in carbon monoxide and hydrocarbons in the atmosphere. The *Personal Responsibility and Work Opportunity Act of 1996* set the goal of getting welfare recipients off cash assistance and into the workforce. This policy also expressed a strong value in work over cash assistance. Some policy statements such as the establishment of holidays express clear values without any specific goal, except perhaps closing public institutions. For example, Memorial Day, Labor Day, and

Martin Luther King Jr. Day are all holidays created by public policy statements. They express values and capture public sentiment—the celebration and recognition of the contributions of military service men and women who sacrificed their lives for their country, of workers who helped build this county, and of a civil rights leader who gave his life so this country could live out the true meaning of its creeds.

Most public **policy activities** involve the allocation of resources, the provision of services, the regulation of behavior, or the distribution of values. They are often designed with specific goals and intentions, for example, to solve problems, enhance the quality of life, make modern conveniences possible, provide safe and secure environments, maintain order, support a stable economy, express values, and so forth. These activities include building and maintaining interstate highways; training people for jobs; providing health insurance through Medicaid and Medicare; sending out Social Security checks, unemployment benefits, supplemental security income checks; funding educational programs such as Head Start; and awarding defense contracts. All of these entail major policy activities and involve the allocation of billions of dollars of federal money.

Policy activities also involve positive and negative sanctions calculated to regulate behavior. Positive sanctions may be a tax cut to encourage business investment in a particular area. A negative sanction may entail financial penalties or incarceration. For example, the Environmental Protection Agency may fine domestic automobile producers millions of dollars for failing to install pollution-control devices. Or the Drug Enforcement Agency may arrest people for selling illegal drugs.

Policy activities can be distinguished in terms of whether they are routine or nonroutine. Routine policy activities rely upon standard practices and are often based on specific rules or formulas, like a federal program that allocates money to local schools based on the number of low-income students. Nonroutine activities are sporadic, such as a project to build a downtown sports arena.

Public policies come from all governmental entities and at all levels: legislatures, courts, bureaucratic agencies, and executive offices at national, local, and state levels. On the federal level, public policies are laws enacted by Congress, executive orders issued by the president, decisions handed down by the U.S. Supreme Court, and regulations issued by bureaucratic agencies. On the local level, public policies include city ordinances, fire codes, and traffic regulations. Also, they are the written rules and regulations of city governmental departments: the police, fire, street repair, or building inspection. On the state level, public policies involve laws enacted by the state legislatures, decisions made by state courts, rules developed by state bureaucratic agencies, and decisions made by governors.

In short, public policies are the authoritative statements and actions of government that reflect what governments decide to do or not do and what they actually do. Policy statements embody governmental decisions, values, and goals and arise during the policy-making phase. Policy activities also occur during the policy implementation phase and embody patterns of governmental actions.

➔ Different Public Policy Typologies

There are many types of public policies and many different ways of classifying them. One way is to distinguish among symbolic, substantive, and procedural policies.

Symbolic, Substantive, and Procedural Policies

Symbolic policy has emotional appeal. It embodies values or ideals. It may demonstrate a commitment to a principle, but have no material impact. For example, the *Employment Act of 1946* expresses a commitment to achieving full employment. Martin Luther King Jr. Day symbolizes our support for King's civil rights ideals.

A **substantive policy** entails the allocation of resources and is expected to have a significant impact. Examples of substantive policies include the *Clean Air Act of 1990,* the *Americans with Disabilities Act of 1990,* the *Civil Rights Act of 1991,* and the Personal Responsibility and Work Opportunity Act of 1996. These acts are expected to reduce air pollution, provide opportunities for people with disabilities, prohibit racial harassment on the job, and assist welfare recipients in getting off welfare.

A **procedural policy** outlines the steps in a process: courtroom procedures, procedures for the government to take people's land and homes (eminent domain) to build an expressway, procedures for which the government bans a particular drug from being sold on the market. Procedural policy often involves the protection of individual rights, like the right to a fair hearing. The *Administrative Procedures Act of 1946* is a procedural policy that outlines the steps a regulatory agency must follow before issuing a regulation. For example, if the Food and Drug Administration (FDA) decides to ban a drug, the law requires the FDA to give the affected pharmaceutical companies an opportunity to present evidence in an open hearing with the FDA.

Distributive, Redistributive, and Regulatory Policies

Another policy classification scheme distinguishes among distributive, redistributive, and regulatory policies. These policies can be distinguished two ways: by the perceived pattern of allocating resources and by the nature of the politics surrounding the policy. Political scientist Theodore Lowi (1979) is credited with originating this typology.

Distributive Policies

Distributive policies appear to allocate benefits or resources to the larger population. A good example of a distributive policy is the interstate highway system. Interstate highways are found in every state and are used by most people. Those who do not use them still benefit from them indirectly because most goods—foods, clothing, automobiles, furniture, and so on—are distributed by way of the interstate highway. Funding for the federal interstate highway system is considered a distributive policy because it allocates governmental resources broadly and benefits the whole population.

Distributive policies are also distinguishable by the pattern of politics surrounding them. Distributive policies generally involve cooperation, nonpartisanship, and close and supportive relations among federal agencies, congressional committees, and interest groups. Everyone works together because everyone benefits.

Redistributive Policies

Redistributive policies appear to shift resources or benefits from advantaged groups to disadvantaged groups. Some students of public policy refer to them as Robin Hood policies because, allegedly, they take from the rich and give to the poor. One example of a redistributive policy is welfare payments for low-income, single women with children. Welfare shifts resources downward from middle- and upper-income families who pay higher taxes to lower-income families who receive the benefits. Affirmative action is another example of a redistributive policy, as this policy (which is designed to improve the employment and educational chances for women and minorities) is perceived to shift privileges from advantaged to disadvantaged groups.

Redistributive policies are distinguished by the contentious pattern of politics surrounding them. They involve partisan disputes between Democrats and Republicans, and ideological conflicts between liberals and conservatives. Indeed, the politics of welfare and affirmative action policies tend to be contentious and divided along ideological lines.

Competitive and Protective Regulatory Policies

Regulatory policies set guidelines for the actions and practices of private individuals, firms, or businesses. They often involve systems of rewards and penalties. For example, regulatory policies may involve issuing licenses to automobile drivers, nurses, doctors, lawyers, cab drivers, and other private individuals seeking to operate a machine or vehicle or to practice a specific profession. These policies may ban the sale and distribution of particular toxic chemicals, specify the conditions under which certain chemicals may be used, or require the use of special gear or garments in particular work areas. Regulatory policies may entail awarding licenses to radio and television stations, with specific guidelines for behavior on the airwaves.

There are two types of regulatory policies: competitive and protective. **Competitive regulatory policies** generally regulate entry into markets and may also regulate prices. An example of competitive regulatory policy is the practice of the Federal Communications Commission (FCC) in issuing licenses to radio and television broadcasting stations to operate on the airwaves and in enforcing rules for operating. By issuing licenses, the FCC determines which companies may or may not enter the broadcasting market. Another example of a competitive regulatory policy is the role of state public utility commissions in regulating the prices of electricity. Electric companies operate as a monopoly. Unchecked, they can charge whatever the market of consumers of electric services is able to bear. In theory, state utility commissions were established to regulate the prices of electric generating monopolies in order to protect the public interest.

The politics surrounding competitive regulatory policies tend to be similar to those surrounding distributive policies. That is, politics tend to be nonpartisan and cooperative even when competitive regulatory policies are controversial. For example, both Democrats and Republicans have favored deregulating select competitive regulatory policies. Indeed, President Carter succeeded in deregulating the Civil Aeronautics Board, the agency that had regulated entry into the airline market and the price of airline tickets.

Protective regulatory policies protect the public from a perceived harm. Examples of regulatory agencies are the Environmental Protection Agency, the Consumer Product Safety Commission, the Occupational Safety and Health Administration, and the Federal Aviation Administration, all of which protect the public from pollution, hazardous products, workplace dangers, and unsafe airplanes. Protective regulatory policies often require a change in behavior brought about by invoking rewards or penalties. Sometimes these policies entail negotiated requests such as an agreement to recall a hazardous product from the market.

The politics surrounding protective regulatory policies tend to be similar to those surrounding redistributive policies; that is, they are partisan and contentious, and policy arguments generally divide along ideological lines.

Allocational and Developmental Policies

Studies of local public policies add two additional policy types: allocational and developmental. **Allocational policies** entail the distribution of urban services: police, fire, parks, museums, libraries, streets, sewers, and others. These policies tend to distribute city services on the basis of professional norms such as greater police services to higher crime areas, or more street repair services to high use areas. **Developmental policies** involve economic revitalization. Often these policies entail solution packages designed to stimulate the expansion of existing businesses, the creation of new businesses, or the location of a new production facility in a particular area of the city. These packages often contain federal dollars and local tax breaks. For example, the City of Detroit used Community Development Block Grant money to assist General Motors to build a new automobile production facility. The city used the money to purchase land and property, demolish buildings and clear the land, build new streets and industrial sewers, and prepare the site on which General Motors built its new facility.

Morality Policies

Morality policies have probably been around as long as there have been public policies. **Morality policies** involve moral issues and notions of right and wrong. They tend to be grounded in religion and entail conflicts over values and principles. Examples of morality issues include abortion, birth control, pornography, homosexual rights, prayer and religion in schools, sex education, and capital punishment.

There are five distinguishing features of morality issues.

1. They tend to be well known. People hear about them on radio and television talk shows.
2. They deal with clear and uncomplicated, black-and-white, right-or-wrong value issues. People tend to be for them or against them and reach their conclusions based on their values and opinions, not on technical information. Moreover, people are not easily persuaded to change their views with additional information.
3. They involve more citizen participation than most other policies.
4. Morality issues are much more contentious and emotional than other issues and people frequently take polarized positions. It is more difficult to reach consensus or to compromise over this type of policy (Mooney 2001).
5. Morality issues are more likely to involve religious organizations and religious views.

There are three similarities between morality and redistributive issues: both involve winners and losers; both issues are highly visible, appearing in the news and discussed frequently on talk shows; and both involve ideological conflicts between liberals and conservatives.

Morality issues differ from redistributive issues in two ways. First, morality policies are more intense and contentious than redistributive issues. While abortion clinics have been bombed, food stamp, Medicaid, or welfare offices have not. It is more difficult to reach consensus over morality issues than redistributive issues. Second, morality issues are explained more by religious factors, whereas redistributive issues are identified more with socioeconomic classes or ethnic groups. Recently, however, religious groups have become involved in changing welfare policies. The extent to which they define welfare as a moral issue will determine whether welfare policy remains redistributive or becomes one of morality.

⇥ *Government, Public Policy, and the Market*

Government enhances the quality of life and makes modern conveniences possible. So why do we need government and public policies? Why can't the free market and private enterprise provide all the conveniences we want?

Theoretically, the market is a place where firms—businesses and industries—sell what consumers want and need—houses, automobiles, household appliances, clothes, food, jewelry, computers, videos, and so forth. The market provides modern conveniences, not government. Moreover, competition constrains firms to provide goods and services efficiently; that is, inefficient firms that provide inferior goods or services at higher prices will lose customers to firms providing better-quality goods or services for lower prices. Eventually, inefficient firms go out of business.

Even though efficient businesses are providing the goods and services consumers want, we still need government for several reasons: (1) law, order, and justice; (2) to prevent unintended market harms; (3) business cycles or economic crises; (4) market disorganization; (5) fair business practices; (6) consumer protection; (7) natural monopolies; (8) public or collective goods; and (9) redistribution.

Law, Order, Contracts, and Justice

Political philosopher **Thomas Hobbes** imagined a state of nature and time before government. Before government, in the state of nature, the lives of people were "solitary, poor, nasty, brutish, and short." The strong preyed on the weak and people fought and killed each other. At some point in history people decided that life without government was chaotic and miserable. Hobbes argued that people gave up their freedom in nature for the security they gain from government. People created government to maintain law and order.

The maintenance of law and order is essential for a free market. Without law and order, trade would be disrupted, goods stolen, and customers intimidated. Markets would collapse. Government protects businesses and consumers from robbers, gangsters, terrorists, and vandals. Without the government to maintain law and order and enforce

Maintaining law and order is one of the most basic functions of government.

contracts between businesses and between businesses and customers, contracts would be meaningless. Moreover, government maintains a uniform system of weights and measures, a monetary system, and other systems that support markets.

Unintended Market Harms

Although markets are efficient at generating the goods and services consumers want, they sometimes have unintended and undesirable outcomes or by-products. The general population ends up paying the cost of these market by-products. The classic example is pollution, the undesirable by-product of the production of steel, paints, plastics, pesticides, electric power, and other desirable products. When pollution is released into the environment, the general population bears the costs. For air pollution, these costs take the form of increased respiratory ailments and dirty air that settles on automobiles, houses, and other forms of property exposed to the air. The costs of pollution must be paid by the firms that cause pollution or by the general public that suffers its impact. The market shifts these costs from the firms to the general public. The government has the power to shift the costs back to the firms or to distribute the costs more equitably.

Externality is another name for these unintended by-products of the market. An **externality** is a cost or benefit that arises apart from the market. That is, it is not reflected in the cost of goods and services sold. Pollution is a cost forced on people against their will. Government and public policies offer some ways of resolving the problems of these unintended harms or externalities.

Business Cycles or Economic Crises

Sometimes the market goes through business cycles or economic crises. A good example is the Great Depression of the 1930s. Many firms went out of business and, at one point, a panic led to the near collapse of the banking industry. People feared that they would lose the money they had deposited in their banks, so they withdrew their deposits. When all depositors demand their money, banks quickly run out of money. People panicked, inciting massive withdrawals which caused other banks to run out of money and go out of business. Neither the market nor the banking industry could respond effectively to this crisis. President Franklin D. Roosevelt declared a bank holiday and prevented further withdrawals and bank failures. The Federal Deposit Insurance Corporation was established in 1933 to insure deposits and help maintain public confidence in the banking industry.

One of the ironies of a free market is that public policies are needed to keep the market competitive and open and to respond to **market failures**. Government responds to other forms of economic crises, especially runaway inflation, through other means. It regulates the supply of money and it negotiates with oil-producing nations to increase the supply of oil in order to slow the rising price of energy.

Market Disorganization and Research and Development

Occasionally, markets respond inadequately in developing new technologies. These occasions arise when the initial costs of the new technology are too high and the risks of investment too great. Under these conditions, government can play a role in stimulating new technology. For example, the government played a role in promoting the development of nuclear energy and in stimulating the rise of computer technology. In many areas of research and development, such as environmental and cancer research, it may take decades for any profits to be made. Government often invests in these important research areas that cannot attract enough private investment.

Fair Business Practices and Consumer Protection

Markets operate under the assumption that firms behave fairly. Fair competition breaks down when firms engage in dishonest and unscrupulous practices. Consider what happens in the market when an unscrupulous firm puts out false rumors in order to destroy competitors who sell better-quality goods for lower prices: The efficient firms go out of business while inefficient and unscrupulous ones thrive. Government plays a role in ensuring fair competition and maintaining efficient markets.

For markets to operate efficiently, consumers must have information about the goods sold so they can make informed judgments about product quality, safety, and cost. Without this information, consumers cannot make informed choices and they become vulnerable to unsafe products. Government also operates to protect the consumer by providing product information.

Monopolies

Although it is generally assumed that the entire economy is an open competitive market, the economy is mixed. Some parts of it are open and competitive with hundreds of businesses operating. For example, any large city has hundreds of restaurants competing with each other in an open market. Other sectors of the economy are dominated by a few large corporations of which none control the market. These economic arrangements are considered oligopolies. Examples of an oligopolistic market include the automobile and chemical industries. Other sectors of our economy are dominated by a single company. These economic arrangements are called monopolies. In some cases monopolies develop naturally, emerging in areas where competition is impractical and initial investment costs are so high that other firms cannot compete. A good example of a natural monopoly is an electric power generating company. Once an electric generating facility is built and electric lines are established, the costs are too high for another competitor to build another facility and install alternative electric lines just to compete with the established company.

Competition compels companies to provide better services for a lower cost. If they fail, their competitors can put them out of business by providing the better services at a cheaper cost. But a monopoly has no competition. In a monopoly, a single firm can offer poor-quality services and charge exorbitant prices and still stay in business because consumers have no alternative. Consumers are at the mercy of the monopoly firm. The only way to protect the consumer is through government and public policies. Thus, another reason for government is to prevent a monopoly from gouging the public and to regulate it in the public interest.

Public or Collective Goods

In markets, firms sell private goods to individual customers. A private good is one that can be sold as a unit exclusively to an individual customer. Those who do not pay for the good do not get the good. Markets work efficiently when firms sell private goods.

This view of the Pentagon in Virginia reminds us of the role of national defense in government.

Markets are not able to provide public or collective goods efficiently. A **public good** is one from which everyone in a community can benefit without necessarily paying for it. Unlike private goods, public goods cannot be divided into units and sold to individuals. Those who benefit from the good without paying for it are called *free riders*. Whereas the private firm cannot easily force the **free rider** to pay for the service, the government can through its tax power. Consider flood control, for example. Flood control is a public good because the entire community benefits from it. It cannot easily be sold in units on the market by private firms to private individuals in the way cars, houses, apples, bread, counseling services, and other private goods and services are sold. Government is more suitable than private firms for providing public goods and getting people to pay for them through taxes. National defense is the classic example of a public good. The entire country benefits from the security of a strong national defense, but defense cannot be divided into individual units and sold.

A road is another example of a public good. Although a private firm can build a road and charge a toll to anyone wanting to use it, governments are better suited for providing roads for several reasons. First, roads are instruments of commerce: They support markets and contribute to the economic vitality of communities. Producers use roads to transport their goods to the market and consumers use them to get to the market to purchase the goods. Roads are essential for the survival of markets.

Second, communities benefit from roads without necessarily using them or paying for their use. Items such as food, building materials, medicine, books, magazines, and other goods are brought into communities by means of roads and contribute to the improvement of life in the community.

Third, governments have the power of eminent domain. **Eminent domain** means governments have the power to seize land and offer just compensation or a fair price. Governments can take tracts of land along a straight line to build a road, as long as they pay the landowner a fair price. Private firms do not have this power; they must buy land where owners are willing to sell. This market requirement would cause firms to build roads that meander because the firms must follow the path where landowners are willing to sell. Such a process makes private road building more inefficient and costly. Thus, since ancient times, usually governments have assumed this function.

There are other public goods that connect producers to markets and that governments are better suited to provide. These goods include harbors, ports, airports, bridges, and tunnels. Public education, and police and fire services are also public goods. Although these services can be sold on the market, they are public goods because the entire community benefits from an educated populace, safe neighborhoods, and fire protection. In some small communities the government taxes homeowners, but contracts with private companies to pick up the trash.

Redistribution

The final reason for government and public policies is to redistribute resources and wealth. Unrestrained markets have a tendency to precipitate uneven development and inequalities in wealth and income. Uneven development refers to a condition in which

This view of the Ambassador Bridge in Detroit is another reminder of an important function of government: building bridges.

one area or region experiences rapid economic growth while another suffers economic decline. Government has operated to stimulate investment in declining areas. Wages in unregulated labor markets tend to fall below subsistence level. For this reason, government establishes minimum wage policies. Government also operates to ameliorate the harsh conditions of poverty. Food stamps, Medicaid, aid to women and infant children, unemployment insurance, and many others public policies serve this purpose.

→ Ideology and Public Policy

Views of government differ along ideological lines. As illustrated in Figure 1.2, four types of ideologies or ideological groups can be identified: conservative, liberal, libertarian, and communitarian. Each ideology can be distinguished by examining whether it favors more or less government on issues of morality and equity policy. Morality issues involve questions of whether particular types of behavior are bad and whether government should regulate the behavior. Equity issues entail judgments about justice and the redistribution of resources or privileges from the more fortunate to the disadvantaged.

FIGURE 1.2
Ideologies and Issues of Equity and Morality

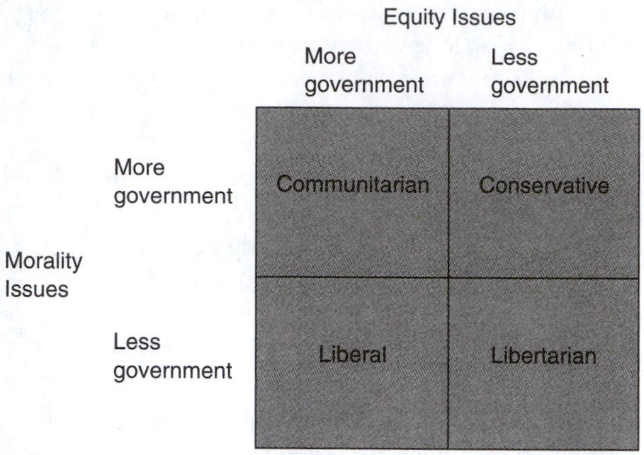

Conservatives versus Liberals

There is a great deal of confusion over the definition of liberals and conservatives. Much of this confusion arises over the tendency of liberals and conservatives to distort each other's positions. Conservatives insist that liberals want big government, more government power, and high taxes. Liberals insist that conservatives lack compassion and sensitivity, especially concerning the poor and less fortunate. Both are wrong.

Conservatives generally want more government to resolve morality issues and less government to resolve equity issues. On the issue of crime, for example, conservatives are likely to support spending more money on police and enlarging police powers to fight crime. With abortion, conservatives support more governmental regulations and powers to protect unborn children. Conservatives also support more governmental power to regulate obscenity and to reduce drug abuse and prostitution. Conservatives are more likely to support capital punishment. Conservatives generally support the expansion of governmental powers and prerogatives to maintain law and order and to regulate immoral behavior.

It is primarily on equity issues that conservatives argue for less government. Conservatives are more likely to support market mechanisms or individual choice over government programs or government regulations. They are more likely to advocate cutbacks in government spending for welfare, food stamps, school lunch programs for students from low-income families, or subsidized housing. Conservatives insist on supporting personal responsibility over welfare dependency. They generally support the reduction of government regulations on the environment, consumer products, and the workplace. They would support market mechanisms such as vouchers, tax breaks, or incentives for companies to reduce pollution.

In contrast, **liberals** favor less government to resolve morality issues and more government to resolve equity issues. Liberals support the privacy of the individual to make his or her own personal choices on morality issues. They are suspicious of increasing police powers, especially where they see the potential loss of civil liberties of all citizens, including those accused of crimes. Liberals are likely to oppose government regulation of what videos or movies citizens may see, what compact disks (CDs) they may hear, or what museum pictures they may view. They oppose the government arresting people for using drugs or getting abortions. Liberals are less likely to support capital punishment. Thus, liberals support individual choice over government intervention, and advocate limiting governmental powers in dealing with morality issues.

On equity issues, however, liberals advocate more government. They call for more spending for welfare, child care, food programs, and subsidized low-income housing. Liberals also support more government regulation of pollution, consumer protection, workplace safety, and others.

Libertarians and Communitarians

Libertarians advocate less government involvement and more individual choice in both morality and equity issues. Like liberals, libertarians oppose government regulation of movies, videos, and CDs. They generally oppose the criminalization of abortion, drug abuse, and prostitution. Like conservatives, libertarians oppose government welfare programs and government regulation of pollution or consumer product safety. In short, libertarians want more individual freedom and less government in all areas.

Communitarians are just the opposite of libertarians. They want more government involvement in all areas. They want greater government regulation of morality issues. They oppose abortion, drugs, and prostitution and want government to do something about these issues. They want more government to promote welfare and to protect the public from pollution and dangerous products (Janda, Berry, and Goldman 2002).

These ideologies have definite public policy implications. Whichever ideology becomes the most pervasive would influence the direction of public policy making. Communitarians would give us more governmental power and activities in all areas while libertarians would give us less. Liberals and conservatives would give us a mix of governmental powers and activities, with liberals giving us more in the equity area and less in the morality area, and conservatives just the reverse.

✢ Explaining Ambivalence toward Government and Public Policies

Government and public policies are an essential and regular aspect of life in a modern, technologically advanced, and democratic society. Nevertheless, Americans have mixed feelings about government and public policies. The question is, what explains this ambivalence? More importantly, what explains the lack of trust and confidence in government? There are several explanations for the ambivalence of Americans toward government. These explanations include past history, recent history, bad policies, and scholars' attacks on government.

Past History

Americans have historically valued freedom, individualism, and limited government. Historians attribute these values to three major factors: the absence of a feudal past, the frontier spirit, and the beliefs stemming from the American Revolution. In Europe during the Middle Ages, feudal lords exercised considerable power over their subjects but assumed responsibility for their welfare. This experience contributed to a political culture in Europe that accepts a strong central government. Because Americans lack a feudal past, a strong central government is not part of our political culture.

The so-called open frontier, although occupied, facilitated a spirit of individualism and self-reliance, as citizens could escape from government and its laws in the east by moving westward. Of course, more recent historians suggest that there may have been much more co-operation among settlers than previously believed.

Historians often attribute our opposition to strong central government to the American Revolution. The revolution was seen as a revolt against King George III, although the British Parliament had as much to do with the enactment of the Stamp Acts, the Intolerable Acts, the embargo of the port of Boston, and many other policies that precipitated the war. Furthermore, Thomas Jefferson, the author of the Declaration of Independence, argued that freedom and democracy could best be achieved with a weak central government and small town meetings. He contributed much to the belief in limited government.

Recent History

A number of events of the late 1960s and early 1970s explain the low levels of trust in government by the end of the 1970s. These events include the Vietnam War, Watergate, and other scandals. Several factors about the Vietnam War contributed to the distrust. The language of the war was deceptive: the war was not a war, but a police action. The troops were initially called advisers, although U.S. servicemen were fighting and dying. The My Lai massacre in March 1968 shocked the American public. Led by Lieutenant Calley, 150 American servicemen assaulted a hamlet in South Vietnam and murdered about 500 unarmed women, old men, and children. The massacre was initially reported as a stunning victory against a Vietcong stronghold. The truth did not become known until after one of the soldiers sent a letter to key U.S. senators prompting a full investigation. In the spring of 1970, President Nixon ordered bombing raids and, later, troops into Cambodia at the same time he claimed to be respecting the country's neutrality. These actions and the continuing war eroded confidence and trust in government.

The Watergate scandal shattered trust in government. This scandal began on the night of June 17, 1972, with the arrest of a group of burglars who broke into the national headquarters of the Democratic Party. The scandal attracted widespread attention as evidence surfaced suggesting that President Nixon had attempted to obstruct the investigation and cover up any connection between the burglars and his election campaign committee. Nixon had taped his White House conversations and initially refused to turn over the tapes to the special prosecutor investigating the scandal. The U.S. Supreme Court ordered Nixon to release the tapes. The tapes provided enough incriminating evidence to force Nixon to resign in order to avoid impeachment. Although his successor, Gerald Ford, pardoned Nixon, some of Nixon's aides were arrested and convicted.

Additional scandals throughout the 1970s contributed further to disillusionment and distrust.

> Between 1975 and 1980 over fifty members of Congress admitted accepting illegal
> campaign contributions; there were several major scandals involving sex and/or alcohol;

and some twenty-five members of Congress were accused of financial indiscretion of one kind or another. In 1981 and 1982 eight members of Congress received jail terms resulting from the FBI's Abscam sting operation. (Rodgers and Harrington 1985, 198)

Confidence in government declined further still during the Carter administration. The perception that his administration responded ineffectively to escalating oil prices, growing inflation, and unemployment rates engendered further distrust in government. Carter lost even more support after 52 Americans in the embassy in Tehran, Iran, were taken hostage in the fall of 1979 and remained hostages for well over a year.

Trust in government increased in the early and mid-1980s under the Reagan administration but declined again by the end of the decade. Several major scandals hit the Reagan administration and explain this decline in trust. One scandal during Reagan's administration was the Iran-Contra Affair (1985–86). This involved National Security Council officials who negotiated the secret sale of military weapons to Iran in exchange for American hostages kidnapped in Lebanon. The profits from the sale of these arms were used to illegally supply the Contras, a group fighting to overthrow the leftist government of Nicaragua. The second scandal involved influence peddling in the Department of Housing and Urban Development (HUD). Here is how historian Haynes Johnson summarized the scandal that only emerged publicly in the spring of 1989 after Reagan left office.

> [C]ongressional investigators began documenting abuses at HUD that would cost the taxpayers billion of dollars in losses . . . the public was given an inside look at the way Reagan HUD officials, former high Reagan government appointees, and Republican officials and former officeholders operated for their mutual self-interest through the awarding and receiving of government contracts. They knowingly profited from poverty. Dozens of former officials, many from HUD and others with close ties to the Reagan White House, earned millions of dollars in consulting fees in return for their efforts in winning HUD housing subsidies and grants for their clients. (1992, 180)

Many of Reagan's appointees had little experience in housing but they made huge sums of money through their political connections. These scandals shook people's faith in government and public policies. They were particularly ironic since Reagan defined government as the problem and insisted that government was wasteful and ineffective.

Scandals cut across party lines. The Clinton administration was replete with scandals. The administration allegedly used the White House to raise campaign money. The scandal involving President Clinton's relationship with White House intern Monica Lewinsky will go down in history. Clinton was impeached but not removed from office. Most people believed Clinton to be guilty but still supported him because of the economic prosperity during his administration. These scandals had perhaps only marginal impact on trust in government.

No doubt a number of government police actions generated antigovernment sentiments. The Ruby Ridge, Idaho, incident occurred in October 1992 when FBI agents attempted to arrest white supremist Randy Weaver on weapons charges. A gun battle ensued in which Weaver's wife and son were killed by FBI snipers. The Waco, Texas, action occurred in April 1993 when Alcohol, Tobacco, and Firearms officers attempted to raid a compound inhabited by members of the Branch Davidians, a religious cult who had allegedly violated federal weapons laws. A gun battle ensued and the compound caught fire. About 80 of the inhabitants died in the fire.

Bad Policies in Government Agencies

Another reason for distrust and cynicism about government is the many cases of bad policies involving government agencies and progams. These make headline news and give public policies an unfavorable reputation. Some of the problems go back to the 1960s and 1970s. For example, the *Comprehensive Employment and Training Act (CETA)* program attracted a great deal of negative publicity. CETA was established in 1973 to provide programs of public service employment, employment training, and summer youth employment for the economically disadvantaged. Cases were reported in which city administrators used CETA money to hire city employees. The city of Cleveland laid off sanitation workers and hired them back as CETA employees. Other cities also used CETA moneys inappropriately.

In response to the CETA scandals, the federal government established independent monitoring units to monitor CETA operations. Many of the problems were corrected, but in 1982 the CETA program ended and was replaced the next year by the *Jobs Training Partnership Act (JTPA)*. The public service program under CETA was eliminated. JTPA provides job training and summer youth employment. Although JTPA is not without criticism, it has been successful in providing summer employment opportunities for economically disadvantaged teenagers and in serving the employment needs of a few local businesses.

Another example is the case of the Occupational Safety and Health Administration (OSHA), established in 1970. Its goals were broad and its methods of achieving them vague. In its early years, OSHA administrators made many serious mistakes. For example, they incorporated fire and building codes from the National Fire Protection Association as OSHA regulations. Many of these codes were obsolete and absurd. Worse, OSHA inspectors had little training and insisted on enforcing trivial and impossible rules such as "a prohibition on using ice in drinking water (originally directed at the nineteenth-century practice of using ice cut from polluted rivers and lakes) and a requirement that all toilets have a 'hinged openfront seat'" (Gerston, Fraleigh, and Schwab 1988, 176–77). Both opponents and supporters of OSHA were angry over the agency's enforcement of these rules. Inspectors appeared more concerned with citing businesses than with improving workplace health and safety. These problems were well publicized and contributed to the negative reputation of public policies.

In 1977 OSHA proposed deleting more than 1,100 regulations, especially the trivial code standards, and by 1990 it had eliminated 900 (Gerston, Fraleigh, and Schwab 1988, 176–77). Thereafter, the agency took a consultative approach to regulations, consulting with both labor and business. The real success story is OSHA's reduction in job-related injuries and fatalities. However, the success of this policy is not well known. When government responds to correct policy problems, the corrections are rarely publicized.

There are many scandals surrounding welfare programs. The severity of the scandals has caused most Americans to believe that welfare programs should be shut down. Some of the horror stories told by political leaders and the media include cases of food stamp recipients who get change from food stamps to buy liquor or drugs, welfare recipients who have babies to get more money, and doctors who make millions of dollars running Medicaid "factories," servicing hundreds of patients without seeing them. The unpopular folklore surrounding these programs does not portray an accurate picture of the majority of recipients. The programs have succeeded in lessening the severity of poverty, eliminating hunger, and reducing the incidence of diseases associated with malnutrition. Nevertheless, the well-publicized scandals have contributed to people's cynicism about government and public policies.

⇢ *Scholars and Government and Public Policies*

Scholars have always been divided over the issue of government and public policies, and they have contributed to the ambivalence of Americans about government and public policies. On one side of the issue are academics who oppose the expansion of government and public policies as threats to individual liberty. They especially oppose welfare and regulatory policies as doing more harm than good, taking money from hard-working Americans and giving it to less-productive Americans. They believe taxes and regulations undermine the incentive system of the private market, destroy individual initiative, restrict freedom of choice, and facilitate a pathological dependency on government. Some consider the expansion of public policies since the 1930s as dangerous forms of centralized governmental powers, diminishing individual freedom. Other scholars see taxation or government regulation as oppressive and a violation of sacred property rights. They view the role of government as limited to maintaining law and order and protecting private property. Anything beyond violates individual liberties. One proponent of this perspective, Robert Nozick, argued that property owners have exclusive authority over their property and that government has no right to take, regulate, or tax private property without the consent of owners. To support this position he cited the 17th-century English philosopher **John Locke,** who inspired Thomas Jefferson (Nozick 1974).

On the other side of the issue are scholars who support the expansion of government and public policies. They see this expansion as necessary to protect the weak and vulnerable from the private sector that undermines individual liberty. For these scholars, the sanctity of private property does not give property owners a license to violate the rights of others or to take advantage of the vulnerable and to abandon community responsibilities. Nor does it excuse government from its responsibility to protect the rights of individuals and promote the welfare of the community. For these scholars, protecting the rights of private property and private markets often requires government to tax and regulate property, even without the owners' permission. A few of these scholars also cite John Locke to support their arguments. Locke wrote:

> [F]or it would be a direct contradiction for any one to enter into society with others for the securing and regulating of property and yet to suppose his land, whose property is to be regulated by the laws of the society, should be exempt from the jurisdiction of that government to which he himself, the proprietor of the land, is a subject. (1690/1952, 69)

Furthermore, "For as a good prince who is mindful of the trust put into his hands and careful of the good of his people cannot have too much prerogative, that is, power to do good . . ." (Locke 1952, 94). Locke believed it was a contradiction for property owners to enjoy all of the conveniences made possible by government and not want to pay for them. Moreover, the use of governmental resources to provide equal opportunities and to develop human potentials enhanced freedom and liberty.

In sum, conservative and libertarian scholars tend to focus on the excesses and the inefficiencies of government, preferring that the private sector, not the government, solve problems. Liberal scholars defend these same powers and policies. Liberals support government intervention when markets fail, when unexpected market harms are produced, when competition breaks down, or when producers act unfairly or endanger the public. These contradictory positions among scholars contribute to Americans' ambiguity toward government and public policies.

Summary

Americans are ambivalent about public policies and government. On the one hand, we don't like government and are distrustful of politicians. Our political culture emphasizes individualism and limited government. We see government as doing too much and as too wasteful, inefficient, and ineffective. Moreover, the Vietnam War, Watergate and other political scandals, scholars' attack on government and policy, and bad publicity and other factors have contributed to current antigovernment sentiments.

On the other hand, we accept the role of government in modern society. Moreover, we believe the government should spend more money for environmental, educational, health care, and other public policies.

Despite our strong mixed feelings about them, government and public policies are an essential part of our lives. Even though we have a strong private market, we need government for many reasons: to maintain law and order; adjust for unintended harms produced by the market; ensure fair business practices, protect consumers, and compensate for monopolies; provide needed public goods that cannot be adequately provided by the market; maintain the viability of markets during economic crises; promote research and development; and guarantee a fair distribution of resources. We have many different types of public policies: distributive, redistributive, competitive regulatory, protective regulatory, morality, symbolic, substantive, to name a few. There are different ideological perspectives on public policies: conservative, liberal, libertarian, and communitarian.

Review Questions

1. What is a public policy?
2. What are some definitions of public policies?
3. What is the difference between policy decisions and policy actions?
4. What are some examples of public policies?
5. How might public policies enhance the quality of life?
6. What are some different types of public policies?
7. Identify symbolic, substantive, and procedural policies. Provide an example for each.
8. Define distributive, redistributive, competitive regulatory, and protective regulatory policies. Provide an example of each.
9. If goods and services are provided in a private, free market, why do we need public policies?
10. Why are Americans ambivalent about public policies and government?

Select Websites

The Roper Center for public opinion research provides information on the general population's attitudes toward government and views toward contemporary public policy issues.
http://www.ropercenter.uconn.edu/

PollingReport.Com is an independent, nonpartisan resource on trends in American public opinion. It covers opinions toward both contemporary issues and presidential candidates.
http://www.pollingreport.com/

This is Randall Ripley's homepage.
http://psweb.sbs.ohio-state.edu/faculty/rripley/rripley.htm

Key Terms

allocational policies
communitarians
competitive regulatory policies
conservatives
developmental policies
distributive policies
eminent domain
externality
free rider
Thomas Hobbes
liberals
libertarians

John Locke
market failure
morality policies
policy activities
policy statements
procedural policy
protective regulatory policies
public good
public policies
substantive policy
symbolic policy

CHAPTER 2

Policy Theory

Theory is a tool that operates like a lens. It focuses attention on some objects, while filtering out others. It contains assumptions about things: what they are and how they are expected to behave. Theory helps to describe, explain, or predict events or phenomena. The following illustration demonstrates the role of theory in describing an object.

Suppose I hire you to measure an elephant. That may sound like a pretty straightforward job description, but think about it for a minute. Do you measure its weight? Height? Length? Volume? Intensity of its color gray? Number and depth of its wrinkles? Or perhaps the proportion of the day it sleeps. In order to measure this creature, you need to select one or a few features from many possibilities. That choice will be determined by your purpose for measuring, or rather mine, since I hired you. If I were manager of a railroad freight department, I would need to know the elephant's height, length, and weight. But if I were a taxidermist, I would be more interested in its volume and wrinkles. As a trainer, I might care more about the proportion of the day it sleeps. As a producer of synthetic animal skins, I would want to know its exact hue of gray. . . . (Stone 1997, 163)

How one describes the elephant depends on one's perspective, purpose, or theoretical orientation. This orientation focuses attention on select aspects of the thing to be described. The same principle applies to public policies. Describing public policies is not a matter of stating facts or citing statistics. The choice of facts to focus on and categories to measure is a function of one's theoretical orientation. Policy theory is an important tool helpful in describing public policies.

Theory also assists in explaining and predicting events. Consider the imaginary story of two sports announcers: a rookie and a veteran. The rookie announced that the Cougars won last night's football game with a score of 36 to the Tigers' score of only 3. The rookie explained that the Tigers lost because they fumbled the ball 15 times, compared to only 2 fumbles for the Cougars. The veteran offered an alternative explanation: The Cougars had started practicing sooner in the season than the Tigers; had trained longer and harder than any other team; had more defensive players with more experience, more weight, and stronger legs than other teams; and had better defensive strategies than most teams. The veteran maintained that the Cougars' defensive team pressured the Tigers into fumbling the ball. He said, "They charged in like a runaway freight train." He also predicted that the Cougars would win next week's football game.

Policy theory assists policy analysts in describing, explaining, or predicting public policies. It focuses attention on what it considers to be the more important aspects of a policy, while detracting attention away from aspects it deems trivial. Theory contains assumptions about the behavioral expectations of a policy. Sometimes theory relies on metaphors to enhance its ability to explain, much like the veteran sports announcer used the metaphor of the runaway freight train.

Public policy theory is most useful in explaining how and why public policies change. There are four major sets of policy theories:

1. State centered and decision theory
2. Elitist and pluralist theory
3. Cyclical models
4. Eclectic theories

Each set focuses on different sources of policy change. State centered theory focuses on the role of governmental institutions and officials. This theory assumes that the way that government is organized and the choices government officials make

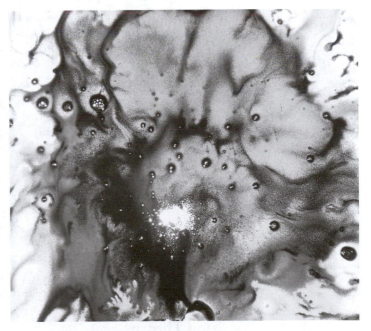

Abstract picture. Political theory is useful in taking an incomprehensible abstraction and making sense out of it.

among policy alternatives explain changes in public policies. Group or pluralist theories concentrate on the role of organized interest groups in changing policies; elite theories generally draw attention to the role of powerful economic elites in changing public policies. Cyclical theories emphasize policy making and change as an ongoing, continuous, and cyclical process. Finally, eclectic theories combine many different theories to explain public policy change.

⇥ *State Centered and Decision Theory*

Institutional, state centered, and decision theory assumes that the way government is organized and the choices individual governmental officials make are key factors in explaining changes in public policies. Because Chapter 3 covers the institutions of government and public policy, aspects of institutional theory will be discussed in that chapter. This section covers state centered and decision theory.

State Centered Approach

State centered theory focuses on the government itself—that is, the role of its organization and key officials in promoting policy change. James Q. Wilson's (1989) study of public bureaucracies is a state centered approach. Wilson insisted that the state is not like a ball bounced around by interest groups or economic arrangements. He argued that state officials often initiate policy change and bring together the political interests essential to produce change. The deregulation of the airline industry illustrates the model. The policy change was led by the staff within the Civil Aeronautics Board (CAB), although it was supported by Congress, the president, and other agencies. Wilson wrote:

> Deregulation was not accomplished until many other actors—two presidents, other federal agencies, several senators and representatives—had played their parts; but the decisive initial steps were taken by staff members who chose to act as if their agency was not in a clientele relationship with industry. (1989, 87)

In 1978 Congress passed the *Air Transportation Deregulation Act* which opened the airline market to competition and allowed airline companies to reduce the price of airline tickets. Wilson insisted that this legislation originated among CAB officials.

Theda Skocpol is another proponent of the state centered approach. She maintained that changes in social welfare policies are best explained by the role of state officials, political parties, and previous policies. Previous policies provide the framework from which subsequent policies emerge. For example, the Aid for Dependent Children (AFDC) program created in 1935 was modeled after the state aid for widows program created during the Progressive Era. Similarly, the 1996 welfare program that limits benefits to two years is modeled after state programs developed in the late 1980s and early 1990s. Skocpol argued that state and local officials, social workers, and professional organizations active in the social welfare area significantly shape welfare policies. Of course, changes in the party in power and in party leadership also contribute to these policy changes. For the most part, state centered theorists see governmental officials as the prime initiators of policy change.

Decision Theory

Decision theory focuses on the manner in which government officials and policy makers decide on policy options. There are many different approaches to the study of decision making.

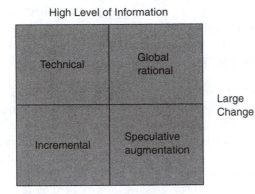

High Level of Information

FIGURE 2.1   *Forms of Decision Making Based on the Amount of Information*

SOURCE: Adapted from *Incrementalism and Public Policy* by Michael T. Hayes, 1992. Reprinted by permission of Pearson Education, Inc.

One approach identifies different methods of decision making depending on the extent of the proposed change and the level of information decision makers possess. Several major decision-making methods can be identified through this approach. The most common methods are (1) rational, (2) incremental, (3) technical, and (4) speculative augmentation. Figure 2.1 illustrates the differences.

Rational Decision Making

The rational decision makers require substantial amounts of information. They must clearly understand the problem they are attempting to solve and the specific policy options open to them. There are many different approaches to **rational decision making**. One popular rational approach is **cost-benefit analysis** which uses a rough formula that compares the benefits of a policy to its costs. Costs are generally estimated by adding the amount of money the government and private businesses must spend to carry out the policy. For example, the costs of implementing clean air policy are estimated in terms of the Environmental Protection Agency's (EPA) budget and the amount of money automobile and utility companies pay for pollution-control devices. Benefits can be estimated in terms of the value of clean air, the decline in health expenses related to air pollution, and the decline in damaged property related to acid rain. The new policy is typically accepted if the benefits are greater than the costs.

Incremental Decision Making

Most decisions over public policy options are incremental; that is, they involve limited information and small tentative adjustments to existing policies. Three practical reasons explain why policy making tends to be incremental. First, it is easier to correct a mistake if the change is small than to correct a large mistake. Second, incremental decision making considers the demands and perspectives of competing interest groups. Rather than seeking the best solution to a policy problem, which may be unacceptable, **incrementalism** strives to satisfy all groups and perspectives, especially established interests, and it involves bargaining and compromise. Students of public policy use the term **satisficing** to describe this process. Finally, policies tend to be incremental because established and powerful interest groups have a stake in maintaining the status quo, especially if existing arrangements favor them. Charles Lindblom used the term "muddling through" to describe incremental decision making. Because decision makers operate in a political environment with little information, few policy alternatives, and a desire to avoid costly errors, they muddle through by making small tentative decisions (Lindblom 1959).

There is one problem with using the incremental decision-making approach: It is difficult to solve major social or political problems. For example, solving the air pollution problem required three nonincremental factors: a radically different approach, a substantial allocation of resources, and a new agency with significant authority. The establishment of a federal agency with the power to impose substantial fines on major automobile producers was a radical break from the incremental approach used before the establishment of the Environmental Protection Agency. It is unlikely that any progress would have been made in addressing this problem without a break with the incremental approach used in the past.

Technical

A technical decision is one based on using substantial information to make a small but important policy change. A good example is the Occupational Safety and Health Administration (OSHA) requiring medical professionals to use latex gloves if it is likely that they will be exposed to blood. The decision was made to reduce the accidental spread of HIV.

Speculative Augmentation

Charles Jones coined the term **speculative augmentation** to describe the process of making nonincremental decisions that involved limited information and required substantial change. When decision makers have little information, they must speculate about the consequences of decisions in a relative vacuum. Because environmental interest groups and public opinion demanded a substantial public response to the pollution issue, policy options expanded well beyond incremental choices. Jones characterized decision making over air pollution in the 1950s and 1960s as incremental, but the process of 1969–70, which culminated in the passage of the Clean Air Act, was speculative augmentation.

Public Choice

Another common approach to decision making is called **public choice**. The public choice theory applies assumptions about the market or economic models to public decision making. Market models assume that decision makers in government and individual citizens pursue their own self-interest. Elected officials strive to get reelected, bureaucrats strive to advance their careers, and citizens strive to advance their positions. Public choice theory assumes that government operates more efficiently when it is decentralized and maximizes the choices of individual citizens. Public choice theory has been challenged on empirical grounds; that is, critics have demonstrated that citizens do not necessarily favor public policies more consistent with their self-interest and that decentralized governments are not necessarily the most efficient.

→ Elitist and Pluralist Theory

For a long time elitist and pluralist theories dominated the debate over policy making. Each theory focused on a different aspect of political power. Advocates of **elitist theory** assumed that power was concentrated in a small group of economic or corporate elites directly involved in making public policies. Proponents of **pluralist theory** assumed that power was dispersed among competing, organized interest groups and that new policies arose from a process of bargaining, negotiation, and compromise.

The Elitist Perspective

Sociologist C. Wright Mills expressed elitist theory in his classic book *The Power Elite* (1973). He identified several types and levels of elites: the corporate and military elites at the national level of government and the economic elites at the local level. Contemporary elite theorists include Thomas Dye and William Domhoff. Dye has written a series of studies of federal policy making focusing on presidents from Nixon to Clinton and the extent to which government officials are drawn from the corporate sector.

William Domhoff (1998; 1996) studied policy making from an elitist perspective. Although he agreed with a number of the assumptions of the pluralist and state centered explanations of policy change, he insisted that these theories grossly underestimate the extent to which leaders from the corporate sector dominate the government and the policy-making process. Summarizing his study of the enactment of Social Security, Domhoff wrote:

> The main work on the program was done by experts from a private organization called Industrial Relations Counselors, Inc., which had been founded in 1921 by John D. Rockefeller, Jr., to search for ways to deal with labor unrest and avoid unionization. The organization was closely linked to both the family's main oil companies (today no longer controlled by the family) and charitable foundations . . .
>
> The legislation that went before Congress had the backing of several major industrialists of the time, who were serving on an advisory commission. These supporters included the chief executive officers of Standard Oil of New Jersey, General Electric, and Filenes Department Store of Boston, all prominent figures in the policy-formation network. (1998, 271)

Domhoff concluded that a rival faction of the dominant class developed Social Security policy. Among this faction were liberal corporate leaders. Other more conservative corporate leaders, the National Association of Manufacturers, and southern plantation owners opposed federal social policies. Domhoff argued that members of the dominant class also influence the policy-making process through their direct involvement in policy-making networks, their support for policy-making foundations and research institutes, their presence in policy-making positions in government, their complex connections with the media, their influence in the electoral process, and their ability to launch public relations campaigns.

Group/Pluralist Theory

Group theory is based on three assumptions about society and government. First, people are social beings and exist in a social or organizational context. They belong to a religious organization (church, synagogue, or mosque), professional association, labor union, block club, social club, sorority or fraternity, or some other form of organization. Even the family is a form of organization.

Second, political interests are expressed in the context of political organizations. As individuals are impacted by issues, they either mobilize the organizations they are a part of or form new organizations. For example, when educational issues impact parents, they get involved in an existing parent organization or they form a new one (Truman 1993).

Finally, group theorists assume that government is responsive to organized political interests that pressure government to respond to their concerns. Sometimes interest groups have mutually exclusive concerns. In these cases, government mediates among the different groups. For example, environmental groups are concerned with the long-term results of the loss of the rain forest. Logging companies are concerned with what they perceive to be excessive regulations that threaten their industry. Proponents of group theory envision government being concerned with both groups, acting as a mediator, and engaging in a process of bargaining and compromise.

Pluralists are group theorists who see the interest group process as an alternative to majoritarian democracy. They argue that most people are concerned only with issues that impact them directly or when they have a stake in the outcome. For example, if a major corporation decides to build a new production facility in a city, then those who may gain jobs or job security from the facility may actively support the project. Restaurant owners who are likely to profit from an increase in business may organize and support the project. Those who might lose their homes or have a stake in preserving the status quo may organize in opposition to the project. Homeowners can go to court to secure a more acceptable price for their homes. Labor unions, business associations, local chambers of commerce, and neighborhood and community organizations may all participate in shaping public policies surrounding the project. As mentioned, pluralists insist that people become involved in the political process when issues affect them directly. Public policy change is explained in terms of the interest group process. The process is democratic so long as people have a right to organize and participate in the policy-making process and so long as government officials respond to the people's interests (Cobb and Elder 1983; Dahl 1970).

Critiques of Elitist and Pluralist Theory

The Pluralist Critique of Elitism

Pluralists are critical of elitists. They maintain that elitists confuse corporate leaders who have a reputation for power with political leaders who actually have a direct influence on the policy-making process. Corporate leaders or economic elites may have little or no interest in most policy areas such as education, forestry, transportation, or highway safety. Pluralists argue that elitists falsely assume that power is fixed and concentrated among the economic elite, when in fact it is fluid, changing from time to time and from one policy area to another.

The Bias of Pluralism

A few scholars have criticized the **bias of pluralism**. These critics have identified two types of biases in the model. The pluralists favor organized groups. E. S. Schattschneider noted, "The range of organized, identifiably known groups is amazingly narrow" (1975, 32). There are many advocacy organizations, such as the Children's Defense Fund or the American Association of Retired Persons (AARP). However, many interests are unorganized and shut out of the interest group arena. They will be ineffective as long as no organizations are present to represent their interests. For example, undocumented workers, homeless people, pregnant teenagers, prison inmates, and food stamp and Medicaid users are rarely organized and, thus, are often excluded from the policy-making process.

Another type of bias is socioeconomic. In this case bias favors upper-strata interests. Schattschneider commented:

The vice of the group theory is that it conceals the most significant aspect of the system. The flaw in the pluralist heaven is that the heavenly chorus sings with a strong upper class accent. (1975, 34–35)

William Hudson (2004) expands on Schattschneider's point. He noted that about 70.0 percent of lobbying groups operating in Washington, D.C., represent business interests, whereas citizen groups account for 4.1 percent and labor unions 1.7 percent. He identified three types of business organizations:

- General business organizations such as the U.S. Chamber of Commerce with about 250,000 members nationally, the National Association of Manufacturers, representing the country's largest industrial firms, and the Business Roundtable consisting of about 200 corporate leaders.
- Trade organizations consisting of groups such as the American Bankers Association and the National Association of Home Builders.
- Lobbyists representing individual corporations or conglomerates such as General Electric and General Motors.

The point is that business and corporate interests tend to dominate the pluralist arena.

Charles Lindblom (1978), a proponent of pluralism, acknowledged the bias and attributed it to the importance of businesses in maintaining a stable economy and generating resources essential for the support of government. Because of the role and function of businesses in a market economy, Lindblom concluded that they have a privileged position in relation to government.

In the eyes of government officials, therefore, businessmen do not appear simply as the representatives of a special interest, as representatives of interest groups do. They appear as functionaries performing functions that government officials regard as indispensable. . . . Any government official who understands the requirements of his position and the responsibilities that market-oriented systems throw on businessmen will therefore grant them a privileged position. (1978, 175)

Businesses employ people and provide the economic base for the taxable revenue that supports government. Moreover, businesses have more resources to mobilize against elected officials who support policies hostile to their interests. For these reasons, the interest group or pluralist process suffers from a business or corporate interest bias.

⇾ Cyclical Theories

There are many cyclical theories of policy change. This section examines two of them: the liberal-conservative cycle and the policy cycle. Both assume that policy making is an ongoing cyclical process.

Liberal-Conservative Cycle Theory

The liberal-conservative theory assumes that public policies change from liberal to conservative and back to liberal again. The theory applies to long-term policy changes occurring over several generations and focuses on the pattern of policy change and less on the factors contributing to the change. Liberal-conservative theory will be used in Chapter 3 to discuss the pattern of policy change in the 20th century. The liberal periods are the 1930s, 1960s, and 1990s; the conservative periods include the 1920s, 1950s, and 1980s.

There are four reasons why policies oscillate from liberal to conservative and back. First, grassroots organizations that produce liberal policies have difficulty sustaining themselves over time. After a liberal policy is established, members of these organizations often lose interest. Membership declines. This happened to environmental groups after the passage of the Clean Air Acts of 1970 and 1990. For another example, after the expansion in the late 1960s of Aid for Families with Dependent Children (AFDC), an income support program for poor families with children, welfare rights organizations that had supported the expansion disappeared by the late 1970s, giving rise to cuts in the program in the early 1980s.

Second, the public has a short attention span. When the public focuses on a problem, government either does something about it or fails to solve it. In either case the public soon loses interest and shifts to another issue.

Third, generational change produces shifts from liberal to conservative policies. The generation of the 1960s produced the Great Society programs. By the 1980s, a new generation emerged to produce the conservative policies of that decade. Also, the conditions that produced the liberal policies of the 1960s no longer existed during the conservative 1980s.

Policy Cycle Model

As shown in Figure 2.2, the **policy cycle model** assumes that policy making is an ongoing and continuous process with different governmental entities and political interest involved at different stages. There are different versions of this model. The simplest version is the three-stage model that entails policy making, policy implementation, and policy impact. Policy is adopted in the policy-making stage. This may involve Congress passing a law or the Supreme Court issuing a decision. Policy is carried out in the implementation stage. For example, an administrative agency may impose fines for not complying with the policy. Not all policies are carried out. If there is no implementing agency or if the agency is uncommitted

FIGURE 2.2   *The Three-Stage Policy Cycle Model*

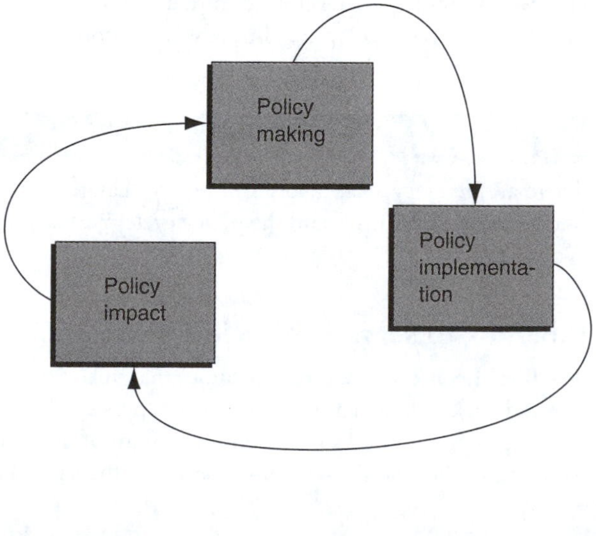

to the policy, the policy is unlikely to be carried out. The final stage has to do with the impacts of the policy. Sometimes there are none or the policy may have an effect opposite to that intended. In either case, the policy moves back to the policy-making stage.

Newer, more elaborate versions of the policy cycle model divide the policy-making stage into several additional stages: problem definition, agenda setting, and policy adoption. Each stage in this model involves different processes and different actors. Interest groups may be involved at every stage, defining policy problems, setting agendas, and securing the adoption of the policy. Government entities are not necessarily involved at the problem definition stage, but they are involved at different stages. The presidency and Congress may be involved at the policy adoption stage. Bureaucratic agencies are often involved in the implementation stage.

Figure 2.3 presents a multistage policy cycle. Each one of the five stages entails complex processes.

Problem Definition

During the first stage, **problem definition**, political leaders define a problem as one requiring a public policy response. Leaders identify its cause, consequences, and solution, and their definition shapes the policy solution.

Most people take political problems for granted. What people accept as a problem today may not have been perceived as a problem 40 or 50 years ago. What people accept as normal today may become a problem 40 or 50 years in the future. For example, today a number of political organizations see drunk drivers as a problem. About a hundred years ago several political organizations saw alcoholic beverages as such a severe problem—the cause of most social ills—that they succeeded in passing an amendment to the Constitution prohibiting the production, distribution, and sale of beer, wine, and liquor. Political leaders identified booze as the problem and created a policy to eliminate it. Of course, 10 or 15 years later political leaders claimed that the solution was worse than the problem. The point is that political leaders play a crucial role in identifying situations and defining them as problems requiring government action.

The study of the problem definition phase of policy making is relatively new. It arises from what some scholars call postpositivism. Positivists take an objective approach to a problem, insisting that a problem is like an object or a condition. You can see it, measure it, take a picture of it, and develop a solution. In contrast to positivists, postpositivists take a cultural approach (Gusfield 1981; Rochefort and Cobb 1994; Stone 1997); they look at how societies and groups define problems. They believe that a problem is a situation that interest groups

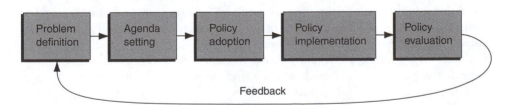

FIGURE 2.3   *Multistage Policy Cycle Model*

define as a problem. Interest groups identify the harm done by the situation, the cause of the problem, and the culprit. They then convince other people to accept the situation as a problem requiring government action. However, different interest groups can see the same situation and interpret it differently. One group might interpret a particular situation as a problem that requires government action while another group will interpret the same situation either as inevitable or as a function of individual choice, therefore not requiring government action. Joseph Gusfield summed up the postpositivist approach as follows:

> Human problems do not spring up, full-blown and announced, into the consciousness of bystanders. Even to recognize a situation as painful requires a system for categorizing and defining events. All situations that are experienced by people as painful do not become matters of public activity and targets for public action. Neither are they given the same meaning at all times and by all peoples. Objective conditions are seldom so compelling and so clear in their form that they spontaneously generate a "true" consciousness. (1981, 3)

Deborah Stone explained the politics of problem definition and the construction of policy cultures:

> Problem definition is a matter of representation because every description of a situation is a portrayal from only one of many points of view. Problem definition is strategic because groups, individuals, and government agencies deliberately and consciously design portrayals so as to promote their favored course of action. (1997, 133)

In other words, interest groups define situations as policy problems. They do this by the way they portray a situation, use images, promote narratives, tell stories, and explain cause and effect—all in ways that favor the policy solutions they advocate.

Take the issue of gun control. Each of the two sides of the gun-control issue is represented by different interest groups, which offer a different story that supports a different set of policy alternatives.

The National Rifle Association (NRA) supports the right to own guns. This organization offers the following story. At one time, in a faraway country, people owned guns. The people were free and violent crime rates low. Then, government took away the people's right to own guns. When people lost this right, horrible things happened. Violent crime rates increased and people lost their freedom. In the United States, the Constitution protects our basic freedoms, among them our right to own guns. The problem is that some politicians would restrict our right to own guns. The solution is to oppose politicians who advocate gun control and support those in favor of the right to own guns.

On the other side of the issue are those interest groups who advocate government regulation of guns. They offer this story: The United States has the highest murder rate among industrialized countries. Most murders are committed with handguns. U.S. gun policy is so liberal that we allow the mentally ill, convicted felons, and emotionally disturbed people to buy guns and kill people. Young children have access to guns without trigger locks. This situation contributes to our higher murder rate. The antigun lobby believes current policies are irrational. Their solution is to require weapons retailers to do background checks on everyone purchasing a gun, to ban assault weapons, and to require gun owners to install trigger locks on guns to prevent children from using them.

The point of the gun-control story is that different interest groups define problems in ways that support the policies they advocate. In defining the problem, they strategically represent it through stories that support their policies.

Agenda Setting

Once a situation is defined as a problem requiring governmental action, the policy-making process moves to the agenda-setting phase. The theory of **agenda setting** examines the process in which issues or problems are raised. Cobb and Elder (1983) identified two major types of political agendas: public and governmental. Public agenda issues are discussed in the media—newspapers, magazines, journals, television, and radio. They are also discussed in places such as homes, restaurants, bars, country clubs, recreational facilities, parks, barbershops, salons, and others. **Government agenda** issues are discussed inside government: Congress, the president's office, bureaucratic agencies, or the courts.

The process of setting the public agenda involves trigger events and initiators. Trigger events dramatize an issue and capture media attention. They make people more aware of the issue (Cobb and Elder 1983). Trigger events are sudden and often traumatic. They include natural disasters, man-made catastrophes, or demographic changes. Hurricanes, tornadoes, and floods are natural disasters. A hurricane precipitated the establishment of the Federal Emergency Management Agency (FEMA). The natural disaster made people more aware of the need for disaster relief.

Man-made disasters include shocking human events such as a bombing, assassination attempt, mass shooting, or a major accident. A good example of a man-made disaster that raised the visibility of an issue and eventually led to major policy changes is mad cow disease, a degenerative and fatal brain disease transmitted to cattle from the brain and spinal cord tissue of infected cattle. Consumer and animal rights groups had been trying to pressure the government to ban the use of cattle brains in cattle feed and to prohibit the slaughter of animals being tested for mad cow disease. A case of mad cow disease was discovered December 9, 2003, in the state of Washington two weeks after the animal had been slaughtered and the beef distributed. The news shocked the nation and made headline news throughout the United States. Several countries banned U.S. beef. In reaction, the secretary of agriculture announced several policy changes that prohibited the slaughter of cows tested for mad cow disease, banned the use of cow brain and spinal cord tissue in cattle feed, and took steps to enforce the ban. Another example of a man-made disaster took place on September 11, 2001. The disaster of 9/11 raised the issue of international terrorism and the need for a homeland security policy. It contributed to the establishment of a new cabinet department, the Department of Homeland Security.

Demographic changes include population growth, population shifts, sudden increases in unemployment, and other similar changes. The sudden increase in the number and proportion of households headed by women and the dramatic increase in the number of welfare recipients in the early 1990s raised the saliency of welfare as an issue. Trigger events, whether natural disasters or demographic changes, dramatize and popularize issues and may act as a catalyst for change.

Initiators are policy leaders who define policy problems, promote public issues, and advocate policy proposals. They operate to raise the visibility of issues, to get them on the governmental agenda, and to navigate them through the policy-making process. John Kingdon insisted that policy initiators inside government are like policy entrepreneurs who take advantage of windows of opportunity to usher policies through Congress (1984).

Policy Adoption

Once a policy gets on the governmental agenda, it moves to the policy adoption phase. **Policy adoption** has to do with a governmental institution creating the policy. Any institution of government can develop and adopt a public policy; Congress, the presidency, the courts, and the bureaucracy make policies all the time. Congress makes public policies when it passes a law that is then signed by the president. The president makes policies by issuing executive orders and by introducing bills to Congress. The Supreme Court makes polices through its decisions. Bureaucratic agencies make policies every time they issue new regulations.

The dynamics of policy adoption differ in the several institutions of government. Interest groups and political leaders play key roles in every institution. The role of interest groups in lobbying Congress and the president is well known. Interest groups are also involved in the decision making of bureaucratic agencies and the courts. Bureaucratic agencies have open hearings when issuing new regulations. Interest groups often testify at these hearings and their testimony influences policy making. Interest groups are involved in the court system in two ways: They bring cases before the courts and they present short papers arguing for their policy preference. Hundreds of different interest groups presented papers or legal briefs in the *Roe v. Wade* decision on abortion. Interest groups thus play a role in defining problems and promoting their policy solutions throughout the policy-making process.

Policy Implementation

Once the policy is made, it enters the implementation stage. **Policy implementation** involves the process of carrying out the policy. Since the proliferation of public policies in the 1960s and 1970s, public policy students have paid more attention to this stage. A focus on the policy implementation stage helps to explain why some policies succeed and others fail. Implementation theory identifies four major factors that explain successful or unsuccessful implementation: (1) statutory, (2) degree of change, (3) environmental, and (4) institutions of government (Mazmanian and Sabatier 1989).

Statutory   Statutory factors are those that policy makers can control. When Congress enacts a law, it can control the goal of the policy, the amount of resources committed to it, and the agency assigned to carry it out. Public policies fail when goals are ambiguous, resources are inadequate, implementing agencies have other priorities, or agencies lack sufficient authority to carry out the policy. Congress has the power to establish clear goals, allocate adequate resources, and assign sufficient authority to the implementing agency.

Degree of Change   Whether a policy goal is reached or not depends on how difficult it is to attain. This difficulty depends on the degree of change required, which in turn depends on two factors: (1) the population that must change and (2) the cost of the change.

The population that must change is called the target population. If the target population is small as a percentage of the total population, then change is more likely to occur. If the target population is large as a percentage of the total population, then change is less likely. For example, to reduce automobile pollution the Clean Air Act of 1970 targeted two populations: automobile producers and automobile drivers. The goal was to get automakers to add pollution-control devices to the automobile and to get drivers to drive less. It was easier to get the automobile companies to change because as a smaller target population, they were easier to identify. It was more difficult to get drivers to change their habits because they constituted a large percentage of the total population.

The costs of change come in two forms: money and values. Money can be measured in terms of the number of dollars required to comply with a new policy. Values are more difficult to measure; they have to do with how strongly people feel about maintaining their traditions. Civil rights laws were resisted because they challenged the southern tradition of segregation, and most southerners felt strongly about maintaining segregation.

Environmental   Environmental factors such as economic arrangements, public opinion, and interest groups play a role in the implementation process. A public policy is less likely to succeed if public opinion or a number of powerful interests are hostile to it. It is more likely to succeed when it enjoys the support of organized interest groups and favorable public opinion. Some policy initiatives are dropped because new issues emerge. For example, the War on Poverty was stalled by the Vietnam War. Clean air policies have been undermined by high unemployment and inflation rates.

Implementing Agency   The implementing agency makes a difference in the success of a policy. If the agency has sufficient resources, adequate authority, and capable administrators, a policy is likely to succeed. The agency must also give the policy a high priority and its leaders must be committed to achieving the goals of the policy.

Policy Evaluation

Once a policy is implemented, it enters the evaluation stage or what has also been referred to as the impact stage. After a policy is implemented it is expected to have an impact. For example, the impact of the Clean Air Act of 1990 is measured in terms of the extent to which acid rain is reduced. The impact of the Personal Responsibility and Work Opportunity Act of 1996 is measured in terms of the reduction of the number of welfare recipients. As in the systems model, policy may impact other interest groups, generate feedback, and start the cycle all over again.

→ Eclectic Theories

Eclectic theories combine many of the earlier theories of public policy change. They provide strong explanations for long-term trends in public policy and are especially useful in explaining the pattern of long-term policy stability, followed by substantial change. Three eclectic theories are covered below: punctuated equilibrium, social movement, and policy regime.

Punctuated Equilibrium

Baumgartner and Jones (1993) use the term **punctuated equilibrium** to describe policy making in the United States. The term refers to long periods of policy stability interrupted by episodes of abrupt and substantial change. The long periods of stability are explained by political power balanced among interest groups. Shifts in public attention and political power explain the episodes of abrupt change.

They examined policy monopolies to explain both stability and abrupt change. A **policy monopoly** is a closed system of policy making—open only to the actors within the close net of decision makers in the system. It consists of bureaucratic, congressional, and interest group leaders who have the same set of beliefs, ideas, and images about a policy. Policy ideas and images include assumptions about the problem addressed by the policy itself. The policy monopoly is similar to iron triangles—close triangular relations among interest group, lower-level bureaucratic, and congressional subcommittee leaders—or subsystems, discussed in the last chapter. Interest groups within the policy monopoly operate to keep other interest groups out and to maintain long-term stability in the policy. Policies change when policy monopolies dissolve and national leaders, the media, and policy makers shift public attention to different aspects of the issue or promote alternative beliefs and policies.

Nuclear energy provides an example of the creation and destruction of a policy monopoly. Originally nuclear energy policy operated in a closed system dominated by "corporate, political, and technocratic elites advocating nuclear power [who] had privileged access to the most insulated and centralized interiors of the policy process" (Campell 1988, 78). Then, several factors contributed to the dissolution of this policy monopoly and brought about policy change: the defection of technical Atomic Energy Commission (AEC) staff members who questioned the safety of nuclear energy, the expansion of the issue as AEC scientists leaked information to excluded organizations such as the Union of Concerned Scientists, the dramatic increase of negative media attention and the image change of nuclear energy from positive to negative, and the creation of new venues as the number of congressional committees and subcommittees overseeing nuclear energy escalated. In 1974 the AEC was dismantled and its regulatory functions assigned to the Nuclear Regulatory Commission; its promotional functions were shifted to the Energy Research and Development Agency.

Social Movement Theory

The **social movement** perspective offers an explanation for both long periods of policy stability and short bursts of policy change. Proponents of social movement theory insist that social movements rarely occur, but when they do, they produce substantial policy changes. These movements are characterized by the rapid growth and mobilization of grassroots organizations. Established organizations move rapidly in attracting new members, distributing information and ideas about their issue and policy solutions, and raising the visibility of their organization. They form coalitions with other organizations and attract media attention to publicize and promote their ideas. Examples of social movements include civil rights, women's rights, environmental protection, consumer protection, and antiwar activism. Some movements were successful in producing new policies. The civil rights movement produced several important civil rights bills, but the movements opposed to strategic arms and nuclear energy were short lived and produced few results.

Piven and Cloward offered a theory of protest movements to explain why they occur sporadically. They argued that social systems are remarkably stable over time because people enjoy stability. People tend to be conformists because conformity gives them a sense of security. The institutional arrangements that regulate their daily lives appear natural and inevitable. Poor and oppressed people tend to accept their lot as they "are led to believe that their destitution is deserved, and that the riches and powers that others command are also deserved" (1979, 6). Protest movements arise only under extraordinary circumstances, such as social dislocation, which takes many forms: sudden increases in mass hardship, rapid institutional changes, breakdowns in daily routines or regulatory institutions, calamitous unemployment rates, rapid urbanization, and others. Social dislocation impacts belief systems and provokes questions concerning the legitimacy of existing arrangements. Changes in belief systems influence changes in behavior. Grassroots organizations help change behavior and beliefs by articulating an alternative worldview and promoting new policy goals.

Policy Regime Theory

The theories discussed here offer some explanation for why and how public policies change. The problem is that each theory focuses on different factors involved in the process of change. For example, the pluralist approach highlights the role of organized interest groups but ignores the role of elites, socioeconomic changes, and policy entrepreneurs in government. Social movement studies tend to ignore the relationship between social movement leaders and government leaders. The state centered approach focuses on decision making, the role of governmental officials, and institutional arrangements, but neglects the role of economic arrangements and social movements in explaining policy change. The policy cycle approach provides a good description of the process of policy change, policy making, and implementation, but offers little explanation. These approaches rarely help us understand periods of long-term policy stability, followed by brief periods of substantial policy change. Cobb and Elder's focus on trigger events, initiators, and agenda building helps to explain periods of policy change, but not necessarily long-term stability.

The Policy Regime Model

The punctuated equilibrium approach of Baumgartner and Jones—with its focus on policy monopolies, venues, ideology, and shifting attention—helps to explain both stability and change. The **policy regime model** builds on this approach. This model is not original but incorporates many different theories of policy change (Harris and Milkis 1996; Wilson 2000). It draws from pluralist, elitist, and state centered theories. It integrates problem definition, agenda setting, policy adoption, and implementation. It also draws from the social movement theory. Because the policy regime model is a composite of different public policy theories, it provides a powerful framework for explaining continuity and change in public policies.

The policy regime model has several dimensions, most notably power arrangements, organizational arrangements, and the dominant policy paradigm. Each dimension explains stability and change in public policy, and each needs to be examined separately.

Power Arrangements   The first dimension is power arrangements. Power arrangements involve patterned ways in which individuals and organizations influence the development and maintenance of a public policy. These patterns may include a small group of influential governmental leaders, a small group of powerful corporate directors, or a wide array of different organized interests.

Organizational Arrangements   The second dimension is organizational arrangements. The organization pertains to the governmental agencies, bodies, and individuals involved in implementing the policy. It also includes private organizations, nonprofit organizations, and citizen groups. Organizational arrangements have to do with government agencies involved with the policy. For example, the EPA is the governmental organization involved with environmental policies.

Policy Paradigm   The third dimension is the dominant policy paradigm. A paradigm is a conceptual framework that contains assumptions about the world. It is like the lens of a camera, focusing attention on particular objects and shaping what one sees. It helps to make sense of the world.

A policy paradigm has much in common with the beliefs, value systems, or ideology of the policy monopoly model or the problem definition of other models. It contains both the definition of the policy problem and the policy solution. The policy paradigm defines the policy problem through the use of stories, language, images, and assumptions that support its policy solutions. For example, the old dominant paradigm on the environment assumed that chemicals were good, that pesticides killed dangerous insects like malaria-carrying mosquitoes, and that critics of the use of chemicals were irrational and stood in the way of progress. The new paradigm on the environment assumed that dangerous pesticides could stick to plant and animal tissue, move up the food chain to people, accumulate in the human body, and cause serious health problems. In the old paradigm, insects were the problem; the solution was potent pesticides. Early pesticide regulations were designed to ensure the potency of the chemical. In the new paradigm, dangerous pesticides were the problem; the solution was to ban the pesticide or restrict its use. The point is that a policy paradigm defines the problem and promotes its own policy solution, depicting alternative policies as irrational. It is a powerful force for maintaining policy stability.

How Regime Theory Explains Periods of Policy Stability

Every aspect of the policy regime contributes to long-term stability: power arrangements, policy paradigm, and organization. Powerful individuals and organizations often operate to preserve the status quo. They exercise their influence to limit the emergence of new policies only to those that are innocuous to their interests. Prior to the establishment of the current environmental policy regime, mining, agricultural, timber, and industrial interests dominated the environmental policy regime until 1970. They kept antipollution issues off the governmental agenda and maintained the status quo. Power arrangements tend to be stable over time. So long as they remain stable, the public policies they support will change very little.

The policy paradigm plays a powerful role in preventing major policy changes. It structures perception of a policy problem in ways that obstruct the emergence of alternative definitions of the problem and alternative policy solutions. The policy paradigm justifies existing policies and contributes to long-term stability.

Government organizations and officials operate to maintain policy stability. Officials generally support the policies they administer precisely because their jobs depend on them. For example, officials involved with implementing the Head Start program—a federally funded program for preschoolers from low-income families—tend to be advocates for this program because their jobs depend on its survival. Organizational arrangement, along with the policy paradigm and power arrangements, operate to maintain long-term policy stability.

Abrupt and Profound Change and the Policy Regime

An abrupt and profound change in a public policy indicates a change in the policy regime. The birth of the Environmental Protection Agency in 1970 provides an excellent example. Throughout most of the 20th century clean air policy was dominated by an old power alignment, an old paradigm, and old governmental organizations uncommitted to clean air policy. From 1900 to 1969, industrial and agricultural interests dominated environmental policies. Environmental organizations such as the Audubon Society and the Sierra Club were weak. Far more influential were the steel, automobile, chemical, and agriculture interests, the dominant power arrangement of the old policy regime.

By the time the Clean Air Act was enacted, power had shifted toward new, more aggressive environmental organizations, which appeared in the late 1960s and grew exponentially, while older organizations (e.g., Audubon Society and Sierra Club) expanded their membership. The environmental policy paradigm also changed. The old paradigm viewed the earth as having unlimited resources, unlimited space, and an unlimited capacity to replenish and purify itself. Science had the capability to solve any problem, including the problem of dirty air, which proponents of the old paradigm believed was a small price to pay for progress and industrial expansion. A new dominant policy paradigm emerged to replace the old one. Its proponents saw the earth as a spaceship with limited resources and space, and faced with the possibility of being completely destroyed by pollution and poisonous chemicals. According to the new paradigm, air pollution could kill, chemicals could accumulate in our bodies and cause cancer and other health problems, and natural resources could be depleted. Whereas the old policy paradigm encouraged governmental inaction, the new paradigm demanded profound policy changes and strong government action to protect the environment. This shift in the dominant policy paradigm indicated a policy regime shift.

The Department of Agriculture, the Department of Health and Human Services (then Health, Education and Welfare), and a few others implemented the old environmental policy. When the old environmental policy regime disintegrated and a new regime emerged, government was reorganized. Responsibilities for environmental policies shifted from the departments of Agriculture and Health and Human Services to the newly created agency, the Environmental Protection Agency (EPA). These three changes—power arrangements, policy paradigm, and organizational arrangements—indicated a shift in the policy regime. This shift explains the big changes in environmental policies. The next section covers the factors that contribute to policy regime changes.

Factors That Produce Policy Regime Change: Stressors

When policies change, change tends to be incremental, changing gradually in small, tentative steps. Policies change slowly for two reasons. First, the policy regime operates to maintain policy stability, a point made earlier. Second, there are advantages to incremental change: Fewer resources are invested which means that when mistakes are made, they tend to be small and easily corrected.

Policy stressors precipitate the big changes or the policy regime shifts. These stressors include demographic shifts, mode of production changes, economic dislocation, catastrophic events, social movements, new technology, and international events.

- *Demographic changes* involve major population movements or shifts. For example, the mass movement of African Americans to urban areas stressed the segregationist regime in the South. The migration of African Americans to cities like Montgomery, Alabama, made the civil rights movement possible. The mass movement of women into the labor force during and after World War II stressed the old women's rights regime.
- A *mode of production* is the way goods are produced, the way production is organized, or the type of machines used in the production of goods. For example, farming using slave labor is one mode of production; farming using migrant labor is another.

The Industrial Revolution marked a profound change in the mode of production. For example, the production of an automobile went from an operation involving 10 to 15 people who assemble the entire car, to an operation involving 15,000 people working at the same production facility, each worker engaged all day in a repetitive task such as installing front seats or a steering wheel. Industrial labor unions and eventually labor policy emerged from this mode of production change.

Economic dislocation encompasses massive unemployment, as in the Great Depression of the 1930s. This type of stressor explains the emergence of New Deal legislation. The change in southern agriculture from a labor-intensive sharecropping system to capital-intensive mechanized farming led to massive outmigration that hastened the growth of the civil rights movement, brought about the destruction of the segregation regime, and contributed to the rise of a new civil rights policy regime.

Catastrophic events are man-made and natural disasters. Examples of natural disasters are floods, hurricanes, tornadoes, earthquakes, mudslides, and others. It was a major hurricane that precipitated the formation of the Federal Emergency Management Agency. The terrorist attack on the twin towers of the World Trade Center in New York City and the Pentagon in Washington on September 11, 2001, is an example of a man-made catastrophic event.

Social movements include the civil rights, women's rights, consumer protection, and environmental protection movements. All of these movements stressed the existing policy regimes and helped bring about policy changes in these areas.

New technology sometimes generates changes in social life. Examples of technological changes of the late 19th and early 20th centuries include the telephone, automobile, and radio. Recent technological changes include the personal computer and the Internet.

International events can also function as stressors. The cold war is a prime example because of its impact on the segregationist regime in the South. U.S. State Department officials had difficulties extolling the advantages of capitalism to Africans, when African Americans could not vote and were barred from public places in the South.

Stressors also include all those factors that produce social movements: sudden increases in mass hardship, calamitous unemployment rates, rapid institutional changes, breakdowns in established institutions, and rapid urbanization. Stressors do not produce public policy changes, but they do impact the regime and enable change. Actual regime shifts are brought about by changes in the dominant policy paradigm and shifts in power and organizational arrangements.

Stressors and Policy Regime Shifts: Two Examples

Civil rights and pro-choice policies illustrate how stressors produce policy change. The old southern civil rights regime collapsed owing to international events, demographic shifts, and mode of production changes. World War II impacted the segregationist regime as African-American servicemen returned from fighting racism in Europe, only to face it at home. We discussed under economic dislocation how demographic changes impacted this regime as African Americans moved into urban areas and took jobs in factories. Mass urban society provided the organizational basis for the mass civil rights movement with the increase of African Americans in industrial labor unions and the marriage of labor unions and civil rights organizations. These changes profoundly affected power arrangements.

Demographic changes were also the major stressor of the old antiabortion regime. The mass movement of families from rural areas, the isolation of the nuclear family (mother, father, and children) from the extended family (grandparents, uncles and aunts, and cousins), the increase in the divorce rate, the movement of women into the labor force, and the increase in women pursuing professional careers—all of these demographic factors contributed to the growth of the women's rights movement and the destabilization of the old antiabortion regime. The disintegration of the old policy regime led to the emergence of policy regimes in favor of abortion legislation and the use of contraceptives.

The policy regime explains long-term policy stability. The dominant policy paradigm and power arrangement maintained the status quo. Periods of substantial policy change indicate regime shifts which are precipitated by stressors. This policy regime model is useful in understanding continuity and change in public policy and can be applied to many different types of public policies.

Summary

Different public policy theories offer different perspectives and different ways of explaining changes in public policies. Different theories focus attention on varying aspects of the change process.

No single theory explains all changes in public policies. Sometimes public officials initiate and promote new policies without strong interest group pressure. In these cases, the state centered theory would be the most appropriate in explaining policy change. Sometimes organized interest groups initiate new policies. In these cases, the pluralist theory would be the most appropriate to use to explain policy change. Sometimes economic elites and social movements are responsible for major policy changes.

Most, but not all, public policies are surrounded by a specific set of ideas or a policy paradigm and specific power and organizational arrangements—that is, identifiable policy regimes. These policy regimes tend to operate to maintain long-term policy stability. They change through a complex process involving stressors, which impact ideas and power arrangements. Policy regime theory combines many of the different theories of public policy change into a larger theory. However, some changes can best be explained by state centered, agenda setting, or other theories.

Review Questions

1. Compare and contrast the pluralist and elitist models of policy making.
2. Why are most federal policy changes in the United States incremental?
3. What are some advantages and disadvantages of incremental decision making?
4. Discuss the role of competing policy paradigms in conflicts over public policies. Use the issues of gun control and abortion to illustrate your point.
5. Public policy making in the United States is characterized by long periods of policy stability and short episodes of substantial change. What factors explain periods of stability? Periods of substantial change?
6. Discuss the policy regime model. How is this model used to explain policy stability and policy change?
7. Some public policies fail to accomplish any of their objectives. Other policies are relatively successful. What factors explain successful or unsuccessful policy implementation? What can policy makers do to improve the chances that their policies would be successfully implemented?

Select Websites

This is the homepage of the Center for American Politics and Public Policy at the University of Washington. Dr. Bryan Jones, one of the most prominent scholars in the area of public policy, is the current director.
http://depts.washington.edu/ampol/navBios/jonesbio.shtml/

This is the Website of the American Enterprise Institute, a conservative public policy think tank.
http://www.aei.org/

This is the Website of the Brookings Institution, a moderate public policy think tank.
http://www.brook.edu/

This is the Website for the Center for Law and Social Policy, a liberal think tank.
http://clasp.org/

Key Terms

agenda setting

bias of pluralism

cost-benefit analysis

decision theory

elitist theory

government agenda

group theory

incrementalism

pluralist theory

policy adoption

policy cycle model

policy implementation

policy monopoly

policy regime model

problem definition

public choice

punctuated equilibrium

rational decision making

satisficing

social movement theory

speculative augmentation

state centered theory

CHAPTER 3

Policy History

This chapter sketches the long-term history of the development of public policies from the late 19th century through the 20th century. Recently, policy theorists have borrowed two models from the natural sciences to understand long-term trends in policy history: the punctuated equilibrium model and the liberal-conservative cyclical theory. These models were discussed in the previous chapter and will be used here to organize the discussion of the history of public policy development.

→ Punctuated Equilibrium and Cyclical Changes

The punctuated equilibrium model derives from the study of evolution. As discussed in Chapter 2, it was once thought that nature evolved slowly, changing imperceptibly over long periods of time. However, natural scientists have recognized episodes of profound, sometimes cataclysmic, change followed by long periods of calm and equilibrium. An example of a cataclysmic change in physics is the big bang that created the universe and set it in motion. The disappearance of the dinosaurs was another cataclysmic change. Scientists call this pattern of evolution *punctuated equilibrium.*

The expression **punctuated equilibrium** also characterizes the process in which public policies evolve (see Chapter 2; Baumgartner and Jones 1993). Public policies are stable for a long period of time and interrupted occasionally by periods of abrupt change. However, during times of crises, public policies change abruptly and substantially.

Another model of change taken from nature is the **cyclical change theory**. Cyclical changes are common in nature. The best example is the changing of seasons, which follow the cycle of spring, summer, fall, winter, and spring again. Historian Arthur Schlesinger (1959) suggested that public policies also change in cycles, alternating between periods of liberalism and conservatism. Liberal periods are characterized by the expansion of welfare and protective and competitive regulatory policies. Conservative periods produce contractions of welfare and protective and competitive regulatory policies. They are also characterized by moral policies, or what critics call moral panics—policies designed to regulate moral turpitude or sin. The liberal-conservative cycle takes about a generation or 30 years. The ideas and conditions that produce either liberal or conservative policies in one decade generally fade by the time a new generation appears.

Although history is far more complicated than the representation of any models, we can identify three periods of liberal policy expansion and three periods of conservatism policy contraction and moral policy. The liberal periods include the Progressive Era of the early decades of the 20th century, the New Deal of the 1930s, and the Great Society of the 1960s. The conservative periods include the 1920s, 1950s, and 1980s.

The two models of long-term change complement each other. The periods of liberal policy expansion in the liberal-conservative cyclical model are the same periods of change in the punctuated equilibrium model. The only difference in the two models is that the cyclical model intimates that policy history, like the seasons, continuously repeats itself in an endless cycle of expansion and contraction. The 20th century had substantially more policies when it ended than it had when it began. Whereas some policies were eliminated or cut during conservative decades, others continued to grow.

⟶ The Progressive Era: 1900–1920

The first two decades of the 20th century was a period of liberal policy expansion known as the **Progressive Era**. Public policies in that period emerged in reaction to three sets of problems: economic, social, and political. The **Progressive movement** was not one political movement, but several movements responding to these different problems. It included remnants of the 19th-century populist movement of farmers against railroads and major corporations. Progressives involved muckrakers, journalists attacking child labor, deplorable working conditions, and the meatpacking industry. The movement consisted of religious organizations concerned about poverty and vice, and women organizations campaigning for women's suffrage and pension programs for mothers. It also involved the municipal reform movement's crusade against corrupt and undemocratic governments and the call for civil service systems, professional administration, merit systems, nonpartisan elections, and more citizen participation in government.

The Progressive movement was most successful in producing new public policies in economic and political areas and least successful in the social realm. Many of the policies are still in place today, but others died during periods of conservative contraction.

Economic Issues: Unregulated Markets and Monopolies

The first two decades of the 20th century was a period of enormous economic development, unprecedented industrial expansion, and unparalleled urban growth. Steel, automobiles, trucks, telephones, electric lines, skyscrapers, and many other things were produced at unbelievable rates. For example, the number of automobiles manufactured increased from about 19,000 in 1904 to well over 1.5 million by 1919 (Kolko 1963, 43). Investment in production facilities almost doubled in the first decade of the century (Blum et al. 1968). Corporations and businesses were consolidating in record-breaking numbers. The most critical economic issue was unregulated markets. The absence of regulations undermined the free and open market in two ways: First, the absence of regulations allowed unintended harms. It allowed diseases or defective products to threaten the lives of consumers. It also permitted unscrupulous producers to take advantage of conscientious producers. Indeed, conscientious producers demanded government regulations.

Historian Gabriel Kolko provides an excellent discussion of some of the problems of the unregulated markets, using the meatpacking industry as an example. In the late 19th century bacteria-infected meat was discovered in meatpacking plants. European governments had banned meat processed in the United States precisely because of the absence of government inspections and regulations. As a result of the closing of the European market to U.S. meat producers, the urging of medical doctors, and the demands of the large meatpacking companies for government inspections, the U.S. government responded with legislation. Kolko described the situation in the 1890s:

> Congress acted to meet the challenge, and in August 1890, responding to the pressure of the major packers, passed a law providing for the inspection of all meat intended for export. But since provision was not made for inspection of the live animal at the time of slaughter, the foreign bans remained in effect. Desperate, in March 1891, Congress passed the first major meat inspection law in American history. Indeed, the 1891 Act was the most significant in this field, and the conclusion of the long series of efforts to protect the export interests of the major American packers. (1963, 100)

Government regulations of processed meat did three things: (1) It protected the consumer from diseased meat, (2) it protected conscientious producers from unscrupulous ones, and (3) it allayed the fears of European consumers and opened up the European market to U.S. meat producers.

The second problem of unregulated markets is the tendency of oligopolies or monopolies to emerge. This tendency is enhanced when markets are unregulated and when price fixing and trusts are allowed. A **monopoly** arises when a single firm controls a market. An **oligopoly** exists if a few firms control a market. A **trust** is a bogus company, generally made up of leaders from other companies who sit on the trust board. A long time ago, trusts were created to manipulate and control markets. **Price fixing** has to do with a group of firms conspiring to increase prices.

Price fixing, trusts, oligopolies, and monopolies were special problems because they undermined and subverted free competitive markets. Either government regulated the market to keep it open and competitive or the unrestrained, unregulated market would deteriorate into oligopolies and monopolies.

Monopolies were special problems in the railroad industry. By the late 19th century this industry had evolved into a monopoly in some regions. As a monopoly, the industry could charge whatever consumers were willing to pay. Farmers, at the mercy of the railroad industry, demanded that the government intercede. Congress responded by establishing the Interstate Commerce Commission in 1887.

Aggressive corporate leaders, committed to eliminating their competitors and controlling their markets, created special problems for the unregulated market during this period. One example is John D. Rockefeller, who founded the Standard Oil Company in 1872. Allegedly, he hated free competition and believed that consolidation was the wave of the future. He used a variety of ruthless methods to eliminate his competitors: rebates, price fixing, price slashing, espionage, bogus companies, and trust companies. He got rebates from the railroad companies that transported Standard's oil. When pipelines became the cheaper mode of transporting oil, he created the United Pipe Line Company and consolidated almost all the pipelines under this company. He used trust companies to control the oil market. The trust board, dominated by Rockefeller, controlled the other companies and the oil market. By the beginning of the 20th century, Standard Oil dominated 90 percent of the nation's oil refining.

Another example is J.P. Morgan, the banker. In the early 1900s Morgan bought out Andrew Carnegie, the founder of Carnegie Steel, and formed the United States Steel Corporation. This company was a giant conglomerate consisting of 138 different companies absorbed by Morgan. It dominated well over 50 percent of the market (Kolko 1963).

This discussion illustrates that a number of practices undermined and subverted free, competitive, and open markets. These practices included price slashing, rebates, price fixing, and trusts. They also included the process of buying out competitors, which left the markets dominated by a few firms or a single firm.

Economic Policies of the Progressive Era

Some business leaders were part of the Progressive movement. They called for government regulation, fair business practices, and stable markets. They wanted protection from unscrupulous competitors and help to enter foreign markets.

Several policies and agencies emerged during this era. The United States Department of Agriculture was created in the 1860s. In 1906 Congress passed the *Food and Drug Act* and the government began inspecting slaughterhouses and processed meats and drugs. The Food and Drug Administration was created much later, in 1931. The Interstate Commerce Commission was established in 1887, especially to regulate railroad monopolies. The Anti-Trust Division of the Justice Department was established at this same time to develop antitrust policies, which were expanded in the early 20th century. The *Sherman Antitrust Act of 1890* was strengthened and clarified by the *Clayton Antitrust Act of 1914*. The departments of Commerce and Labor were created at the beginning of the century, and were separated into two distinct departments in 1913. Also, in 1913 the Federal Reserve Board was created to regulate the banking industry. The Federal Trade Commission was created a year later to promote fair trade practices.

By the 1920s the federal government was regulating railroads, inspecting meats, monitoring drugs, investigating monopolies and trusts, and encouraging fair trade practices. Although the effectiveness of government in these areas has been disputed, there is no doubt government had expanded into several new areas. It had enacted new policies and created new government agencies. Expansion was not part of any governmental conspiracy, but largely the result of political pressure from the public, interest groups, or business leaders. It arose from the Progressive movement.

Social Issues: Workplace Safety, Child Labor, and Urban Housing

In addition to economic issues, a number of social issues confronted the nation during this period: hazardous working conditions, child labor, poverty, and overcrowded slums. Some of these issues overlapped. For example, hazardous working conditions often contributed to accidents on the job. These accidents often left families destitute.

In 1906, for example, Adam Rogalas was working for the Iron City Grain Elevator Company in Pittsburgh where he earned $1.60 a day. His income equaled the national average for industrial workers and it supported his wife and four children. Unfortunately, Rogalas was killed on October 16, 1906. While working in a grain storage building, the floor above him collapsed and the falling grain crushed him to death (Moss 1996, 1). Rogalas's children and pregnant wife were left without a provider, savings, or insurance. His widow was unable to support herself and her children. The family became destitute. Stories like this illustrate the connection between hazardous working conditions and poverty.

Child labor was a special problem of this period. The children of industrial workers and coal miners worked full time. Less than one-tenth of them completed high school. Four million children worked between 54 and 60 hours a week, and half a million worked between 60 and 70 hours. Working conditions were hazardous. Children, like adults, suffered job-related injuries.

The Hammer and Dagenhart decision of 1918—the Supreme Court case that invalidated a federal child labor act of 1916—further illustrates the problem of child labor. The U.S. Supreme Court claimed that the law exceeded the federal powers under the commerce clause and the reserve powers clause of the Tenth Amendment, that the regulation of child labor did not fall under the commerce clause, and that only the states had the power to regulate in this area. The case arose when Roland Dagenhart, an employee at Fidelity, a cotton mill in North Carolina, challenged the law on behalf of his two sons who worked for the mill as well as cotton manufacturers. Five years after the court struck down the law, a journalist interviewed Reuben Dagenhart, Roland's son. Reuben said:

> Look at me! A hundred and five pounds, a grown man, and no education. I may be mistaken, but I think the years I've put in the cotton mills have stunted my growth. They kept me from getting any schooling. I had to stop school after the third grade and now I need the education I didn't get. (Epstein and Walker 2000, 200)

Having children work long hours and exposing them to hazards such as cotton dust stunted their growth, prevented them from attending school, and obstructed their development.

The rapid growth of urban areas during this period created special problems of overcrowded housing and poverty. Cities were particularly hard hit by the panic of 1907. Local governments were ill prepared to deal with these problems. Widows were particularly vulnerable, as women were barred from many jobs and professions.

Social Policies of the Progressive Era

Progressive organizations representing industrial workers, women, social workers, and religious groups mobilized to secure the passage of social policies. Social reformers advocated programs to assist widows, orphans, and other poor people. They demanded child labor laws, a minimum wage, maximum working hours, and sanitary working conditions, particularly in the meatpacking industry. They succeeded in establishing the Children's Bureau, a new federal agency, in 1912. They prevailed upon many state governments to establish pension programs for widows. The federal government had pension programs for veterans. While social reformers secured the passage of state laws regulating child labor, working conditions, working hours, and minimum wages, these laws were short-lived, killed by a conservative Supreme Court. In 1921 Congress passed the *Maternity and Infant Protection Act*. This act provided a small amount of money to states for programs to assist mothers with infant children. It too was dead by the end of the 1920s, a victim of conservative contraction.

Political Issues: Municipal and Electoral Reform

Another major issue of the Progressive period was corruption in city government. Local political parties, generally organized at the county level, tended to dominate city governments. Their goal was to acquire and maintain power over city governments, and they used different strategies to achieve their goals. To get votes, local parties provided services and favors for constituents, many of whom were immigrants. They used patronage, giving jobs to party loyalists regardless of their qualifications. The parties had reputations for corruption—voter fraud, bribery, and kickbacks. Critics claimed that the Philadelphia political machine used the names of dogs and children to win elections and the Chicago machine used names from gravestones.

The Progressive movement encompassed municipal reform. This movement targeted urban machine governments and state political parties. It promoted many policies designed to weaken the power of state and local political parties. Reformers demanded the establishment of nonpartisan elections, primary elections, and professional bureaucracies. A nonpartisan election is one in which party labels do not appear on the election ballot. In a primary election voters, rather than the party leaders, nominate candidates for political office. Bureaucratic reform calls for the establishment of civil service systems, which hire and promote personnel on the basis of merit rather than party loyalty. Reformers also called for the creation of referendum, initiative, and recall elections. The referendum is a special election in which voters can vote directly for a law. Initiatives are devices in which citizens initiate or propose legislation. Recalls are special elections to vote an elected official out of office or recall the official.

Political Policies of the Progressive Era

The municipal reform movement succeeded in getting state legislatures to pass a series of laws reforming elections. Today most states have primary elections and some have nonpartisan local elections. All state and most local governments have civil service systems that hire people on the basis of merit. Many states have the referendum and the recall. A few have initiatives.

Liberal Ideology and Public Policy

Liberal ideas supported the Progressive movement. Liberal scholars of this period included Thorstein Veblen, Richard T. Ely, John Dewey, and William Willoughby. Like the conservatives and libertarians, liberals supported free, open, and competitive markets, private property, and individualism. They differed with conservatives over the role of government. Liberals believed that government was needed to secure individual freedom, protect private property, and provide welfare for the people. For example, Richard T. Ely argued, "Regulation by the power of the state … is a condition of freedom" (Fried 1998, 29).

Other Progressives complained about the growth of inequality in the distribution of wealth and income. They believed that unrestrained markets helped the rich get richer and the powerful more powerful, leaving the poor vulnerable and unprotected. Progressives attacked conservative and libertarian ideas as anachronistic. They argued that in the agrarian societies of the 17th and 18th centuries, too much government threatened individual liberty. However, in the industrial early 20th century, too little government allowed for the growth of inequality, the exploitation of child labor, and unfair business practices.

Some Progressives insisted that even Adam Smith, often considered a conservative-libertarian, favored government regulations to protect the rights of workers and to prevent extreme inequality. They quoted Smith: "[W]hen the regulation, therefore, is in favour of the workmen, it is always just and equitable; but it is sometimes otherwise when in favour of the masters." Smith also said, "No society can be flourishing and happy, of which the far greater part of the members are poor and miserable" (Smith 1776/1952, 61, 78–79).

As we have seen, Progressive scholars supported antitrust regulations, the prohibition of rebates and price fixing, the regulations of railroad shipping costs and fares, and the inspection of meat. They also supported workers' compensation, child labor laws, public education, public works, and public welfare. Socialist ideas were popular at this time but had little influence on public policies.

Mixed Success of the Progressive Era

The Progressive movement was successful in some areas but unsuccessful in others. It helped initiate a few social programs at the state and local level, and it had some success in the creation of regulatory agencies. The Sixteenth and Seventeenth Amendments were added to the Constitution during the Progressive Era. The Sixteenth Amendment gave the federal government the power to tax people directly and the Seventeenth Amendment provided for the popular election of senators. The Nineteenth Amendment granting the right to vote to women was ratified in 1920, at the end of the era.

The Progressive movement failed in the area of social issues. For a brief moment, it secured the passage of state and federal legislation concerning child labor, minimum wages, and maximum working hours. However, the U.S. Supreme Court struck down these laws in a series of cases representing the triumph of conservative ideology of the 1920s.

⟫ *The 1920s: Conservative Contraction*

The 1920s was a period of economic expansion and conservative policy. With the exception of a slump in 1921, unemployment was low. By 1923 wages were almost double what they were in 1914 and they continued to rise throughout the decade. Production and profits also increased. Conservative ideas and moral issues dominated the period, contributing to the contraction of Progressive policies and the expansion of moral issues. Many of the social policies of the Progressive period were terminated. In 1919, the Eighteenth Amendment banned the manufacture, distribution, and sale of intoxicating beverages.

Conservative Ideas of the Period

Whereas conservatives emphasized individual liberty, limited government, efficiency, and high moral standards, their philosophy may be found in three major strands: social, business, and constitutional.

Social Darwinism, a social philosophy originated by the British scholar Herbert Spencer, was the dominant form of social conservatism of this period. Spencer, a relative of Charles Darwin, coined the term "the survival of the fittest" to characterize his theory of government and society. Spencer believed that beyond protecting private property, enforcing contracts, and maintaining national defense, government should do nothing. Just as the strongest survive competition in the animal world, the strongest people would survive the competition of the human world. Spencer used the term *liberalism* to describe his belief in individual liberty and opposition to state coercion. Spencer ascribed to the belief in inferior and superior races, believing that the inferior races would die out. Graham Sumner, a follower of Herbert Spencer, promoted Social Darwinism in the United States. Like other conservatives, he advocated **laissez-faire capitalism** and individualism, and considered state intervention in the market dangerous.

Business conservatives rejected the notion of survival of the fittest, believing instead that programs that benefited businesses favored the entire country. Characterizing this belief, President Calvin Coolidge said, "The business of America is business." Moral conservatives explain social problems like poverty or divorce in terms of immorality: laziness, promiscuity, drunkenness, and other vices.

Constitutional conservatives killed many of the Progressive policies enacted in the early part of the century: minimum wage, child labor, and others. These conservatives used two legal arguments to inflict their mortal blows: contract and states' rights. The contract argument is that child labor, the minimum wage, maximum working hours, and other such policies violated contract rights. The *Lochner v. New York* (1905) and *Adkins v. Children's Hospital* cases illustrate the use of this argument. The *Lochner* decision struck down a New York law that limited the number of hours an employer could require a worker to work. The *Adkins* decision (1923) invalidated a District of Columbia statute establishing minimum wages for women. In both cases, the Supreme Court argued that the laws interfered with workers' rights to contract for as many hours and as high a wage as they could negotiate with their employers. The Court claimed that these state and local laws violated the individual right of workers to freely contract with their employer. The Court did not consider the individual to be an equal in negotiations with an employer. The employer had the power to fire the individual worker who refused to agree to the employer's terms. Because many other workers are standing in line for the job and because a fired worker has diminished opportunities to support himself and his family, an employer is placed in a superior position over a single worker in negotiations over wages, working conditions, and working hours.

The states' rights argument is that any federal law to protect child labor, establish minimum wages, and set maximum working hours is a violation of the Tenth Amendment which states, "The powers not delegated to the United States by the Constitution, nor prohibited by it to the States, are reserved to the States respectively, or to the people." The constitutional conservative interpretation of this amendment was that if the Constitution does not explicitly give the power to the federal government, then the federal government is prohibited from exercising that power. As you have read, the *Hammer v. Dagenhart* decision struck down the federal child labor law primarily on the grounds that it violated the Tenth Amendment.

Conservative Policies of the 1920s

During the 1920s, almost all of the social policies of the Progressive Era were terminated. The Supreme Court struck down child labor, minimum wage, and maximum working hours laws. Congress repealed the Maternity and Infant Protection Act. Policy makers emphasized cutting government spending and relying more on the private sector. Congress also introduced the Eighteenth Amendment (Prohibition) and the states ratified it in 1919.

→ The 1930s: The Great Depression and the New Deal

The 1930s was a decade of profound policy expansion. No doubt the Great Depression influenced the growth of public policies. In reaction to this crisis, Franklin D. Roosevelt's administration produced an avalanche of new policies. Also, the Twenty-first Amendment repealed national Prohibition, the Eighteenth Amendment, in 1933.

The Great Depression

The **Great Depression** followed the stock market crash of October 1929, pushing the nation to the brink of economic and social collapse. Rates of business failure and unemployment were higher than at any time in the nation's history. The gross national product (GNP) declined by almost 50 percent. The GNP measures the health of the economy in terms of the total value of goods, services, and structures produced. GNP declined from $103.4 billion in 1929 to $55.8 billion in 1933.

National unemployment rates reached 25 percent. This rate measured the percentage of those who had been working, were out of work, and were seeking employment. It did not measure those who had never worked or those who became so discouraged that they had dropped out of the labor force. It also did not measure the extent of poverty among migrant workers, farm workers, or sharecroppers. Poverty was much more pervasive than the unemployment rate indicated.

Some cities suffered unemployment rates of over 50 or 60 percent. A number of cities went bankrupt. Families foreclosed on homes in record-breaking numbers. Thousands of people lost their farms. The banking industry almost collapsed, as people lost confidence in the security of their deposits and withdrew their funds. More than 5,000 banks failed between 1929 and 1932.

The Depression precipitated social turmoil. Conflicts between management of major industries and newly forming labor unions reached warlike levels. Pitched battles were fought in Detroit and Flint, Michigan, between the United Auto Workers and Ford Motors, General Motors, and other automobile producers. There was an urgent need for the federal government to take action. Arthur M. Schlesinger, Jr., summed up the situation:

> It was hard to understate the need for action. The national income was less than half of what it had been four short years before. Nearly thirteen million Americans—about one

quarter of the labor force—were desperately seeking jobs. The machinery for sheltering and feeding the unemployed was breaking down everywhere under the growing burden. And a few hours before, in the early morning before the inauguration, every bank in America had locked its doors. It was now not just a matter of staving off hunger. It was a matter of seeing whether a representative democracy could conquer economic collapse. It was a matter of staving off violence, even (at least some so thought) revolution. (1959, 3)

The Depression was a national disaster. People demanded that the federal government take action.

Hoover's Response

Herbert Hoover was president at the time of the stock market crash. Operating under the conservative ideology of the time, he responded with a series of policies to address the growing problems of the Depression.

- Tried to balance the budget.
- Cut taxes to stimulate the economy.
- Persuaded New York bankers to create a National Credit Association.
- Established the Reconstruction Finance Corporation to make loans to banks, railroads, and insurance companies.
- Opposed federal relief on grounds that it was a local responsibility.
- Established the Emergency Committee for Employment, which recommended a federal public works program, but Hoover rejected that.

Hoover vetoed a bill to give bonus payments to war veterans. In the spring of 1932 thousands of veterans marched on Washington, set up camp near the White House, and occupied a number of public buildings. Efforts to evict them led to riots. In July Hoover used the army to drive the "Bonus Army" veterans from Washington.

Hoover believed that the Depression was temporary. He encouraged people to be patient and told them that prosperity was just around the corner. The Depression only worsened. State and local governments had few resources to assist their needy citizens. Private charities were overwhelmed by the need for food. Big cities were marred by scenes of long soup lines, children rummaging through garbage looking for food, and old women begging for a piece of bread.

Farmers were particularly hard hit. The 1930s was a period of severe drought which destroyed both crops and livestock. Moreover, in some areas erosion and overgrowing of crops depleted the topsoil. The area from the Southwest to the Midwest became a dust bowl. Hoover was more predisposed to intervene to assist farmers and supported legislation to loan money to them. However, he opposed legislation to distribute surplus wheat to the unemployed. Critics ridiculed him for feeding the cattle but refusing to feed starving women and children.

The turmoil worsened. Labor-management conflicts intensified. Farmers in some areas used guns to defend their farms from foreclosure. Farmers in other areas threatened to disrupt traffic until they got some relief from the federal government. State and local political leaders, charities, union leaders, and even some business leaders demanded that the federal government do something. People became increasingly dissatisfied and public pressure for federal intervention mounted. Hoover no longer had the public's confidence.

Franklin D. Roosevelt was elected in 1932 by an overwhelming margin. The Democrats captured the presidency and both houses of Congress. Congress and the president began working together to solve the problems of the Great Depression.

Roosevelt and Keynes

Roosevelt offered the **New Deal** as an alternative to Hoover's policies. In the election campaign he advocated federal relief programs, government regulation of utilities, government regulation of agricultural production and prices, public works programs, forest conservation, flood control, and the development of waterways. He also advocated the repeal of Prohibition, the constitutional amendment that prohibited the sale and distribution of alcoholic beverages.

A new economic theory emerged to support Roosevelt's more aggressive public policy approach to the Depression. **John Maynard Keynes** offered an alternative to the conservative economic view of the Depression. Conservative economists saw the Depression as a natural process in which inefficient businesses went out of business and more successful businesses survived. Government interference in this process would do more harm than good.

Keynesian economics, on the other hand, argued that the Great Depression was symptomatic of overproduction and underconsumption. Firms could not maintain high sales so they responded by cutting back production and laying off workers. This response increased unemployment, which in turn decreased the amount of money available for workers to purchase goods. Rising unemployment set in motion a downward spiral of declines in sales followed by cuts in production and worker layoffs, which increased the number of unemployed and reduced the number of consumers.

Keynes insisted that the Depression was not necessarily temporary: It could get worse, markets could collapse, and doing nothing would only make matters worse. To save the market and prevent its collapse, the government had to take action. Like conservative economists, Keynes supported tax cuts to stimulate the economy. However, he believed that this approach was too slow and would not have a significant impact. A faster, more effective approach was to put money directly into the hands of consumers. Keynes expressed it this way:

> If the Treasury were to fill old bottles with banknotes, bury them at suitable depths in disused coal mines which are then filled up to the surface with town rubbish, and leave it to private enterprise on well-tried principles of *laissez-faire* to dig the notes up again . . . , there need be no more unemployment and, with the help of the repercussions, the real income of the community, and its capital wealth also, would probably become a good deal greater than it actually is. It would, indeed, be more sensible to build houses and the like; but if there are political and practical difficulties in the way of this, the above would be better than nothing. (1936, 129)

When unemployed workers are given a job, even a meaningless one, they earn money and become consumers and are able to purchase things. If they purchase more things, producers would increase production and hire more workers. For Keynes, government had an obligation to act during depressions. This action could take the form of public works or relief programs.

Keynes did not write his major work, *The General Theory of Employment, Interest, and Money*, until 1936, but he had published several books and articles throughout the 1920s. Whether the ideas directly influenced the development of New Deal policies is open to debate. But there is no debate that Keynesian economics supports the New Deal programs and a new era of liberal public policy making.

Public Policy Response: The New Deal

In the first few months of his administration, Roosevelt addressed the banking problem. People had lost confidence in banks. They feared that if banks went out of business, they would lose their life savings deposited there.

Indeed, large numbers of people panicked and withdrew their money, and banks went out of business in massive numbers. Roosevelt declared a bank holiday and, with support from major bankers, closed the banks to prevent further massive withdrawals and the collapse of the banking industry.

Roosevelt next created the Federal Deposit Insurance Corporation (FDIC). This federal agency insured bank deposits and restored people's confidence in the banking industry.

Roosevelt opened the floodgates that ushered in several new public policies. The list that follows shows some of the major legislation and agencies created.

1. The *Agricultural Adjustment Act* assisted farmers and stabilized farm prices.
2. The *National Industrial Recovery Act* set up the National Recovery Administration to stimulate industrial production and reduce unemployment.
3. A number of public works programs were created, most notably the Works Progress Administration (WPA), the Public Works Administration (PWA), and the Civilian Conservation Corps (CCC).
4. The *Federal Emergency Relief Act of 1933*, which provided assistance to the unemployed and their families, involved the federal government in the relief business.
5. The *Social Security Act of 1935* established old-age and survivors insurance, unemployment insurance, aid for women with children, and aid for the blind and disabled.
6. The **Federal Housing Administration (FHA)** and the **Public Housing Authority (PHA)** addressed the housing needs of both low- and middle-income families. The FHA guaranteed mortgages for middle-income homebuyers, and the PHA built housing projects for poor families.
7. The *Wagner Act* established the National Labor Relations Board to help ameliorate labor conflicts.
8. The Civil Aeronautics Board (CAB) regulated airline prices and flights.
9. The Securities Exchange Commission (SEC) regulated the stock market.
10. The Tennessee Valley Authority was set up to build dams and power plants to develop the seven states in the Tennessee River watershed. Among its goals was a rural electrification program.

With this enormous explosion in the growth of public policies, Roosevelt formed the Executive Office of the President to help him manage the enlarged government.

The U.S. Supreme Court

The Supreme Court, dominated by conservative justices, struck down most of the New Deal policies enacted in Roosevelt's first term in office. For example, it struck down provisions of the Agricultural Adjustment Act (*U.S. v. Butler* 1936), a program to assist farmers, and parts of the National Industrial Recovery Act (*Panama Refining Co. v. Ryan* 1935), a set of rules regulating oil prices. It invalidated policies establishing minimum wages and maximum working hours (*Schechter Poultry Corp. v. U.S.* 1935). However, the Court switched its position in 1937 when it upheld a state minimum wage law (*West Coast Hotel Co. v. Parrish* 1937). This same year the Court upheld the Wagner Act and National Labor Relations Board regulations in the *National Labor Relations Board v. Jones and Laughlin Steel Corporation* (1937) decision. By the end of the decade the Court had reversed most of its previous decisions. It upheld federal laws designed to assist farmers, regulate industries, and establish minimum wages and maximum working hours.

Although New Deal programs stimulated the economy somewhat and reduced unemployment rates, only the high level of government spending during World War II took the nation out of the Depression. The workforce needs of both the war and war production created a labor shortage. Wartime unemployment rates dropped below 2 percent, the lowest rate of the century. Many of the New Deal public works programs disappeared during the war, as they were no longer needed. The CCC, PWA, and WPA were eliminated. The War Production Board, created to coordinate wartime production, was dismantled after the war.

✧ The 1950s: Conservative Contraction

The post–World War II period was a time of economic expansion. Wages rose and productivity and profits increased. Military spending declined somewhat, but remained well above prewar levels because of the cold war. The high level of spending, no doubt, helped to stimulate the economy. With a few exceptions, the economy did well throughout the entire decade. Unemployment rates generally remained below 5.0 percent.

Dwight Eisenhower was elected president in 1952 and served two full terms. He considered himself a conservative, and advocated a conservative policy agenda. He called for efforts to balance the budget, cut taxes, devolve federal programs to the states, and shift some federal functions to the private sector. The federal deficit declined. Taxes were cut, but mostly for the well to do. Eisenhower created a special committee, the Commission on Intergovernmental Relations, to identify federal programs to return to the states.

Many of the New Deal programs that survived World War II continued to grow gradually under Eisenhower. These included programs under the Social Security Act of 1935—Social Security, aid for dependent children, unemployment insurance, aid for the disabled, and aid for the blind.

One of the most significant New Deal programs that impacted society in the 1950s was the federal housing program. The Federal Housing Administration, established in 1934, guaranteed the loans for families to purchase homes. This policy was expanded under Eisenhower and precipitated a boom in suburban housing development. The 1950s was known as a period of rapid suburbanization.

In 1954 the Supreme Court ordered southern school districts to stop the practice of segregating their students into all-white schools and all-black schools. Eisenhower was not enthusiastic about school desegregation, but he became involved symbolically in civil rights policies. In 1957 Arkansas Governor Orval Faubus used the Arkansas National Guard to prevent a few African-American high school students from enrolling in Central High School in Little Rock. After rioting broke out, Eisenhower deployed federal troops, placed the National Guard under federal control, and imposed martial law on the city. Troops escorted the students into the school.

A number of new agencies emerged in the late 1940s and the 1950s. The Atomic Energy Commission was created in 1946 to promote the development of peacetime nuclear energy. In 1956 the Federal Aviation Administration was created to compel the airline industry to protect the safety of the public. The CAB regulated the price of airline fares and shipping costs.

Despite calling himself a conservative, Eisenhower initiated one of the most far-reaching highway programs in the history of the country with the *Interstate Highway and National Defense Act of 1956*. Today interstate highways are visible everywhere.

McCarthyism and Moral Panic

The 1950s was hit by a moral panic, which is like a witch hunt. It is characterized by a pervasive fear of something evil or sinful that must be stopped at all cost. The moral panic of this decade was **McCarthyism**, but it did not begin with Senator Joseph McCarthy. It began in the late 1940s, arising from the cold war and a fear of international communism and nuclear war after the Soviet Union acquired the atomic bomb. The panic reached its peak when Senator McCarthy gave a speech in which he claimed to have the names of several officials of the State Department who had ties to the Communist Party. It involved a series of hearings by the House Committee on Un-American Activities and was sensationalized with the confession of a German-born scientist, Klaus Fuchs, working at Los Alamos, a nuclear facility in New Mexico. The scientist confessed that he had sold atomic secrets to the Soviet Union.

In 1947 President Harry Truman had established a federal loyalty program that required his Attorney General, Tom Clark, to compile a list of subversive organizations. Any federal employee who had an association with any one of the organizations on the list was to be fired. As a public policy McCarthyism led to the government requiring public employees to take loyalty oaths, targeting those employees suspected of being disloyal, and firing those having any links to radical or left-wing political organizations. Two thousand federal employees were fired and over 200 resigned.

McCarthyism spread across the country like wildfire. Many state and local governments adopted the federal policy. Illustrating the tragedy of this policy, social critic and historian Marty Jezer cited the following story:

> The Detroit city government purged leftists from civil service jobs and, in the process, helped destroy the United Public Workers Union. One of the workers fired in Detroit was a black garbage man who had worked for the city since 1925. He was a thirty-second degree Mason and had a son fighting in Korea. But he had also supported Henry Wallace, had attended a Paul Robeson concert, and had gone to meetings of a group, the Civil Rights Congress, which appeared on Attorney General Tom Clark's list of subversive organizations. (1982, 91)

Henry Wallace, former vice president (1941–1945), ran for president in 1948 as an independent under the Progressive Party, a liberal party that supported New Deal programs. Most of Wallace's supporters were liberals, but many were socialists and a few were Communists. Just before the Progressive Party's national convention, the Communists were arrested for being members of the Communist Party—and thus regarded as subversives.

Senator McCarthy had chaired a Senate committee investigating un-American activities. He had destroyed the careers of many people by raising suspicion of their Communist affiliations. He was finally discredited by the Senate in the mid-1950s, after attacking high-ranking military officials with stellar records. Of course, some aspects of McCarthyism remained as the FBI investigated civil rights organizations along with any other organization that threatened the status quo throughout the 1950s and 1960s.

→ The 1960s and 1970s: Liberal Policy Expansion

The 1960s and early 1970s was a time of prosperity and political turmoil. The economy continued to expand. Average income, even after adjusting for the cost of living, increased. Suburban areas continued to explode in population. Unemployment rates remained as low as they were in the 1950s.

This period of prosperity was also one of social movements such as the civil rights, antipoverty, women's rights, anti–Vietnam War, environmental protection, consumer protection, gay and lesbian rights, and other movements. With these social movements came an expansion of public policies, especially during the Johnson and Nixon administrations.

Johnson: A Flood of New Policies

Past presidents used short phrases to characterize their domestic public policy programs. For example, Woodrow Wilson used the expression New Freedom. Roosevelt used the term New Deal. Kennedy coined the phrase New Frontier. Johnson called his domestic policies the Great Society.

Although many of the policies of the 1960s had roots in the Roosevelt administration, John F. Kennedy and Lyndon Johnson opened the public policy floodgate, which initiated many new policies. This flood of new policies entailed three major currents of domestic policies: civil rights, antipoverty, and urban development.

Civil Rights Legislation

Congress, at Johnson's urging, passed three major civil rights bills: the *Civil Rights Act of 1964,* the *Voting Rights Act of 1965,* and the *Fair Housing Act of 1968.* These bills constituted the most expansive civil rights legislation of the 20th century. They prohibited racial discrimination in hotels, restaurants, movie theaters, parks, beaches, amusement parks, swimming pools, and other public places. The Civil Rights Act of 1964 prohibited employment discrimination on the basis of race, religion, national origin, and gender. The Voting Rights Act expanded the right to vote of African Americans and other minorities. The Fair Housing Act prohibited racial discrimination in the housing market. Several new agencies were created to carry out civil rights laws. The Equal Employment Opportunity Commission was established to implement Title VII of the 1964 Civil Rights Act. The Office of Civil Rights was created in the Department of Health, Education, and Welfare, primarily to carry out the *Brown* decision. In *Brown v. Board of Education of Topeka* (1954), the U.S. Supreme Court ruled that separate schools for African American students were unconstitutional. The Court also played an active role in upholding these laws and extending federal powers in the area of civil rights. (See Chapter 7.)

Antipoverty Policies

The second stream of public policies was a set of antipoverty programs. The federal government had rediscovered poverty in the 1960s. A federal task force of physicians and government officials documented the severe and debilitating health effects of poverty in the United States. They discovered among children a range of diseases associated with poverty and common in underdeveloped nations.

In response to these discoveries, Johnson declared war on poverty. In his War on Poverty, he sponsored a series of bills concentrated in health, nutrition, jobs, education, and community participation. In the area of health, Medicaid was established as a health program for the poor while Medicare was created for the elderly. In nutrition, Johnson promoted the enactment of the food stamp and federal school lunch programs. He supported and expanded upon job development and job training programs, many of which originated in the Kennedy administration such as the *Manpower Development and Training Act.* In the area of public education, Johnson sponsored two major programs: Head Start and the *Elementary and Secondary Education Act (ESEA).* Head Start was a preschool program for children from low-income families. ESEA provided federal money for schools with significant proportions of children from low-income families. Another part of Johnson's War on Poverty addressed the political inactivity of poor communities. He called for "maximum feasible participation" within these communities and established community action agencies to facilitate this participation.

Urban Development Policies

The third stream of Johnson's domestic policies was urban development. The hallmark of this policy was "Model Cities." Johnson envisioned revitalizing cities that would be integrated in terms of race and class.

Johnson decided not to run for re-election in 1968 because his administration had become bogged down in the Vietnam War, as well as continued civil rights agitation and other domestic issues. Vice President Hubert Humphrey ran against Richard Nixon and lost.

Nixon: Modification of Public Policies

Nixon, who had served as Eisenhower's vice president in the 1950s, was elected president in 1968 and again in 1972. He served until he resigned in 1974, under the cloud of the Watergate scandal. Nixon was a conservative Republican who opposed big government. Nevertheless, he claimed to be a supporter of Keynesian theory. He was an astute politician, sensitive to political pressures. Nixon modified some of Johnson's programs and introduced some new initiatives.

Program Changes under Nixon

Programs Nixon modified were those in the War on Poverty. He eliminated the Office of Economic Opportunity. He changed the rules on Aid for Dependent Children to penalize states for giving benefits to ineligible recipients. This reduced the rate of increase in this program.

Nixon introduced **block grants**, a program formed by combining several categorical grants in the same policy area. Many of the antipoverty programs of the 1960s were categorical grants, which are grants for narrow purposes or specific objectives established by the federal government. Generally federal money was targeted toward poor people who were neglected by local government. Local governmental officials had little control over categorical programs. Nixon changed this by combining many categorical grants in a particular policy area into a block grant. The block grant enabled local officials to have more control over the programs.

Examples of block grants are the *Community Development Block Grant (CDBG) of 1974,* which included Model Cities, infrastructure grants, and community action agency grants, and the Comprehensive Employment Training Act (CETA) of 1973, which combined job training, public employment, job development, and summer youth employment.

The CDBG still exists but CETA was eliminated in 1982 and replaced during the Reagan administration by the Jobs Training Partnership Act. Nixon also established the General Revenue Sharing program which allocated federal money to state and local governments. Local administrators could spend the money however they wished.

The Influence of Social Movements

The social movements of the late 1960s and early 1970s influenced Nixon. These movements prodded elected officials to support new environmental protection, consumer protection, and occupational health and safety policies. With these movements in the background, Nixon created the Environmental Protection Agency, the Occupational Safety and Health Administration (OSHA), and the Consumer Products Safety Commission. Indeed, federal policies and agencies proliferated under his leadership.

❖ The Late 1970s and 1980s: A Renewed Conservative Contraction

The period of liberal policy expansion ended in the late 1970s, but the conservative contraction began with Carter, not Reagan. Several factors contributed to the new conservative era: the economic crisis of the late 1970s, the crisis of Keynesian economic theory, and the emergence of new conservative ideas and public awareness of problems with the programs of the 1960s.

The late 1970s was a period of stagflation characterized by a combination of high rates of unemployment and inflation. Stagflation created a crisis in Keynesian economic theory because it defied Keynesian expectations. Keynes predicted an inverse relationship between prices and unemployment; if unemployment declined, prices were expected to rise. The reason for this relationship is simple. If more people were employed, then more people would have money to buy goods at higher prices. By the mid-1970s, however, both unemployment and inflation rates had increased. This trend contradicted the expectations of Keynesian economic theory, hastening the emergence of an alternative conservative/libertarian theory.

The alternative theory was the old theory of the 1920s, but with some revisions and a new name. Neoconservative or supply-side economic theory attributed the simultaneous occurrence of high unemployment and high inflation rates, or stagflation (see Chapter 15), to excessive government regulations, high taxes, and bloated government. The public policy solution was to eliminate regulations, cut taxes (especially corporate taxes), and reduce the size of the federal government. Neoconservatives proposed reducing the size of the government by cutting the national budget, chopping government programs, shifting government programs to the private sector, devolving federal programs to the state level, and making government more efficient.

Federal programs came directly under attack. Newspapers and magazines published articles on the waste, mismanagement, and ineffectiveness of various federal programs, especially the Great Society programs of the Johnson administration. They reported cases of money mismanaged in the CDBG and CETA programs. Several cities had used CETA money to hire city workers such as police officers, city engineers, and sanitation workers. Others had misappropriated CDBG moneys. Critics accused the federal government of throwing money at social problems and wasting taxpayers' money.

Liberals also criticized federal programs. They criticized welfare policy for invading the privacy of welfare recipients through surprise home inspections. Consumer advocate Ralph Nader joined conservatives in attacking ineffective government agencies such as the Interstate Commerce Commission and the Civil Aeronautics Board. They said that these agencies had lost their sense of public purpose and regulated industries for the benefit of industries, not the public.

Carter's Initiatives

Jimmy Carter was elected president in 1976, at the time of stagflation and the challenge to Keynesian economic theory. There were three aspects of Carter's public policy initiatives in this crisis. First, Carter increased funding for public works, especially highway development, and public employment programs. Second, Carter deregulated select competitive regulatory programs, most notably the Civil Aeronautics Board (CAB) and the Interstate Commerce Commission. The Carter administration secured the passage of legislation which reduced the powers of, and eventually eliminated, these two agencies. The deregulation of the CAB allowed for price competition and permitted new airlines to fly intercontinental routes. The deregulation of the ICC encouraged competition in the trucking industry.

Third, Carter supported policies designed to make government more efficient and effective. He created the Regulatory Analysis Review Group (RARG) to review a small number of regulatory proposals. The group studied the economic impacts of major changes in regulatory rules.

Carter reorganized a number of cabinet departments to make them more effective. For example, he reorganized the Department of Labor. He created independent monitoring units to monitor the implementation of the CETA program and two new cabinet-level departments: Education and Veteran Affairs.

Reagan's Attack on Government Regulation and Programs

Ronald Reagan campaigned on a distinctively conservative platform. He advocated cutting taxes, especially for corporations, reducing the size of government, rolling back federal regulations, devolving national programs to the state level, and shifting programs to the private sector, where feasible. He defined government as the problem and criticized it for being too large, wasteful, inefficient, and intrusive. Reagan insisted that welfare programs undermined individual initiative and facilitated dependency on government. He believed in strengthening national defense and increasing military spending. He supported more aggressive police action against crime and tougher sentences for criminals. Like traditional conservatives, he opposed abortion and supported raising the minimum drinking age from 18 to 21.

Reagan targeted social programs and protective regulatory policies. He attempted to reduce the number of recipients of Supplemental Security Income (SSI), which provides benefits to the disabled, because this program had many abuses. Believing that many of the recipients were faking disabilities, he required them to report to the government office for reassessment and terminated the benefits of those who missed their appointments. The courts ordered him to reinstate those recipients terminated from the program. Reagan tried and failed to cut food stamps, Medicaid, and unemployment benefits because Congress did not support the cuts. Some social programs continued to grow under Reagan, although not as fast as in past decades. Congress increased spending but at a much slower rate than in previous years.

Reagan went after protective regulatory policies. He established a policy to subject all new federal regulations to a cost-benefit test. He ordered the Office of Management and Budget (OMB) to monitor federal regulatory agencies and to determine if the costs of new regulations outweighed the benefits. This order had a chilling impact on new regulations and the number declined sharply. Whereas President Carter targeted economic regulations, Reagan attempted to deregulate both economic and protective regulations.

The environmental protection policy was one of Reagan's most controversial efforts at deregulation. He tried to reduce environmental regulations by appointing people opposed to the EPA.

Reagan was successful in cutting taxes and increasing defense spending. He believed that cuts in other domestic programs could compensate for increases in defense spending. However, the cuts were too small to make a difference. Spending increased, revenue from taxes decreased, and, consequently, the budget deficit doubled (Vig and Kraft 1984).

Reagan was successful in increasing the minimum drinking age from 18 to 21. He did so by pressuring state governments. The states were given a choice: Increase the minimum drinking age or lose significant amounts of their federal highway money.

→ The 1990s: Bush and Clinton

Although the 1980s was a conservative decade, policies changed gradually and the liberal programs of previous decades were not dismantled. Some programs were cut, others remained the same, and others expanded. The CETA program was terminated and replaced by the Jobs Training Partnership Act of 1983, administered under Private Industry Councils (PICs) consisting of community leaders.

Public policies continued to expand in the 1990s, even though a few programs experienced cuts. Congress enacted several important bills in the early 1990s, most of which expanded policies already in place.

- The Clean Air Act of 1990 expanded the Clean Air Act of 1970 and addressed the issue of acid rain.
- The Americans with Disabilities Act of 1990 required employers and public agencies to make reasonable accommodations to people with disabling conditions.
- The National Labeling and Education Act of 1990 established national standards for labeling and providing nutritional information on processed foods.
- The Civil Rights Act of 1991 expanded the Civil Rights Act of 1964 by prohibiting racial harassment on the job and providing guidelines for demonstrating illegal forms of employment discrimination.

These policies are discussed in more details in later chapters.

Welfare programs were reduced in the late 1990s. The Personal Responsibility and Work Opportunity Act of 1996 set time limits for women with children receiving welfare benefits. The old Aid for Families with Dependent Children (AFDC) became the Temporary Assistance for Needy Families (TANF) program. Under TANF, recipients can receive benefits for only two consecutive years, although many states extended this limit to three years, and a lifetime limit of five years. By 2000 the number of TANF recipients had declined substantially.

The 1990s was a period of experimentation with market mechanisms to deliver public services. Most states created charter schools, private schools funded by state money. Typically, a charter school would contract with a local school district, a county school district, a university, or a state department of education to provide educational services.

Some states initiated voucher systems for education. Parents could use federal vouchers to send their children to parochial schools. Because most of the voucher money went to church schools, the voucher system created constitutional issues of church and state separation. Nevertheless, the Supreme Court upheld the constitutionality of vouchers in the summer of 2002.

✧ 2001 and Beyond: George W. Bush

War on Terrorism

President George W. Bush's administration was rocked by the September 11, 2001 (9/11) catastrophe, in which terrorists crashed aircraft into the World Trade Center in New York and the Pentagon in Washington, killing 3,000 people in the planes and on the ground. In response to 9/11, Bush supported the Uniting and Strengthening America by Providing Appropriate Tools Required to Intercept and Obstruct Terrorism Act *(USA PATRIOT Act)*, established the Department of Homeland Security, and invaded Afghanistan where al-Qaeda terrorists had been given sanctuary. The USA PATRIOT Act, passed in 2001 less than two months after 9/11, enjoyed bipartisan support in the U.S. Senate and House of Representatives. The Justice Department's Website claims that this Act improves counterterrorism efforts in several ways:

- Expands the power of federal law enforcement officials to use surveillance and gather information.
- Allows domestic and foreign law enforcement and intelligence-gathering agencies to share information and cooperate with each other.
- Increases the penalties for terrorist acts and expands federal police powers.

The Bush administration insists that this expansion is reasonable and necessary to effectively fight terrorism.

A number of interest group organizations such as the American Civil Liberties Union (ACLU) and the American Library Association (ALA) expressed strong concern over the USA PATRIOT Act. These organizations claimed that major provisions of the act violate the Constitution, which protects freedom of speech and guards against unreasonable search and seizures. The ACLU claims that the Act violates the Fourth Amendment because it allows the Federal Bureau of Investigation (FBI) to obtain credit card and medical records without a search warrant or to engage in secret searches of suspects' homes. Both the ACLU and the ALA maintain that the law violates the First Amendment protection of free speech because it prohibits librarians from talking about FBI investigations of library patrons.

Also in response to 9/11, the Bush administration established a new cabinet department, the Department of Homeland Security. Many existing agencies such as the Immigration and Naturalization Service, the U.S. Customs Service, and others were moved into the new department.

Congress created a special 9/11 Commission to investigate what happened, why it happened, and what needs to be done to prevent it from happening again. The commission noted problems of communications and coordination between federal agencies involved in combating terrorism, including the Central Intelligence Agency (CIA) and the FBI. It recommended the establishment of an intelligence czar and Bush created the new position by executive order.

In early 2003 the Bush administration invaded Iraq as a preemptive strike. Officials in the Bush administration initially argued that Saddam Hussein's regime had weapons of mass destruction and direct ties with al-Qaeda, the terrorist group responsible for 9/11. To date, the administration has not been able to substantiate either one of these claims officially. The war effort diverted public attention and resources from many of Bush's domestic programs and generated antiwar sentiments. Nevertheless, he pursued a decidedly conservative policy agenda, much in the tradition of Ronald Reagan. Bush's economic and budget programs emphasized cuts in taxes and increases in military spending. This policy contributed to larger budget deficits.

Domestic Policies

Bush's social policy proposals included **faith-based initiatives**—efforts to allocate federal money to church organizations to provide social services and community development programs. Bush continued the welfare reform program of the Clinton administration, which emphasized getting people off welfare and into the workforce.

One of the crowning achievements of the Bush administration's domestic policies was the establishment of a discount prescription drug program for Medicare recipients and federal subsidies for low-income recipients. The program enjoyed the support of the American Association of Retired Persons (AARP) and the pharmaceutical industry. Critics attacked the program for failing to effectively address the problem of the high prices of prescription drugs and for refusing to allow the federal government to negotiate lower prices with the drug companies.

Bush pursued a conservative agenda in regard to morality policies. He supported a constitutional amendment to ban same-sex marriages. He opposed abortion and secured the passage of a federal law prohibiting partial-birth abortions, even though the U.S. Supreme Court had struck down a similar state law.

Bush insisted that he supports environment policies, but not at substantial costs to industry. He advocated opening up the Arctic National Wildlife Refuge to oil drilling, opposed an international agreement to reduce the emission of greenhouse gases reputedly responsible for global warming, and favored relaxing clean air policy regulations. Like Reagan, he cut funding for select units of the EPA such as research.

He argued for a strong national education policy, which included national educational standards and national tests. He supported charter schools, but abandoned the proposal for federal school vouchers, a program to compensate families $1,500 for the cost of tuition to a private or parochial school. He proposed increasing funding for traditional black colleges such as Tuskegee Institute.

Summary

This chapter provided a brief sketch of the evolution of public policies. Public policies developed in cycles. Liberal periods of policy expansion have been followed by conservative periods of policy retrenchment. The liberal periods corresponded to the episodes of explosive policy expansion of the punctuated equilibrium model. The first two decades of the century, the Progressive Era, was a time of policy expansion. The 1920s was a period of policy contraction, when many of the child labor, minimum wage, and working hour laws enacted earlier were struck down. The 1930s, the decade of the New Deal, was another liberal period of policy expansion. The 1950s was a conservative period, the era of McCarthyism, a trend consistent with the liberal-conservative cycle theory. However, the decade was also one of policy expansion, a trend that contradicted the liberal-conservative model. The 1950s was the decade of the *Brown* decision, the interstate highway system, and the Federal Aviation Administration. Policies continued to expand, but not as substantially as during liberal periods.

The liberal decade of the 1960s and early 1970s brought an avalanche of new policies: civil rights, antipoverty, environmental protection, consumer protection, and others. This trend was consistent with the cycle theory. The late 1970s and 1980s was a conservative period of policy contraction in which some programs were eliminated while others grew more slowly. Policies continued to expand in the 1990s especially with the addition of disabilities rights, nutrition labeling, and environmental policies against acid rain. Nevertheless, this decade was mixed with the contraction of welfare policy and the introduction of market models in education. Policies grew throughout the 20th century, but they grew in spurts as predicted by the punctuated equilibrium model.

By the beginning of the 21st century, the public policy state was well in place. If the last decade of the 20th century is any indication of what is to come in this century, then students of public policy can expect continuous changes in public policies, but perhaps not as dramatic as those of the Progressive, New Deal, or Great Society periods.

Despite pundits' interpretation of the 2004 election results as a mandate for President George W. Bush to push for a more conservative political agenda, exit polls indicate that most voters, including those who voted for Bush, support most of the policies already in place and favor bipartisanship (see Table 3.1). Moreover, a win by only 51 percent of the vote is not a decisive victory. Despite the talk about morality issues and the 2004 election, most Americans believe that abortion should remain legal or mostly legal. Although eleven states passed propositions to ban same-sex marriages and benefits associated with civil unions, this issue is likely to remain on the political agenda for some time in the future. Most Americans remain concerned about defending the country from future terrorist attacks. However, they are also concerned about the environment, the job market, Social Security, education, health care, and other policy issues.

TABLE 3.1

Select CNN Exit Poll of the 2004 Presidential Election

	Candidates		
Vote Summary	**Bush**		**Kerry**
Total Votes	60,608,582		57,288,974
Percent of Summary	51%		48%
Electoral Votes	286		252
Vote by Gender	**Bush**	**00**	**Kerry**
Male (46%)	55%	+4	44%
Female (54%)	48%	+5	51%
Vote by Race	**Bush**	**00**	**Kerry**
White	58%	+4	41%
African American	11%	+2	88%
Latino	44%	+9	53%
Asian	44%	+1	56%
Income	**Bush**	**00**	**Kerry**
<$15,000	36%		63%
$15–30,000	42%		57%
$30–50,000	49%		50%
$50–75,000	56%		43%
$75–100,000	55%		45%
$100–150,000	57%		42%
$150–200,000	58%		42%
$200,000+	63%		35%
Education			
<HS	49%		50%
HS	52%		47%
Some College	54%		46%
College Grad	52%		46%
Post Grad Studies	44%		55%
Religion			
Protestant	59		40
Catholic	52		47
Jewish	25		74
Other	23		74
None	31		67
White Evangelical/Born Again	78		21

continued

TABLE 3.1 (continued)

Select CNN Exit Poll of the 2004 Presidential Election

| Most Important Issue | | Candidates | | |
Issue	%	Bush	00	Kerry
Moral Values	22	80		18
Economics/Jobs	20	18		80
Terrorism	19	86		14
Iraq	15	26		73
Health Care	8	23		77
Taxes	5	57		43
Education	4	26		73
Abortion Should Be				
Always legal	21	25		73
Mostly legal	34	38		61
Mostly illegal	26	73		26
Always illegal	16	77		22
Policy toward Same-Sex Couples				
Legally marry	25	22		77
Civil unions	35	52		47
No legal recognition	37	70		29
Vote by Size of Community				
Big cities	13	39		60
Smaller cities	19	49		49
Suburbs	45	52		47
Small towns	8	50		48
Rural	16	59		40
Vote by Church Attendance				
More than weekly	16	64		35
Weekly	26	58		41
Monthly	14	50		49
A few times a year	28	45		54
Never	15	36		62
Weekly	41	61		39
Occasionally	40	47		53
Never	14	36		62

continues

TABLE 3.1 (continued)

Select CNN Exit Poll of the 2004 Presidential Election

	Candidates	
Vote by Race in Select States	Bush	Kerry
Michigan		
White	54	44
African American	10	89
Latino	36	62
Asian		
Other		
Illinois		
White	51	48
African American	10	89
Latino	23	76
Asian		
Other		
Ohio		
White	56	44
African American	16	84
Latino	35	65
Asian		
Other		

SOURCE: U.S. President/National/Exit Poll, *CNN.com*, November 2, 2004,
www.cnn.com/ELECTION/2004/pages/results/states/US/P/00/epolls.0.html.

Review Questions

1. Name some of the social and economic problems of the first two decades of the 20th century.
2. What were some of the public policy successes and failures of the Progressive movement?
3. Why was President Hoover reluctant to respond to the economic crisis of the 1930s?
4. Name some of the policies enacted under President Roosevelt to address the economic crisis of the 1930s.
5. How did the ideas of John Maynard Keynes influence the development of public policies throughout the 20th century?
6. What were the three streams of public policies enacted under the Johnson administration?
7. Discuss the formation of block grants. What are the advantages and disadvantages of block grants and categorical grants?
8. Discuss the policy agendas of Presidents Ronald Reagan, George H. W. Bush, and Bill Clinton.
9. Discuss the policy agenda of President George W. Bush.

Select Websites

Findlaw.com is one of the best Websites for finding U.S. Supreme Court decisions.
http://www.findlaw.com

For an excellent list of books and syllabi on the Progressive Era visit this social science and historical Website:
http//www.Swarthmore.edu/SocSci/rbannis1/Progs

The Franklin D. Roosevelt Presidential Library and Museum Website offers biographical information on Franklin and Eleanor Roosevelt and some information on the New Deal.
http://www.fdrlibrary.nurist.edu

Key Terms

block grants
cyclical change theory
faith-based initiatives
Federal Housing Administration (FHA)
Great Depression
John Maynard Keynes
Keynesian economics
laissez-faire capitalism
McCarthyism
monopoly

New Deal
oligopoly
price fixing
Progressive Era
Progressive movement
Public Housing Authority (PHA)
punctuated equilibrium
Social Darwinism
trust

CHAPTER 4
⚜

National Institutions of Policy Making

Previous chapters covered theories of public policy and examined long-term policy change. This chapter looks at the institutions of policy making. Its purpose is to examine how these institutions operate and interact with each other and with organized interest groups to produce, sustain, or change public policies. It takes somewhat of a theoretical approach in surveying the Constitution and governmental institutions. It examines policy making within the context of a federal system, but this chapter is not comprehensive; an entire textbook is needed to provide a full discussion of the federal government and its policy-making process. This chapter also looks at the role of the states and local governments in the process of making and carrying out national policies, reviews the Constitution and the changing system of federalism, and focuses on the organization of Congress, the presidency, the bureaucracy, and the courts.

Several major features of the federal government militate against major policy changes and operate to ensure stability in policy making and incremental change. The U.S. Constitution, which provides for a system of checks and balances and separation of powers; the decentralized organization of Congress and its partisan divisions; the division of governmental powers between the federal and state governments—all of these factors have historically operated to inhibit policy change and have contributed to the pattern of long-term policy stability and gradual change.

→ *The U.S. Constitution*

The Constitution, the legal foundation of the national government, provides for three branches of government, a system of checks and balances, protection of basic rights, and a federal system. The term **separation of powers** means that each branch of government is separate from the other branches; that is, each has a different method of selecting its members, a different set of powers, and different methods of making public policies. Members of Congress are elected by popular vote. Representatives serve a two-year term, senators six. The Electoral College elects the president. Each state is allotted a number of electors equal to the state's total number of senators and representatives in Congress. The president appoints Supreme Court justices, with the advice and consent of the Senate.

The Constitution gives different powers to different institutions of government. It gives Congress, the legislative body, the powers to make laws, to lay and collect taxes, to provide for the common defense and general welfare of the nation, to borrow money, to regulate commerce, to coin and regulate money, to make rules for government, to declare war, and to raise and support armed forces. The long list of powers delegated to Congress suggests that the framers of the Constitution intended to make Congress the more powerful body.

The Constitution provides a shorter list of powers and responsibilities for the president. It makes the president the commander in chief of the armed forces and the chief officer of the executive branch. It gives the president the power to pardon people for federal crimes; to make treaties; and to nominate ambassadors, including independent commission and cabinet departments, federal judges, Supreme Court justices, and heads of federal agencies, with the advice and consent of the Senate.

The Constitution gives the judicial branch the power to interpret the law and to mediate conflicts. The Supreme Court also has the power to review laws enacted by Congress or state legislatures and to determine if those laws violate the Constitution. If the Court rules that a law violates the Constitution, then that law becomes null and void. You will read more about the *Supreme Court and policy making later in this chapter.*

Presidential scholar Richard Neustadt disputes the traditional notion of separation of powers.

> The constitutional convention of 1787 is supposed to have created a government of "separate powers." It did nothing of the sort. Rather it created a government of separate institutions sharing powers. (1990, 29)

The Constitution provides for a system of **checks and balances;** that is, it gives each branch some powers over the other branches. As Congress has the power to enact laws, the president has the power to veto them. Congress has the power to override the veto. As the president has the power to nominate officials, the Senate has the power to approve or reject them. As the president is the head of the armed forces, Congress has the power to control the defense budget and to declare war. As Congress has the power to impeach and try the president, the Chief Justice of the Supreme Court presides over the Senate in any trial to remove the president from office. The Court has the power to order presidents to turn over documents to Congress, to interpret laws, and to rule laws unconstitutional.

✦ *Constitutional Changes*

The Constitution is not engraved in stone. It changes as new amendments are added and as the Court changes its interpretation of this document. Although there have been many changes in the Constitution, three changes are most important in any discussion of public policy making: (1) the growth of individual and civil rights, (2) the shift of power from Congress to the president, and (3) the shift of power and policy-making responsibilities from the states to the federal government.

The Growth of Individual and Civil Rights

The first fundamental change in the Constitution came with the introduction of the **Bill of Rights,** the first 10 amendments. These amendments provide basic freedoms and rights.

1. First amendment—Provides for the freedom of speech, press, assembly, and religion and the right to petition the government.
2. Second Amendment—Protects the right to bear arms for protection of the state by means of a regulated militia.
3. Third Amendment—States that soldiers will not be quartered in homes without the owner's consent.
4. Fourth Amendment—Safeguards individuals from unreasonable police searches.
5. Fifth Amendment—Protects individuals from self-incrimination and double jeopardy.
6. Sixth Amendment—Guarantees the accused in criminal prosecutions the right to a speedy trial and an attorney.
7. Seventh Amendment—Guarantees a trial by jury for certain common law cases.
8. Eighth Amendment—Prohibits excessive bail and cruel and unusual punishment.
9. Ninth Amendment—States that rights listed in the other amendments do not preclude the existence of rights not listed in the Constitution.
10. Tenth Amendment—Protects the powers of the states.

A number of later amendments further extended civil rights. The Thirteenth Amendment ended slavery and the Fifteenth Amendment prohibited states from denying any individual the right to vote on account of race, color, or previous condition of servitude. The Fourteenth Amendment defined anyone born or naturalized in the United States as a citizen. It also guaranteed all citizens equal protection under the law and prohibited the government from depriving any individual of life, liberty, or property without due process of law. The Nineteenth Amendment gave women the right to vote. The Twenty-fourth Amendment prohibited the use of poll taxes. (Civil rights are discussed in Chapter 7.)

The Shift of Power from Congress to the President

At the beginning of the 20th century, Congress shifted some of its policy-making responsibilities and powers to the president. It did so for three reasons: Congress had become disorganized, the government had grown too large, and issues had become too complex. Congress shifted powers to the president with the expectation that the president would take the initiative in a number of policy areas. For example, in 1921 Congress passed the *Budget Act.* This act created the Bureau of the Budget, which is now the Office of Management and Budget. Congress gave this agency and the president responsibility for initiating the federal budget. Today, the president is responsible for writing the federal budget and submitting it to Congress, for developing a national domestic policy agenda, and for introducing legislation.

Presidential war powers have also grown substantially during the 20th century, especially in the post–World War II era. After the war, the United States emerged as a world power and became embroiled in the cold war. Congress and the public expected the president to respond quickly and decisively to international crises and to deploy troops if necessary. Congress legalized this practice with the War Powers Resolution of 1973 which allows the president, in the absence of a formal declaration of war from Congress, to send troops to foreign lands to protect the lives of American citizens. It requires the president to inform Congress within 48 hours of sending troops, thus allowing the element of surprise. Congress has the power to bring the troops home after 90 days.

The 9/11 catastrophe also increased the powers of the president. Today the president is expected to protect American lives at home as well as abroad. Working with the Justice Department and the Department of Homeland Security, the president is expected to initiate effective antiterrorists policies.

Federalism and Shifts of Powers from the States to the National Government

The Constitution provides for a **federal system,** one in which sovereignty or governmental powers are divided between the national and state governments. Initially, and until 1937, the United States operated under a system of **dual federalism.** The term implies a system of dual sovereignty that divides policy responsibilities between the states and the national government. Under this form of federalism, state governments dealt with most domestic policies. The national government handled foreign policy and managed national territory and relations with Native Americans. Most domestic policy areas—which included criminal justice, education, health, social welfare, and transportation—were the exclusive domain of the states. Although the national government provided some land for universities, assisted with the building of the railroads, helped former slaves during the Reconstruction period, and assisted in a few other domestic policy areas, prior to the 1930s state governments dominated the domestic policy area.

Under dual federalism, the Tenth Amendment was used to restrict the powers of the national government and enhance those of the states: "The powers not delegated to the United States by the Constitution . . . are reserved to the States . . ." Opponents of federal power have interpreted the **delegated powers** clause to mean that unless the Constitution explicitly gives the power to the national government, it belongs *only* to the states. The Supreme Court used this amendment to strike down federal civil rights, child labor, minimum wage, maximum working hours, and major pieces of New Deal legislation in Franklin D. Roosevelt's first term in office.

By 1937 dual federalism had ended and **cooperative federalism** had emerged. The new form of federalism was characterized by federal involvement in most domestic policy areas and by a cooperative arrangement between the states and the national government. Three factors explain this change: (1) a shift in the Court's focus from the Tenth Amendment to the commerce clause, (2) an increase in federal funds allocated to state and local governments, and (3) the emergence of national issues.

The Shift from the Tenth Amendment to the Commerce Clause

In Roosevelt's second term, the Supreme Court shifted its focus from the Tenth Amendment to the **commerce clause.** Because the national government has supremacy in the regulation of interstate commerce, this shift allowed for a tremendous increase in federal powers. The Court's new focus on the commerce clause allowed it to uphold national minimum wage, maximum working hours, and child labor laws. The Court argued that goods manufactured in one state are generally sold in other states and consequently involve interstate commerce. Moreover, since the goods made by adult and child laborers are entangled in interstate commerce, the national government has the power to regulate minimum wage, maximum working hours, and child labor laws.

Eventually, the Court applied the commerce clause to civil rights policies, particularly to uphold federal laws that prohibited racial segregation or discrimination in public accommodations. For example, in the *Heart of Atlanta Motel, Inc. v. United States,* the Court argued that people who use motels are generally traveling from one state to another and are therefore engaged in interstate commerce. Motel owners interfered with interstate commerce when they refused to rent rooms to African Americans. In prohibiting racial discrimination in public accommodations, the federal government was exercising its powers under the commerce clause. Hence, the Supreme Court increased federal powers in many policy areas by shifting its focus from the Tenth Amendment to the commerce clause.

Increase in Federal Funds Allocated to State Governments

A great deal of the increase in federal powers is explained by the increase in federal money allocated to state and local governments. Most of this increase was made possible by the Sixteenth Amendment (1913), which allowed Congress to levy and collect taxes on income. The tax generated substantially expanded federal revenue.

At the beginning of the 20th century, few federal dollars were available for state and local governments. With the enactment of federal urban renewal programs, the interstate highway system, and several other programs, federal money allocated to state and local governments increased to more than $10 billion by the early 1960s. Today the federal government allocates more than $100 billion to state and local governments (Janda, Berry, and Goldman 2002).

This increase in federal money has meant an increase in national powers. The federal government has used this money to exercise power over the states and to get them to adopt national policies. A prime example is highway money and the minimum drinking age. In the 1980s the Reagan administration asked states to raise the minimum drinking age from 18 to 21; if the states refused, Reagan threatened to reduce their federal highway money. Many state governors felt the federal government was dictating to them, in violation of the Constitution. The Supreme Court disagreed with the governors and pointed out that the states had a choice of accepting or rejecting the federal money.

Civil rights policies offer another example. State and local institutions receiving federal funds are subject to losing this money if they engage in discrimination based on race, nationality, religion (Title VI of the Civil Rights Act of 1964), gender (Title IX of the Education Amendment of 1972), or physically disabling conditions (Title V of the Rehabilitation Act of 1973).

Money allocated for federal programs generally promotes national goals. For example, the federal government allocates billions of dollars under its compensatory education program. This program mandates the creation of additional education programs for low-income school children, primarily through additional hours of math and reading instructions. These programs probably would not exist without federal money.

The Emergence of National Issues

The emergence of a national economy and complex issues cutting across state lines created pressures for a greater involvement of the federal government in domestic policies. Economic crises like the Great Depression cut across state lines and enveloped the entire country. States with the most severe economic problems had the least resources. Many of these states teetered on the brink of bankruptcy. They turned to the federal government for help.

Air and water pollution cut across state lines. Acid rain develops in one state but damages property and vegetation in other states. Sources of water pollution are sometimes found in one state, but polluted rivers often run through several states. These types of problems cannot be adequately addressed by individual states and can be more effectively handled at the national level.

The Important Role of State and Local Governments

Although policy-making responsibilities have shifted from the states to the national government, states continue to play an important role in domestic policies. Just as the federal government has become more active in making domestic policies, so have the states played a greater role in carrying out national policies. State bureaucracies have grown much faster than the federal bureaucracy, as state agencies implement more federal programs and as states continue to initiate new policies themselves. Whereas the number of federal employees has declined between 1990 and 2004, the number of state and local employees has increased.

State governments play a major role in implementing federal programs. States have always administered the federal Aid to Families with Dependent Children (AFDC), now the Temporary Assistance for Needy Families (TANF) program. Within the past 15 years, states have assumed responsibilities for monitoring and administering other federal programs such as the Jobs Training Partnership Act and the Elementary and Secondary Education Act.

State governments are today and have always been what Ira Sharkansky called laboratories of democracy—that is, many new federal policies originated as experimental programs at the state and local level. Sharkansky added, "Virtually all major Federal grants in aid borrowed heavily from the experiments of state governments" (1978, 96). He noted that 10 states had old-age pension programs before the federal government adopted the Social Security program. Another example is the 1996 welfare reform bill. Several states had established experimental workfare programs and time limits years before the enactment of the federal program. The term **innovation and diffusion** characterizes the process in which a new or experimental program is established in one state and then gradually spreads to other states. Charter schools, which began as a small experimental program in one state, illustrate this process.

The Supreme Court has set new limits on federal powers and has recognized policy areas that are the exclusive domain of state governments. For example, in the *Printz v. U.S.* (1997) decision, the Court struck down the provision of the Brady gun-control bill that mandated local police to perform background checks on prospective gun buyers before local gun dealers sell them weapons. In *U.S. v. Lopez,* the Court struck down a federal law banning the possession of a gun in or near a school. The Court claimed that there was a limit to the types of situations in which the commerce clause could apply.

Today state and local governments play a major role in shaping federal policies. Organizations of governors, state legislators, and mayors constitute powerful political forces in Washington, D.C. For example, the National Governors Association played a key role in the passage of the Personal Responsibility and Work Opportunity Act of 1996 (PRWO). The National League of Cities and the National Council of Mayors play a major role getting federal aid programs for cities.

→ The Organization of the Federal Government and the Process of National Policy Making

Although state governments continue to play an important policy-making role, the federal government is a major domestic policy player. Congress, the presidency, the courts, and the bureaucracy make national policy. Understanding the organization and operation of these institutions is essential in understanding the policy-making process.

Congress

Congress consists of internal and external organizations. There are three major types of internal organization within Congress: (1) committee organizations, (2) party organization, and (3) caucuses. External organizations are bureaucratic governmental agencies that are extensions of Congress and assist the lawmakers in their policy-making functions.

Internal Organization of Congress

Congress consists of two chambers: the House of Representatives and the Senate. The House is the largest chamber, with 435 members based on population in each state as of the most recent census. The Senate has 100 members, two from each state. Because of its large size, there is a greater need for stronger leadership and formal procedures in the House of Representatives. The strong leadership comes from the Speaker of the House who presides over this body. This is a powerful position. The Speaker is the leader of the majority party, who

Congress is the hub of the federal policy-making process.

TABLE 4.1

Summary of House and Senate Differences

	House	Senate
Number of members	435	100
Number of committees	19	16
Term of office	2 yrs.	6 yrs.
Representation	District	State
Rules Committee	Powerful	Weak
Debate rules	Usually limited to 1 hr.	Unlimited
Assignment of bills to committee	Speaker assigns bills	Assignments debated
Age qualification	25 yrs.	30 yrs.
Citizenship qualification	7 yrs. as citizen	9 yrs. as citizen

chairs the party's steering committee and provides leadership for the party's policy agenda. The Speaker has the power to assign bills to committees.

Because of its smaller size, the Senate can afford to be more informal. According to the Constitution, the vice president presides over the Senate and votes only in the case of ties. The president pro tempore presides in the absence of the vice president. In practice, the vice president is generally absent. The president pro tempore is a ceremonial position. The real leadership comes from the leader of the majority party. See Table 4.1 for a summary of differences between the House and Senate. Table 4.2 provides a summary of house and senate standing committees.

The Committee System

The House and the Senate are organized in a committee system. There are three major types of committees: standing, joint, and select. **Standing committees** are permanent committees where most congressional policy making occurs.

There are 19 standing committees in the House. Most have subcommittees, which represent even more specialized policy areas. For example, the House Committee on Resources has five subcommittees: (1) Energy and Mineral Resources; (2) Fisheries, Wildlife, and Oceans; (3) National Parks, Forests, and Lands; (4) Native American and Insular Affairs; and (5) Water and Power Resources.

The Senate has 17 standing committees, each representing a different policy area and most with more specialized subcommittees. For example, the Senate Committee on Environment and Public Works has four subcommittees: (1) Clean Air, Wetlands, Private Property, and Nuclear Safety; (2) Drinking Water, Fisheries, and Wildlife; (3) Superfund, Waste Control, and Risk Assessment; and (4) Transportation and Infrastructure.

Congress also has **joint committees,** which consist of members from both the House and Senate. A good example of a joint committee is the Joint Budget Committee. A **conference committee** is also a joint committee. It is created for a short period of time to work out the differences between the House and Senate versions of similar bills. Before a bill becomes a law, both houses of Congress must approve the same version of the bill.

TABLE 4.2

Summary of House and Senate Standing Committees

House Committees	Senate Committees
Agriculture	Agriculture, Nutrition, and Forestry
Appropriations	Appropriations
Armed Services	Armed Services
Banking and Financial Services	Banking, Housing and Urban Affairs
Budget	Budget
Energy and Commerce	Commerce, Science, and Transportation
Education and the Workforce	Health, Education, Labor, and Pensions
International Relations	Foreign Relations
Resources	Energy and Natural Resources
Transportation and Infrastructure	Environment and Public Works
Rules	Rules and Administration
Judiciary	Judiciary
Small Business	Small Business
Ways and Means	Finance
Government Reform	Governmental Affairs
Veterans Affairs	Veterans Affairs
House Administration	No comparable Senate committee
Science	No comparable Senate committee
Standards of Official Conduct	No comparable Senate committee
No comparable House committee	Indian Affairs

Select committees are established for a short period of time, generally to investigate issues not covered by standing committees. These committees hold hearings, gather information, and make recommendations. For example, the Senate Select Committee on Whitewater was the select committee that investigated President Clinton's financial affairs in Arkansas.

Party Organizations and Leadership

The Democratic and Republican parties are well organized in Congress. Each party has its own leaders, its own process for appointing its members to committees, and its own policy committees. Parties are playing a stronger role in setting the legislative agenda and in getting bills passed consistent with that agenda. One of the best examples of the role of parties in promoting a policy agenda occurred in the early 1990s with the Republican party in the House of Representatives under Speaker Newt Gingrich's leadership. Gingrich put together a document titled *Contract with America,* which outlined the party agenda of House Republicans. The party was successful in getting many of the agenda items through Congress, although many were modified to persuade some Democrats to support them.

Each party has its leaders and assistant leaders. There are majority and minority leaders and assistants. Assistant leaders are called whips, but this term is losing its popularity. As of 2005, the Senate majority leader is Bill Frist and the assistant leader is Mitch McConnell.

Harry Reid is the minority leader. The Speaker of the House of Representatives is Dennis Hastert. The majority leader and whip in the House are Tom Delay and Roy Blunt. The minority leader and whip are Nancy Pelosi and Steny Hoyer.

Caucuses

Another type of congressional organization is the **caucus.** Examples of caucuses include the Black Caucus, the Congressional Caucus on Women's Issues, and the Hispanic Caucus. There are also regional caucuses such as the Sunbelt Caucus and state caucuses. These caucuses play an important role in setting the agenda for Congress and shaping legislation. For example, the Congressional Caucus on Women's Issues played a major role in securing the passage of the following bills: the *Violence Against Women Act of 1999,* the *Child Care Infrastructure Act of 1999,* and the *Public School Modernization Act of 1999.* Although the Black Caucus has a broad political agenda, it is known for promoting issues that impact African Americans.

External Support Organizations

Several organizations provide support for Congress. The two most important support agencies are the General Accounting Office and the Congressional Budget Office. The **General Accounting Office (GAO),** established in 1921, provides two important functions for Congress. It audits federal agencies to determine if they are spending their money appropriately and it evaluates federal programs to determine if they are operating in the manner that Congress intended. The GAO reports to Congress and its reports are available to the general public. Periodically, we read about cost overruns in defense contracts; the GAO conducts the audits that find the overruns.

The **Congressional Budget Office (CBO),** created in 1974, assists Congress in formulating the federal budget. Of course, the president, with the assistance of the Office of Management and Budget, writes the first draft of the budget that is presented to Congress. The Congressional Budget Office analyzes this draft and makes recommendations to Congress.

Members of Congress also have their own personal staff—actually two sets of staff, one at the home office in the member's state, the other in Washington, D.C. The home office staff provides services for the constituency. For example, veterans having difficulties getting benefits to which they are entitled may contact their congressperson at the home office where staff members can assist them. Staff members also might help a community organization in getting a federal grant. The staff in Washington assist members of Congress in doing research on a bill or in helping to write legislation.

Congress and Policy Making

The policy-making process in Congress is complex and varies from bill to bill. A bill can be introduced in either the House or the Senate; once introduced, it is assigned to a committee. The committee chair then assigns it to a subcommittee, where most of the work is done. When the subcommittee completes its work and approves the bill, it goes back to the committee. Most bills don't make it this far and the bill dies. If the committee approves the bill, it then goes to the House Rules Committee.

The House Rules Committee, one of the most powerful committees in the House, regulates the flow of bills to the House floor and assigns two major types of rules: debate and amendment. The debate rule limits the time of debate. The amendment rule determines whether amendments may be added when the bill is sent to the House floor. When the Rules Committee approves the bill and assigns rules to it, the bill goes to the House floor where members debate the bill. When the time for debate ends, members vote on the bill. If the majority of the members present vote in favor of the bill it goes to the Senate.

In the Senate the bill goes to the committee, the subcommittee, and back up to the committee. If the committee approves the bill, it goes to the Senate floor. The Senate Rules and Administration Committee does not play a role here. There is no limit to debate in the Senate unless three-fifths of the members vote to end debate. This vote is called the **closure rule.** About 41 Senators can keep debate open and prevent a vote on the bill. The tactic of unending debate is called a **filibuster.** It is a way a minority of senators can talk a bill to death. Generally when the Senate approves a bill that originated in the House, it is a changed bill. However, before the bill can become law, the House and Senate must approve identical bills.

A conference committee, made up of members from both the House and the Senate, negotiates the differences between the House and Senate versions of the bill and produces a compromise bill. The compromise bill is sent back to the floor of both houses of Congress. If both houses approve the bill, it is sent to the president for his signature. It becomes a law when the president signs it. It also becomes a law automatically if the president does not sign it and Congress remains in session for more than 10 days after sending the bill to the president. If Congress adjourns within the 10 days, the bill is vetoed. The president has the power to directly veto the bill. It takes a two-thirds majority in the House and the Senate to override a presidential veto.

In the past, most policy making inside Congress was decentralized. Most of the detailed work on bills occurred within the specialized subcommittee whose members became experts within the narrow policy areas of the committee. Historically, when bills came before the House or Senate floor, it was not uncommon for members to defer to the judgment of the subcommittee.

New Trends in Congressional Policy Making

Recently, two trends have characterized the new policy-making process in Congress: (1) submission of bills to multiple committees and (2) increased party conflict. Barbara Sinclair noted that congressional rule changes in the mid-1970s permitted the submission of a bill to more than one committee and the practice of multiple submissions began to increase in the late 1980s and early 1990s (Sinclair 2000). This increase in the number of committee submissions has contributed to a more fragmented policy-making process and has reduced the chances of passing new legislation. Research into multiple committee assignments found that even though the Americans with Disabilities Act (ADA) of 1990 and the Health Care Reform Bill of 1993 were both opposed by the business sector, the ADA passed but the health care bill died. The ADA was submitted to a single committee; the health care bill was submitted to 10 different committees (Krutz 2001).

The other recent trend in congressional policy making is heightened partisan conflict, a trend that became evident in the early 1980s and intensified during the Clinton administration. This heightened conflict has meant two things: First, political parties are playing a more centralized role in the policy-making process, especially over the more controversial bills.

Second, heightened party conflict has meant an increase in deadlocks, which have paralyzed the policy-making process. For example, in 1994 conflicts over the federal budget had become so intense under the Clinton administration that Congress and the president were unable to reach an agreement until December, almost three months after the last year's budget had expired September 30. Although spending for most programs was extended, some government agencies closed down because funding had run out.

Of course, there have been a few cases of bipartisan cooperation, including the passage of the *Social Security Act of 1983,* the Civil Rights Act of 1991, and the Personal Responsibility and Work Opportunity Act of 1996. There also tends to be bipartisan support for the president's national security and foreign policy proposals, as indicated by the almost unanimous support for the invasion of Afghanistan and the 2002 resolution authorizing the invasion of Iraq.

The Presidency

The organization of the presidency consists of two major divisions: the cabinet-level departments and the Executive Office of the Presidency. There are 15 departments such as the State Department, the Department of Education, and the Department of Health and Human Services. The full list of cabinet departments is given below.

Cabinet Departments		
Agriculture	Health and Human Services	Justice
Commerce	Homeland Security	State
Defense	Housing and Urban Development	Transportation
Education	Interior	Treasury
Energy	Labor	Veterans Affairs

The White House: The center of executive powers.

Each **cabinet department** contains several agencies, each with different functions. Some agencies provide services to clients; others have regulatory powers. Examples of service-providing agencies include the Federal Crop Insurance Corporation in the Department of Agriculture. This agency provides crop insurance for farmers. Another example is the Census Bureau in the Department of Commerce, which takes the census every 10 years. Regulatory agencies include the Federal Aviation Administration (FAA), in the Department of Transportation, and the Food and Drug Administration (FDA), in the Department of Health and Human Services.

The newest cabinet department is the Department of Homeland Security (DHS), formed in reaction to 9/11. This department has three major divisions: Border and Transportation Security (BTS), Emergency Preparedness, and Science and Technology. A listing of some of the agencies in the BTS division illustrates the extent to which agencies were moved from other departments to form the DHS. BTS houses the U.S. Customs Service, from the Department of Treasury; the Immigration and Naturalization Service, from the Department of Justice; and the Animal and Plant Health Inspection Service, from the Department of Agriculture.

The other division of the presidency is the **Executive Office of the President,** established in 1939 to assist the president in developing policies and running the government. Today, there are 11 Executive Office units which are listed below.

Executive Office of the White House	
Office of Management and Budget	Office of the United States Trade Representative
Office of the Vice President	Office of Science and Technology
Office of Policy Development	Council of Economic Advisers
Office of Administration	Council on Environmental Quality
National Security Council	White House Office Staff
Office of National Drug Control Policy	

The **Office of Management and Budget (OMB)** has two major functions. It assists the president in writing the draft of the national budget which it does in consultation with the president and the Council of Economic Advisers. The OMB also assists the president in managing the federal bureaucracy. It monitors federal agencies and reviews new regulatory proposals.

The **Council of Economic Advisors (CEA)** assists the president on economic policies. Presidents Kennedy and Clinton hired economists who had earned the Nobel Prize in Economics to head the CEA.

The **National Security Council (NSC)** consists of the president, vice president, the secretary of state, secretary of defense, the National Security Adviser, the chair of the Joint Chiefs of Staff, the director of the Central Intelligence Agency, and various assistants. The council advises the president on foreign policy matters and occasionally coordinates and carries out foreign policy initiatives. The White House Office includes the president's closest advisers, personal attorney, legislative liaison aides, press secretary, and others.

The Presidency and Policy Making

The president plays a central role in national policy making. The modern president's most important power in making public policy arises not from the Constitution, which gives the president few powers, but from the president's ability to persuade (Neustadt 1990). This power to persuade comes from a number of sources: the ability of the president to communicate effectively, to bargain and negotiate, to build support and popularity, and to convince others of the reasonableness and necessity of the policy proposals.

In exercising the power to persuade and in promoting their policy proposals, presidents use several strategies. They use radio and television to communicate directly to the public. President Franklin D. Roosevelt initiated the process of talking directly to the public through the radio in regular fireside chats. Presidents Ronald Reagan, George H. W. Bush, Bill Clinton, and George W. Bush have all used the radio. Reagan and Clinton were most effective in engaging the public through television.

Communicating directly to the people helps build public support. Presidents use this support as a resource to persuade key members of the opposite political party to switch over and support the president's policy proposals. This strategy worked well for Reagan, as many Democrats switched to support Reagan's budget cuts and policy proposals in the early 1980s, partly out of fear of public reaction for not supporting him. When President Bill Clinton locked horns with Speaker of the House Newt Gingrich over the federal budget in the fall of 1995, it was the shift in public opinion against Gingrich and in support of Clinton that persuaded Congress to compromise with the president. Presidents use other strategies in the policy-making process: They operate to set the governmental agenda, to lobby members of Congress, and to use the administrative process.

Agenda Setting

Presidents influence the policy-making process through the agenda-setting strategy. Presidential candidates campaign with a domestic policy agenda. When elected, presidents articulate this agenda through State of the Union addresses at the beginning of every year. They set the congressional agenda when they introduce new legislation. They influence the policy-making process as they push their policy initiatives and lobby members of Congress.

Direct Lobbying

Presidents engage in lobbying Congress directly. They have their own lobbyists called the **legislative liaison staff** who contact key members of Congress to persuade them to support the president's bills.

Presidents also lobby members of Congress directly. President Johnson, who had served as majority leader in the Senate, was effective in communicating directly to members of the Senate during his administration. He had a reputation for an intense, engaging, and persuasive style of communicating. Sometimes presidents engage in quid pro quo (this for that) negotiations. President Reagan called key members of Congress on the telephone to persuade them to vote for his Social Security bill (Light 1995). In return for their support, the president would promise support on a bill or proposal important to those key members. Presidents sometimes used close advisers or top-level administrators as lobbyists. A good example of this form of indirect lobbying was David Stockman's secret meetings with Senator Moynihan over Reagan's Social Security bill in 1983. Paul Light provides an excellent discussion of this process in *Still Artful Work* (1995).

Administrative Strategy

The president engages in an administrative strategy for making public policy. The president makes law directly by issuing executive orders. This power, common with the modern president, arises from the president's power as chief executive. Examples of executive orders include

Roosevelt's prohibition of racial discrimination in firms receiving major defense contracts, Truman's integration of the armed forces, and Reagan's requirement that regulatory agencies subject proposed regulations to cost-benefit analyses.

Presidents also influence policy making through the appointment process. They can alter the direction of public policies by changing the people who run the responsible agencies. For example, Reagan tried to change the direction of environmental protection policies by appointing officials sympathetic to industry and hostile to environmental laws. A president can make a single appointment to the Supreme Court that can shift the political balance and generate important policy changes.

Trade-offs and Paradoxes of Presidential Policy Making

Presidents face a number of trade-offs in the policy-making area. One trade-off is between domestic policy making and foreign policy making. Presidents have an advantage in the formation of foreign policy because Congress and public opinion tend to give the president full support over foreign policy matters, especially when the president decides to commit armed forces. Presidential scholar Aaron Wildavsky (1995) has documented this foreign policy advantage. The president's popularity tends to increase dramatically when he sends troops to a foreign country. Military action tends to galvanize public support behind the troops and the president. For example, Reagan's support increased when he sent troops to Grenada. President George H. W. Bush's popularity increased dramatically during the first Gulf War in 1991. President George W. Bush's popularity increased when he sent troops to Afghanistan and Iraq. However, foreign policy ventures often overshadow domestic policy initiatives. For example, the Vietnam War overshadowed Johnson's Great Society programs, and the Iraq war of 2003 overshadowed Bush's domestic policy agenda.

Presidents sometimes experience trade-offs between making public policies and administering the government. This trade-off was most evident in the Johnson administration. Despite Johnson's reputation as a successful legislator, his reputation as an administrative president was less impressive. Some scholars, like Martha Derthick (1972), suggested that some of the failures of policies of the 1960s were the result of Johnson's lack of attention to the details of administration. Having expended so much time and resources on policy making, he had little time and few resources left for policy administration. Of course, presidents from Ronald Reagan to George W. Bush have attempted to address the administration problem by appointing top-level officials committed to the president's agenda and delegating more administrative responsibilities to them.

The Bureaucracy

There is no provision in the Constitution for the federal bureaucracy. However, the bureaucracy has become such a regular feature and a powerful force of the contemporary state that it is often considered the fourth branch of government. A **bureaucracy** is a large organization characterized by a hierarchical structure, specialized divisions, selection and promotion on the basis of merit, and written rules and routines. Hierarchical structure refers to a chain of command, with a top-level department head, lower-level supervisors, and several subordinates. Merit means that people are hired based on their credentials, specialized skills, or test performance. The bureaucracy is the nonelected part of government. The General Accounting

Office is an example of a bureaucratic organization because it is large, selects employees on the basis of merit, has a hierarchical structure, performs specialized tasks, and is governed by written rules and routines. There are many different ways of classifying government organizations and many different types of bureaucratic agencies, which we will examine next.

The Independent Commissions, Boards, Agencies, and Administrations

Commissions, boards, agencies, and administrations can be identified most often by their titles. Examples of **independent commissions** include the Federal Trade Commission, the Equal Employment Opportunity Commission, and the Federal Communications Commission. The National Labor Relations Board is an example of an **independent board.** These agencies, like most commissions and boards, have regulatory power. Some, like the Civil Rights Commission, only have power to investigate issues and write reports.

Presidents have less control over boards and commissions because commissioners or board members serve for longer terms than the president and it is difficult for presidents to remove them. They serve five- or seven-year terms.

Most, but not all, **independent agencies** have the word *agency* in their titles and they have a range of different functions. Examples of independent agencies include the Environmental Protection Agency (EPA), the Central Intelligence Agency (CIA), and the Federal Emergency Management Agency (FEMA). The EPA is a regulatory agency. The CIA is a government support agency that carries out covert operations in foreign countries and gathers information to aid in the formulation of foreign policy and national security decisions. FEMA provides services and assistance to victims of national disasters.

Administrative agencies have the word *administration* in their titles and are generally nested inside a cabinet department. Examples include the Federal Aviation Administration (FAA), the National Highway Traffic Safety Administration (NHTSA), and the Food and Drug Administration (FDA). The FAA and the NHTSA are nested inside the Department of Transportation. The FDA is located inside the Department of Health and Human Services.

Sometimes agencies have been consolidated into cabinet departments or, alternatively, administrative agencies have been separated from a department and have become independent. The creation of the Department of Veterans Affairs is an example of the former and the separation of the Social Security Administration (SSA) from the Department of Health and Human Services (HHS) in 1995 is an example of the latter.

Just as agencies can be classified by title, they also can be identified by function. The types of functions of agencies include support, corporate, service, regulatory, and enforcement.

Support Agencies, Government Corporations, and Service Agencies   **Governmental support agencies** help elected officials develop public policies or administer the government. These agencies include those associated with Congress, such as the General Accounting Office (GAO) and the Congressional Budget Office (CBO). They also include those associated with the president such as the OMB or the CEA. They evaluate issues and make policy recommendations. **Government corporations** operate as quasi-private businesses. They provide most of their own revenue. A good example of a government corporation is the U.S. Postal Service.

Service Function   Service agencies provide benefits and services to their clients. These agencies are sometimes called **clientele agencies.** The best examples of clientele agencies can be found in cabinet departments like the Department of Agriculture and the Department of Veterans Affairs. For example, the Agricultural Stabilization and Conservation Service provides price support payments to grain producers who are the clients that receive the benefits. The Department of Veterans Administration provides medical benefits to veterans who are the clients receiving the benefits. The Social Security Administration (SSA), now separate from HHS, sends out Social Security checks to senior citizens who are the clients of the SSA.

Regulatory Functions and Agency Policy Making

Regulatory agencies are a special category of bureaucratic entities. They have the power to issue regulations. Many of the independent commissions or boards, independent agencies, and administrative agencies have regulatory powers. The Federal Communications Commission (FCC) regulates television, radios, cable television, citizens band (CB) radios, and any other audio or visual communications medium, including computers. The National Labor Relations Board regulates labor-management relations, the EPA regulates the environment, and the Occupational Safety and Health Administration (OSHA) regulates health and safety in the workplace.

The regulations of these agencies have the force of law, just as if Congress had passed a bill signed by the president. This body of regulatory law is called administrative law. These agencies acquire their lawmaking powers from Congress. Members of Congress—realizing that they are not biologists, pharmacists, or chemists—delegate the power to make technical decisions to regulatory officials who are biologists, pharmacists, or chemists. These agencies then issue rules and regulations governing the use of toxic substances (EPA), dangerous drugs (FDA), cotton dust in the workplace (OSHA), and others.

The process of making administrative law is described in the Administrative Procedures Act of 1946. All proposed regulations are published in the *Federal Register* before they become final. This publication alerts those interests affected by the proposed rule and gives them an opportunity to express their concerns and influence the development of the new policy. The act requires agencies to hold open and public hearings on the proposed rule. At this time interested parties have a chance to respond and raise objections. Final regulations are published in the Code of Federal Regulations, which includes executive orders and proclamations.

Regulatory agencies sometimes work with Congress in passing bills. Often Congress calls agency heads to testify and give their expert opinions. Sometimes agency heads submit proposals that find their way into actual legislation.

Enforcement Agencies

There are several federal police or enforcement agencies. Examples include the Federal Bureau of Investigation (FBI), the Bureau of Alcohol, Tobacco, Firearms and Explosives (ATF), and the Drug Enforcement Administration (DEA), all located in the U.S. Department of Justice.

The Courts

The court system, consisting of state and federal courts, plays a major role in making public policies. State courts include criminal courts dealing with felonies, misdemeanor courts dealing with petty crimes, juvenile courts dealing with delinquents, probate courts handling wills, family courts taking care of divorces and child custody cases, civil courts handling

The Supreme Court is the highest court in the nation and the center of judicial policy making.

major lawsuits, and small claims courts dealing with lesser lawsuits. State courts are organized on three levels: lower courts, appellate courts, and the state supreme court.

The federal judicial system has three levels—lower, appellate, and supreme. The major lower courts are the **federal district courts** consisting of about 94 district courts in the United States, one in Puerto Rico, and one in the District of Columbia. In addition to the district courts, there are other lower federal courts such as the U.S. Claims Court and the U.S. Tax Court. The district courts handle cases involving federal crimes, civil cases involving federal law, and bankruptcy cases. There are also 12 federal appellate courts and, at the top, the U.S. Supreme Court.

The Supreme Court

The U.S. Supreme Court has original jurisdiction in cases involving ambassadors, other public ministers, and consuls and suits involving states as parties. Other types of cases reach the Supreme Court on appeal from the U.S. appellate courts or from state supreme courts. The Supreme Court consists of one chief justice and eight associate justices, all with equal voting power. The chief justice presides over Court proceedings. When the chief justice is in the majority on a Court decision, he assigns the task of writing the majority opinion. When the chief justice is in the minority, the senior ranking associate justice in the majority decides who will write the majority opinion.

The Supreme Court and Policy Making

The United States Supreme Court is a powerful policy-making body. In a few areas the Court has been the primary policy-making body. For example, in the *Miranda v. Arizona* decision the Court required police to read suspects their rights before arresting them. This policy was not created by Congress, the president, or an administrative agency, but it was made by the Supreme Court.

The Court creates new policies two ways: judicial interpretation and judicial review. Judicial interpretation involves the court clarifying the law. When the law is ambiguous, the court makes the law as it decides on its meaning. If the Court's interpretation is different from what was intended by Congress, Congress has the power to enact new laws to clarify its intention. For example, in the *Grove City College v. Bell* decision, the Court decided that Title 9 of the *Education Act of 1972* prohibited gender discrimination in the finance office of a university, but not in athletic programs or anywhere else in the university. Congress responded by passing the *Civil Rights Restoration Act of 1988* clarifying its intent to prohibit gender discrimination throughout the university, including within athletic programs and scholarships.

Judicial review is the power of the Court to determine whether a law is valid under the Constitution or not. The power of judicial review was not granted in the Constitution but emerged as far back as 1803 in the Supreme Court case of *Marbury v. Madison.* However, some of the biggest changes in public policies of the 20th century occurred through the Court's exercise of judicial review: the *Brown v. Board of Education* decision, which desegregated public schools; the *Roe v. Wade* decision, which legalized abortion; and the *Miranda* decision.

The process of the Court making public policy is called judicial activism. Critics of judicial activism insist that the Court should leave the lawmaking process up to Congress. Originally, conservatives used the term to attack what they perceived to be a liberal Court. However, the Court today is largely conservative and it still engages in judicial activism.

Interest Groups and the Court

Another aspect of judicial policy making is the role of interest groups. This aspect is often ignored because it is generally assumed that justices are insulated from politics. However, interest groups play a major role by pursuing cases all the way up to the Supreme Court and by writing briefs or statements supporting one side of an issue or another.

> Interest groups from the entire political spectrum look to the Court to decide issues of public policy: from business organizations and corporations in the late nineteenth century to the Jehovah's Witnesses in the 1930s: the ACLU and NAACP in the 1950s and 1960s; "liberal" women's rights groups and consumer and environmental protection groups, such as the National Organization for Women (NOW), Common Cause, "Nader's Raiders," the Sierra Club, the Environmental Defense Fund, and the Natural Resources Defense Council; as well as a growing number of conservative "public-interest" law firms like the Pacific Legal Foundation, the Mountain States Legal Foundation, and the Washington Legal Foundation. (O'Brien 1990, 248)

The role of interest groups can be seen in the *Regents of the University of California v. Bakke* case involving reverse discrimination where 120 organizations joined 58 amicus (friends of the court) briefs; of the interest groups, 83 were for the University of California, 32 for Bakke, and 5 urged the Court not to take the case. In the *Webster v. Reproductive Health Services* decision on abortion, 78 briefs were filed (O'Brien 1990, 248).

→ Patterns of Policy Making

Now that we have discussed how Congress, the presidency, the bureaucracy, and the courts make laws, we can examine how they interact with each other in the policy-making process. Several patterns of policy making can be identified involving different combinations of governmental and nongovernmental agencies. These patterns include iron triangles, issue networks, and the policy cauldron. Each pattern involves governmental entities and interest groups.

Iron Triangles

The **iron triangle** involves a long-term, stable, and closed relationship between a bureaucratic agency, a congressional subcommittee, and special interest groups. The interest groups tend to remain for long periods of time, which explains stability. Triangles tend to be closed systems because they provide benefits to a narrow select group of interests. For example, the Army Corp of Engineers is responsible for dredging harbors. Only those cities with harbors and the private companies involved with harbors benefit from the policy. When dredging is required, "the Corps' water resource programs operate through a well-established network of ties between individual members of Congress seeking projects for their districts, congressional committees (the House and Senate public works committees and the House Public Works Appropriations Subcommittee), officials of the Corps of Engineers, and representatives of affected local interests and national lobbying organizations . . ." (Ripley and Franklin 1984, 114). Because it involves the congressional subcommittee and a single bureaucratic agency, the triangle is often called a subgovernment.

This triangular relationship between interest groups, agency, and subcommittee is powerful for many reasons.

1. It is a cooperative, mutually supportive relationship. All three cooperate for their mutual benefit. Interest groups support the bureaucratic agency and members of the congressional subcommittee. In return, the agency and subcommittee develop policies beneficial to the interest groups.
2. Iron triangles tend to make policies quietly and outside of public view, often without media coverage. This occurs primarily because of the absence of conflicts.
3. Interest groups within these triangles are powerful: They have considerable resources and influence.
4. Members of Congress tend to defer to the judgment of the subcommittees within these iron triangles because subcommittee members become knowledgeable in their respective areas and other members of Congress trust their judgment.

There are many examples of iron triangles. Ripley and Franklin illustrated one involving price support in agricultural policy.

> The price-support subgovernments are several, and there is a variant for each major crop or supported item. The basic participants are relevant specialists in the Agricultural Stabilization and Conservation Service (in the Department of Agriculture), the members of the various commodity subcommittees of the House Agriculture Committee and representatives of the interest groups for the various crops and commodities (such as the National Association of Wheat Growers, the National Wool Growers Association, the Soybean Council of America, and the National Milk Producers Federation). . . . each commodity subgovernment works to obtain the most favorable support possible for the producers of the commodity, both in terms of acreage allotments and target prices set for crops. (1984, 107–108)

The House and Senate tend to defer to the judgments of the congressional subcommittees in a particular iron triangle.

Price-support payments were severely curtailed under the Reagan, Bush, and Clinton administrations. The Reagan administration even tried to eliminate them, but they have persisted into the 21st century because of the power of the iron triangle.

Issue Networks

Policy analyst Hugh Heclo originated the term *issue networks* (1992). Whereas iron triangles involve a small, closed circle of participants, **issue networks** entail a larger, more open community of loosely connected participants and higher levels of government. Although there are many different patterns of issue networks, the two most noticeable are the shared action coalition and the kaleidoscopic patterns.

Social Security is a good example of the shared action coalition issue network. Social Security policies are not made in a closed triangle involving a closed circle of interest groups. Rather, the making of Social Security policy has involved the Social Security Agency, close advisers to the president, the director of the Office of Management and Budget, economic advisers to the president, local Social Security offices throughout the country, a cadre of specialists in the area, and several different interest groups on both sides of the issue, including the Business Roundtable, the National Association of Manufacturers, the American Association of Retired People, and several labor unions. According to Heclo, issue networks involve people who may not necessarily agree, but who are knowledgeable about the policy. In a shared-coalition issue network, there may be general consensus on the policy among different interest groups.

An example of the kaleidoscopic issue network is provided by energy policy. Heclo insisted that energy policy cannot be simplified into a division between big oil companies and consumer interests, or liberals versus conservatives. Rather, it involves many different types of interests such as the environment, tax reform, civil rights, and nuclear power (Heclo 1992).

Policy Cauldron

The major difference between coalition and kaleidoscopic networks is that there is consensus in the coalition and continual conflict within the kaleidoscopic networks. Knowledge and information is used to settle disputes within issue networks (Helco 1992). The implication is that disputes over energy policy can be settled with information and expertise, just as information and expertise helped create consensus over Social Security policies. However, some policies with conflicting values, such as moral policy, cannot be settled with information and expertise. Abortion is a good example. The differences between pro-life and pro-choice groups cannot be settled by information. The conflicts between these two groups are intense and sometimes violent. The term **policy cauldron** characterizes the pattern of policy making in this issue. It is like a pot with volatile substances coming to a boil.

Summary

For the most part, the Constitution and organization of government operate to inhibit changes in public policy. The system of checks and balances, the division of powers between the states and the national government, partisanship, and the decentralized organization of Congress—all of these factors have operated to inhibit policy change. Nevertheless, change has occurred, especially when presidents have been persuasive, when support has cut across party lines, or when external political pressures have been strong enough to overcome institutional barriers.

Different types of policies have been characterized by different patterns of policy making. These patterns include the iron triangle, issue network, and the policy cauldron; they involve different patterns of power arrangements; and they arise from different types of policies. Iron triangles entail arrangements among subcommittees, interest groups, and lower-level bureaucratic agencies and they arise out of distributive policies. Issue networks entail higher levels of government and professional organizations and they arise out of redistributive policies. Policy cauldrons entail higher levels of government and usually arise from contentious moral policies.

Review Questions

1. Why did the Federalists favor strengthening national powers?
2. Why did critics of the original U.S. Constitution claim that this document was flawed?
3. What three factors contributed to the growth of federal powers?
4. Discuss iron triangles and issue networks.
5. Discuss the policy-making process of Congress, the presidency, the Supreme Court, and the bureaucracy.
6. Discuss the organization of Congress. Explain how a bill becomes law.
7. Discuss the powers and role of the president in the policy-making process.
8. Discuss how bureaucratic agencies make law.
9. How does the Supreme Court make policy?
10. In what ways did the shift of powers from the states to the federal government impact on national policy making?
11. Discuss the role of state governments in the period of growing federal powers.

Select Websites

This is the official Website for the White House.
http://www.whitehouse.gov

Firstgov.gov operates as a portal into the national government. It takes visitors to anywhere inside the government.
http://www.firstgov.gov

Thomas is a good Website for following bills recently introduced into Congress.
http://www.Thomas.loc.gov

These are the official Websites for the Congressional Budget Office and the General Accounting Office:
http://www.cbo.gov
http://www.gao.gov

This is the Website of the United States Supreme Court.
http://www.supremecourtus.gov

Key Terms

Bill of Rights
bureaucracy
cabinet departments
caucus
checks and balances
clientele agencies
closure rule
commerce clause
conference committees
Congressional Budget Office (CBO)
cooperative federalism
Council of Economic Advisers (CEA)
delegated powers
dual federalism
Executive Office of the President
federal district courts
federal system
filibuster
General Accounting Office (GAO)

government corporations
governmental support agencies
independent agencies
independent board
independent commission
innovation and diffusion
iron triangles
issue networks
joint committees
judicial review
legislative liaison staff
National Security Council
Office of Management and Budget (OMB)
policy cauldron
regulatory agencies
select committees
separation of powers
standing committees

PART II

CHAPTER 5

Social Welfare Policy

Social welfare policies are about helping people in need: the homeless, unemployed, underemployed, disabled, blind, aged, mentally ill, widows, children of poor parents, and others. These policies are designed to lessen the severity of poverty and make life livable for people who are poor or destitute. Social welfare policies are expected to act as a safety net to catch people and keep them from falling into the abyss of human suffering.

Social welfare is classified as a redistributive policy. It shifts resources downward, from the advantaged to the disadvantaged. It generally involves ideological disputes and high levels of conflict. It entails issue networks with social welfare professionals at the local, state, and national levels who interact with each other.

The 19th and 20th centuries saw several social welfare policy regimes: the preindustrial (1700–1870s), industrial (1870s–1900), Progressive (1900-1935), New Deal (1935–1965), and Great Society (1965 to current period) regimes. The passage of the Social Security Act of 1935 inagurated the New Deal regime and established the national social welfare state. The creation of food stamps and Medicare and Medicaid in 1965 set forth the Great Society regime. These regimes are distinguishable by the dominant ideas about poor people and the economy, by specific relations of power, and by the mix of the policies of the period. Specific stressors triggered policy regime changes. The Industrial Revolution and urbanization incited the change from the preindustrial to the industrial regime. The Progressive movement precipitated the change from the industrial to the Progressive social policy regime. The Great Depression undergirded the change from the Progressive to the New Deal regime. The social movements of the 1960s initiated the change from the New Deal to the Great Society regime.

→ The Preindustrial and Industrial Policy Regimes

The preindustrial social welfare regime rested on an agrarian society with small towns and communities in which everyone knew each other and in which most people lived in rural areas. For the most part, neighbors helped one another during times of crisis—natural disasters, accidents, illnesses, fires, and other calamities. Some charity organizations were present in larger towns.

Ideas about poor people distinguished between the deserving poor and the undeserving poor. The deserving poor included people who were blind, disabled, and orphaned. People who could work were expected to work. Poor people who did not work were considered undeserving and were viewed as defective or immoral. Although local communities had some charity organizations, it was not uncommon for a community to banish the undeserving poor. Communities had mixed feelings about widows. In most cases, well-to-do widows managed well and poor widows were expected to work.

Industrialization and urbanization ended the preindustrial policy regime and contributed to the emergence of the industrial policy regime of the late 19th century. Industrialization accelerated after the Civil War and generated a massive migration to cities which exploded in population. Table 5.1 illustrates the extent of the population growth for select fast-growing cities.

Between 1860 and 1920, the populations of these cities increased by a factor of five or more. Chicago's population increased by a factor of about 20. The expansion of industries and the need for workers attracted immigrants from Europe and migrants from rural America to urban America. In 1870 barely 25 percent of the U.S. population lived in cities. By the

TABLE 5.1

Population Change in Select Cities, 1860–1920

City	Population in 1860	Population in 1920
Chicago	109,260	2,701,705
Detroit	45,619	993,678
New York	805,651	5,620,000
Philadelphia	565,651	1,823,779

SOURCE: Klebanow, Diana, Franklin Jonas, and Ira Leonard. *Urban Legacy: The Story of America's Cities.* New York: The New American Library Inc, 1977.

end of the century over 40 percent of the population lived in cities. By 1920 most Americans lived in urban areas (Klebanow, Jonas, and Leonard 1977). Urbanization was a major stressor that altered the reality of poverty. It produced mass urban communities of strangers and large numbers of poor people. It precipitated the change from the preindustrial to the industrial policy regime.

Under the industrial policy regime, state governments, private organizations, and the national government produced a mix of new social welfare policies. In the early 1870s the number of private charity organizations increased dramatically, especially in large cities like New York, Chicago, Philadelphia, and Detroit. Because of concern over the duplication of services and possible abuse by recipients, an organization called the Charity Organization Society (COS) was established in 1877 in Buffalo, New York. The COS kept records on charity recipients and coordinated charitable services. By the 1880s about 25 other cities had established COSs; by 1900 that figure had grown to about 138 (Klebanow, Jonas, and Leonard 1977).

The federal government created two social welfare programs just after the Civil War. One program was the Freedmen's Bureau which provided assistance to former slaves until 1872. The other federal program provided benefits for veterans of the Civil War. By 1920 the program had expanded to include the veterans of the Spanish-American War and World War I. Veterans benefits had emerged as one of the largest federal social programs by 1920.

Just as the Industrial Revolution was characterized by large organizations, state governments responded to the problems of poverty by creating large institutions. Asylums, orphanages, and poorhouses emerged in the late 19th century. This institutional response to poverty, along with private charities, defined the industrial policy regime.

Welfare Institutions of the Industrial Era

Poorhouses

Poorhouses provided a refuge for poor people. State government provided the money; county governments administered the programs. Most poorhouses provided temporary shelter for the jobless, especially during economic depressions. They were places of last resort for the elderly, the sick, the mentally ill, the blind, and the disabled.

Conditions within poorhouses varied. Some were decent and fairly clean. A few offered some medical services (Trattner 1999, 60). Some poorhouses were poorly kept; some were dirty and vile. A turn of the century New York legislative committee report on poorhouses claimed that in the county poorhouse might be found:

> . . . the lunatic suffering for years in a dark and suffocating cell, in summer, and almost freezing in the winter—where a score of children are poorly fed, poorly clothed, and quite untaught—where the poor idiot is half starved and beaten with rods because he is too dull to do his master's bidding—where the aged mother is lying in perhaps her last sickness, unattended by physician, and with no one to minister to her wants. . . . (Trattner 1999, 60)

Trattner claimed that poorhouses were receptors for different people: the sick and the healthy, young children, women and old men, the sane and the insane, good citizens and hardened criminals, as well as alcoholics and drug addicts.

> Male and female, all thrown together in haphazard fashion. Nakedness and filth, hunger, vice, and other abuses such as beatings by cruel keepers were not uncommon in many of these wretched places, vile catchalls for everyone in need, defined by contemporaries as "living tombs" and by another as "social cemeteries."(Trattner 1999, 59)

The Progressive movement contributed to poorhouse reform. It succeeded in banning children from them and in creating asylums for the insane. New Deal programs eventually made poorhouses obsolete, as federal programs eventually provided direct support for the un-employed, the blind, single mothers, the elderly, and the disabled. Some historians claim that poorhouses disappeared, others that they evolved into nursing homes.

Orphanages

Orphanages expanded at the end of the 19th century. They were not only for children with-out parents; they became a warehouse for children whose parents could no longer afford to care for them. It was not uncommon for a widow to put her children in an orphanage be-cause she was unable to care for them and earn enough to survive. Orphanages as social wel-fare programs were extremely inefficient. It was substantially cheaper to give families food and housing assistance than to institutionalize the children. Moreover, while orphanages were private organizations, they received state money. The more children they had, the more state money they would receive. This type of arrangement encouraged the overcrowding of or-phanages and the underfeeding and neglect of the children.

Charities

Most cities had charity organizations to assist the needy. Most charities were associated with churches and focused on specific needs. For example, some charities helped the blind only and some helped widows. Private charities were not obligated to help the poor. Most did not provide assistance to able-bodied men or unmarried pregnant women. Many required clients to attend Christian training or church services before providing assistance. Major business leaders often contributed substantial sums of money to them.

Settlement Houses

Settlement house programs emerged in response to the deplorable housing conditions in the rapidly growing industrial central cities. Several programs first appeared in the late 1880s pri-marily to assist poor immigrants. Jane Addam's settlement house in Chicago, the Hull House, is one of the best known.

Many low-income families in big cities like New York lived in overcrowded tenement or apartment houses. Patterson described a family of nine—husband, wife, grandmother, and six children—crowded into a two-room tenement house on the east side of New York City at the beginning of the 20th century. One room was only

> ten feet square that served as parlor, bedroom, and eating room, the other a small hall-room made into a kitchen. . . . The rent was seven dollars and a half a month, more than a week's wages for the husband and father, who was the only breadwinner in the family. That day the mother had thrown herself out of the window, and was carried up from the street dead. She was "discouraged," said some of the other women of the tenement. (1994, 1)

Patterson cited cases of dirty working conditions and disease-ridden factories; a case of a young woman, ill with tuberculosis, sewing at home to make money to survive, but dying within three years; and cases of little children working to help support their families. Of a 1905 case he wrote:

> The other day a girl of 8 years was dismissed from the diphtheria hospital after a severe attack of the disease. Almost immediately she was working at women's collars although scarcely able to walk across the room. (1994, 4)

⇢ *Social Policy and Dominant Ideas*

Traditional ideas operated as powerful barriers preventing the emergence of social policies. There were four strands of traditional theories which acted as barriers to new social programs: classical economic theory, traditional conservatism, racialism, and Social Darwinism.

Classical Economic Theory

Classical economic theory is covered in more detail in Chapter 14, as it is too involved to cover here. Nevertheless, three aspects of this theory operated to restrain social welfare policy. First, classical economic theory rejected the notion of involuntary unemployment. It assumed that unemployed workers would get jobs if their wages were reduced—much like bargain stores reduced prices to sell overstocked merchandise.

Second, classical economic theory included the ideas of Thomas Malthus. He believed that population increases contributed to poverty, that poverty was inevitable, and that increasing wages would only allow workers to have more children, which in turn would cost more money and thus absorb the increase in wages. Conservative Malthusians believed that government antipoverty programs would encourage poor people to have more children and would not reduce poverty.

Finally, classical economic theory assumed that depressions were natural periods in which the market purged itself of inefficient and wasteful businesses. Government interference with this process would do more harm than good and cause markets to operate inefficiently. Social welfare programs would promote dependency and produce unnaturally high wages.

Traditional Conservatism

Traditional conservatives emphasized limited government, individualism, and hard work. They opposed government intrusion into the market, but supported government regulation of morals. They saw poverty not as a sign of problems within the market, but as a consequence of the values, attitudes, and behavior of poor people. The conservative view of the **culture of poverty** presumed that poverty resulted from laziness, impulsiveness, hedonism, and lack of education. Conservatives preferred charities that provided food, shelter, and religious instructions. Giving poor people too much help would discourage work and facilitate dependency. A good example of the conservative culture of poverty perspective is found in Edward Banfield's classic book *The Unheavenly City* (1974). A more liberal perspective of the culture of poverty is found in Oscar Lewis's *The Children of Sanchez* (1961).

Racialism

Racialism or racism played a major role in obstructing the formation of social welfare policies throughout the 20th century. **Racialism** was not based on ignorance or hatred, but on the use of labels and stereotypes, classifying a group of people as belonging to a separate human species and ascribing negative behavioral traits onto the group. Labels such as inferior, untrustworthy, conniving, impulsive, unintelligent, savage, emotional, and dangerous evoked feelings of revulsion and hostility. These racial stereotypes operated as powerful barriers to social welfare programs. For example, stereotypes of African-American welfare queens incite hostility toward welfare programs today.

Social Darwinism

Herbert Spencer, the father of **Social Darwinism,** opposed any form of government programs, including old-age pensions, widows' benefits, minimum wage, workers' compensation, and public education. He argued that the solution to poverty is to let the poor starve. Spencer is known for the expression "the survival of the fittest," in which society, like nature, involved a struggle between the strong and the weak, the fit and the unfit. The strong and the fit would survive this struggle; the weak and unfit would perish. He insisted that the whole society evolves through this process and that any government interference with it would be disastrous, the destruction of civilization.

Some American Social Darwinists conceded some support of the poor to prevent starvation. For example, William Graham Sumner, a Social Darwinist and founder of American sociology, supported charity to prevent starvation. He also supported public education, but opposed most other government programs, especially the minimum wage and maximum working hours. Social Darwinism died out by the middle of the 20th century. However, traces of it are reflected in the thought of contemporary intellectuals and political leaders who argue for the complete elimination of welfare.

❖ *The Progressive Movement*

The Progressive movement impacted the industrial policy regime and stimulated the rapid expansion of social welfare programs. This movement was not one but several movements, including municipal and social reformers. Municipal reformers focused on cleaning up corrupt city governments, creating professional city administration, establishing nonpartisan elections, civil service systems, and many other reforms.

Social reformers included labor unions, muckrakers, (journalists who were social critics), women's organizations, professional social workers, the Social Gospel movement, and the settlement house movement. Industrial unions advocated the eight-hour workday, minimum wage legislation, unemployment compensation, workers' compensation, and antipoverty programs. Muckrakers like Upton Sinclair dramatized the horrible and hazardous conditions of industrial workers and the high rates of industrial accidents. Some muckrakers attacked urban poverty and supported the settlement house movement.

Several women's organizations emerged in response to the problems of child labor, the hardships of widowhood, and other issues concerning the welfare of women and families:

- Women's Trade Union League (WTUL)
- National Child Labor Committee (NCLC)
- National Congress of Mothers (NCM)
- American Association for Labor Legislation (AALL)

The AALL was founded to research labor issues. It campaigned for minimum wages, workmen's compensation, unemployment benefits, and old-age pensions. It also advocated replacing poorhouses with national welfare programs. The WTUL, NCLC, and NCM promoted child labor and mothers' pension programs (Gordon 1994). Women's organizations like the NCM argued for programs to educate and assist mothers and protect children. They were successful in getting a number of states to establish these programs.

Religious organizations began to change at the beginning of the 20th century. The Social Gospel movement emerged among Protestant religious organizations responding to the need of the rapidly rising industrial working class living in central cities and in poor rural areas. The movement emphasized the new mission of churches to help the poor and the needy. In response, urban churches established many social service programs.

Social reformers argued for expanded state and federal antipoverty programs. They supported workmen's compensation, widow's benefits, and old-age pensions. Appalled by the poorhouses and orphanages that characterized the industrial policy regime, they attacked the institutional approach to poverty.

Progressive Ideas

The Progressive movement involved not only a political struggle over policies but also a war over ideas—traditional ideas versus social reform ideas. Social reformers fought against the traditional ideas, especially Social Darwinism, racialism, and conservatism. Muckrakers such as Upton Sinclair blamed poverty on corporate greed and inhumane working conditions. Henry George identified features of the modern economy that contributed to poverty—low wages, business failure, industries shutting down, and inequality. George's work *Progress and Poverty: An Inquiry into the Causes of Industrial Depressions and of Increase of Want with Increase of Wealth* anticipated Keynesian theory which emerged in the 1930s. Industrial labor leaders attacked the traditional views with a passion. For example, Eugene V. Debs, an early 20th century labor leader, demanded higher wages for workers and an eight-hour working day. He attacked racism, called for equal rights, and proclaimed that all workers were equal, regardless of race, national origin, or gender. He advocated industrial workers joining industrial unions. Debs was one of the founders of the Industrial Workers of the World and ran for president as the Socialist Party candidate. Other Progressives, particularly President Teddy Roosevelt, attacked Debs for his membership in that party. He was arrested for giving a speech against the U.S. involvement in World War I.

Debs was also influenced by the ideas of Thomas Paine, one of the intellectual leaders of the American Revolution. Paine blamed poverty on inequality. In his essay "Agrarian Justice," he insisted that no human life should be more miserable than it was in the state of nature. He suggested that civilization brings inequality, making some people more affluent and others more wretched. Paine supported a stronger role for government in shifting wealth downward. He believed that helping poor people should not be just a matter of charity, but a government obligation. He advocated government programs for the blind, aged, and disabled.

These social Progressive ideas had limited influence, primarily because of divisions among Progressives and the popularity of the dominant ideas of the period—conservatism, racialism, Social Darwinism, and classical economics. Social reformers fought bitterly against these ideas. Other Progressives, especially municipal reformers, ascribed to many of the dominant views and provided little support for the social program. Nonetheless, there were some successes in policy initiatives.

Progressive Policies

Social reformers were successful in expanding social programs such as religious-based social services, private charities, and settlement houses. They encouraged the emergence of the social work profession. They were successful in removing children from poorhouses and in securing the enactment of many important state-level social programs. By 1920 workmen's compensation programs had been established in 45 states. By the end of the 1920s, about eight states had old-age pension programs. By 1931, 46 states had aid for mothers or pension programs for widows (Gordon 1994, 185; 226).

The Progressive movement produced several new federal programs. In 1912 Congress created the **Children's Bureau** to promote issues pertaining to women with children (Gordon 1994). It administered educational programs for mothers in order to reduce infant mortality rates, but it was not a welfare agency. In 1921 Congress passed the *Sheppard-Towner Act,* which allocated some money to assist women with children. As Congress became more conservative and concerned about spending too much money, it terminated this program in 1929.

Despite the successes of the social reformers, there were many holes in the social safety net through which several groups fell: poor farmers, low-wage unskilled workers, the unemployed, unmarried women with children, and the aged. There was no unemployment insurance. The Supreme Court killed minimum wage, maximum working hours, and child labor laws. Private charity and religious organizations provided some social programs. Rural areas had few programs. Although several states had small programs for widows, there were no programs for unmarried women with children. On the national level, there was no comprehensive social welfare program: no federal relief programs and no unemployment benefits. Some programs established in the early years of the 20th century were gone by the end of the 1920s.

→ *The Social Welfare Policy Regime of the New Deal*

The Great Depression was like an earthquake; it shook the foundation of the Progressive policy regime and ignited explosive political movements. It changed the way people thought about poverty and government responsibility and created conditions ripe for a policy regime change.

In the early years of the Depression, most people ascribed to traditional views and blamed themselves for their poverty and unemployment. However, as the ranks of the poor and unemployed expanded, people began to blame the system more and themselves less. Unemployment rates reached 25 percent nationally, and exceeded 50 percent in some cities. Local charities were overwhelmed and could not handle the demand for assistance produced by massive unemployment. The unemployed began to organize, first locally, then nationally as they found unemployment and poverty in common with others. Renters began organizing and demanding fair rent and affordable housing. Poor people's organizations were formed at the local level demanding increases in relief benefits. National organizations emerged later (Piven and Cloward 1979).

In the early 1930s a number of cities like New York, Philadelphia, Chicago, and others experienced rent strikes, food riots, and relief insurgency (Piven and Cloward 1979). Riots involving thousands of people broke out in reaction to the eviction of families from their homes. The *New York Times* in 1932 described the riot accompanying the eviction of three families as follows: "Probably because of the cold, the crowd numbered only 1,000 although in unruliness it equaled the throng of 4,000 that stormed the police in the first disorder of a similar nature on January 22" (quoted in Piven and Cloward 1979, 53). Large crowds attacked trucks carrying food and organized groups converged on relief agencies demanding support. Several national organizations of the unemployed emerged by the mid-1930s: The Unemployed Councils of the U.S.A. (1930), the Federation of Unemployed Workers Leagues of America (1932), the Eastern Federation of Unemployed and Emergency Workers (1934), and the Workers' Alliance of America (1935). By the end of 1936 the National Workers' Alliance Convention (NWAC) claimed 1,600 locals with 600,000 members in 43 states (Piven and Cloward 1979, 76). Leaders of NWAC demanded an increase in relief benefits, the establishment of a federal relief program, the creation of federal unemployment benefits, and federal housing assistance.

Industrial labor unions increased organizing efforts during the Depression. Some industries cut wages substantially, which incited union organizing and provoked strikes. Unions became more organized, aggressive, and demanding, especially of social programs like minimum wage, unemployment benefits, a Progressive social security system, and many other programs. (See Chapter 9.)

Traditional groups supported these movements to get the federal government to assist the poor and unemployed. Mayors, governors, social workers, and other professionals sympathized with these movements and supported efforts to get the government to help poor people. With the massive job losses brought about by the Depression and with millions of people begging for work, the notion that poverty and unemployment were the result of laziness, vice, or inferiority lost all credibility. The need for expanded welfare programs became most evident.

Keynesian Theory, Franklin D. Roosevelt, and the New Deal

The ideas of economist John Keynes dominated the social welfare policies of President Roosevelt's **New Deal.** (Keynes is discussed in more detail in Chapter 14.) Keynes argued that the most effective way of stimulating the economy was to put more money in the hands of consumers through government jobs or government cash transfer payments. Government projects employed people to build roads, bridges, ports, and government buildings; to plant trees and clear land; and to engage in other similar activities. Cash transfers involved old-age retirement, unemployment benefits, aid for the blind, and others.

There are three views of the enactment of New Deal programs: elite, social movement, and state centered. Elite theorists insist that liberal corporate leaders played a key role in shaping New Deal social programs. William Domhoff, a proponent of the elitist view, said this:

> I claimed in my first effort that corporate moderates had significant involvement in the
> process through an organization called the American Association for Labor Legislation . . .
> and the Business Advisory Council . . ., and that Gerard Swope, a member of both
> forenamed organizations . . . was influential in reinforcing Roosevelt's business-oriented
> views on how old-age pensions and unemployment compensation should be funded. I also
> said that ultraconservative businessmen, epitomized by the National Association of
> Manufacturers, and southern plantation owners made the legislation even more conservative,
> leading to my conclusion: the act was shaped by rival segments of the ruling class within the
> context of the pressure of major social disruption. . . . (1996, 118)

The second view emphasizes the role of the social movements of the period. No doubt the rent strikes, the food riots, and the labor wars created an urgency for federal action. Grassroots organizations demanded policy change.

The state centered view, promoted by Theda Skocpol (1992), insisted that officials inside the Roosevelt administration were largely responsible for the policy changes of this period. These officials were social workers and former state officials who had promoted state-level social programs. Skocpol maintained that Roosevelt and the Democratic Party played a key role in establishing the New Deal social programs.

Roosevelt himself played a key role as a policy entrepreneur and in 1932 had campaigned on a promise to attack the problem of the Depression. He aggressively pursued New Deal policies and since his party, the Democrats, enjoyed a substantial majority in Congress, the passage of most New Deal bills was ensured.

There is evidence to support all three views. The truth is probably a combination of them.

The Social Security Act of 1935

The Social Security Act of 1935 was the hallmark of Roosevelt's social programs. This act established the federal social welfare system and signaled the formation of a new social welfare policy regime. This act created four new federal programs:

1. Old-Age Assistance, now Social Security
2. Aid for Dependent Children
3. Aid to the Blind
4. Unemployment compensation

The Old-Age Assistance program was a national version of the old-age pension program formerly administered by state governments. It is today known as Social Security and has gradually expanded. In 1939 Congress added survivors and dependents of Social Security recipients to the program. Later it became Old Age Survivors and Disability and Health Insurance (OASDHI). Medicare was added in the mid-1960s.

The Aid for Dependent Children (ADC) program was modeled after the former state-level mothers' pension or widows' programs. Initially, the program was for mothers who lost their husbands through death or desertion. It evolved into a program primarily for poor single mothers. Congress amended the program in 1961 to allow states to give benefits to unemployed fathers, although only a few states adopted this provision. In 1962 it became **Aid for Families with Dependent Children (AFDC).** Like most other social welfare programs, the number of recipients expanded dramatically in the late 1960s. Today, AFDC is the **Temporary Assistance for Needy Families (TANF).**

The Social Security Act also provided benefits for the blind under the Aid to the Blind (AB) program. In 1950 Congress added a fifth program to the Social Security Act: Aid to the Permanently and Totally Disabled (APTD) program. This program provided benefits to recipients with physical or mental disabilities.

Unemployment compensation provided financial assistance to working people who had lost their jobs. Employers paid into the program for their employees. Workers became eligible for the benefits if they were laid off or the company closed down.

Other Major New Deal Programs

Work Programs

Keynes recommended work programs and Roosevelt proposed several programs as part of his New Deal. These programs included the Civil Conservation Corps (CCC), the Works Progress Administration (WPA), and the Public Works Administration (PWA). The CCC provided conservation jobs such as planting trees. Most WPA and PWA jobs involved building public buildings. For example, in Toledo, Ohio, WPA workers built many of the structures on the University of Toledo campus, the Toledo Zoo, and others. These public employee workers built bridges, federal buildings, and highways. The New Deal work programs provided meaningful jobs for the unemployed. They lasted until the early 1940s when World War II made them no longer necessary.

Public Housing

In 1937 Congress passed the *Public Housing Act.* This program initially provided billions of dollars to build and subsidize high-rise apartments for low-income families. Many of these apartments were built in high-poverty, inner-city areas of the nation's largest cities. Public housing was a means-tested program—that is, a recipient had to demonstrate low income to qualify for public housing. However, poverty status did not guarantee access to the housing. In most cities, low-income families were placed on a long waiting list because there were far more families in need of subsidized housing than there were units to accommodate them.

During the 1960s public housing acquired a reputation for being concentrated in racially segregated, crime-infested, inner-city areas. The Chicago Housing Authority (CHA), established to manage Chicago's public housing projects, was found guilty of deliberately segregating the public housing projects. The Supreme Court required the CHA to scatter public housing throughout the Chicago metropolitan area. Most suburban areas successfully resisted the establishment of housing projects within their jurisdictions, but during the late 1970s and the 1980s a few public housing and federally subsidized housing projects were scattered in select central cities. Funding for new public housing was cut substantially in the early 1980s.

In the early 1970s, President Nixon established a housing voucher program called **Section 8** which provided vouchers for low-income families seeking homes in the private rental market. Today Section 8 serves more families than public housing.

Food Programs

In 1933 Congress established the Federal Surplus Relief Corporation. This agency was responsible for distributing surplus commodities to poor families. These commodities included surplus food, coal, and blankets. The program continued after World War II, but it focused on distributing nonperishable surplus agricultural products like powdered milk, powdered eggs, cheese, and others.

The federal government experimented with a food stamps program from 1939 to 1943. There were two types of food stamps. One type was free and could be used in exchange for surplus food. The other type had to be purchased by beneficiaries and could be used to buy food in grocery stores. The food stamp program was ended in 1943 but revived in the 1960s.

Social Insurance, Public Assistance, Cash, and In-kind

Many of the New Deal social programs can be classified as either social insurance or public assistance. **Social insurance** programs operate like private insurance; that is, to be eligible for the benefits, you or your employer must pay into the program and the level of benefits tends to be related to the amount paid into the program. Social Security and unemployment compensation are social insurance programs.

Public assistance programs are based on need. AFDC (now TANF) is a public assistance program. Although recipients pay taxes, they do not have to contribute to the program to become eligible for benefits. Eligibility for public assistance is based on need, as measured by income.

Programs that pay money directly to recipients are called **cash assistance** programs. TANF is an example of a cash assistance program. Programs that do not provide cash, but offer benefits, are called **in-kind benefits programs.** Examples of in-kind programs include food stamps, public housing, and Medicaid.

→ The Great Society Policy Regime

Several stressors impacted the New Deal policy regime and precipitated a rapid and substantial expansion of social welfare programs. These stressors included economic changes, social movements, and the new social welfare research. These stressors provided the fertile ground for President Johnson's Great Society programs.

Economic Stressors

A number of economic changes of the 1940s and 1950s impacted the New Deal regime. The labor-intensive sharecropping system (see Chapter 7) was destroyed by the expanded use of farm machinery and chemical pesticides. Large plow and harvest machines replaced farm workers and pushed thousands of sharecroppers off the farms and into the cities. Like earlier urbanization movements, this process changed the nature of poverty. The New Deal social welfare regime had excluded farm workers and sharecroppers, an exclusion that barred many poor blacks from federal welfare programs. The movement of poor blacks from rural areas of the South to urban areas of the North and South put more pressure on the social welfare system by placing poor blacks in a more favorable position to obtain social support.

Social Movement Stressors

Several social movements impacted the New Deal policy regime: the civil rights, women's rights, antipoverty, and industrial labor movements. The civil rights movement peaked in the 1960s (Chapter 7). The industrial labor movement (Chapter 9), which had expanded during the 1930s, had continued throughout the 1960s. Both civil rights and industrial labor leaders had turned their attention to poverty issues by the late 1960s.

The civil rights movement was not limited to civil rights issues, as civil rights leaders also called for social justice. The 1963 march on Washington, D.C., focused national attention on poverty as well as civil rights issues. Before his assassination, Martin Luther King, Jr. had focused on low-income and poverty issues. He was assassinated in Memphis where he had come to assist city sanitation workers obtain a fair contract. Labor unions and church organizations emerged in the late 1960s as part of the antipoverty coalition.

The women's movement raised issues about the work of mothers—caring for children and families—as uncompensated labor. Of course, the women's movement was split on this issue, as many feminists promoted the right of women to enter the job market and to pursue professional careers. The National Organization for Women (NOW) provided a little support for welfare programs, although this organization of middle-class women focused more on breaking down barriers for professional women.

New organizations such as the Welfare Rights Organization and the Welfare Rights Union emerged in the late 1960s. These organizations demanded that the federal government expand AFDC benefits and relax eligibility rules to make it easier for women in need to obtain and maintain benefits. They specifically opposed the man-in-the-house rule and the residency requirement. The former rule terminated the benefits of any woman who had a man living in the house. The latter rule required prospective recipients to reside within the state for six months or more before becoming eligible for benefits.

Poverty Studies of the 1960s

Three types of poverty studies impacted the New Deal regime: those that exposed the extent and severity of poverty, those that attacked racism as a source of poverty, and those that attacked traditional conservatism. Michael Harrington's book *The Other America: Poverty in the United States* (1962) fell into the first category. Harrington documented poverty in key geographical regions, particularly the rural South, the Appalachians, and urban areas of the North. Harrington attacked the conservative notion that people are poor because of character defects such as laziness or drug addiction. He documented the association between the rise of new agricultural farming technology and rural poverty. He showed how poverty contributed to disease and mental illness. He related how the Social Security payments of the elderly poor were so low they could not afford food. He discussed the way affluent suburbs zoned out low-income housing and left the urban poor isolated and concentrated in inner cities.

Harrington claimed that the New Deal social welfare programs were inadequate. Social Security was regressive; that is, it gave more money to the elderly rich and less money to the elderly poor. He insisted that the Public Housing Authority responded only to the needs of a small fraction of low-income families. The AFDC program did not reach many poor women with children in need and the benefits per family were too low. Harrington's study influenced President Kennedy and precipitated other studies.

In the mid-1960s the Senate created a special ad hoc committee on poverty. The committee hired four medical doctors to conduct a study that focused on poverty among Head Start children in Mississippi. The results embarrassed senators Eastland and Stennis from Mississippi. They vehemently denied that poverty was a problem in their state and insisted that the study was subversive and slanderous (Rodgers 1979, 6–7). The Senate committee held well-publicized hearings, which precipitated a follow-up study by a larger group of medical doctors called the Physician Task Force.

The task force expanded the original study to the entire nation. It described a population of poor people throughout the United States, suffering chronic hunger and malnutrition associated with a range of maladies: anemia, growth retardation, protein deficiencies, parasitic and worm infestations, scurvies, rickets, marasmus, and kwashiorkor. Scurvies results from a lack of vitamin C. Its symptoms include a weak body, anemia, and swollen and bleeding gums. Marasmus and kwashiorkor result from gross deficiencies in calories, protein, and other nutrients over a period of several months. Marasmus generally afflicts malnourished infants from three months to about two years and is characterized by the wasting away of muscle tissue. The Physician Task Force also documented cases of poor children with distended bellies, bulging eyes, and other features characteristic of children in the poorest underdeveloped countries (Rodgers 1979, 7–8). It reported cases of elderly people who could not afford to buy solid meals and children who went to school without breakfast, could not afford lunch, and returned home to dinners without meat or green vegetables.

These studies shocked the nation and generated a groundswell of support for antipoverty programs. People believed that the federal government should do more to attack poverty, and labor unions, religious organizations, and civil rights groups pressured the federal government to take action. The Johnson administration initiated the War on Poverty.

Gunnar Myrdal's book the *American Dilemma* (1948) exposed racialism as a source of poverty. Myrdal demonstrated that many African Americans had been trapped and impoverished in the sharecropping system of the South. When this system collapsed, they moved into the cities and took the unskilled, lower-paying, and least desirable industrial jobs. Myrdal insisted that the pervasiveness of racial prejudices and patterns of discrimination contributed to high levels of poverty among African Americans.

In *Talley's Corner*, Elliot Liebow (1967) attacked the culture of poverty explanation for black poverty, challenging the stereotypical notion that blacks suffered poverty because they were lazy, impetuous, or immoral. Liebow engaged in intensive interviews and long-term observations of blacks in a high-poverty, inner-city area. He insisted that the people of Talley's Corner had values and aspirations no different than those of middle-class or any other people. Poor blacks valued hard work and money, but they operated within a different social context and opportunity structure. They had few opportunities for the development of skills that qualified them for higher-paying jobs, but they had ample opportunity for low-income, temporary jobs, with spells of unemployment. Liebow's study indicated that poverty was not a function of race or culture, but of the lack of opportunities to develop marketable skills and the absence of decent-paying and secure jobs.

Lyndon Johnson and the War on Poverty

Poverty studies along with the antipoverty, civil rights, and women's rights movements of the 1960s stressed the New Deal policy regime and created strong pressures for policy regime change. President Johnson played the key role of a policy entrepreneur. As a New Deal

Democrat committed to the programs initiated by Roosevelt and as a self-styled poor boy from Texas who sympathized with the civil rights leaders and believed in antipoverty programs, Johnson declared war on poverty. His previous experience as majority leader in the Senate and the Democratic control of both houses of Congress ensured the passage of many of his Great Society proposals which we will discuss below.

Food Stamps and Other Nutrition Programs

In response to the well-publicized evidence of hunger in the United States, Congress reestablished the food stamp program, created the **Women, Infants and Children (WIC)** program, and expanded the school nutrition program. Congress passed the *Food Stamp Act* in 1964, which created a program administered by the Department of Agriculture. **Food stamps** are distributed on the basis of need, which is determined by income and family size. Generally, food stamps accompany other benefits such as AFDC, unemployment compensation, or Supplemental Security Income (SSI). Initially, families had to buy the food stamps, although the cost varied with their income and needs. However, the *Food Stamp Act of 1977* made free food stamps available to low-income families lacking the money to buy the stamps.

Women, Infants and Children was created by Congress in 1972 as a pilot program. It became permanent in 1974. This program entitled women who were pregnant or had infant children to vouchers for milk, eggs, cheese, baby formulas, and other food items.

The School Nutrition Program was established just after World War II. This program subsidizes school lunches for low-income students. These students are entitled to free or reduced-cost lunches, depending on their income. In 1966 Congress created the School Breakfast Program, which is similar to the lunch program.

Medicaid and Medicare

Medicaid and Medicare (discussed in more detail in Chapter 6) were enacted in 1965. Medicaid is based on need and it is generally associated with the TANF program or with nursing homes. Medicare is for the elderly and is associated with Social Security. These programs have emerged as the most costly social welfare programs.

Job Training Programs

Several **job-training programs** emerged in the 1960s and early 1970s. The Manpower Development and Training Act allocated federal money to local agencies to provide job training for unemployed individuals. Congress also established summer employment programs for low-income teenagers. Some of these jobs involved cleaning up vacant lots, streets, or expressways. **Public employment programs,** which appeared in the early 1970s, enabled local governments to use federal money to hire low-income individuals to work for city governments. The Nixon administration consolidated these programs into a block grant under the Comprehensive Employment and Training Act (CETA) of 1973. CETA expanded throughout the 1970s.

Community Action Agencies

A major feature of Johnson's War on Poverty was the political empowerment of poor people through community action agencies. **Community action agencies** gave low-income residents an avenue to develop their communities and to negotiate with local governments. These agencies were controversial, as they allowed neighborhood groups to challenge city hall. The Nixon administration gave local government power over these programs, and the ideal of the political empowerment of the poor soon disappeared. By 1974 many of these programs were combined with slum clearance and economic development programs to form the Community Development Block Grant (see Chapter 4).

Supplemental Security Income

Supplemental Security Income (SSI) was formed out of the consolidation of programs designed to assist the disabled such as Aid for the Blind and Aid for the Permanent and Totally Disabled programs. SSI was based on need and disability status. Disability is determined by a physical or mental condition that impairs or prevents a person from engaging in one or more life activities such as walking, seeing, hearing, speaking, learning, or working (DiNitto and Dye 1987, 98). The disabled include the blind, deaf, dumb, paraplegic, or quadriplegic. It also includes those with life activity impairments such as heart disease, multiple sclerosis, muscular dystrophy, cerebral palsy, and others. Disability includes mental impairments related to mental retardation or drug or alcohol addiction.

Aid for Families with Dependent Children (AFDC)

The AFDC program expanded tremendously in the late 1960s. In 1965 a little more than a million families received AFDC benefits; by 1974 this figure had increased about 250 percent to 3.5 million families. By 1980 3.7 million families received AFDC benefits. Several factors contributed to this rapid increase.

1. Racially discriminatory practices, which had excluded many black families from the program, were outlawed with the passage of civil rights laws of the 1960s.
2. The policy that barred farm workers from the program was eliminated. The elimination of this barrier meant that sharecroppers, migrant farm workers, and farm workers would be eligible.
3. Restrictive eligibility rules unrelated to poverty status were relaxed or removed. The man-in-the-house rule and long-term residency requirements were eliminated.
4. The number of female-headed households and unemployment rates increased. These increases meant that more families would become eligible for AFDC benefits. The number of families needing these benefits has been strongly associated with the unemployment or poverty rate since the early 1970s.

Nixon had attempted to stop the increase in the number of recipients. He imposed rules to penalize states financially for awarding benefits to ineligible families (Randall 1979). In the early 1970s Nixon introduced a proposal to create a minimum guaranteed family income, the Family Assistance Plan. The proposal died because both liberals and conservatives opposed it—liberals because they did not trust Nixon and felt that the benefits would be too low, conservatives (Moynihan 1973) because it looked too liberal. Nixon had succeeded in slowing the increase in the number of recipients.

→ Social Programs since the 1980s

Social programs came under attack in the early 1980s. President Reagan was elected under the promise of reducing the size of government and cutting social programs. In many cases congressional Democrats joined Republicans in support of the cuts.

TABLE 5.2

Expenditures for Federal Income-Tested Job Training Programs

Year	Expenditures (In millions of constant 2000 dollars)
1980	18,416
1985	6,240
1990	5,277
1995	5,217
2000	6,219

SOURCE: U.S. Census Bureau, *Statistical Abstract of the United States*, 2003.

Changes in Employment Training Programs: From CETA to JTPA

Employment training programs changed in 1983. Spending for public service employment had been cut in 1980 under the Carter administration and completely eliminated in 1982 under Reagan. The CETA program also ended in that year. In 1983 Congress enacted the Jobs Training Partnership Act (JTPA). This new program changed the terms of its organization within the intergovernmental system. The CETA employment training programs were targeted primarily on large cities with high unemployment rates. CETA money flowed straight from Washington to these areas. The Jobs Training Partnership Act required the creation of state JTPA offices and local private industry councils (PICs). Federal dollars now flowed from Washington to the state JTPA officers and were then redistributed throughout the state. The money was more broadly distributed than under CETA.

In addition to organizational changes, job-training programs also declined. Spending for job training had been cut in the early 1980s. Funding continued to decline throughout the 1990s (see Table 5.2).

Minimum Wage

The minimum wage was increased in 1996, from $4.25 to $4.75. This increase seemed substantial. However, liberals insisted that in constant dollars (i.e., what the dollar could purchase), the minimum wage of $4.25 was the lowest it had been since 1954 and that this low wage was largely responsible for high rates of poverty. The minimum wage was raised again in 1997 to $5.15. Conservatives were reluctant to raise the minimum wage because they believed it would cause an increase in unemployment, especially among teenagers. Refer to Table 5.3 for a 50-year history of the minimum wage in actual and constant 2002 dollars.

Social Security in Crisis

By the 1980s Social Security was in crisis. It was paying out more money in benefits than tax revenues brought in. Three factors contributed to this crisis. First, the number of recipients increased dramatically as life expectancy increased. More people were living past age 65 than ever imagined. In 1940 there had been about 222,000 recipients. By 1980 there were almost 40 million (DiNitto and Dye 1987, 73). Second, benefit levels had increased. In 1977 Congress

TABLE 5.3

Minimum Wage: In Actual and Constant 2002 Dollars

Date	Actual	Constant 2002
1954	$ .75	$4.80
1958	1.00	6.56
1962	1.15	6.56
1966	1.25	6.64
1970	1.60	7.10
1974	2.00	6.99
1978	2.65	7.00
1982	3.35	5.98
1986	3.35	5.26
1990	3.80	5.01
1994	4.25	4.94
1995	4.25	4.80
1996	4.75	5.21
1997	5.15	5.53
1998	5.15	5.44
1999	5.15	5.32
2000	5.15	5.15

SOURCE: U.S. Census Bureau, *Statistical Abstract of the United States*, 2003.

indexed Social Security benefits to inflation at a time the inflation rate exceeded 9 percent. Consequently, benefits increased automatically each year by this amount. Finally, Social Security revenue declined in the early 1980s with the economy. As unemployment increased, the number of people paying into Social Security declined. By 1980 the Social Security program was spending $10 billion to $15 billion more than it was taking in. Its reserve funds were dwindling rapidly. The program was expected to go broke by the mid-1980s.

In response to this crisis, President Reagan created a special task force, the National Commission on Social Security. It consisted of key White House officials and prominent senators and representatives of both parties. Senators Robert Dole (R) and Patrick Moynihan (D) played key roles on this Commission. At one point, Moynihan, a former Harvard professor, worked with his former student, David Stockman, Reagan's director of the OMB. They worked together to build a bipartisan coalition and pass a bill to reform Social Security (Light 1995).

Lobbying over the bill was fierce. A strong coalition of organizations named Save our Social Security (SOS) emerged to defend Social Security and lobby against any Social Security tax increase. This coalition consisted of groups such as the American Association of Retired Persons (AARP), the National Council of Senior Citizens, the AFL-CIO, the United Auto Workers, the National Education Association, the National Farm Union, and several others. Business organizations also lobbied against any Social Security tax increase. These organizations included the National Association of Manufacturers, the Chamber of Commerce, and the National Federation of Independent Business.

The National Commission on Social Security proposed delaying cost-of-living adjustments in Social Security benefits, taxing benefits over $7,000, increasing Social Security taxes, and raising the retirement age in the future to 67 by 2027. Congress followed the recommendations and passed the Social Security Act of 1983. These changes slowed the increase in costs and generated more revenue. They resolved the crisis and saved Social Security—in the short term.

In the long term, these changes did not save Social Security. Experts predicted that another crisis would arise with the retirement of the baby boomers, the large number of people born just after World War II, from 1946 through 1956. This generation will begin retiring at age 65 in 2011. At that time, a record-breaking number of people will be retiring and applying for Social Security. This crisis can be avoided, but any proposal for saving Social Security will be controversial. Social Security taxes can be raised, new sources of revenue can be found, the age of retirement can be increased, or money can be shifted from the general federal budget to fund Social Security.

Some conservatives have proposed to either privatize Social Security or allow recipients to use part of their Social Security retirement money to invest in annuities (retirement savings accounts), bonds, or stocks. President George W. Bush has supported this proposal, but no proposals had been presented to Congress at the end of 2004.

Welfare Reform or Attack on Welfare: From AFDC to TANF

Welfare came to be associated with the Aid for Families with Dependent Children. AFDC has always been a controversial program involving conflicts between liberals and conservatives. This program came under fierce conservative attack during the 1980s and 1990s. In his first term of office, President Reagan attempted to turn this program into a block grant in order to give state governments more discretion over it. He also attempted to reduce the number of recipients. He reduced the income level that determined eligibility in order to make it more difficult to qualify for benefits. Reagan did not succeed in converting AFDC into a block grant, but he did succeed in reducing the number of recipients.

President Clinton had campaigned on a promise to change welfare as we know it. Like Reagan, Clinton proposed to convert AFDC into a block grant and establish work requirements and time limits. The Republican party in Congress also promoted similar proposals. Supporters considered these proposals as part of welfare reform. Opponents considered the same proposals an attack on welfare.

In 1996 Congress passed the *Work Opportunity and Personal Responsibility Act (WOPRA)*. This act, often called the welfare reform bill, did several things. First, it replaced the AFDC program with the Temporary Assistance for Needy Families (TANF) program. Second, it established time limits for recipients: two consecutive years and a lifetime limit of five years. Third, it established work requirements. Recipients are now required to seek a job to be eligible for benefits. Fourth, it converted the old AFDC program into a block grant, replacing the entitlement aspect of the program with a discretionary program. Under the TANF block grant program, the federal government does not increase funds as needs increase. Instead it caps the amount of money allocated to states. Moreover, states are encouraged to reduce the number of recipients. The new program initially barred immigrants, but this provision was eliminated in 1997.

These substantial changes in the AFDC/TANF can be explained by three factors: shifts in power, changes in media depiction of welfare recipients, and the emergence of studies critical of welfare. Increases in the cost of the program and the number of recipients cannot adequately explain this change.

Program Costs and the Number of Recipients

The need for AFDC/TANF benefits is largely associated with the economy (see Table 5.4). As unemployment rates go up, the demand for the program increases. Of course, Reagan was successful in reducing the number of recipients in the early 1980s, despite the rising unemployment rates from 1981 to 1983. The number of AFDC/TANF recipients again increased in the early 1990s, as unemployment rates rose. The number of recipients began to decline by 1996, as unemployment rates declined, and they continued to decline throughout the rest of the decade and the early years of the 21st century. Conservatives claim this decline indicates that the workfare program is working. Liberals maintain that it means fewer mothers in need are getting assistance.

When the number of AFDC/TANF recipients increases, political leaders are concerned; they are also concerned about increases in benefits. However, when the cost of living is taken into account, the real value of these benefits actually declined. Unlike Social Security, AFDC/TANF benefits were not indexed to inflation. Senator Moynihan pointed out in *Family and Nation* that despite the decline in the real value of the benefits of this program by about 40 percent, most members of Congress believed that benefits had actually increased (Moynihan 1987).

Unlike Social Security, AFDC/TANF benefits varied from state to state. Benefits levels were more than $500 a month in states like California and Alaska and as low as $100 a

TABLE 5.4

Number of Families and Recipients Receiving AFDC/TANF Benefits

Year	Number of Families	Number of Recipients	Year	Number of Families	Number of Recipients
1980	3,712	10,774	1991	4,467	12,930
1981	3,835	11,079	1992	4,829	13,773
1982	3,542	10,258	1993	5,012	14,205
1983	3,686	10,761	1994	5,033	14,161
1984	3,714	10,831	1995	4,791	13,418
1985	3,701	10,855	1996	4,434	12,321
1986	3,763	11,038	1997	3,740	10,381
1987	3,776	11,027	1998	3,050	8,358
1988	3,749	10,915	1999	2,253	6,822
1989	3,799	10,993	2000	2,215	5,778
1990	4,057	11,695	2001	2,104	5,359

SOURCE: U.S. Census Bureau, *Statistical Abstract of the United States,* 2003.

month in Mississippi and Texas. Benefits were hardly excessive. AFDC costs increased primarily because of increases in the number of recipients.

Conservative Literature and the Assault on AFDC

Conservative literature attacked AFDC relentlessly. Martin Anderson (1978) insisted that AFDC benefits, when combined with other programs, were too generous. Charles Murray (1984) argued that welfare created a perverse incentive system. It provided inducements for having children out of wedlock and for not working. Murray insisted that the welfare system as a whole produced increases in female-headed households, teen pregnancy, and joblessness. In their controversial book *The Bell Curve,* Richard Hernstein and Charles Murray (1994) suggested that the unemployed, single mothers on welfare or working in low-income jobs and other poor people are more likely to have low intelligence and that government assistance did more harm than good. This view was somewhat reminiscent of the old Social Darwinist perspective.

Other conservative critics of AFDC insisted that the program facilitated dependency. George Gilder noted that at least 25 percent of AFDC recipients were long-term dependents and this dependency was carried over from one generation to the next. He believed that women on welfare have children who grow up and become dependent on welfare (Gilder 1981). He suggested that these long-term recipients never held full-time jobs. Other critics insisted that the program was filled with abuse and fraud.

These arguments promoted efforts to reform welfare. They supported the proposals to establish time limits for obtaining benefits, to require recipients to work, and to reduce the number of recipients.

Conservative Shifts in Political Power

Political power surrounding AFDC shifted in favor of new conservative organizations that appeared in the 1980s and 1990s in opposition to AFDC/TANF. These organizations included the Christian Coalition and the Coalition of Family Values which opposed AFDC primarily because they believed the program caused the breakup of families and the rise of female-headed households. Conservative think tanks—the Cato Institute, the Hoover Institution, the American Enterprise Institute, and others—opposed AFDC. State government and business organizations—the National Governors Association, the National Association of Manufacturers, the Business Roundtable, the U.S. Chamber of Commerce, and others—joined in the campaign against AFDC. Policy changes in the late 1980s allowed states to establish experimental work programs. During the early 1990s a number of governors had set up experimental welfare reform programs with work requirements and time limits for AFDC recipients. Business and conservative leaders concerned with the impact of welfare on the job market and wages believed that overly generous benefits would drive up labor costs. These leaders emerged to dominate the policy-making process and succeeded in securing the passage of the Work Opportunity and Personal Responsibility Act of 1996.

Media Depiction of AFDC Recipients

In his book *Why Americans Hate Welfare,* Martin Gilens (1999) insisted that the media is responsible for Americans' hatred of welfare. He documented through content studies of magazines, newspapers, and other sources that the media image of poor people changed after the late 1960s. Prior to that time, most poor people and most AFDC recipients portrayed in the media were white. This portrayal reflected reality. After the riots of the late 1960s, the image of most poor people and AFDC recipients presented in the media changed from white to black, although most, in reality, were white. Gilens also noted that after the late 1960s, most stories about poor people and AFDC recipients presented in the media were negative. For example, the media presented stories of recipients with large families, yet most recipients had about two children; recipients were said to be on welfare for extended periods of time—for 10, 20, or 30 years or for multiple generations—yet most recipients were off the program in two years. And the media told of recipients who defrauded the government, yet actual cases of fraud were rare.

Liberal and Feminist Support for AFDC/TANF

Liberal and feminist support for the AFDC/TANF program declined substantially, but survived and continues today. Welfare rights organizations active in the 1960s and 1970s were gone by the early 1990s. Civil rights organizations that supported AFDC/TANF shifted their focus to other issues. The Children Defense Fund (CDF) and the National Organization for Women (NOW) continued to support the program, although they did not oppose the work requirements for TANF. The CDF was most concerned about the rising poverty rates among children and supported AFDC because this program helped poor children. NOW supported it because it gave women greater independence from men and assisted women in getting out of abusive relationships.

NOW joined labor and civil rights organizations in lobbying for increases in the minimum wage and in federal subsidies for child care. They argued that in constant dollars, the minimum wage was the lowest it had been since the 1950s and was largely responsible for high rates of poverty. Congress authorized a significant increase in the minimum wage the same year it passed the welfare reform bill of 1996. Liberal and feminist organizations were also successful in convincing Congress that if poor mothers were to work, they needed affordable child care. Congress then increased spending for child care after the passage of WOPRA.

The Scholars' Argument   Feminist and liberal scholars have vigorously defended AFDC. They have disputed every conservative criticism of the program: that the program breaks up families, facilitates dependency, and encourages young girls to get pregnant and older women to have more babies, quit their jobs, and cheat the government.

Many feminist scholars see the attack on the program as misogynist. In her book *Keeping Women and Children Last,* Ruth Sidel (1996) responded to the common belief that TANF/AFDC encourages teenaged women to have babies. She cited Representative Shaw, the chair of the Ways and Means Committee, who did most of the work on WOPRA, saying that denying cash benefits to teen mothers would take away the "lure of the cash" and that without the money "the mothers are going to be more careful and use contraceptives" (1996, 119). Sidel argued that there is no evidence to support this view and that over 85 percent of teen pregnancies are unintended because many teenagers have misconceptions about contraceptives and sexual reproduction, arising from the absence of sexual education. She blamed men for getting young girls pregnant and insisted that in most cases these women were sexually abused and impregnated by adult men.

Sidel maintained that by making it more difficult to get AFDC/TANF benefits and emphasizing the preservation of marriage, the welfare reform movement constrains women to remain in physically abusive marriages.

Nancy Rose challenged the campaign against welfare cheats. Most state and local authorities have increased efforts to prosecute recipients for fraud. She argued that this campaign against so-called welfare cheats is based on prejudice and stereotypes of AFDC/TANF recipients and that cases of fraud in the program are greatly exaggerated; more money is lost through fraud in other federal programs than through AFDC. She argued further that many of the cases prosecuted for fraud involved women who were forced to work because benefits were inadequate for survival or eligibility workers who committed errors in processing welfare applications. For example, "As Elizabeth Briano, who received AFDC for four years, explained, 'I was forced to do *fraud* [italics added] in order to survive'" (Rose 1995, 160). Rose adds the following:

> Welfare recipients were arrested even if eligibility workers made mistakes in their calculations and paid recipients more than they were entitled to receive. Due to the complexity of applications for AFDC and food stamps, as well as the inferior treatment (too many cases and low wages) of eligibility workers, this was a common occurrence—in fact, it accounted for more than half of all fraud cases in California. (1995, 160)

Arresting and jailing mothers for working to get extra money for their families or because of mistakes made by eligibility workers discourages mothers from applying for welfare benefits in the first place and sends a powerful and threatening message to would-be welfare cheats.

Liberal scholars have also criticized the workfare programs, claiming that they are exploitive. Piven and Cloward made the following point:

> In New York City, some 45,000 people, mainly women, sweep the streets and clean the subways and the parks. They do the work once done by unionized municipal employees. But instead of a paycheck and a living wage, they get a welfare check that leaves them far below the poverty level, and they have none of the benefits and protections of unionized workers. Perhaps just as bad, they have become public spectacles of abject and degraded labor—of slave labor, many of them say. (2001, xi)

Feminists and liberals took issue with conservatives on every point in the welfare debate. They insisted that only a small percentage of recipients, 25 percent, are long-term dependent. Rather than destroying families, the program helps abused women leave violent men. Rather than encouraging girls to have babies, it gives mothers who had been sexually abused by men ways of escaping the abuse and building a new life. Feminists and liberals insisted that there is little abuse in this program, and that the campaign against welfare cheats is driven by stereotypes of welfare recipients. In some cases benefits are so low that they constrain women to get money elsewhere in order to survive. Feminists argued that child poverty rates are high in the United States because benefits for poor families or single women with children are so low.

Table 5.5 gives an abridged summary of the conservative critique of welfare and the liberal and feminist response.

TABLE 5.5

Pros and Cons over Welfare

Conservative Critique	Liberal and Feminist Response
The program facilitates dependency.	Even Gilder's figures indicate that only 25% of recipients are long-term dependent.
The program causes families to break up.	The program helps women leave abusive men.
The program encourages young girls to have babies.	Most young girls having babies have been sexually abused and most are impregnated by adult men.
The program provides incentives for women to have more babies.	Since there is very little additional money for more babies, the program hardly provides these incentives.
The program encourages joblessness.	The lack of health care in the private sector, not welfare, encourages women to stop working.
The program is full of abuse.	There is little abuse in this program. There is more abuse in defense contracts.
The program is too generous.	Compared to programs in other countries, this one is the stingiest in the world.

➔ Policy Regime Shift and Other Social Welfare Policy Changes

To some extent the changes from AFDC and TANF constituted a policy regime shift, with power moving from liberal to conservative groups. The policy paradigm changed from defining the welfare problem as one of insufficient support for the poor to one of getting people off welfare and into the job market.

The change from CETA to JTPA also represented a policy regime change. Community action agencies and public service jobs disappeared. Ideas about jobs programs changed from empowering the poor people to training the unemployed for jobs that serve the interests of local businesses. The organization of job training changed from a federally controlled program to a state-controlled one.

Other social programs changed incrementally. Funds for food stamps and unemployment compensation fluctuated, rising and falling in small margins with the unemployment rate. Funds for child care increased measurably. The federal minimum wage rate increased significantly in 1996, although its real value today is a little below what it was during the 1980s. Social Security increased, but gradually. It may undergo additional but incremental changes in the first two decades of the 21st century.

Social Welfare and the Debate on Poverty

Today there is still intense debate over the causes of poverty. Conservatives still blame poverty on the morals and values of poor people. They expect poverty to decline when poor people

TABLE 5.6

Poverty Rates by Age Group, 1959–2003

Year*	Persons under 18 %	Persons over 65 %		Persons under 18 %	Persons over 65 %
1959	27.3	35.2	1996	20.5	10.8
1960	26.9	N/A	1997	19.9	10.5
1965	21.0	N/A	1998	18.9	10.5
1970	15.1	24.6	1999	17.1	9.7
1975	17.1	15.3	2000	16.2	9.9
1980	18.3	15.7	2001	16.3	10.1
1985	20.7	12.6	2002	16.7	10.4
1990	20.6	12.2	2003	17.6	10.2
1995	20.8	10.5			

*People as of March of the following year.

SOURCE: U.S. Census Bureau, *Statistical Abstract of the United States,* 2003.

get jobs. Many liberals blame poverty on low minimum wages, poor performance of the economy, economic dislocation, low government transfer payments, and single-parent families. They expect poverty to decline with an increase in the minimum wage and a boost in the performance of the economy. Some moderate scholars like William Julius Wilson attribute poverty to a mismatch between the high level of education required for knowledge-intensive jobs of the 21st century and the low level of education attained by people living in concentrated poverty areas of the central cities (Wilson 1987).

Social welfare programs have not eliminated poverty. Of course, this was never their goal. These programs have reduced poverty rates and ameliorated the harsh conditions of poverty. They have improved the quality of the lives of people whose incomes have fallen below the poverty line. The food stamp and Medicaid programs have succeeded in substantially reducing hunger in America and in eliminating diseases associated with malnutrition.

In 1964 the Social Security Administration (SSA) established a standard measure of poverty, based on a simple calculation. The SSA first determined the cost for a low-budget, nutritionally adequate diet for one person, for one day. It then multiplied this figure by three, based on the assumption that a poor family spent one-third of its family budget on food, the rest on shelter, clothing, transportation, and other living expenses. The SSA then multiplied this figure by 365, the number of days of the year, to calculate the annual poverty index. Each year the SSA adjusts the poverty index to the consumer price index (CPI) to account for the increase in the cost of living.

Poverty rates have come down since the mid-1960s, especially among the young and, most notably, among the elderly, which is perhaps an indication of the success of the Social Security program. (See Table 5.6.) Child poverty rates declined measurably during the 1960s, but after an interim period of increase and decline, these rates have gradually increased since 2001.

Summary

The United States has experienced several major social welfare policy regimes: preindustrial (1700–1870), industrial (1870–1900), Progressive (1900–1935), New Deal (1935–1970), and Great Society (1970–present). The preindustrial regime involved people in rural communities and small towns working together to assist each other in times of need. The Industrial Revolution and urbanization wiped out this regime and gave rise to the industrial policy regime, which took an institutional approach to social welfare—poorhouses, orphanages, city charities, and others. The Progressive movement transformed the industrial regime, took children out of the poorhouses, reformed orphanages, introduced settlement houses, expanded private charities, and established state workers' compensation and widows' pension programs. About eight states had old-age pension programs. These policy changes characterized the Progressive policy regime, which also introduced laws to prohibit child labor and set minimum wages and minimum working hours, although the Supreme Court later killed these programs.

Despite the efforts of Progressive reformers, several paradigms dominated the first few decades of the 20th century and operated to block the development of more expansive social welfare policies. These paradigms included classical economics, traditional conservatism, racialism, and Social Darwinism.

The massive poverty, unemployment, and misery produced by the Great Depression refuted many of the assumptions of these paradigms, pulverized the intellectual barrier to more expansive social welfare programs, and provoked multiple social movements. The Depression triggered rent strikes, food riots, and labor wars and spawned grassroots movements among the poor, unemployed, and workers—all demanding national policy solutions.

President Franklin D. Roosevelt played the role of a policy entrepreneur in the introduction, with congressional support, of an avalanche of new programs: Social Security, ADC, unemployment, aid to the blind, child labor, minimum wage, public housing, and work programs. The New Deal social welfare policy regime did not replace Progressive programs; it built upon them, adding new programs, some of which were initially introduced by Progressive reformers. This regime lasted from 1935 to about 1970.

The social research and social movements of the 1960s contributed to another policy regime change. Social research undercut racialism and discovered cases of poverty in the United States as severe as those found in underdeveloped nations. It created the intellectual basis for further expansion in social programs. The social movements of the 1960s—the civil rights, antipoverty, and welfare rights movements—created strong pressures for expansion in social welfare programs.

The Great Society policy regime expanded upon the New Deal programs. It added food stamps, Medicaid, Medicare, Head Start, job training, and other programs. The introduction of antipoverty programs continued into the 1970s with the establishment of SSI, CETA, and others.

To some extent the change from AFDC to TANF in 1996 constituted a policy regime shift. Power had shifted from liberal to conservative groups. The policy paradigm changed from defining the welfare problem as one of insufficient support for the poor to one of getting people off welfare and into the job market. TANF established time limits and work requirements and changed welfare from a categorical program to a block grant.

Other social programs changed incrementally. Funds for food stamps and unemployment compensation fluctuated, rising and falling in small margins with the unemployment rate. Funds for child care increased measurably. The federal minimum wage rate increased significantly in 1996. Social Security also increased, but more gradually. It may undergo additional but incremental changes in the first two decades of the 21st century. With huge numbers of baby boomers retiring soon, the chairman of the Federal Reserve Board said that Social Security benefits might eventually have to be cut. Just after his reelection in November 2004, President G. W. Bush announced that he would not increase Social Security taxes, but would propose allowing taxpayers to use a small proportion of their Social Security funds to invest in the private sector. This investment option proposal has already generated opposition from Social Security supporters such as the AARP. Health care policies will be discussed in the next chapter.

Review Questions

1. What were some sources of poverty at the beginning of the 20th century? the beginning of the 21st century?
2. What factors contributed to the change from the preindustrial to the industrial policy regime?
3. What factors contributed to the rise of the New Deal social policy regime?
4. How do liberals and conservatives differ in their explanation of poverty?
5. How did social welfare policies change in the 1930s? the 1960s? the 1990s?
6. What factors explain the changes in social welfare policies in each of these decades?
7. Discuss the differences between liberals and conservatives over welfare reform.
8. Discuss how racial views influenced social welfare policies.

Select Websites

This is the Website for the U.S. Department of Health and Human Services.
http://www.hhs.gov

Key Terms

Aid for Families with Dependent Children (AFDC)
cash assistance
Children's Bureau
community action agencies
culture of poverty
food stamps
in-kind benefits programs
job-training programs
New Deal
poorhouse

public assistance
public employment programs
racialism
Section 8
Social Darwinism
social insurance
Supplemental Security Income (SSI)
Temporary Assistance for Needy Families (TANF)
unemployment compensation
Women, Infants, and Children (WIC)

CHAPTER 6

❧

Health Care Policy

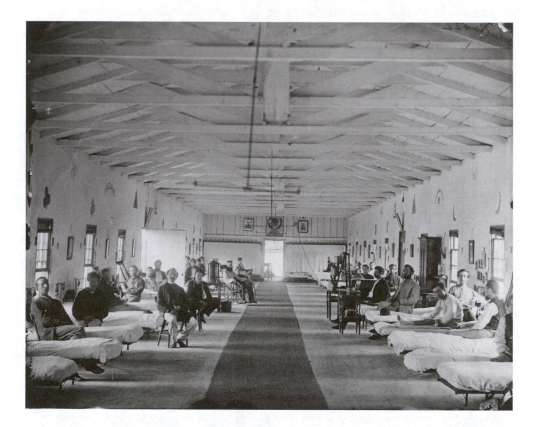

Health care policy involves promoting public health and providing medical assistance to people who are injured, ill, or infirm. This policy had moved from the distributive to the redistributive policy category, as it shifted from one policy regime to the other. There were two major health care policy regimes of the 20th century: the solo doctor or Progressive regime and the Medicaid/Medicare regime. The solo doctor regime was characterized by public health, municipal and private nonprofit hospitals, and solo doctors. Local governments established public health departments to prevent epidemics and to promote public health. This was a distributive policy, as public health benefits the entire population.

The Medicare/Medicaid policy regime emerged out of the social movements of the 1960s. Medicaid is primarily for Temporary Assistance for Needy Families (TANF), Supplemental Security Income (SSI), and nursing home clients. Medicare is primarily for Social Security recipients. These programs fall into the redistributive policy category as they shift resources from the advantaged to the disadvantaged and involve ideological disputes and political conflicts. This regime has remained in place since 1965, although there have been significant changes in national health care policies over the past 45 years.

The Medicare/Medicaid policy regime addressed problems of providing health care coverage for the poor and the elderly, but avoided the issue of universal health care coverage. Health care policy changed incrementally. These changes included the expansion of Medicaid to include children from families just above the poverty level, the creation of cost controls, the use of private health maintenance organizations (HMOs) to assist in delivering Medicaid and Medicare services, and the establishment of pharmaceutical drug coverage for Medicare recipients.

→ The Solo Doctor Policy Regime

The independent family doctor and local health departments characterized health care during the late 19th and early 20th century, the period of the solo doctor policy regime. Most doctors were in family practice and operated independent of hospitals. Doctors made house calls and treated most people in their homes. Doctors controlled their own profession and dominated health care politics. The **American Medical Association (AMA),** formed in 1847, represented medical doctors and dominated the political arena at least until the last third of the 20th century.

The number of hospitals increased "twenty fold between 1860 and 1910" (Klebanow et al. 1977, 203). Many military hospitals were built during the Civil War, such as the Armory Square Union hospital shown on the opening page of this chapter. Most hospitals built during this period were private and nonprofit. By the first decade of the 20th century, most cities had established health departments and built municipal hospitals. Local spending for public health increased exponentially in this period. With thousands of people living in close proximity to each other—a product of urbanization—epidemics could spread rapidly with devastating consequences. With the discovery of bacteria, viruses, and sterilization, health departments emerged to help prevent and manage the spread of diseases in large cities. Local health departments provided public health services such as immunizations, tests for communicable diseases, the regulation of local restaurants and private establishments, the monitoring of local diseases, and the collection of health records and statistics.

With the exception of military hospitals and land grants for medical colleges, federal health care was practically nonexistent. National health care proposals were introduced to Congress during the Progressive period and the New Deal era. However, the American Medical Association (AMA) played a key role in pushing the issue of national health care off the federal agenda.

There were two federal programs before 1965. Congress passed the *Hill-Burton Act of 1946* (officially, the *Hospital Survey and Construction Act*) and the *Kerr-Mills Act of 1960*. The Hill-Burton Act provided assistance for the construction of hospitals, with the expectation that hospitals would provide some charity for poor people in need of emergency hospital care. To assist in providing health care for the poor and the elderly, the Kerr-Mills Act set aside federal money to be matched by state funds.

For the most part, health care before 1965 remained a private affair, involving a close relationship between the family doctor and the individual patient. There were some local public health programs and some state or local support for hospitals.

The modern day hospital complex is a product of technological changes that occurred in the first half of the 20th century.

The dominant idea of the solo doctor was that local governments promoted public health, but the unregulated private market provided health care. The market consisted of the doctors, who were the providers, and the patients, who were the consumers. The AMA, fearing government control of the medical profession, vigorously opposed federal health insurance programs which it branded as socialized medicine.

Explaining Policy Regime Change

The solo doctor policy regime lasted until about 1965, with the birth of the new Medicare/Medicaid regime. Three factors contributed to the big change in health care policy and the new policy regime.

Technology and Medical Specialization

First, technological and specialization changes in the medical profession impacted the health care market and the role of doctors. Medical knowledge and technology advanced tremendously throughout the 20th century. X rays, discovered in the late 1890s, emerged as an indispensable diagnostic tool during the 1930s. Sonar, discovered in the early 20th century, emerged as ultrasound in the mid-1950s, an important diagnostic tool for gynecologists. By the 1950s advancements in medical technology had produced new fields of medical specialization—cardiology, dermatology, gynecology, pediatrics, and many others—and new support technicians such as X-ray technicians and laboratory technicians. Because of the cost and complexity of modern medicine, doctors were constrained to become part of a larger medical complex, which included hospitals, technicians, and specialists. By the 1960s most doctors were tied to a medical complex. Advances in medical technology had ended the era of the solo doctor who made regular house calls.

Rise of New Medical Organizations

The second factor that contributed to the changes in health care policy was the rise of new organizations. Many health insurance companies like Blue Cross and Blue Shield emerged in the 1930s. They were controlled by doctors or by hospitals. It was not until the rise of **health maintenance organizations (HMOs)** in the 1970s that doctors began to lose some control over their own profession. However, health insurance had a subtle impact on the rise of the Medicare and Medicaid programs. By the 1960s the high cost of medical care made private health insurance coverage essential for health care. Other organizations such as the American Hospital Association (AHA) and the American Association of Medical Schools (AAMS) emerged during the 1950s. The rise of these organizations meant that the AMA now shared power in the health policy area.

The Antipoverty Movement

The third factor that contributed to the big policy change was the antipoverty movement of the 1960s. As noted in Chapter 5, the discovery in America during the 1960s of diseases associated with poverty, diseases afflicting children and the elderly, and diseases as severe as those in the poorest underdeveloped countries precipitated changes in the dominant way of thinking about health care policy. These health care issues among children and the elderly were well publicized by the Physician Task Force, Senate hearings, and popular books. The problem of nutrition and disease was aggravated by the lack of health care insurance and access to medical care, except for state or county hospitals, among most of the poor and the elderly. The publicity of the problems of the elderly and poor combined with the antipoverty social movement of the 1960s to create strong pressures for the establishment of some sort of federally funded health care program for the poor and the elderly.

⇢ *Medicare/Medicaid Policy Regime*

In response to these pressures, President Lyndon B. Johnson and Congress passed in 1965 Title XVIII and Title XIX of the Social Security Act, creating the Medicare and the Medicaid programs, respectively. These new policies initiated a major change in federal health care policy and introduced the Medicare/Medicaid policy regime.

Medicare is a national program, financed exclusively by the federal government. It is associated with the Social Security program and is primarily for Social Security recipients. It was expanded in 1972 to include people suffering from kidney disease and, more recently, a subsidy and discount for prescription drugs.

Medicare has evolved into a complex program with several parts. **Medicare Part A** covers most medical costs associated with hospitalization: the cost of surgery, intensive care, hospital-related diagnostic tests, medical treatment, prescription drugs, other hospital-related medical services, and a semiprivate room. Part A does not cover physician care.

Medicare Part B is optional. It operates like physician care insurance, with co-payments and deductibles. The federal government pays a large share of the premium. The recipient pays the balance. Part B covers visits to the doctor's office, outpatient hospital services, laboratory and diagnostic tests, and ambulance services.

Medicare Part C, sometimes called Medicare Plus Choice, was introduced in 1997. It gives Medicare recipients the option of joining an HMO or another insurance option in lieu of the fee-for-service plan provided by Medicare.

The *Medicare Modernization Act of 2003* established **Medicare Part D.** It allowed Medicare recipients to purchase a discount drug card in the spring of 2004, but the major provisions of this part will not go into effect until 2006. This bill will be discussed in more detail later. Medicare Part A covers prescription drugs associated with hospital care and Part B covers them as part of outpatient care, but otherwise Medicare beneficiaries had to pay out of pocket for prescription drugs, at least up to 2006. Medicare does not cover long-term care. A few Medicare recipients purchased additional private insurance to cover services not covered by Part A or B. This additional private insurance was called **Medigap,** as it was purported to cover gaps in Medicare.

Medicaid has been associated with the poor, with the idea that it would be primarily for AFDC and SSI recipients. Like the AFDC/TANF program, Medicaid funding was split between the federal government and the state governments, with the federal government contributing the larger share. The program expanded rapidly throughout the late 1960s and early 1970s, especially as the number of AFDC and SSI recipients increased.

A significant proportion of Medicaid recipients are children. Other recipients include the low-income elderly, blind, physically and mentally disabled, and other adults. Freund and McGuire claimed:

> Children constitute 49 percent of Medicaid recipients, but consume only about 16 percent of Medicaid funds; the elderly used 31 percent of Medicaid dollars, representing only 11.5 percent of those eligible. . . . Thus, Medicaid has *not* functioned primarily as a source of health care for lower-class persons, especially children, among whom poverty rates are at a 30-year high. Rather, its main recipients appear to be those who were made poor by the costs of health care in disability and old age. (1999, 293)

Most of the Medicaid funds go to the blind and disabled, as health care programs serving this population tend to be more intense, long term, and costly. At one time more than 50 percent of Medicaid funds went to long-term care (Coughlin, Ku, and Holahan 1994). Today the figure is around 35 percent (Burwell, Eiken and Sredl 2002). Eligibility for long-term Medicaid assistance is determined by financial and medical need.

Medicaid coverage is comprehensive. It covers most services associated with hospital care: surgery, recovery, intensive care, radiology, and laboratory and diagnostic tests. It also covers physician care: prescription drugs, prosthetic devices, dental service, home health care, and nursing facilities.

Changes in Medicaid and Medicare

After cutting social welfare programs in 1981, Congress expanded Medicaid eligibility standards to cover more low-income children and pregnant women. Three years later Congress expanded Medicaid coverage to include all children meeting state AFDC/TANF eligibility standards and pregnant women who would qualify for AFDC/TANF after giving birth.

In 1988 Congress passed the *Medicare Catastrophic Coverage Act (MCCA),* which expanded Medicaid coverage to include all pregnant women and infant children whose family income was below the federal poverty line. It also expanded Medicaid eligibility because some state eligibility standards for TANF and Medicaid were below the federal poverty line. MCCA did many other things.

- Assisted low-income Medicare recipients in paying Part B premiums.
- Created special health care surtaxes and provided coverage for sudden and catastrophic illnesses that bankrupted families.
- Most important, it expanded Medicare coverage, but Medicare recipients were required to pay an increased premium for the additional benefits. Part B premiums were scheduled to increase in 1989 and Part A enrollees would pay a supplemental premium. The rate of this premium would depend on the Medicare recipients' income or federal income tax liability.

Kart added:

For the first time, older people alone (and really only those with annual income tax liability) were being asked to underwrite an expansion in the Medicare benefits. Faced with pressure from politically active older adults and their organizational representatives, who were upset about the funding mechanisms for these expanded benefits, Congress passed the Medicare Catastrophic Coverage Repeal Act of 1989 and repealed the Medicare catastrophic benefits legislated in 1988. (2001, 500)

Thus, the MCCA was repealed and most provisions were terminated, except for the expansion of coverage to low-income children and pregnant women.

→ *Insurance and Health Maintenance Organizations*

Health care policy involves both the public and the private sectors. Medicaid and Medicare cover about one-third of the population. Most people are covered by private insurance. Today the health insurance industry is dominated by health maintenance organizations.

Health insurance emerged in the early 20th century, but the industry did not begin to grow until the 1930s, with the formation of hospital and physician insurance formed by organizations of hospitals and doctors. Hospitals created the hospital insurance called Blue Cross. The American Medical Association formed Blue Shield, a physician insurance. With this insurance, the client would pay the insurance organization an annual fee or premium. In exchange for the fee, the insurance organization would promise to cover most, but not all, of the client's hospital and doctors' expenses. Until the late 1960s, Blue Cross/Blue Shield dominated the private health insurance market. Other large commercial insurance companies such as Metropolitan Life, Prudential, and others competed with Blue Cross/Blue Shield.

In 1973 Congress passed the *Health Maintenance Organization Act* in response to escalating health care costs and to calls for national health care for people who were not poor or elderly. The act offered federal financial assistance to develop health maintenance organizations.

The problem with escalating health care costs was that health insurance companies paid the physicians and hospitals whatever they charged. Neither the patient nor the insurance company looked for cheaper rates and there was little competition. The costs of physician and hospital services increased much faster than the rate of inflation. Health insurance companies did little to control costs and there were no market mechanisms to do so. The plan was to get HMOs to compete among themselves to reduce health care costs and provide cheaper health care coverage.

There are about four different types of HMOs:

1. The staff type of HMO hires individual physicians to work for the organization in a facility it either owns or leases. The HMO pays the doctors a fixed salary, generally regardless of the number of patients. Sometimes the HMO pays a bonus for efficiency in service delivery.
2. The group type of HMO owns or leases the facility, but contracts with a group of physicians to provide medical services, with a set limit for doctor fees.
3. With the individual practice association, the HMO pays physicians a set fee for service.
4. The network type involves a few groups of physicians leasing their own facilities and contracting with the HMO.

In addition to the HMO arrangement, physicians have organized their own insurance groups called **preferred provider organizations (PPOs).**

HMOs dominate the private health care market. Because of recent changes in federal policies, a few HMOs have begun covering some Medicare and Medicaid recipients. The HMO would provide health care coverage for the Medicare or Medicaid recipient, and Medicaid or Medicare would pay the HMO. This connection between HMOs and federal health care programs represented an important change in the Medicare/Medicaid policy regime.

In 1974 Congress passed the *Employee Retirement Income Security Act (ERISA),* largely to protect the retirement funds of people employed in private companies. It also allowed employers with large numbers of employees to pool resources and to provide their own employee health care program. The law prohibits state governments from taxing the premiums employers pay on health insurance policies and restricts the ability of states to regulate the self-insured health program.

→ Health Care Crisis

Despite the emergence of HMOs, current health care policy is in crisis. There are three dimensions of this crisis: a crisis of costs, a crisis of access, and a crisis of quality. The cost of health care has been increasing geometrically over the past two decades. More Americans are now without health care insurance than there were 10 or 20 years ago. Although Americans spend more on health care than most other developed countries, life expectancy is lower and infant mortality higher in the United States compared to those developed countries.

The Cost Problem

Health care costs have risen in terms of total spending and in terms of spending as a percent of GNP (gross national product), the total amount spent in the nation on goods and services. In 1960 total health care costs annually represented a little more than 5 percent of GNP, or about $27.0 billion. It had increased to 7 percent of GNP and $73 billion by 1970, and to about 9 percent of GNP and $246 billion by 1980. Today it hovers around 18 percent of GNP, or over $1.9 trillion. (See Table 6.1.) Summarizing the magnitude of the increases in health care costs, health policy analyst Mark Peterson wrote:

> Health care expenditures emerged as a major concern in the 1970s, but by the early 1990s many business leaders, citizen group advocates, and policy makers had concluded that nothing short of government intervention would stem the tide. Medical inflation was 12 percent or higher each year, typically twice the overall consumer price index. Between 1970 and 1989, employer spending on wages and salaries, controlling for inflation, went up just 1 percent, but for health benefits, it rose 163 percent. (1998, 183)

TABLE 6.1

Health Care Costs from 1960 to 2005

Category	1960	1970	1980	1990	2000	2005
Total expenditures (In billions of dollars)	27	73	246	696	1,310	1,907*

*Projected figure.

SOURCE: U.S. Census Bureau, *Statistical Abstract of the United States,* 2003.

There are several explanations for the escalating health care costs. Whereas inflation in the general economy is a major factor, health care costs have increased well beyond what is explained by inflation. The other factors include demographics, medical technology, third-party payers, Medicare/Medicaid, and perverse market incentives.

Demographic Factors

Two demographic factors contributed to the increase in health care costs: the aging of the general population and the rise of costly epidemics. More people are living past age 65 than ever before. More people living longer means more diseases related to old age: heart disease, strokes, Alzheimer's, dementia, and others. These diseases often require long-term care and contribute substantially to rising health care costs.

Epidemics of the late 1990s have driven up health care costs even more than old age. For example, the rise of the AIDS (acquired immunodeficiency syndrome) epidemic has drive up health care costs. Full-blown AIDS patients require expensive drugs and long-term hospital care.

Medical Technology

Another explanation for the increase in health care costs is the growth in investment in medical technology. There are two major areas of medical technology: diagnostic and treatment. Diagnostic technology includes the development of such devices as computerized axial tomography, better know as the CAT scan. Recent technological developments have been in the area of high-resolution computer tomography and magnetic resonance imaging (MRI), that is, more sophisticated scanning with more detailed and colorful images for the diagnosis of disease. Other developments have included the use of computers in laboratory work.

Treatment technology includes the development of laser surgery, pacemakers, organ transplants, and artificial body parts such as knee joints, hips, and others. These technological developments required the investment of billions of dollars in medical research. A single transplant alone can cost hundreds of thousands of dollars.

In some cases, new technology initially lowers costs. For example, the CAT scan lowers costs because its use avoids expensive and invasive exploratory surgery. However, once in place, its use has become routine and frequent. Moreover, it has generated a whole new category of health care specialists, just as the invention of the X ray contributed to the rise of the X-ray technician profession. For another example, the creation of devices to improve breathing contributed to the rise of the inhalation therapy profession. The increased use of the technology and the growth in the number of new specialists associated with it add to health care costs.

Third-Party Payers: HMOs and Private Insurance

HMOs and private insurance have operated to control costs. The federal government had supported the growth of HMOs, particularly to control health

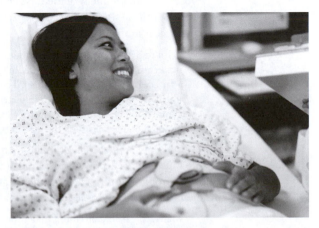

A pregnant woman sees her baby on ultrasound.

care costs. HMOs have been successful in controlling costs in some areas, but they have been unsuccessful in others as their expenses, particularly administrative costs, have risen. Summarizing their assessment of private insurance and HMOs, Freund and McGuire reached the following conclusion:

> The U.S. system of private insurance is structurally inefficient and expensive to administer because it is based on the exclusion and discrimination of denying coverage to precisely those who need the most health care. . . . To screen all claims by insured patients to enforce these exclusions and other restrictive terms, commercial insurance companies spend 33.5 cents for each dollar of benefits provided. These administrative costs are 14 times those of Medicare (2.3 cents per dollar) because all persons covered by Medicare have the same coverage and terms. (1999, 289)

HMOs have tried to control costs, but they have reduced costs by decreasing some services.

Increases in Medicare/Medicaid

Medicaid and Medicare costs have soared over the past 20 years. The federal government's share of Medicaid in 1988 was $30 billion. It rose to $82 billion six years later. In the same period Medicare rose from $86 billion to $159.5 billion (McKenna 1998, 628). Spending for Medicare increased from $197.4 billion in 2000 to about $270.5 billion in 2004 (Statistical Abstract 2004). Federal spending for Medicaid increased from $117.9 billion in 2000 to $160.7 billion in 2003 (U.S. Congressional Budget Office 2004).

The increase in Medicaid was due to two factors: the increase in the number of recipients and the increase in health care costs, especially hospitalization and long-term care, such as nursing homes.

Both programs, combined with the growth of private insurance, expanded the health care market. The rapid expansion of public spending in this field, without cost controls, has encouraged price increases beyond the rate of inflation (Coughlin, Ku, and Holahan 1994).

Perverse Market Incentives

Robert LeBow, president of the Physicians for a National Health Program, suggested that the high cost of American health care is partially the result of perverse market incentives and a religious faith in the market.

> With respect to the financing of health care, "the market" has been an abject failure. The market may work well with automobiles, housing, and fast food. But buying health care is a far cry from buying a hamburger. The much-vaunted advantage of market "competition" in health care has only resulted in increased woes for providers and patients. With competition being almost exclusively based on cost, the result has been the creation of oligopolies, the control of the market by large corporations. (2003, 18)

LeBow argued that although managed care temporarily controlled inflation in health care prices, "the effect was short lived" (2003, 18). He suggested that HMOs tried to control costs through cutting back on the length of stay in hospitals, cutting back on reimbursements, and denying some services. He added:

> Managed-care organizations underpriced their products to gain market share and, as a result, half of them lost money in the late '90s. Many continue to lose money today.

Moreover, the popular backlash to the abuses of managed care forced managed-care organizations to abandon many of their rationing mechanisms. Maybe the forces of competition could lead to better outcomes if quality were the issue, but with cost and profits as the motivators, "the market" in health care has lead to . . . a marked decrease in choice . . . increased diversion of resources to administration, marketing, and profits, with less money left for patient care . . . decrease in quality care, expansion of for profit HMOs . . . [and] frustrated physicians because administrative demands have limited the amount of time they are able to spend with patients. (2003, 19–20)

Compared with other countries, including those with universal health care, the United States pays a substantially higher percentage of administrative costs.

The Impact of Costs

The increase of health care costs has had three major impacts. First, it has impacted the economy; a greater share of GNP now goes to health care. This increase has also impacted the cost of production and the profits of major corporations. Corporations had to spend more money on health care, as insurance premiums increased. In *Health of Nations: An International Perspective on U.S. Health Care Reform,* Laurene Graig argued that health care costs impact American businesses much more than they impact businesses in other countries. Private businesses in the United States pay for health care as part of their benefit packages for their employees. In

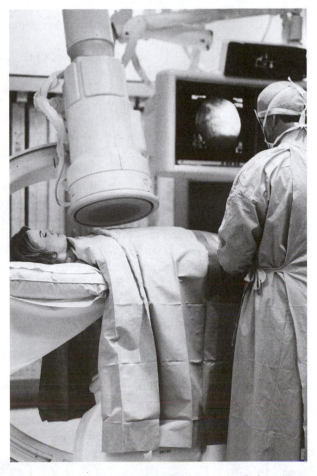

Advances in medical technology provides clearer images for better diagnosis.

contrast, the national government pays for these costs in other developed countries. The high cost of U.S. health care leaves American businesses at a competitive disadvantage compared to their foreign competitors.

The burden of health care costs in other nations is spread across the entire population, and no one industry or sector is overburdened. In the United States, on the other hand, industries with older work forces, such as steel and autos, do pay significantly higher health care costs. Indeed, in industries such as automobile manufacturing, health benefits costs are the largest nonwage factor in production costs. (Graig 1993, 23)

The second impact has been on state governments, which have been hard hit by increases in Medicaid costs, driven up by the increasing cost of nursing homes, hospital care, and more recipients.

The third impact has been on individuals and families. Many companies have begun shifting health care costs to their employees. This shift has meant that employee medical benefits have declined and that employees pay more money out of pocket for the health care they do get.

Bonser, McGregor, and Oster (1996) discussed several cases that illustrate the impacts of health care costs on families and individuals. One involved a family in which two sons, three and six years old, were diagnosed with cystic fibrosis. The family paid $1,500 a month for the medicine to treat the disease. Fortunately, their insurance covered the cost of the drugs.

Another case involved a 39-year-old married woman who had a stroke and required constant care. The couple's private health insurance did not cover long-term care at home or a nursing home. The husband's income disqualified her for Medicaid and she was too young for Medicare. The family attorney advised the husband to divorce his wife so that she might qualify for Medicaid and go into a nursing home.

Another case involved a married couple priced out of insurance. The wife was 59 years old and the husband 63. They were not eligible for Medicare or Medicaid. In 1988 their insurance cost $3,578 annually, with a $500 deductible for hospital coverage. By 1992 it cost $10,500 with a $2,000 deductible.

Cost Controls

Both the private sector HMOs and the public sector Medicaid and Medicare programs have been successful in controlling health care costs in a number of areas. They have set limits on the number of hospital days they would pay for. This practice has provided incentives to shift patients from the more expensive hospital care facilities to the less expensive outpatient care facilities. HMOs have used family or primary care physicians to regulate costs. For example, HMOs have refused to pay for the services of medical specialists unless authorized by the primary care physician. Furthermore, some HMO arrangements require the primary care physician to get authorization from the HMO before recommending specialists or special forms of treatment.

In 1983 Medicare replaced the fee-for-service system of reimbursement with a new prospective payment system. Under the fee-for-service system, Medicare paid hospitals whatever they charged. Under the prospective payment system (PPS), rather than paying hospitals whatever they charged, Medicare established set prices for specific medical services. These prices involved diagnostic-related groups (DRGs), a list of specific ailments with a corresponding list of the price of treatment. The government would pay out the set rate for the specific diagnosis. If physicians generally charged more, they would still get the established rate, and suffer a

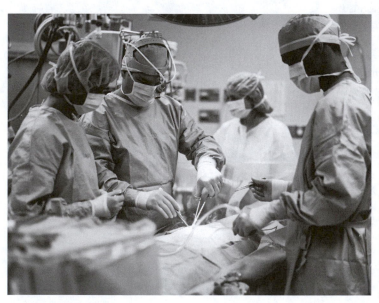

This hospital operating room illustrates the complex medical technology that contributes to rising health care costs.

loss. If the physicians generally charged less, they would get the higher amount and enjoy the gain. The use of DRGs provided incentives to control costs.

Despite these efforts, health care costs have continued to rise even though the rate of increase had slowed. High health care costs remained a problem.

The Access Problem

The crisis in health care costs has contributed to another crisis: a crisis in access to health care. Most people find health care too expensive to pay for out of pocket. Despite the range of people covered by private insurance, Medicare, and Medicaid, the number of people without any health care coverage—private or public—has increased. Table 6.2 lists the groups covered by Medicaid and Medicare.

The Uninsured

As Table 6.3 shows, more people are without any health care coverage today than 15 years ago. Moreover, the numbers and percentages are still increasing.

TABLE 6.2

Groups Covered

By Medicaid	By Medicare
TANF recipients*	Elderly
SSI recipients*	Low-income elderly
Pregnant women qualified for TANF after giving birth*	End-Stage Renal Disease
Children age six and under at 133 percent of poverty level*	
Children age 18 and under below the poverty level	

*Low-income Medicare beneficiaries.

TABLE 6.3

People with No Health Insurance

Year	Not Covered (In millions)	Percent
1990	34.7	13.9
1994	39.7	15.2
1996	40.6	15.4
1997	41.7	15.6
1998	43.4	15.6
2001	41.2	14.6
2002	43.6	15.2
2003	45.0	15.6

SOURCE: U.S. Census Bureau, *Statistical Abstract of the United States,* 2003.

The number of people without any health care covered increased from 34.7 million in 1990 to 45.0 million by 2003. The proportion of the uninsured increased from 13.9 percent in 1990 to 15.6 percent by 2003.

Several reasons explain the recent growth of the uninsured. One reason has to do with the area in which people are employed. Most adults without health care insurance do have jobs. An estimated 75 percent of the uninsured population consists of employed persons and their dependents (Freund and McGuire 1999, 295). The uninsured just happen to work in occupations unlikely to provide health care insurance: the self-employed, part-time workers, small businesses, the service sector, and others. The self-employed include independent truckers, mechanics, or contractors. The owners of these businesses have to purchase their own health insurance or manage without it. Many do without. Neighborhood stores, restaurants, and other small businesses have too few employees to get the type of health insurance discounts given to large companies with well over a hundred employees.

Another reason for the rising number of the uninsured is the shift of jobs from the industrial sector to the service sector. Many people who have lost jobs with benefits in the unionized industrial sector—steel, automobiles—have obtained jobs without health care benefits in the service sector. Service sector jobs include security guards, maintenance workers, restaurant workers, or the retail clerks—jobs that come with lower pay and no benefits.

Health care policy analyst Vicente Navarro provides several examples illustrating the increase in the uninsured, resulting from the contraction in the industrial sector. All of Navarro's examples are from Baltimore, Maryland. In 1990 John Dunlop was laid off from the Bethlehem Steel mill where he had worked for over 20 years. Not only had he lost his job, but he lost his health insurance as well.

> He could no longer receive the care he needed for a heart condition because he could not afford the insurance. He died in May 1993 from a stroke. He was one of the 100,000 people who die in the United States each year because they cannot afford medical care. (1993, 9)

Many underemployed workers have no health care insurance. The underemployed are those with part-time jobs, but prefer full-time work. More businesses have employed people part-time, usually 35 hours a week, in order to avoid having to pay health care benefits. This practice has increased the ranks of the uninsured.

Anne Lorraine is an example of an underemployed worker with no health insurance. She is a single, African-American woman with three children. She has two jobs, one of which is as a custodial worker at Johns-Hopkins Hospital. Neither of her two employers pays health benefits for her or her family and Lorraine cannot afford to pay the premiums on her own. About 32 percent of all health care workers in the United States have no health insurance (Navarro 1993, 10).

The Underinsured

The problem of the uninsured has been aggravated by the underinsurance problem. The Congressional Budget Office defines the *underinsured* as those who pay more than 10 percent of their annual income on health care (Calkins, Fernandopulle, and Marino 1995, 179). Several factors contribute to this problem. Probably the number one factor is the absence of coverage for long-term care. Few private policies cover long-term care. Medicare does not. Medicaid covers it, but only for the medically needy who meet financial eligibility requirements. Another factor producing underinsurance has been the practice of shifting health care costs from the employer to the employee. This practice generally results in employees with higher premiums, fewer benefits, and greater deductibles. One example sited earlier is the case of a family with a $500 deductible in 1988 which rose to a $2,000 deductible in 1992. A deduction of $2,000 constitutes underinsurance for those with incomes of $20,000 or lower. It can be a serious financial burden even for middle-class families.

Mary McCormick of Baltimore illustrates the problem of the underinsured. Mrs. Mc-Cormick was an administrator at the Maryland National Bank where she had full health care coverage for physician and hospital care.

> On January 27, 1992, she had a stroke that left her so seriously handicapped that she needed long-term care. But her health insurance did not include this benefit. She had to sell almost everything she owned to make herself eligible for government assistance. And in order to protect her husband's assets—their home and car—she had to divorce him. In March 1993 Mary killed herself. She was one of the 202 million people in the United States whose health benefits do not include long-term care. (Navarro 1993, 10)

Holes in Medicaid and Medicare

Medicaid and Medicare operate to some degree as a safety net to catch the poor and elderly who ordinarily would not have any health care at all. However, there are several holes in the Medicaid and Medicare safety net.

1. Medicaid does not cover the working poor. It does not cover adults without children whose incomes fall below the poverty line. It does not cover childless adults who are unemployed or who work but earn less than the poverty level.
2. Medicaid does not cover children ages 7 to 18 whose family incomes are just above the poverty level.
3. Medicaid does not work as effectively as private insurance. Since it usually pays only 60 percent of doctor fees, many doctors will not accept Medicaid patients. Many Medicaid beneficiaries do not have primary care physicians and use Medicaid primarily for emergency care. This problem impacts the quality of health care received by Medicaid recipients.
4. Finally, recent studies of poor children indicate that many families eligible for Medicaid do not even apply for benefits. In some cases, parents are not aware that they and their children are eligible for Medicaid; in other cases, the difficulty in obtaining coverage discourages families from applying.

Medicare has one main hole in its coverage. It does not cover long-term nursing care.

Underinsurance also affects Medicare recipients. Freund and McGuire provided examples to illustrate this problem. Dorothy and Frank are a married couple in their 70s with a monthly income of $1,400 in Social Security benefits.

> They have Medicare coverage, but noncovered health care expenditures consume about 50 percent of their entire family budget, leaving them scrimping to pay for food, utilities, and other basic needs. Their monthly costs include modest Medigap insurance policy, $200; Medicare premiums, $85; prescriptions and other medicine, $250; deductibles and other charges not covered by Medicare or Medigap, $50; long-term care insurance (for Dorothy; Frank is not eligible because of preexisting health conditions), $200. . . . (1999, 291)

Another example is that of an 85-year-old widow, Clarissa, who lives alone on Social Security payments of $650 per month.

Her health care needs not covered by Medicare consume 40 percent of her fixed income. They include Medicare premium, $42; prescriptions and other medicine, $120 (but she spends only $80, because she can't afford prescription painkillers for her arthritis); Medigap insurance, $80 (for a minimal policy); other charges not covered, $20. (1999, 291)

The Quality Issue

Political leaders have debated the issue of whether access to health care impacts health status or health outcomes. On one side of the argument, political leaders insist that health status is a function of lifestyles. Lifestyles include eating habits, exercise, smoking, and drug and alcohol abuse. They say that poor health has little to do with access to health care, as the poorest uninsured person has access to emergency care. They contend that if Americans have a lower life expectancy than people in other countries, it may be that Americans eat more red meat, consume more high-fat foods, smoke more, and exercise less. High-fat diets and the lack of exercise contribute to obesity and related health problems such as diabetes, high blood pressure, and heart disease. High rates of disease are often attributable to alcohol and drug abuse. These factors affect the health status of Americans regardless of the high quality of health care in the United States.

On the other side of the argument, critics of the U.S. health care system insist that public policy makes a difference in health status. For example, Patel and Rushefsky (1995) argued that the uninsured suffering from an acute illness are less likely to seek medical attention than those with private insurance. "For example, uninsured and Medicaid patients suffering from appendicitis are more likely to experience a ruptured appendix than privately insured patients" (p. 111). Also babies from uninsured families and Medicaid-insured babies "are likely to be discharged from hospitals sooner than privately insured babies" (Patel and Rushefsky 1995, 112).

Other critics maintain that the United States has the most expensive and technologically advanced health care system in the world, yet Americans have unimpressive health indicators. Table 6.4 compares the per capita spending, life expectancy, and infant mortality of the United States and a number of industrialized countries. Americans spend more on health care than any other country in the world. In terms of per capita spending—the amount spent per person—the United States spends three times what Great Britain spends; more than twice what Japan, Austria, and the Netherlands spend; and almost double what Germany, Norway, France, Sweden, and Switzerland spend. The only country that comes close to U.S. spending levels is Switzerland, but the United States outspends this country by $1,300 in per capita health care costs.

The higher U.S. spending levels do not translate into better health indicators. Out of 22 developed countries, the United States ranks 18th in female life expectancy and 21st in male life expectancy. Only the Czech Republic has a lower male life expectancy than the United States. It should be noted that the Czech Republic also has the lowest per capita health care spending.

The United States has the highest infant mortality rate among the other 21 developed countries: 7.8 per 1,000 live births. The United Kingdom is ranked 21st with an infant mortality rate of 6.1 (see Table 6.4).

Infant mortality rates are higher in American cities than in the country at large. These rates are higher among African Americans than those of some Third World countries. For example, the infant mortality rate for Mexico is 17.0 per 1,000 live births (Anderson and Poullier 1999). Table 6.5 shows that the rate for African Americans is 17.5 for Washington, D.C., 17.6 for Buffalo and Chicago, 17.8 for Cincinnati and Detroit, 18.0 for St. Louis, and 18.8 for Memphis.

White Americans have infant mortality rates lower than blacks in select cities, but substantially higher than those found in developed countries. For example, the infant mortality rate for whites is high in cities like Buffalo, Detroit, Cincinnati, and Norfolk. These rates for

TABLE 6.4

Health Status Spending and Outcomes in Selected Industrialized Nations

Nations	Per Capita Spending 1997 ($)	Life Expectancy 1996 (Years)		Infant Mortality* 1996 (%)
		Female	Male	
Australia	1,805	81.1	75.2	5.8
Austria	1,793	80.2	73.9	5.1
Belgium	1,747	81.0	74.3	6.0
Canada	2,095	81.5	75.4	6.0
Czech Republic	904	77.2	70.5	6.0
Denmark	1,848	78.0	72.8	5.2
Finland	1,447	80.5	73.0	4.0
France	2,051	82.0	74.1	4.9
Germany	2,339	79.9	73.6	5.0
Greece	974	80.4	75.1	7.3
Iceland	1,374	78.5	73.2	3.7
Italy	1,589	81.3	74.9	5.8
Japan	1,741	83.6	77.0	3.8
Luxembourg	2,340	80.0	73.0	4.9
Netherlands	1,838	80.4	74.7	5.2
New Zealand	1,352	79.8	74.3	7.4
Norway	1,814	81.1	75.4	4.0
Spain	1,168	81.6	74.4	5.0
Sweden	1,728	81.5	76.5	4.0
Switzerland	2,547	81.9	75.7	4.7
United Kingdom	1,347	79.3	74.4	6.1
United States	3,925	79.4	72.7	7.8

*Per 1,000 live births.

SOURCE: Anderson and Poullier. "Health Spending, Access, and Outcomes: Trends in Industrialized Countries," *Health Affairs* *18*(3), 1999.

TABLE 6.5

Infant Mortality Rates in Select U.S. Cities, 1995–1998 (Per 1,000 Live Births)

City	Total	White	Black
Atlanta	11.7	6.7	14.6
Boston	6.7	4.8	10.0
Buffalo	12.0	8.1	17.6
Chicago	11.5	7.0	17.6
Cincinnati	12.9	8.4	17.8
Dallas	6.4	5.4	9.6
Detroit	14.4	8.2	17.8
Indianapolis	9.2	7.5	14.0
Memphis	15.4	7.2	18.8
Milwaukee	8.9	6.3	12.0
New Orleans	9.4	6.4	10.4
New York	7.4	4.5	12.1
Norfolk	14.0	11.6	16.5
Philadelphia	12.0	6.7	16.6
St. Louis	8.9	7.5	18.0
San Francisco	4.6	2.6	12.3
Tampa	7.4	5.4	15.8
Toledo	7.5	5.6	12.2
Washington, DC	—	—	17.5
Wichita	8.3	7.6	14.7

SOURCE: Centers for Disease Control and Prevention 2002.

whites are no doubt associated with low incomes, which may be related to poor diet and inadequate access to medical care (see Tables 6.5 and 6.6).

Improvements in Health Status over Time

Despite the poorer health outcomes for the United States compared with other developed countries, the health status of Americans has improved substantially throughout the 20th century. Infant mortality rates have declined substantially over the past 30 years and life expectancy rates have increased throughout the past century. Infant mortality rates have declined from 20 per 1,000 in 1970 to about 6.8 today (see Table 6.6). Life expectancy rates increased from 47.3 years in 1900 to 68.2 years in 1950. They have continued to increase and today they are around 76.7, about 74 for men and 79.4 for women (U.S. Census Bureau 2002).

Several factors have contributed to improved health over the years, most of which are related to improved standards of living. Some of these factors are economic such as increased wages and purchasing power. Some have to do with the expansion of public amenities and modern facilities: electricity, refrigeration, indoor bathrooms, gas stoves, running water, and sewer and sanitation services. Others are related to public policies such as workplace safety,

TABLE 6.6	
Infant Mortality Rates in Select Years (Per 1,000 Live Births)	
Year	**Rate (%)**
1950	29.2
1960	26.0
1970	20.0
1980	12.6
1990	8.6
1995	7.6
1998	7.2
1999	7.1
2000	6.9
2001	6.8

SOURCE: U.S. Census Bureau, *Statistical Abstract of the United States,* 2002.

the minimum wage, maximum working hours, child labor, and other related policies. Public health policies such as immunization and disease control also have contributed to higher life expectancy.

As you have read, the debate over whether lifestyles or public policies are responsible for health status continues. Lifestyles indeed impact health conditions. At the same time, public policies such as food stamps, nutrition programs for women and children, and Medicaid and Medicare have contributed to declines in infant mortality rates and possibly to a marginal increase in life expectancy.

⇢ *Health Care Policy Initiatives of the Late 20th Century*

There were three major health policy initiatives of the late 1990s: the failed Health Security Act of 1993, the Health Insurance Act of 1996, and the health care rights movement.

The Health Security Act of 1993

The defeated *Health Security Act of 1993* was one of the most important health care policy initiatives of the late 20th century. President Bill Clinton, who had campaigned on a promise of providing national health care, introduced it. The idea was that this bill would be the social security act for health care. It was designed to address the problems of costs and access. It was an ambitious piece of legislation, over 1,300 pages long. It underscored six principles: security, savings, quality, choice, simplicity, and responsibility.

The first principle, security, was designed to provide health insurance coverage for every American. It proposed to cover people through existing private health insurance organizations such as HMOs. It prohibited private insurance companies from refusing to cover people because of preexisting conditions. It would guarantee continuous coverage for those who lost their jobs, switched jobs, or started a small business. The bill covered the following:

- Preventive care (i.e., screenings, physicals, immunizations, mammograms, prenatal care)
- Doctor visits
- Prescription drugs
- Hospital services
- Emergency/ambulance services
- Laboratory and diagnostic services
- Mental health and substance abuse treatment
- Expanded home health care

The second principle, savings, was designed to control health care costs. It limited how much insurance companies could raise premiums. States would be required to create health alliances to oversee competition among HMOs or private insurance companies and to provide consumers with information on costs and quality. The goal was that health alliances would facilitate competition among the insurance companies in ways that would encourage lower prices.

The third principle, quality, was expected to improve quality by emphasizing preventive care and guaranteeing a wide range of benefits. The Health Security Act would enhance the fourth principle, choice, by preserving the right to choose one's own physician. The Executive Summary of the Health Security Act said this about choice:

> The proposal ensures that you can follow your doctor and his or her team to any plan they might join. Today, more and more employers are forcing their employees into plans that restrict your choice of doctor. After reform, your boss or insurance company won't choose your doctor or health plan—you will.

Simplicity involved reducing paperwork, requiring insurance companies to use a single claim form, streamlining billings, and others. Responsibility, the last principle, entailed making health care everyone's business and producing health care cards for everyone.

Most Americans favored the ideal of national health insurance. Most expected the federal government to solve the cost, access, and quality problem of health care. Most initially supported the Health Security Act, yet the bill was defeated. Three factors contributed to its demise: (1) interest group opposition and support, (2) a divided Congress, and (3) the complexity of the bill.

Interest Group Opposition

By 1990 the political landscape involving national health care politics and traditional interest groups had changed. The American Medical Association was not as influential as it had been in the past. Fewer physicians were members. New organizations of physicians had emerged to challenge its leadership. Moreover, the rise of HMOs had changed the medical profession in ways that reduced the power of doctors. In the interest of controlling costs, HMOs challenged more of the decisions made by doctors. Summing up the situation with the AMA, Peterson wrote:

> The previous alliance of medical, business, and insurance interests that had always prevented the federal government from enacting comprehensive reform was split in every conceivable way. For example, the membership of the American Medical Association (AMA) declined from an estimated 90 percent of physicians in private practice to over two-thirds of all physicians as recently as the 1960s to 41 percent in the 1990s. Scores of

specialty organizations with an invigorated Washington presence, including the American College of Surgeons and American Academy of Family Physicians, challenged the AMA's position on health care reform and its role as medicine's voice. (1998, 184)

The AMA, joined by insurance and business organizations, initially supported the Health Security Act. A new organization, the Physicians for a National Health Program (PNHP), was formed to support universal health care. It appeared that the Medicaid/Medicare policy regime was going to collapse and give way to a new national health care regime.

Nevertheless, the old regime held together. A few interest groups opposed to national health care policy mobilized. They initiated a three-pronged attack on the new policy: They attacked the policy directly in the media, mobilized to rebuild the coalition of the old regime, and lobbied directly to defeat the bill.

The political organization that first attacked the Health Security Act was the National Federation of Independent Business (NFIB). "With 600,000 members scattered across every state and congressional district, and with millions of dollars committed to its two-stage campaign of grassroots mobilization and heavy inside lobbying against the president's proposal, the NFIB alone was a formidable source of opposition" (Peterson 1998, 194).

The NFIB worked with several other organizations to create a coalition opposing the Health Security Act. These included the National Restaurant Association, the Independent Insurance Agents of America, and the Christian Coalition. Television and lobbying campaigns hostile to the act were launched. The coalition opposed to the Health Security Act was called the No Name Coalition. Its leaders conducted focus group interviews and discovered that although Americans favored national health care, they were worried about big government and the competence of the federal government. "Bombarded with the message that Clinton proposed a government takeover of medical care that even threatened doctors and patients with jail terms if they violated the rules, the public grew increasingly worried about the ramifications of reform" (Peterson 1998, 195). Congressional leaders opposed to the bill contacted leaders in the AMA and the U.S. Chamber of Commerce and succeeded in persuading them to change their position and join the opposition. A powerful coalition emerged to oppose the bill.

Organized support for the bill was weak. The organizations expected to support the bill included consumer interest, organized labor groups, and senior citizen groups. There were three problems with this support. First, organized labor was weak and divided. The AFL-CIO leadership supported the bill, but they had some difficulty in getting support among local and affiliated labor unions. The length and complexity of the bill created problems in generating support. Also, more liberal groups favored more government support and less involvement of private insurance companies. The bill failed precisely because it had strong interest group opposition and weak interest group support.

Divided Congress

The second reason the bill was defeated is that opposition to the bill in Congress was united and support was divided. Republican Party leader Newt Gingrich, Speaker of the House at the time, was a very organized and influential leader and mobilized House Republicans to defeat the bill.

Democrats were divided over the bill. Liberal Democrats, such as consumer interest groups, wanted a bill with more federal involvement and more federal subsidies. "The pivotal point in the debate came in the spring of 1994, when John Dingell, the powerhouse chairman of the House Energy and Commerce Committee and long-time advocate of health care reform, could not overcome the opposition of key moderate Democrats to muster the majority needed to report a bill" (Peterson 1998, 196).

Complexity of the Bill

The complexity of the Health Security Act contributed to its demise. Leaders of political organizations that supported the bill first had to read it and understand it, then explain it to their constituents before they could build support. They had difficulties countering the opposition because the bill was so complex.

Clinton had introduced the bill in 1993. It was stalled in the House Energy and Commerce Committee in 1994. When the Republicans took control of the House and Senate after the 1994 election, the bill was dead by the end of the year. The submission of the bill to multiple committees also contributed to its death, a point noted in Chapter 4. The bill was submitted to about 10 different congressional committees.

Kennedy-Kessebaum Act of 1996

A year after the demise of the Health Security Act, senators Edward Kennedy and Nancy Kessebaum introduced the Health Insurance Portability and Accountability Act, perhaps better known as the *Kennedy-Kessebaum Act of 1996*. This act attempted to address the twin problems of portability and accountability. The portability problem has to do with workers who are offered a new job, but are faced with the possibility of losing their current health care coverage. The new law required the health care insurer to continue coverage for workers changing jobs. The accountability problem refers to a new health care provider refusing to cover previously existing health conditions. The law prohibited employers from refusing to cover preexisting conditions for new employees who had been covered elsewhere within 63 days of starting the new job.

Several amendments to the Kennedy-Kessebaum Act were proposed, but only a few were approved. One major amendment allowed the establishment of tax-exempt medical savings accounts (MCAs). Only a limited number of MCAs would be approved for Medicare recipients and they would operate like retirement accounts. The MCAs were strongly supported by the Republicans, who had a narrow majority. Kennedy and Kessebaum accepted the MCA provision as a compromise to ensure the passage of the bill. Senate Majority Leader Bob Dole played a key role in forging the compromise, producing bipartisan support and getting the bill through the Senate.

The Medicare Modernization Act of 2003

President George W. Bush introduced the Medicare Modernization Act of 2003, another complicated bill that added drug coverage and introduced changes in Medicare. The bill had five noteworthy aspects.

1. The bill provides a drug discount card, which seniors can purchase for $30 a year. It provides discounts of 10 percent to 25 percent for prescription drugs.
2. The bill provides a drug coverage option to Medicare recipients under Medicare Part D. Recipients would pay a premium of $35 a month. After a $250 deductible,

Medicare would pay 75 percent of the costs of drugs up to $2,250. There is no coverage for the cost of drugs between $2,250 and $5,000. Medicare will pay 95 percent of the cost of drugs costing more than $5,100.

3. The bill provides a sliding scale of benefits for low-income recipients. Medicare recipients whose income falls below the poverty line and who qualify for Medicaid would be exempt from paying premiums and deductibles. They would pay a one dollar co-pay for the drugs. Medicare recipients with incomes below 135 percent, but above 100 percent of the poverty line and with assets below $6,000 would also be exempt from premiums and deductibles, but would have to pay a $2 co-pay for drugs. As income and assets increase, premiums, deductibles, and co-pays would also increase.

4. The bill offers subsidies of up to $86 billion to employers who provide prescription drug benefits to retirees who are over 65 and eligible for Medicare.

5. Finally, the bill encourages Medicare recipients to move into HMOs. In this sense, it expands on the Medicare changes of 1996, which established Medicare Part C.

There was a great deal of conflict over the Medicare Modernization Act, not just between liberals and conservatives but also within each group. The American Association of Retired Persons supported the bill; although the bill was not what they wanted, it was a beginning. They had fought a long time for prescription drug benefits. The Alliance for Retired Americans opposed the bill and issued a press release stating, "Under the proposed bill, Medicare as we know it will cease to exits." They were especially concerned with the privatization of Medicare or the shifting of a fee-for-service program into HMOs. They also complained that the bill does not control the cost of drugs and precludes seniors from getting cheaper drugs from Canada.

Some conservatives were divided over the bill, primarily because of its projected costs: about $400 billion over a 10-year period. President Bush emphasized the privatization provision to obtain support from conservatives and the prescription drug coverage to obtain support from liberals. Corporate leaders supported the bill because of its allocation of $86 billion in subsidies to industries that provide prescription drug coverage for their retired workers.

Bush persuaded most Republicans, a majority in Congress, to support his bill. A few Democrats joined the Republicans, guaranteeing its passage.

Summary

The 20th century saw two major health care policy regimes: the solo doctor or Progressive regime and the Medicare/Medicaid regime. The solo doctor policy regime was characterized by local public health programs designed to prevent epidemics and reduce the spread of diseases, by local public and private nonprofit hospitals, and by solo doctors. Health care policy had changed little up to 1965. National health care proposals were introduced during the Progressive era and again during the New Deal, but they failed. Health care remained a private affair between doctor and patient. State and local governments, with some federal support, assisted in the construction of hospitals and provided a little assistance to poor people for emergency hospital care. The American Medical Association had fought bitterly against any proposal for a national health care system which it characterized as socialized medicine, a violation of the free market, and a dangerous interference with the private relationship between doctor and patient.

In 1965 the passage of Title XVIII and XIX of the Social Security Act, which established Medicare and Medicaid, marked a policy regime change. Several factors stressed the old Progressive policy regime and facilitated the change. First, technological and organizational changes in medical practice impacted the world of the physician, transforming the solo doctor into an associate of a large medical complex with hospitals, expensive medical machines, and a host of medical specialists. These changes contributed to substantial increases in health care costs. Second, the rise of health care insurance and later health maintenance organizations (HMOs) provided coverage for upper- and middle-class families, but left the poor and elderly without health care. Third, the antipoverty movement of the 1960s focused public attention on the health care issues of the poor and elderly people. These changes helped to produce the Medicare/Medicaid policy regime.

Medicare provided health care coverage for the elderly. Medicaid provided coverage for the disabled, for poor families with children, and for poor people needing long-term nursing home care. Medicare and Medicaid changed incrementally from 1965 to the present.

The Clinton administration added some minor protections for people covered by private insurance. The Kennedy-Kessebaum Act prohibited employers from refusing to cover preexisting conditions for new employees who had previous coverage. The Bush administration added a seminal prescription drug program. The Medicare/Medicaid policy regimes remain intact.

Efforts to establish a national universal health care system failed in the 1990s. Although powerful organizations like the AARP and the AFL-CIO supported such a system, other powerful organizations were opposed to it. These organizations included the National Federation of Independent Business, the National Association of Manufacturers, the Pharmaceutical Manufacturers Association, and the Health Insurance Association of America. Nevertheless, the cost and access crises in health care will continue to exert strong pressures for substantial policy changes. A few states have already moved in the direction of universal health care coverage.

Review Questions

1. How does health care at the beginning of the 21st century differ from health care at the beginning of the 20th century?
2. What factors contributed to the health care crises of cost and access?
3. How does the cost and quality of health care in the United States compare with the cost and quality in other developed nations?
4. What is Medicaid? Medicare? Who are the recipients of each?
5. What is the Health Security Act? What did it propose? Why was it defeated?
6. Discuss the Medicare Modernization Act of 2003. Why was this policy so controversial?

Select Websites

This is the Medicaid homepage.
http://www.cms.gov/medicaid/

This is the Medicare Website.
http://www.medicare.org

Key Terms

American Medical Association
health maintenance organizations (HMOs)
Medicaid
Medicare Part A
Medicare Part B

Medicare Part C
Medicare Part D
Medigap
preferred provider organizations (PPOs)

CHAPTER 7

Civil Rights Policy

Civil rights policy is about extending the same political rights enjoyed by one group of people to other groups of people. It is about the government protecting the rights of minority populations, identifiable by gender, race, nationality, religion, physical conditions, sexual preference, or any other characteristic different from majority or more powerful groups. Civil rights have been about the right to vote, own property, enter into contracts, serve on juries, purchase homes, pursue a quality education, and obtain a decent job. It is about the right to be free from harassment or violence. In a broad sense, civil rights have been about the government providing equal opportunities for all citizens.

Civil rights policies have been classified as either redistributive or protective regulatory, having some features of each policy type. Affirmative action, an aspect of civil rights policy, is redistributive, in so far as it is hotly debated and involves ideological disputes. Title VII of the 1964 Civil Rights Act is a protective regulatory policy in so far as it involves the Equal Employment Opportunity Commission (EEOC) operating to protect people from employers who would otherwise exclude them from jobs on the basis of race, religion, nationality, or gender.

✷ The Struggle of Minorities against Prejudice and Injustice

The history of civil rights has been a history of struggle against prejudice and injustices by groups identifiable by race, national origin, ethnicity, religion, sexual orientation, disabling conditions, and other factors. Many different groups have suffered from prejudices and injustices. A few examples include Irish Americans, Native Americans, Asian Americans, and African Americans. Each group suffered different experiences of prejudice and injustices and requires separate discussions.

Irish Americans

In the 16th century, when the English were conquering Ireland, they defined the Irish as a separate race. The English dehumanized the Irish with demeaning stereotypes and prejudices, often referring to the Irish as savage (Smedley 1993). Many Irish came to North America as indentured servants where they worked in large plantations until the 1690s when plantation owners began to rely exclusively on African slaves. In the 19th century Irish Americans suffered from prejudice and discrimination. Irish Americans were encouraged to lose their identity as Irish and to become Americans and blend into the so-called melting pot.

Native Americans

Native Americans have suffered centuries of prejudice and violence. In 1836 Congress passed the *Indian Removal Act.* Insisting that this act would benefit the Native Americans, President Andrew Jackson ordered them to move from their land in the southeastern United States to territory west of the Mississippi River in what is now Oklahoma. The Cherokee Nation sued the national government for violating treaties that guaranteed the Cherokees the right to remain in possession of their land. The U.S. Supreme Court ruled that the treaties were valid and that the Cherokees could keep their land. With contempt for the Court ruling, Jackson ordered the U.S. Army to remove the Cherokees. Many died as they were forced at gunpoint to leave their lands.

In the late 19th century, Native Americans were forcibly removed from their western lands and placed on reservations. In 1887 Congress passed the *Dawes Act.* This act broke up communally owned Native American land for resale to settlers. Moreover, the act allowed Native Americans to become citizens only if they completely lost their Native American cultural identity, by giving up their dress, religion, and language. Those who kept their identity were not considered citizens of the United States, even after the ratification of the Fourteenth

Amendment, which granted citizenship to anyone born in the United States. Citizenship rights were not extended to Native Americans who maintained their identity until Congress passed the *Indian Citizenship Act of 1924.*

The *American Indian Movement (AIM)* emerged along with the civil rights movement of the 1960s. Title II of the *Civil Rights Act of 1968* applied the Bill of Rights to Native American tribal governments. In 1970 the Native American Rights Fund was established to raise money to pursue the civil rights of Native Americans.

Asian Americans

Asian Americans suffered from prejudice and discrimination, especially in the late 19th century and throughout the 20th century. Just after the Civil War, Chinese were brought to the United States in large numbers to work on building the transcontinental railroads in the West. The *Chinese Exclusion Act of 1882* barred Chinese immigrants from becoming U.S. citizens. The *Immigration Act of 1924* limited immigration mostly to people from northern Europe.

In the 1930s and 1940s Asian Americans suffered forms of segregation and discrimination similar to those experienced by African Americans. Southern schools classified Asians as colored and barred them from white schools. During World War II, Japanese Americans were placed in internment camps because of the fear of Japanese spies. Only recently were they compensated for property losses. Immigration laws did not give non-European immigrants an equal opportunity to become American citizens until the passage of the *Immigration and Naturalization Act of 1965.*

Other groups also have been victimized by prejudices. Mexican Americans have been targets of prejudice and stereotypes; Jewish Americans suffered the indignities of anti-Semitism; and, in the aftermath of the September 11, 2001 terrorist attacks, Arab Americans have been frequent targets of prejudice.

Because of the color of their skin, African Americans have stood out. They have suffered more severe and enduring forms of prejudice and injustice. In the past, they were denied the right to vote, excluded from many skilled trades, and concentrated in the sharecropping system of the South. Worse, they were the targets of lynchings and mass violence.

✦ *African Americans and Civil Rights Policies*

A large part of this chapter covers the emergence of civil rights policies affecting African Americans. Of course, the civil rights movement of the 1960s and advancements in civil rights laws affected other groups. The contemporary civil rights regime has expanded civil rights protection for minorities regardless of race, nationality, religion, gender, sexual orientation, or physical condition.

Civil rights policies addressing the issues of African Americans developed in four stages, representing four different policy regimes: slavery, Reconstruction, segregation, and fair play or rights. A major upheaval marked the change from each policy regime. The Civil War marked the change from the slave regime to the Reconstruction regime. The overthrow of the Republican Party in the South and the reemergence of the planter class marked the change from the Reconstruction regime to the segregation regime. The disintegration of the sharecrop system marked the change from the segregation regime to the fair play regime.

The Slave Regime

The slave regime has been characterized by several factors: the plantation system, the conditions of the slaves, the slave laws and power arrangements, and the slavery paradigm. This regime collapsed with the Civil War.

The Plantation System and the Status of African Americans

Slavery as an institution in the United States was based primarily on the plantation system. This system had two distinguishing characteristics. First, it was a cash crop (e.g., cotton or tobacco) agricultural economic system common in the deep South, based on the use of large amounts of land (over 1,000 acres) and large numbers of slaves (over 100). Second, plantation slavery was an inflexible and permanent racial system. Slaves were identifiable by the color of their skin. Slavery was considered a permanent status, a life sentence that carried over into the next and future generations. Of course, a few slaves obtained their freedom by running away, by purchasing it, or by the generosity of their masters. Also, not all of the slaves lived on plantations; some lived on small farms with only a few slaves, some worked as servants, and some had specialized skills like carpentry. However, most slaves worked and lived on the large plantations in the South (Stampp 1956).

Conditions of Slaves

There has been a great deal of debate over the conditions of the slave. Some scholars, such as Eugene Genovese (1965), argued that slaves were well taken care of, well treated, and well fed because they were expensive property. Other scholars, such as Kenneth Stampp, argued that slaves were overworked and sometimes suffered horrendous cruelty. Stampp argued that economic gain was an incentive to work the slaves as hard as possible without killing them.

Slave Laws

National and state laws supported the institution of slavery. The U.S. Constitution and federal fugitive slave laws required free states to return runaway slaves to their owners. In the *Dred Scott v. Sanford* decision, Chief Justice Roger B. Taney made it clear that slaves were property, were not citizens of the United States, and had no rights under the Constitution. Taney made the racial aspect of this system clear:

> They [blacks] had for more than a century before been regarded as beings of an inferior order; and altogether unfit to associate with the white race, either in social or political relations; and so far inferior that they had no rights which the white man was bound to respect and that the Negro might justly and lawfully be reduced to slavery for his benefit . . .

Southern states denied rights to those who sympathized with slaves. Many states outlawed abolitionist speech and writings. For example, in Louisiana anyone found guilty of speaking in a public place in a way that might incite slave rebellions or insubordination among slaves could be executed. The possession or distribution of abolitionist literature was illegal in most southern states.

Power Arrangements of the Slave Regime

The planter class dominated the slave regime. This class consisted of those who owned more than a 1,000 acres of land and more than 100 slaves. It dominated southern politics and

African American Union Infantry soldier.

exercised considerable influence at the national level. A significant proportion of southern governors and U.S. senators from the South came from this class.

Slave Policy Paradigm

The slave policy paradigm emerged with plantation slavery to rationalize slavery. There were two major strands of this paradigm. The first told tales of how awful things were in Africa, how Africans were cannibals, and how Africans enslaved each other. Of course, these were largely myths and lies about Africa and Africans, but these were promoted to make it appear that slavery in the United States was better than freedom in Africa. It was not.

The second strand claimed that Africans were an inferior race, a subspecies of humanity. There is no scientific basis to this claim, but the assumption made it easier to treat Africans like animals. The idea that dark-skinned people belonged to an inferior race was invented to justify slavery.

The End of the Slave Regime

The Civil War was a major social upheaval that destroyed the slave regime. The war destroyed the power of the planter class and changed the way people thought about the South and African Americans. For a brief moment after the war, Confederate leaders were disenfranchised and blacks were enfranchised. Power had shifted from the planter class to blacks who were former slaves and whites who were poor, landless, or owners of small farms. This shift in power contributed to the emergence of the Reconstruction regime.

The Reconstruction Regime

The Reconstruction regime was the first civil rights regime and it produced a flood of civil rights policies. Just after the Civil War, Congress proposed several civil rights amendments to the Constitution and passed several civil rights laws. The **Thirteenth Amendment** ended slavery. Lincoln's Emancipation Proclamation only freed slaves in areas in rebellion against the United States. The **Fourteenth Amendment** did three things. First, it made anyone born or naturalized in the United States a citizen of the United States. This amendment was proposed in direct reaction to the *Dred Scott* decision, which had denied citizenship to African Americans. Second, it contained a due process clause, which stated that the government could not take life, liberty, or property without due process of law. Third, this amendment contained an equal protection clause: Government cannot deny any individual equal protection under the law. The **Fifteenth Amendment** prohibited states from denying individuals the right to vote on account of race, color, or previous condition of servitude.

Congress passed four major civil rights laws: the Civil Rights Act of 1866, the Enforcer Acts of 1870 and 1871, and the Civil Rights Act of 1875. The *Civil Rights Act of 1866* prohibited states from denying individuals, on account of race or color, the right to enter into private contracts, to sue people in court, and to buy, lease, own, or sell property. It requires fair and equal treatment of all people regardless of race or color. The civil rights acts of 1870 and 1871, the *Enforcer Acts,* prohibited organized attacks on blacks in the South. The *Civil Rights Act of 1875* prohibited segregation in public accommodations. Clearly, the Reconstruction regime attempted to protect the rights of former slaves.

The power base of the Reconstruction regime was the Republican Party of the South and the social groups and alliances that supported it: blacks who were former slaves and whites who were poor, landless, or owners of small farms. This party was racially integrated and promoted black and white candidates.

Disintegration of the Reconstruction Regime

The Reconstruction regime was short lived. It began breaking up in the 1870s and was gone by the end of the century. Several factors, or stressors, contributed to its demise. First, the federal government withdrew its support for Reconstruction. President Rutherford B. Hayes pulled federal troops out of the South by 1877; there were already too few troops to protect the former slaves by the mid-1870s. The former slaves were now completely vulnerable to the former Confederate leaders.

Second, former Confederate leaders took extralegal and legal steps to destroy the Reconstruction regime and the southern wing of the Republican Party. They used bribery, threats, intimidation, and violence to get people to vote Democratic candidates into office. Once they secured a majority in state legislatures, they took legal steps to achieve their goals. They passed laws to disenfranchise Republican and Populist (a party that emerged in the 1870s) voters.

Morgan Kousser, a political scientist, examined the social background of the state legislatures and the voters who supported the disenfranchisement movement and concluded:

> Not only did the vast majority of the leaders reside in the black belt, almost all of them
> were affluent and well educated, and they often bore striking resemblances to antebellum
> "patricians." Indeed, almost every one was the son or grandson of a large planter, and
> several of the older chiefs had been slaveholders before the war. (1974, 247)

Kousser demonstrated not only the positive association between wealthy landowners and the vote to disenfranchise blacks, but also that whites who owned small farms voted against disenfranchisement.

Other scholars have shown that the disenfranchisement of blacks also meant the disenfranchisement of whites. For example, in Texas from 1900 to 1904, when blacks lost the right to vote, voter participation declined among whites from 80 percent to 27 percent. Many whites who were poor lost the right to vote when blacks were disenfranchised (Bloom 1987).

To get around the Fifteenth Amendment, southern states used various legal devices to deny people the right to vote: literacy tests, poll taxes, character tests, and grandfather clauses.

These devices gave local officials the power to deny anyone the right to vote. If they thought you were not likely to vote for the Democratic candidate, the local registrar would fail you on the literacy test, refuse to accept your poll tax, or reject you as a bad character and not allow you to vote.

Finally, the U.S. Supreme Court played a major role in dismantling the Reconstruction regime. It attacked civil rights laws and promoted segregation. In the *U.S. v. Cruikshank,* the Court struck down provisions of the Civil Rights Act of 1871. The Supreme Court invalidated the Civil Rights Act of 1875, which prohibited private individuals or businesses operating public accommodations (e.g., restaurants, hotels, amusement parks) from segregating or excluding people on account of race. The Court claimed that the Fourteenth Amendment applied to state governments, not to private individuals or businesses. Moreover, the Court argued that the Civil Rights Act of 1875 violated the reserved powers clause of the Tenth Amendment, which specified that all powers not granted to the federal government were reserved to the states.

After mutilating civil rights laws, the Court supported racial segregation. In 1896 it created the **separate but equal doctrine** in the *Plessy v. Ferguson* decision. This case involved a Louisiana state law segregating the railroads. Homer Plessy, who claimed to be seven-eighths white, was arrested for sitting in the passenger car designated for whites only. Plessy's attorney argued that the law violated both the Thirteenth and Fourteenth Amendments. When the state forced the segregation of blacks from whites, it created a badge of servitude for blacks and violated the Thirteenth Amendment. By arresting Plessy, the state treated him worse than others and therefore violated the equal protection clause of the Fourteenth Amendment. The Court's majority opinion dismissed the Thirteenth Amendment argument without any discussion, and stated that segregation did not violate the equal protection clause of the Fourteenth Amendment so long as the segregated facilities were equal. The court provided the legal basis for the emergence of the segregation regime. The *Plessy v. Ferguson* decision encouraged the enactment of other segregation laws.

The Segregation Regime

By the beginning of the 20th century, the Reconstruction regime was gone. Power had shifted from lower-income whites and blacks back to major landowners. Civil rights protections disappeared. The segregation regime was well in place.

By the 1900s blacks were denied the right to vote. Almost every aspect of public life in the South was racially segregated: parks, restaurants, schools, residential areas, restrooms, theaters, hospitals, beaches, amusement parks, and other public places were split into those reserved for whites and those reserved for blacks. There were public restrooms for whites only and for blacks only. There were public drinking fountains for whites only and for blacks only. The balconies of movie theaters were generally reserved for blacks only. It was illegal for a black child to go to an all-white public school. In some states it was illegal for blacks and whites to meet in large numbers in public gatherings. Interracial marriages were felonies in most southern states. The segregation regime remained in place until the passage of the Civil Rights Act of 1964 and the collapse of the sharecropping system. The next section defines the sharecropping system and the section after that discusses the dominant paradigm of the segregation regime.

The Sharecropping System

For the first half of the 20th century, many rural southern blacks and whites were trapped in constant poverty through debt peonage in the sharecropping system. The **sharecropping system** worked as follows: A poor family that owned nothing—whites and blacks suffered in the same position—would work on a parcel of land owned by a planter. The family members would get everything they needed from the planter: the house they lived in, food, clothing, tools, and other supplies—all on credit from the landowner. The family would owe the landowner for the rent, food, supplies, clothes, and tools for the year. To pay this debt, the family would work the land year-round. Family members would clear the land, and plant, weed, and harvest the crops—cotton, for example. The landowner would tally the value of the harvested crop and subtract that value from the amount of money the family owed. If the value of the crop was less than what the family owed, the family would be in debt to the landowner. Debt peonage arose when state law prohibited families from leaving the land until the debt was paid. The family would work harder the next year, but no matter how hard they worked, they usually remained in debt.

The Segregation Policy Paradigm

There were three strands of the segregation policy paradigm: eugenics, Social Darwinism, and cultural segregation. Eugenicists believed that there was a hierarchy of races arranged from the superior to the inferior. Eugenicists thought that the people of Western Europe were the superior race, followed by Eastern Europeans, Jews, Asians, Native Americans and Africans. They believed that the superior races surpassed those below them biologically, intellectually, and morally. Eugenicists argued that government should force the separation of the races to maintain the purity of the superior races. They supported laws that mandated segregation and prohibited interracial marriage. Some promoted abortion and sterilization among those deemed most inferior. A few advocated social programs for the least fortunate.

Like the eugenicists, Social Darwinists believed in a hierarchy of the races and in laws segregating the races and prohibiting interracial marriage. However, Social Darwinists opposed programs that helped the less fortunate races, because they believed such programs interfered with nature and the Darwinist notion of the survival of the fittest.

Cultural segregationists believed that the so-called lower races were culturally inferior. They felt that African Americans were lazy, immoral, dirty, unlawful, and dangerous. Their view of the culture of African Americans helped to promote segregation.

Changes in Civil Rights Policies

Changes in civil rights policies from 1900 to 1950 were incremental. This point can be made by examining the role of Congress, the Supreme Court, and presidents during this period.

Congress   Congress passed no civil rights laws from 1900 to 1956. Southerners committed to segregation dominated key committees in Congress. They were successful in keeping civil rights off the congressional agenda. Congress did not begin to enact civil rights laws until the *Civil Rights Act of 1957*. This law created the Civil Rights Commission and the Civil Rights Division of the Justice Department. The job of the **Civil Rights Commission** was to study the race problem. The Civil Rights Division could investigate cases of state-supported racial violence.

Courts   For the first half of the 20th century, the U.S. Supreme Court allowed segregation. It interpreted the Constitution to permit most aspects of segregation and most practices denying voting rights to African Americans. It supported the segregation of public accommodations and facilities. It upheld literacy tests, poll taxes, and character tests. It tolerated states laws that made interracial marriage a felony.

Beginning in the 1940s, the Court began to gradually chip away at segregation policies, when it prohibited primary elections for whites only. In 1954 it overturned the "separate but equal" principle in the *Brown v. Board of Education of Topeka* decision. The Court ordered public schools to desegregate with all deliberate speed. However, desegregation came slowly in the South, where there was massive resistance to desegregation efforts. A few black students attended all-white high schools, but in some cases they had to be escorted by the National Guard. Citizen councils were established specifically to maintain segregation. In a few cases, entire school systems were shut down to avoid complying with the *Brown* decision. Significant change did not occur until the Civil Rights Act of 1964 was passed.

Presidents   Presidents from Theodore Roosevelt to Dwight Eisenhower were reluctant to get involved in civil rights issues. Woodrow Wilson even supported segregation. Franklin Roosevelt was the first president in the 20th century to exhibit concern about civil rights issues. He appointed blacks to advisory positions in his administration. In response to a planned march on Washington organized in 1941 by A. Philip Randolph, the president of the Brotherhood of Sleeping Car Porters—one of the largest black labor unions in the nation—President Roosevelt established the **Fair Employment Practices Commission (FEPC).** This

Ku Klux Klan marching in Washington, D.C.

agency was responsible for studying the problem of racial discrimination in the job market, but it had no enforcement power and lasted only from 1941 to 1946. President Truman ordered the integration of the armed forces and supported desegregation cases. Eisenhower was reluctant to move too rapidly on civil rights matters, although he used National Guard troops to protect black students entering an all-white high school. The segregation regime disintegrated during the Kennedy-Johnson term.

The Disintegration of the Segregation Regime

Three stressors contributed to the disintegration of the segregation regime: (1) international events: World War II and the cold war; (2) mode of production and demographic changes; and (3) social movements.

International Events   World War II and the cold war impacted the segregation regime by dramatizing this profound contradiction: Americans had fought a war against fascism and racism in Europe, but maintained segregated armed forces, denied African-American service men and women the right to vote at home, and sanctioned racial segregation in the South. The segregation regime hindered America's postwar propaganda campaign against communism. The United States had promised to offer a just alternative to communism among people of color in Asia and Africa, but denied equality and justice to people of color on its own soil.

Mode of Production and Demographic Changes   As you read earlier, the sharecropping system was the dominant mode of production in the South to the mid-20th century. The collapse of this system doomed the segregation regime and stimulated the mass movement of African Americans into urban areas and into industrial jobs. African Americans were no longer isolated on a small plot of land in the sharecropping system, but now lived near each other in large numbers in urban areas. Thus, urbanization created the basis for a mass social movement against segregation. The movement of African Americans into industrial jobs joined the labor movement to the civil rights movement.

Social Movements   The civil rights movement was characterized by the dramatic expansion of older, generally conservative civil rights organizations, the rapid growth of new, more assertive civil rights organizations, and the formation of a broad-based national coalition of organizations. The older organizations included the **National Association for the Advancement of Colored People (NAACP),** established in 1910. The NAACP had pursued a legal strategy, filing multiple lawsuits throughout the first half of the century. The **Congress on Racial Equality (CORE)** was formed in the early 1940s, the **Southern Christian Leadership Conference (SCLC)** was organized in the 1950s, and the **Student Nonviolent Coordinating Committee (SNCC)** was established in the early 1960s.

The industrial union movement of the 1930s and 1940s impacted the civil rights movement. Whereas African Americans faced extreme racial discrimination in the skilled trade unions, they often found jobs in steel mills, jobs that were dangerous and unpopular. The movement to organize industrial unions in the 1930s and 1940s also meant organizing African-American workers into these unions. Consequently, industrial unions tended to be more supportive of civil rights issues than skilled trade unions. By the 1950s and 1960s, industrial unions had become part of the civil rights movement, as union organizers often assisted civil rights organizers. The movement gained momentum with the *Brown* decision and the bus boycott in Montgomery, Alabama, in the early 1950s. The struggle intensified in the 1960s with the formation of SNCC and its more aggressive organizing and voter registration drives in the Deep South.

By the 1960s there was a broad and powerful civil rights coalition. It consisted of several old and new civil rights organizations, industrial unions, religious organizations, and civic organizations. The civil rights movement even had the support of a few key industrial leaders. It had strong support in the Kennedy and Johnson administrations.

⇢ Civil Rights since the 1960s

The segregation regime had disintegrated by the mid-1960s and was replaced by the fair play civil rights regime. Power had shifted, a new policy paradigm had emerged, and new civil rights laws were enacted.

Fair Play Civil Rights Regime

The civil rights coalition shifted power. This coalition consisted of a broad array of organizations across the nation with millions of constituents. It consisted of civil rights organizations such as CORE, NAACP, SCLC, SNCC, and many more. It included many different types of religious organizations. Large and powerful labor unions such as the United Automobile Workers (UAW) and key industrial union leaders also became part of this coalition.

Fair Play Civil Rights Policy Paradigm

Several scholars contributed to the emergence of the fair play civil rights policy paradigm. Gunnar Myrdal's *American Dilemma* (1944) had a profound effect on thinking about race relations. Myrdal presented substantial evidence that challenged the segregation regime. He demonstrated that high poverty rates among African Americans were not a function of bad biology or bad culture, but a function of blocked opportunities, substantial job market discrimination, and the sharecropping system. Myrdal concluded that African Americans were not treated fairly and had been denied opportunities that others enjoyed.

Historians such as W. E. B. DuBois (1946/1976) and, more recently, Frank Snowden (1991) have demonstrated that ancient Greeks and Romans considered variations in skin color to be nothing more than variations in exposure to the sun and that the notion of basing racial differences on skin color emerged with the African transatlantic slave trade. The modern concept of basing racial differences on skin color has no basis in science. Moreover, scholars in the United Nations Educational, Scientific and Cultural Organization (UNESCO) have long insisted that there was no scientific basis to the concept of different races.

Sociologist Kenneth Clark refuted the segregationist paradigm. Clark had testified in the *Brown* decision and demonstrated that state-mandated segregation had a detrimental effect on the psychological development of black children. It instilled within them an inferiority complex. Clark's book *Dark Ghetto* (1965) documented the impact of housing and job market discrimination on African Americans in urban areas. It blocked their opportunities and reduced their chances for economic advancement. Studies such as these supported aggressive civil rights policies.

Political leaders also contributed to the development of the fair play paradigm. Martin Luther King, Jr. eloquently articulated this paradigm. He challenged other political leaders to carry out the true meaning of the American creed: that all people are created equal. He insisted that government has an obligation to protect the rights of all of its citizens.

This short list of a few thinkers cannot do justice to the avalanche of writers who contributed to this paradigm shift. The literature on antiracism included both fiction and nonfiction. A sample of fiction writers would include Zora Neale Hurston, *Their Eyes Were Wathcing God* (1937/1978); Ralph Ellison, *The Invisible Man* (1952/1972); Richard Wright, *Native Son* (1940/1989); and James Baldwin, *Go Tell It on the Mountain* (1953/1969). These fiction writers also contributed to nonfiction antiracist literature and helped change people's thinking about race and racism.

The works of scholars explaining the extreme anti-Semitism in Europe during the 1930s and 1940s also contributed to the antiracist literature. These studies include Gordon Allport (*The Nature of Prejudice*), Theodor Adorno (*The Authoritarian Personality*), and Eric Fromm (*Escape From Freedom*).

Congress, the Supreme Court, and Civil Rights Policies

In the 1960s Congress and the Supreme Court promoted aggressive civil rights policies. Congress continued to support civil rights policies throughout the late 20th century and into the 21st century. The Court, on the other hand, changed in the mid-1980s when it began hacking away at civil rights policies. Congress responded by restoring many of the policies the Court destroyed. Once the fair play civil rights regime was in place, most of the policy changes were incremental.

Congress enacted the Civil Rights Act of 1964 which prohibited racial discrimination in public facilities and accommodations. Title VI of this act prohibited racial discrimination in programs receiving federal funds. Title VII prohibited discrimination based on race, nationality, religion, or gender in employment. The **Equal Employment Opportunity Commission (EEOC)** was established to implement Title VII of the act.

Civil rights policies can be divided into several specialized areas such as education, voting, and employment. These areas can also include the issues of affirmative action and the conflict between Congress and the Court.

Education

Public education and civil rights involved the implementation of the *Brown v. Board of Education of Topeka* decision of 1954. As noted earlier, this decision repudiated the separate but equal principle and ordered southern school districts to desegregate. By 1964 most southern school districts had not complied with the order. Many districts had eliminated the mandatory segregation policy and established freedom of choice plans. Black families could choose to send their children to all-white schools, but too often these schools had no openings for black students. Hostility against desegregation had persisted into the 1960s and southern schools remained segregated.

A number of policy changes of the 1960s enhanced the implementation of school desegregation efforts. The Office of Civil Rights (OCR) was established in the Department of Health, Education and Welfare to desegregate public schools. This agency aggressively investigated cases of noncompliance with the *Brown* decision. It negotiated with local school systems to desegregate their schools, turning over the worse cases of noncompliance to the Justice Department.

In the 1970s the Supreme Court continued to take an active role in desegregating public schools. The Court distinguished between de jure and de facto segregation. *De jure* segregation was segregation by law or segregation produced by deliberate government policy. *De facto* segregation was segregation after the fact or segregation produced by factors other than government policy. A good example of de facto segregation in the schools was produced by residential segregation.

In the *Swann v. Charlotte-Mecklenburg* decision of 1971 the Court ordered the integration of a school district found guilty of de jure segregation. The Court also defined the meaning of integration in concrete terms. Since the school district was approximately 30 percent black and 70 percent white, the Court ordered a 30 to 70 percent range for the racial composition of its schools; that is, no school would have less than 30 percent of the children of one race and no more than 70 percent of the children of another race. Since the school district had used busing to maintain segregation, it was ordered to use busing to achieve integration.

The *Keyes v. Denver School District Number 1* (1973) was the first Supreme Court decision involving a northern school district. The Court found the Denver school district guilty of de jure segregation although there were no laws on the books mandating segregation. The Court ordered the district to bus students to achieve racial balance as a remedy for de jure segregation.

The Supreme Court found many other northern school districts guilty of de jure segregation, and it ordered busing as a remedy in several northern school districts including Cleveland, Detroit, Boston, and many more. By the 1990s, however, the Court was no longer supporting busing. School desegregation efforts had been successful in some areas and less successful in others. While many southern school districts were integrated, not all northern school districts were. However, because of the migration of whites out of central cities and because of segregated residential patterns, many school districts, such as Detroit, were as segregated in 2005 as they were 50 years earlier.

Voting Rights

The Voting Rights Act of 1965 addressed the issue of discrimination in voting. It contained a clause that triggered a federal response if less than 50 percent of the eligible voters in a southern county were registered to vote. This response entailed the observation of county election procedures by federal officials or the replacement of local officials in order to register people to vote. The Voting Rights Act also contained a preclearance section that required southern counties to obtain approval from a federal district court before making any changes in voting policy.

The Voting Rights Act of 1965 was one of the most successfully implemented civil rights policies. It had clear goals and substantial support among civil rights groups. The impact of this act was significant.

> By far the biggest increases in black registration took place in the seven Southern states covered by the Voting Rights Act. More than one million new blacks were registered in these states between 1964 and 1972, increasing the percentage of eligible blacks registered from about 29 percent to almost 57 percent. (Bullock and Lamb 1984, 41)

This act was amended several times—in 1970, 1975, and 1982. The *Voting Rights Act of 1975* required counties to accommodate minorities who spoke a language other than English, if they constituted a significant percentage, more than 5 percent, of the county population.

In the *Mobile, Alabama v. Bolden* case, civil rights groups challenged the at-large election structure of Mobile on grounds that it discriminated against African Americans. Because districts represented neighborhoods or sections of a city, city councils based on district elections were more likely to mirror the diversity of different ethnic or racial groups in the city. Justice O'Connor delivered the Court's majority opinion that the Voting Rights Act of 1975 did not guarantee the election of minorities. She argued that this act only prohibited state and local governments from discriminating against minorities.

Congress responded to the *Bolden* decision with the *Voting Rights Act of 1982.* This act did not outlaw at-large elections, but it outlined the conditions under which they could be challenged in court. These conditions were the following:

1. Where no minority was represented on the city council, even though minorities constituted a significant proportion of the population.
2. Where there was evidence of racial polarization in voting patterns—that is, whites voting for white candidates and blacks voting for black candidates.
3. Where evidence showed racial tensions within the city.
4. Where racial tensions existed within local political parties.

The 1982 act encouraged states to put forth efforts to increase black representation in the U.S. Congress. After the 1990 census, a number of states redrew their congressional district lines. Some states gerrymandered the district lines to increase black representation. The term **gerrymander** came from Gerry and salamander. Elbridge Gerry (1744–1814) was the governor of Massachusetts who drew boundary lines that shaped districts like a salamander. In the past, a number of southern states had engaged in racial gerrymandering in order to reduce the power of the black vote. In the early 1960s the Court had ruled that gerrymandering to reduce the power of the black vote was illegal. In the late 1990s the Court decided that it was also illegal for states to gerrymander districts to increase the number of black representatives.

Voting rights have been expanded through means other than the Voting Rights Act. The Twenty-fourth Amendment outlawed poll taxes. Other reforms have made it easier for people to register to vote and have expanded the number of voters, including registration drives at banks, supermarkets, and college campuses. The national driver's license registration program has also increased the ranks of voters. Many of the voting rights problems have been resolved.

Florida, the Presidential Election of 2000, and Electoral Reform

The U.S. Civil Rights Commission has expressed concerns about Florida and the 2000 presidential election. After the November election the commission conducted hearings to investigate voting rights complaints. The commission reviewed more than 100,000 pages of documents and listened to more than 20 hours of testimony from over 100 witnesses. It concluded, "Statistical data, reinforced by credible anecdotal evidence, pointed to the widespread denial of voting rights" (U.S. Civil Rights Commission 2001, 2). The commission identified several specific problems:

1. Purging
2. Police presence
3. Driver's license registration
4. Accessibility
5. Poll closings
6. Rejected ballots

Purging   The State of Florida had contracted with a private firm to purge the state's voter registration rolls of ineligible voters: deceased persons, convicted felons, individuals declared mentally incompetent, duplicate registrants, and others. The company matched the list of convicted felons with the list of registered voters. Voters without felonies were purged if they happened to have the same name and race of a felon. Thus, thousands of law-abiding eligible voters without a police record were purged and prevented from voting. A disproportionate number of those denied the right to vote were African Americans (Civil Rights Commission 2001).

Police Presence   The Civil Rights Commission report reads: "On the afternoon of the election day, the Florida Highway Patrol received notice of a complaint to the attorney general's office that Florida State troopers had hindered people of color from arriving at the polling places due to the Oak Ridge Road checkpoint. . . . troopers conducted an unauthorized vehicle checkpoint within a few miles of a polling place in a predominantly African American neighborhood" (Civil Rights Commission 2001, 9). Several African-American voters who were stopped claimed that the checkpoint was on a major thruway to a predominantly African-American polling place and many testified that they felt intimidated. The head of the Florida State Troopers insisted that although the checkpoint was unauthorized, it was legal and should not have prevented anyone from voting.

Driver's License Registration   The commission report cited a problem with the program of registering people at state motor vehicle driver's license offices. Several people who claimed to have registered were not on the list of registered voters at the polling place and they were not allowed to vote.

Accessibility   Several people testified that polling places had failed to accommodate people with disabilities. Polling places were not wheelchair accessible.

Poll Closings   A few people complained that they were denied the opportunity to vote because the polling place closed early and refused to let them in. Some complained they were unable to vote because the place moved and had not notified them.

Rejected Ballots   Compared with white voters, a disproportionately greater number of votes cast by black voters were rejected and a disproportionately higher percentage of black voters were purged from the registration rolls. Some voters were purged from the rolls because they were not legally eligible to vote. However, a much greater percentage of the purged black voters were purged in error compared with the percentage of purged white voters. This meant that a much higher percentage of black voters who were legally eligible to vote were denied the right to vote.

> Statewide, . . . black voters were nearly 10 times more likely than non-black voters to have their ballots rejected. . . . However, poorly designed efforts to eliminate fraud, as well as sloppy and irresponsible implementation of those efforts, disenfranchise legitimate voters and can be a violation of the VRA [Voting Rights Act]. During the November 2000 election, Florida's overzealous efforts conducted under the guise of an anti-fraud campaign resulted in the inexcusable and patently unjust removal of disproportionate numbers of African American voters from Florida's voter registration rolls. (Civil Rights Commission 2001)

Congress responded to the commission's report by enacting the *Election Reform Act of 2002,* which required states to provide provisional ballots for voters erroneously purged from the rolls. Their votes will count after their eligibility is verified. In the November 2004 presidential election there were over 130,000 provisional ballots in the state of Ohio.

Discrimination in Employment

Title VII of the Civil Rights Act of 1964 prohibits discrimination in employment, but it did not provide a clear definition of employment discrimination. Initially, the Equal Employment Opportunity Commission (EEOC) had difficulty implementing this title. The agency was overwhelmed in its first few years. Summarizing the problem of this agency, Bullock and Lamb wrote:

> For most of its life, EEOC has proven inadequate to fulfill its mandate. Its problems have been numerous. First, EEOC adopted the mostly passive approach of complaint processing. From the beginning EEOC received far more complaints of discrimination than had been anticipated. . . . The EEOC did not have enough employees to investigate all the complaints, many of its employees were poorly trained, and the general disorganization of the Commission caused a rapid turnover in personnel and a great deal of tension. (1984, 96)

The initial strategy of the EEOC did not work. In its first few years of operation, it pursued employment discrimination on a case-by-case basis. It looked for cases of **individual discrimination** which occurs when an employer expresses a prejudice against minorities and acts on that prejudice by refusing to hire them. Victims of individual discrimination often do not know why they were denied a job.

Institutional discrimination occurs when the hiring practices of an organization are unrelated to job performance and operate to exclude a prospective employee on the basis of race, nationality, religion, or gender, even when the people in the organization are not prejudiced. There are many examples of institutional discrimination. For example, some firms had never advertised for a job in the local media but would hire new people on the basis of recommendations from current employees. Minorities who were unaware of job openings and who were unrelated to and had no contact with the firm's current employees were excluded from the hiring process. Another example of institutional discrimination occurred in local police departments which used height requirements, often over 6 feet in hiring police officers. Whereas white and black men passed the height standard, women were often excluded from police jobs. Women successfully challenged the standard because it was unrelated to job performance (cities could not demonstrate that taller people made better police) and it discriminated against women.

The *Griggs v. Duke Power Company* case (1971) was the first in which the Supreme Court recognized institutional discrimination. Black males had filed suit against the Duke Power Company on grounds that the company had engaged in discriminatory practices. The company had routinely excluded blacks from janitorial jobs. After the passage of the Civil Rights Act of 1964, the company changed its practice and required a high school diploma and a high score on an aptitude and personality test. Chief Justice Warren Burger acknowledged that employers must be able to hire the best-qualified people and to do so they needed hiring standards. However, hiring standards must be related to the job. They cannot discriminate on the basis of race or gender. For example, an employer must be able to give typing exams to hire the best-qualified secretary. The typing exam is related to the job because good secretaries must be good typists. However, a test that measures whether a person likes or dislikes golf is not relevant to a clerical job. If such a test excludes qualified racial minorities, then it is racially discriminatory and constitutes an illegal form of institutional discrimination.

The best way to detect institutional discrimination is to compare the proportion of minorities in a firm with the proportion of qualified minorities in the job market. If minorities constitute 10 percent of the job market but zero percent of the employees in the firm, then institutional discrimination is likely occurring. To avoid institutional discrimination the EEOC looks at statistical patterns. It requires employers to use standards that are validly related to job performance and to advertise in ways that encourage minority candidates to apply.

Affirmative Action

Many employers established **affirmative action** programs to combat institutional discrimination. Today affirmative action is controversial because it means different things to different people. Supporters see affirmative action as an antidiscrimination policy; opponents see it as a form of reverse discrimination. The problem with affirmative action is that it is not one thing. Affirmative action may have about five definitions.

1. Affirmative action means taking positive steps to hire qualified minorities. In many cases, firms discriminated against minorities by not even letting them know when there were job openings. Sometimes firms did not hire minorities because minorities never applied for the jobs, and they did not apply because the firm had a reputation for not hiring minorities. Affirmative action is a set of practices involving the advertisement of job openings in minority communities, the recruitment of minority candidates through professional associations, and the encouragement of minorities to apply for jobs. This type of affirmative action arose in the Johnson administration, as the president ordered firms receiving contracts from the federal government to take positive steps to recruit, hire, and promote qualified minorities.

2. Affirmative action means developing strategies and establishing timetables for hiring qualified minorities. Just encouraging minorities to apply for jobs had sometimes been ineffective. Firms considered developing long-range plans that included outreach strategies for recruiting minorities.

3. Affirmative action means hiring the minority individual if all other things are equal and minorities are underrepresented in the firm. A prime example of this form of affirmative action is the case of *Johnson v. Transportation Agency* (1987). In this case, women were concentrated in lower-paying clerical jobs in the Transportation Agency

of Santa Clara County in California. Diane Joyce was a clerk who had applied for a dispatcher job, operating a radio. She was told that she lacked experience working on the highway road crew and that this experience was a qualification for the job. Women had been barred from working on the road crew, in direct violation of the Civil Rights Act of 1964. This job requirement appeared arbitrary and irrelevant to the job. Nevertheless, Joyce applied for a road crew job to get the experience for the dispatcher job. She worked on the road crew for several years, occasionally as a substitute dispatcher. When a dispatcher position became available, she applied again. Several other people, including Paul Johnson, also applied. Paul Johnson had been a road yard clerk, who, like Joyce, had occasionally worked as a substitute dispatcher. He believed that he was the best-qualified person for the job; Diane Joyce believed that because of her clerical experience she was the best-qualified person. Each candidate appeared separately before an interview panel which gave Joyce a score of 73 and Johnson 75. Joyce contacted the director of affirmative action because there were no women on the interview panel, one panelist had commented on her wearing a skirt, and she believed the panel was biased against her. Joyce argued that the interview scores were assigned arbitrarily and that the candidates were equally qualified. The director made an affirmative action decision to give the job to Diane Joyce. Johnson sued the county Transportation Agency. The Supreme Court ruled in favor of the county's affirmative action decision.

4.   Affirmative action means establishing quotas or set-asides. A quota is a goal expressed as a percentage. For example, a university may set aside 16 percent of its freshmen openings for minority students—a 16 percent quota. A local government may set aside 10 percent of the dollar value of its contracts for minority contractors—a 10 percent quota.

5.   Finally, affirmative action has meant hiring minorities even if they are less qualified than other candidates. This is a controversial form of unbalanced preference, often referred to as reverse discrimination. The Supreme Court generally disallows quotas and unbalanced preferences.

The Bakke Decision and the Future of Affirmative Action

A discussion of affirmative action would be incomplete without a discussion of the *Bakke* decision—*University of California Board of Regents v. Bakke,* 1978. This was the first case in which the Supreme Court commented on affirmative action. This case involved a white male, Allen Bakke, who had been refused admission to the medical school at the University of California at Davis. He claimed that the medical school's affirmative action program was responsible for his rejection and sued on grounds that the school violated his civil rights. There were two controversial aspects of this case. First, the school had a dual admissions process: a regular admission and a special admission. Students rejected through the regular admissions process could apply through the special admission process which gave preference to minorities. Second, the school set aside 16 seats of a total of 100 freshmen seats for students to be admitted through the special admissions program. Justice Powell, writing for a divided court, rejected the medical school's affirmative action program. He was especially disturbed by the school's dual admissions process and agreed that the medical school's affirmative action program unfairly rejected Bakke. At the same time, he did not reject all forms of affirmative action. He used the Harvard University affirmative action program as a model of an acceptable policy.

Harvard had only one admissions program. It looked at each student individually and considered a range of factors in its admission decision. Along with tests scores and grade point averages, Harvard also examined candidates' attitudes toward medicine, the type of doctor they were likely to be, what type of experience they could bring into the classroom, the region they were from, and where they were likely to practice medicine. Harvard's affirmative action program also considered the race, ethnicity, and economic status of candidates. In short, the *Bakke* decision struck down the University of California Medical School's affirmative action program, but upheld the legality and constitutionality of many other forms of affirmative action.

The U.S. Supreme Court has issued several decisions on affirmative action, establishing guidelines on acceptable and unacceptable policies. It has allowed the use of quotas when they are used as a remedy for demonstrated and clear cases of discrimination. The recent campaigns against affirmative action would eliminate all forms under any circumstances. The antiaffirmative action laws passed in California outlaw even the modest affirmative action programs allowed in *Bakke*.

The University of Michigan Cases

The Court revisited the affirmative action issue and reaffirmed the *Bakke* decision in the summer of 2003 when it decided two separate cases involving the University of Michigan. *Gratz v. Bollinger* concerned the University of Michigan's undergraduate program, which used a formula based on a point system to determine admission into the university. Gratz, who was denied admission, sued Bollinger, the president of the university. In *Gratz,* the Court struck down the undergraduate program's use of race because it was not narrowly tailored enough to the problem it was designed to address and because it imposed too great a burden on non-minority students. The formula allocated 20 points to minority students in a system based on a total of 150 points—a system that was too expansive and gave too much weight to race.

In the second decision, *Grutter v. Bollinger,* the Court upheld the University of Michigan law school's use of race because it was much like the Harvard model in the *Bakke* case. In making admission decisions, the law school looked at test scores and grade point averages. It conceded that the best student is not necessarily the one with the highest test score or grade point average, but may be the candidate most passionate about the study of law or most enthusiastic about principles of justice. It looked at student backgrounds—school of origin, region, and income—and considered race along with these factors. It was committed to achieving a diverse student body for the purpose of an enhanced educational experience. The Court ruled that achieving diversity was a compelling purpose and that the University of Michigan law school's admissions process was narrowly tailored to achieve that goal.

The Conflict between Congress and the Supreme Court

In the 1950s the Supreme Court initiated government support for civil rights policies and continued this support throughout the 1960s and 1970s. By the 1980s, however, the Court began chipping away at civil rights policies. It limited the scope of Title IX, which prohibited gender discrimination in programs receiving federal funds. The Court interpreted this policy to mean that in a large organization like a university, the law applied only to that part of the organization receiving federal funds, not the entire organization. Congress responded to this decision with the passage of the Civil Rights Restoration Act of 1988, which applied Title IX to the entire organization. In 1989 the Court claimed that civil rights policies did not prohibit racial harassment on the job and it rejected the *Griggs* principle that prohibited institutional discrimination. Congress responded by passing the Civil Rights Act of 1991. This act prohibited racial harassment on the job and restored most of the principles determined in the *Griggs* decision. This principle required businesses with hiring policies having a discriminatory impact to demonstrate that the policies are necessary and nondiscriminatory. Congress continued to support civil rights policies into the 21st century.

→ *Women and Civil Rights*

Volumes have been written about women's rights. It is difficult to cover this issue in a single chapter and impossible in a small section, so that which follows is a short commentary on the subject. Whereas the women's rights movement was separate from the civil rights movement, the shift from the segregation regime to the fair play civil rights regime also impacted women's rights. During the segregation regime, women had been barred from voting, excluded from particular professions, denied property rights given to men, and subjected to wage discrimination.

Women and Job Discrimination

Women did not gain the right to vote until 1920, with the ratification of the Nineteenth Amendment. However, women continued to suffer exclusion from particular professions, gender segregation in the job market, and discrimination in wages. This treatment was supported by the dominant policy paradigm, the Supreme Court, and power arrangements.

The dominant policy paradigm was paternalism. *Paternalism* was the belief that women were not only different from men, but physically, emotionally, and intellectually inferior. It depicted women as the weaker sex who needed to be protected by men. This paradigm was reflected in major Supreme Court decisions pertaining to gender equity issues. Summarizing the legal status of women, James Foster and Susan Leeson wrote:

> In the view of many women's rights advocates in the nineteenth century, the legal condition of women was basically the same as that of slaves. Women lost both their legal identity and their property when they married. Under the common law doctrine of coverture, married women were treated as though they were legally dead. (1998, 580–81)

The 1873 case of *Bradwell v. Illinois* further illustrates this point. Myra Bradwell challenged a state of Illinois law that barred women from practicing law. With her husband, a judge, she edited and published the *Chicago Legal News,* a prestigious Midwestern law journal. When her husband died, she decided to practice law to support herself. Although she passed the Illinois bar examination, she was prevented from practicing law because she was a woman. Bradwell took her case to the Supreme Court which upheld the Illinois law. Justice Joseph Bradley reflected the paternalistic paradigm in this decision:

> Man is, or should be, woman's protector and defender. The natural and proper timidity and delicacy, which belongs to the female sex evidently, unfits it for many of the occupations of civil life. The constitution of the family organization, which is founded in the divine ordinance, as well as in the nature of things, indicates the domestic sphere as that which properly belongs to the domain and functions of womanhood. The harmony, not to say identity, of interests and views which belong, or should belong, to the family institution is

repugnant to the idea of a woman adopting a distinct and independent career from that of her husband. (quoted in Foster and Leeson 1998, 583)

Expressing the assumptions of this paradigm, members of the Court concluded that for the sake of the family, women must not have careers independent from their husbands.

The Paradigm Shift in Women's Issues

This view of women began to change during World War II as women moved into traditionally male factory jobs, replacing men who went off to war. The paradigm shift was helped by a dramatic increase in books on women's issues and in women's rights organizations during the 1960s and 1970s. This new literature and the women's movement assaulted the paternalist paradigm and promoted equal rights for women. This shift was helped further by the women's rights movement.

Congress enacted a number of women's rights policies. It passed the *Equal Pay Act of 1963*, which prohibited employers from paying women less than men for doing the same job, with the same qualifications, credentials, and experience. It enacted Title VII of the 1964 Civil Rights Act, which prohibited gender discrimination in the job market, and Title IX of the 1972 act, which forbade gender discrimination in programs receiving federal funding.

The Court has changed its position on women's rights. It promotes equal treatment and fair play policies, and no longer tolerates the exclusion of women from key professions. The number of women in those professions has increased dramatically.

One of the most controversial gender equality cases is *Virginia v. United States* (1996). This case involved the prestigious Virginia Military Institute, which had long excluded women. The state justified the exclusion by arguing that it provided a separate but equal military academy for women. The Court rejected the separate but equal argument and ordered the state to admit women to the Virginia Military Institute.

➔ Civil Rights and Disabling Conditions

In the early 1970s Congress began addressing the issue of discrimination against people with disabling conditions. The *Rehabilitation Act of the 1973* prohibited firms receiving federal funds from discriminating on the basis of these conditions. The *Americans with Disabilities Act of 1991* prohibited discrimination against individuals with disabilities and required public agencies and employers to make reasonable changes to accommodate them. This act has been used to challenge employers who have fired employees exclusively because of a disability or illness. For example, this law prohibits an employer from firing an employee simply because the employee has AIDS. It has also required local governments to make public buildings and the curbs on public streets wheelchair accessible.

➔ Civil Rights and Sexual Orientation

Today the most contested and divisive public issue involves the rights of gays and lesbians. This issue moves civil rights policies into the realm of moral policies and embroils the nation in what some religious conservatives call the cultural wars, the battle for the soul of the nation. There are two major aspects of this issue: marriage and special rights.

Gay and lesbian marriage is a hotly burning issue. Although marriage has been a state issue, it has flared up on the national agenda. In 1993 the supreme courts of Hawaii and Alaska decided that the banning of gay and lesbian marriages in their states violated the equal rights provisions of their state constitutions. In reaction to the actions taken in these two states, Congress in 1996 enacted the *Defense of Marriage Act,* which defined marriage as a union of a man and a woman, not of two people of the same sex. It also declared that states do not have to recognize same-sex marriages from another state. Of course, the full faith and credit clause of the Constitution—which requires that each state recognize marriages from other states—may soon invalidate the act. Also, Hawaii and Alaska changed their state constitutions to limit marriage specifically to heterosexual couples. Over 35 states have enacted laws or amended their constitutions to ban same-sex marriages. In the November 2004 election 11 states had proposals on the ballot to ban same sex-marriage. Every proposal passed.

Opposition to same-sex marriages has been fierce. A number of religious and political leaders condemned the Massachusetts Supreme Court decision to allow same-sex marriages. Many opponents of same-sex marriage cite the Bible as the source of their opposition. The Massachusetts Catholic Conference issued a statement calling the court ruling in that state a tragedy and urged people to demand a constitutional amendment banning gay and lesbian marriages. President George W. Bush weighed in on the side of the religious organizations defining marriage as a union between a man and a woman and favored a constitutional amendment promoting this definition.

Gay and lesbian organizations have defined the same-sex marriage issue as a civil right. To them banning gay and lesbian marriages amounts to denying to a minority the rights given to the majority. Most states today explicitly prohibit same-sex marriages, but about seven states have legalized domestic partner health benefits.

Another issue involving gays and lesbians is their right to enjoy other forms of government protection, especially protection against violence and employment discrimination. On one side of the issue are those who believe that government should protect the civil rights of gays and lesbians. On the other side are those who believe that gays and lesbians should not constitute a minority group requiring government protection. Proponents of this view believe that when the government provides special protection for gay and lesbian citizens, it inadvertently promotes and encourages gay and lesbian lifestyles.

A good example of this issue took place in the state of Colorado where in the early 1990s a few cities passed laws protecting the civil rights of gays and lesbians. In reaction to these laws, conservative groups launched a statewide campaign for a constitutional amendment that would prohibit any state agency or subdivision from enacting or enforcing "any statute, regulation, ordinance, or policy whereby homosexual, lesbian, or bisexual orientation, conduct, practices, or relationships would constitute or otherwise be the basis of or entitle any person or class of persons to have or claim any minority status . . . or claim of discrimination" (*Romer v. Evans* 1996). This constitutional amendment thus prohibited cities from protecting the civil rights of its gay and lesbian residents. The amendment was challenged in federal court in *Romer v. Evans* and in 1996 the U.S. Supreme Court struck it down on grounds that it violated the equal protection clause of the Fourteenth Amendment.

Since that time, a number of states have passed special hate crime laws protecting gays and lesbians from violence. Michigan recently passed an antidiscrimination law protecting the rights of gays and lesbians.

Summary

There have been several civil rights policy regimes: the slave, Reconstruction, segregation, and fair play civil rights regimes. The Civil War destroyed the slave regime and gave rise to the short-lived Reconstruction regime. This regime collapsed when the North withdrew its troops and the former plantation owners reemerged and captured state governments and exercised considerable influence in Congress. These owners were largely responsible for establishing the segregation regime, promoting ideas of black inferiority, and disenfranchising poor blacks and poor whites. The segregation regime remained in place up to the 1960s.

Several factors contributed to the demise of this regime: the collapse of the sharecropping system, the mass movement of African Americans into urban areas, World War II against fascism, the cold war with international communism and the political war to offer American democracy as an alternative to communism, the civil rights movement, and an avalanche of antiracist literature. These factors acted as stressors, sufficient to collapse the segregation regime and allow the emergence of the fair play rights regime. This regime introduced a flood of civil rights policies, most notably, the Civil Rights Acts of 1964, Voting Rights Act of 1965, the Fair Housing Act of 1968, and many Supreme Court cases.

The civil rights movement had a spillover effect. It contributed to the passage of the Immigration and Naturalization Act of 1965 and encouraged other movements including the American Indian Movement and the women's movement. These movements produced other policy regime changes.

Several factors contributed to the rise of the women's rights regime: the labor shortage of World War II, the movement of women into jobs that were traditionally men-only jobs, the rise of feminist literature during the 1960s, and the feminist social movement. Civil rights laws incorporated women's rights, especially Title VII of the 1964 law, which prohibited employment discrimination based on gender, and Title IX of the Education Act of 1972, which prohibited gender discrimination in programs receiving federal funds. To a large extent, the rights movements of women, African Americans, Native Americans, and many others are part of the larger contemporary civil rights regime.

This regime has expanded the civil rights protection for minorities regardless of race, religion, nationality, gender, sexual orientation, or physical conditions. Despite the protection of everyone under civil rights policies, disputes continue. Battles rage over protecting the rights of gays and lesbians, and continue to be fought over affirmative action. These fights are likely to continue.

Review Questions

1. Discuss the factors that explain the disintegration of the slave regime and the formation of the Reconstruction regime.
2. Discuss the stressors that contributed to the destruction of the segregation regime and the formation of the fair play civil rights regime.
3. Discuss the similarities and differences in the civil rights struggle for women and for African Americans.
4. What is the difference between individual and institutional discrimination and how has the EEOC responded to both?

5. What is affirmative action? Why is this policy so contentious? What does the Supreme Court say about this policy?
6. What civil rights conflicts are likely to continue well into the 21st century? Why?

Select Websites

This is the Website for the U.S. Civil Rights Commission.
http://www.uscer.gov

This is the Equal Employment Opportunities Commission's Website. It posts up-to-date information on employment discrimination laws and regulations.
http://www.eeoc.gov

This is the Website of the National Association for the Advancement of Colored People (NAACP).
http://www.naacp.org

This is the official Website for the National Organization for Women (NOW).
http://www.now.org

Key Terms

affirmative action
Civil Rights Commission
Congress on Racial Equality (CORE)
Equal Employment Opportunity
    Commission (EEOC)
Fair Employment Practices Commission
    (FEPC)
Fifteenth Amendment
Fourteenth Amendment
gerrymandering
individual discrimination

institutional discrimination
National Association for the Advancement
    of Colored People (NAACP)
separate but equal doctrine
sharecropping system
Southern Christian Leadership Conference
    (SCLC)
Student Nonviolent Coordinating
    Committee (SNCC)
Thirteenth Amendment

PART III

Protective and Competitive Regulatory Policy

CHAPTER 8

Environmental Protection Policy

Environmental protection policy is about protecting air, water, land, and other natural re-sources. It is about the conservation and preservation of nature; the establishment of city, state, and national parks; the creation of wildlife reserves; the regulation of hunting and fish-ing; and the restoration of forests and soil. It is about removing hazardous substances from the air people breathe, from the water people drink, from the homes people sleep in, and from the earth people live on.

Environmental issues have been around as long as people had established farms, do-mesticated animals, and built cities. Early environmental issues included concerns about the disposal and recycling of animal waste, obtaining safe drinking water, eliminating human waste, and establishing healthy surroundings. Some of these environmental issues were a mat-ter of life and death, particularly at a time when diseases associated with poor environments had decimated urban populations.

Most environmental historians have identified three waves or generations of environ-mental policies (Dowie 1996).

This text takes a different approach, identifying and focusing on three environmental policy regimes, characterized by a dominant paradigm and definite power arrangements: in-dustrial (1800–1900), conservationist (1900–1970), and environmental (1970–present).

The industrial paradigm assumed that the earth was dead matter with unlimited re-sources that needed to be exploited for progress and that science and technology were always progressive and beneficial. Farming, mining, and industrial interests substantially dominated this regime and there were few environmental policies.

The conservationist paradigm retained many of the assumptions of the industrial par-adigm, except it maintained that the earth was to be exploited in a wise and manageable way. Industrial, farming, mining, and timber interests worked with conservationists and preserva-tionists, but still dominated the policy-making process. Environmental policies consisted pri-marily of establishing national parks, assisting timber interests in managing their forests, helping cattle owners manage grazing land, and other conservationist projects. Industrial in-terests used their power to keep clear air and clean water issues off the political agenda.

The environmental paradigm assumed that the earth had limited resources and that it was finite, interconnected to ecosystems full of life, and fragile. Poisoning one sector of the environment impacted the other sectors and eventually poisoned people. Environmentalist organizations challenged the power of industries and produced policies concerning clean air, clean water, pesticides, and hazardous wastes.

❖ The Industrial Policy Regime

At the beginning of the 20th century the Industrial Revolution was having its most severe im-pact on the environment. This revolution meant the emergence of mass assembly-line pro-duction involving thousands of people. It produced sprawling urban areas with populations well over a million. It created hundreds of skyscrapers, millions of new automobiles, and mil-lions of new household products and other things. Rapid industrial expansion had environ-mental consequences. Industries had a rapacious appetite, consuming resources at levels unimagined in the past century; relentlessly devouring land, guzzling fossil fuel, and using up natural resources such as timber, copper, iron, and tin at unbelievable rates. Industries by themselves created new and more severe air and water pollution problems. Territorial expan-sion, population explosion, urban sprawl, soil exhaustion, insatiable appetites for commodities (household appliances, automobiles, clothing, etc.)—all accompanied the Industrial Revolution and impacted the environment. By the beginning of the 20th century, agricultural areas were overworked, wilderness areas had shrunk, forests were dwindling, and natural geological features unique to North America were threatened. Natural resources and game animals were depleted. A number of animal species were hunted to the brink of extinction. The bison that once thundered across the plains were nearly silent. A number of species of birds had disappeared. Urban areas languished under blankets of suffocating smoke. Rivers and streams suffered from industrial runoff.

The Industrial Paradigm and Policies

The industrial paradigm was the dominant perspective of this period. It had a number of assumptions about the environment and government. First, this paradigm assumed that the earth had unlimited resources and an unfathomable capacity to replenish itself and to absorb waste. Second, the paradigm assumed that pollution was the cost of progress. People saw thick smoke covering cities as an indication of a booming economy: more air pollution meant more people employed and a prosperous economy.

Third, industrialists had tremendous faith in science and technology. They believed scientists could solve any problem, that any advancement in technology indicated progress, and that all chemicals were good for humankind. This faith in science has also characterized the conservationist paradigm and has persisted throughout much of the 20th century.

Fourth, industrialists assumed that state and local governments, not the federal government, were responsible for pollution policies. Industrialists assumed that it was inappropriate and unconstitutional for the federal government to regulate pollution. Many of these assumptions persisted throughout the conservationist period.

Enlightenment philosophers contributed to this paradigm. For example, Sir Isaac Newton often used metaphors of the earth as dead, as a machine, or as a clock. John Locke considered unused land as wasted land. Descartes referred to the earth as dead and animals as soulless.

The industrial paradigm covered the 19th century, an era preoccupied with Manifest Destiny, the idea that the nation was destined to cover the entire continent from the Atlantic Ocean to the Pacific Ocean, seizing land, annexing territory, and building cities. Industrialists keep environmental issues off the public agenda, except for issues harmless to industry such as eliminating animal waste from city streets.

⇢ Conservation Policy Regime

The first real environmental policy regime emerged out of two movements at the turn of the century: the conservationist and preservationist movements. Both conservationists and preservationists were critical of the excesses of the industrial policy regime. Conservationists were committed to the use of natural resources, but also to seeing that they were replaced. Preservationists were committed to a hands-off policy toward the environment. The whole idea of conserving or preserving the environment represented a policy paradigm shift. For the early 20th century, these ideas were revolutionary.

Conservationists were critical of the excesses of industrialism, of what they believed to be the senseless and destructive way industries exploited nature and depleted natural resources. Conservationists advocated the wise use of nature. For example, **George Perkins Marsh** documented in *Man and Nature* (1864) the catastrophic effect of human destructiveness on nature. He insisted that when all the trees on a hilly forest were cut down, rain would erode the soil and turn the hills into barren rock. Marsh believed that the problem was not the use of trees, but the senseless and ruthless exploitation of nature. Conservationists advocated the wise management of land: limiting its use, replacing cut forests, preventing soil erosion, and other similar measures.

Preservationists believed in the complete protection of nature, pristine wilderness areas, and animals in danger of extinction. They lobbied for the establishment of national parks. **John Muir**, one of the founders of the Sierra Club, is a good example of a preservationist. He wrote books extolling the inherent beauty and value of nature. He believed in the spiritual aspect of nature: Nature was food for the soul and we need it just as we need bread. In *The Yosemite,* Muir wrote, "Everybody needs beauty as well as bread, places to play in and pray in, where Nature may heal and cheer and give strength to body and soul alike" (quoted in Clarke and Cortner 2002, 113).

Occasionally, conservationists and preservationists clashed, particularly over the commercial use of virgin parks, which preservationists opposed. For example, conservationist Gifford Pinchot and preservationist John Muir fought over the grazing of sheep in national forests. Muir believed that the sheep would destroy the forest; Pinchot believed that allowing sheep grazing was a prudent use of the forest.

Some of the early environmentalist organizations were preservationists. One of the oldest is the Sierra Club, founded in 1892, which campaigned to get the federal government to designate select wilderness areas as **national parks**. Once the parks were established, the Sierra Club operated to protect them and to support federal management of them. At the beginning to the 20th century, it vigorously protested efforts to reduce the size of Yosemite National Park. It fought to establish **national forests**, persuade the federal government to purchase and preserve the redwood trees in California, designate the Grand Canyon as a national park, and create Glacier National Park and many others.

Another preservationist organization, the National Audubon Society, was established in 1905 with the merger of several local organizations outraged over the senseless slaughter of birds. It campaigned for the passage of laws protecting birds and their natural habitat. It secured the passage of the *Federal Migratory Bird Treaty Act of 1918* and supported efforts to prevent the extinction of endangered birds.

The conservationist Izaak Walton League was formed in 1922 by a group of some 50 fishermen, hunters, and sportsmen concerned about the decimation of populations of fish, deer, ducks, and other game animals. The league advocated the protection of wildlife and the establishment of wildlife refuges. In 1936 the National Wildlife Federation was founded by conservationists. It campaigned to educate people about wildlife and conservation.

There were other environmental organizations during the first few decades of the 20th century, both preservationists and conservationists, although conservationist interests prevailed (see Table 8.1).

Industry-Dominated Conservationist Regime

Although there were several environmental organizations in existence, environmental policies were restricted to land management, and land was managed in ways beneficial to industry.

TABLE 8.1	
Select Environmental Organizations	
Name	**Year Established**
Sierra Club	1892
National Audubon Society	1905
National Parks and Conservation Association	1919
Izaak Walton League	1922
Wilderness Society	1935
National Wildlife Federation	1936
Environmental Defense Fund	1967
Friends of the Earth	1970
National Resources Defense Council	1970
Greenpeace (worldwide)	1971

Industry substantially dominated environmental policies during the first half of the 20th century. Its power was evident in four major policy areas: land management, air pollution, water pollution, and pesticides.

Land Management

Most of the land management policies emerged from the conservationist and preservationist movements of the turn of the century. These policies included the establishment of national parks, monuments, and forests and the creation of several federal land management agencies. The Bureau of Reclamation was created in 1902, the U.S. Forest Service in 1905, and the National Park Service in 1916. A number of national parks were created: Yosemite in 1891, Mount Rainier in 1899, and the Grand Canyon in 1908. President Theodore Roosevelt played a major role in getting land designated as national parks. Most federal policies dealt with conservation.

Political scientist George Gonzalez held that business interests dominated the process of making land management policy and that economic elites often played key roles in conservationist and preservationist organizations. One example was Gifford Pinchot who not only had training in forestry, but also had close ties to the economic elite such as George Washington Vanderbilt. He managed Vanderbilt's extensive forests in North Carolina and the landholdings of other railroad leaders. Pinchot's term as director of the Department of Agriculture's Forestry Division illustrated the direct connection between conservationist policy and economic interests, as the Forestry Division assisted the timber industry in managing its land. Gonzalez concluded that "a policy network, led by economic elites, intervened directly to mold the profession of forestry into a discipline that served the needs of the U.S. timber industry" (2001, 26, 41).

A number of business interests were active in working with conservationists and in shaping land management policies, including the American Cattle Growers Association, the National Wool Growers Association, the National Lumber Manufacturers Association, and the Forest Industries Council. Conservationists supported the lumber industry's cutting trees in national forests, so long as care was taken to plant new trees. Cattle and sheep growers sometimes formed alliances with conservationists who supported the opening of federal land for cattle and sheep grazing, so long as the land was managed wisely. Agricultural interests and farm organizations later worked closely with federal agencies on soil conservation (Kraft 1996).

A number of conservation policies emerged in the 1930s. The Civilian Conservation Corps (CCC), established in 1933, was designed to conserve the national forests and parks and provided employment during the depression. Many CCC workers planted trees in national forests and parks. The Federal Grazing Service, created in 1934, worked with cattle interests to regulate grazing on federal land. The Soil Conservation Service (1935) worked primarily with farmers to carry out a national soil conservation policy. President Franklin Roosevelt played a key role in developing these policies. There were other minor developments in land policy throughout the 1940s and 1950s.

Air Pollution Policy

For the first half of the 20th century, the federal government avoided the issue of air pollution. Industrial interests and the industrial paradigm kept it off the national agenda. But air pollution did emerge as a local issue; a few local governments had begun passing air pollution ordinances as early as the 1880s.

Air pollution was a visible problem, especially in cities with steel mills. Blast furnaces often accidentally released massive pillars of black smoke into the open air. The black, dirty smoke damaged homes and soiled clothes. It caused serious respiratory problems. It got so bad in cities like Chicago, Pittsburgh, St. Louis, and Gary that residents raised the issue with their city councils. A number of these cities passed dirty air ordinances: Chicago in 1881 and Los Angeles in 1905 (Switzer 1994, 194). However, most of these ordinances failed to address the issue of industrial pollution.

Political scientist Matthew Crenson demonstrated that industry was the primary source of air pollution.

> All three steel mills in northwest Indiana in 1966 were located in either Gary or East Chicago. They accounted for almost 70 per cent of the particulate pollutants, about 56 percent of the nitrogen oxide emissions, and about 20 per cent of sulfur oxide emissions. . . . Emissions from East Chicago refineries accounted for about 44 per cent of all hydrocarbons released in northwest Indiana. (1971, 39)

East Chicago's city council passed an air pollution abatement ordinance in 1949. Representatives from East Chicago's Chamber of Commerce, local industries, and businesses played an active role in writing the ordinance. The ordinance required the inspection of new industrial facilities and would fine a mill $300 for blast furnace slips. This was probably the most aggressive air pollution ordinance in the industry up to 1970. The pollution problem in Gary, Indiana was worse than in East Chicago, but Gary had no pollution control ordinance. The presence of U.S. Steel had a silencing impact on local policy makers who kept the air pollution issue off the local agenda out of fear of a hostile reaction from the corporation. Thus, most local air pollution policies failed to address industrial sources of pollution.

Federal policy makers began to pay some attention to the issue of air pollution in the 1950s and 1960s when Congress passed two laws that allocated money for air pollution research.

- *Air Pollution Control Act of 1955*
- *Clean Air Act of 1963*

Two additional acts provided money to study the feasibility of establishing federal emission standards for motor vehicles and encouraged the establishment of state, local, and regional air pollution programs.

- *Motor Vehicles Air Pollution Control Act of 1965*
- *Air Quality Act of 1967*

These laws gave the federal government no power to regulate pollution (Jones 1976).

That industries continued to dominate the environmental policy regime up to 1970 was demonstrated in the politics behind the passage of the Air Quality Act of 1967. In congressional hearings, a few scientists testified that there was a connection between air pollution and lung disease. When the Johnson administration proposed an amendment requiring industrial polluters to disclose what they were emitting into the atmosphere, representatives of major industries such as the chemical, coal, paper, and electric industries converged on Congress urging policy makers to reject the proposal (Jones 1976). The amendment was quashed. Beyond the federal government encouraging research and requesting state and local governments to take action, there was little federal involvement in air pollution regulation.

Water Pollution Policy

Water pollution policies were similar to air pollution policies. For the first half of the 20th century, the industrial paradigm and industry operated to keep water pollution off the national policy agenda, but there were some early national efforts. Congress passed the *Refuse Act of 1899,* which prohibited the dumping of solid waste into commercial waterways (Switzer 1994, 170). Established in 1912, the U.S. Public Health Service also began to examine water and air pollution issues.

In the 1920s the Izaak Walton League published a report documenting the water pollution problem. Summarizing the report and its impact, Jacqueline Switzer wrote:

> The Izaak Walton League was among the first to draw attention to the contamination problem, noting in a report published in the late 1920s that 85 percent of the nation's waterways were polluted and that only 30 percent of all municipalities treated their wastes, many of them inadequately. Industrial interests like the American Petroleum Institute, the American Iron and Steel Institute, and the Manufacturing Chemists Association insisted, "streams were nature's sewers" and convinced key legislators industrial dumping posed no environmental threat. (1994, 172)

The Izaak Walton League report pointed to several water pollution problems. Most local governments did not have waste treatment facilities and those that did exist were inadequate. Industrial waste was a major source of water pollution, but, as with air pollution, representatives and experts representing industrial interests appeared before Congress to discredit the water pollution report and succeeded in convincing national policy makers that water pollution was not a serious problem.

Nonetheless, in 1948 Congress passed the *Water Pollution Control Act,* which provided a small amount of money to begin researching the water pollution problem and to provide a little assistance to local governments with sewage treatment (Switzer 1994, 172). In the 1960s Congress provided money to assist local governments with water pollution. The *Clean Water*

Restoration Act of 1967 allocated $3.5 billion to assist local governments in the construction of sewage treatment plants. From 1948 until 1972, there were few federal water pollution policies. The federal government provided some financial assistance to local governments to study the problem, but it made no direct effort to stop water pollution.

Pesticide Policy

Pesticides were not a problem in the early part of the 20th century. Most of the early pesticides were made with arsenic, copper, lead, manganese, or zinc, with little concern about their hazards. The big issue was whether pesticides were potent or not. Agricultural and chemical interests, dominating this policy area, worked closely with the U.S. Department of Agriculture. These interests secured the passage of laws that ensured the potency of pesticides, but did not regulate their safety.

With the development of organic chemicals, the situation with pesticides changed during World War II. These chemicals had a carbon base that bonded to plant and animal tissue. **DDT** (dichloro-diphenyl-trichloro-ethane) was a popular organic pesticide and was instrumental in reducing the population of malaria-bearing mosquitoes. It was effective in killing lice and ending the postwar typhus epidemic in Europe. After the war, army officials sprayed DDT to eliminate all sorts of pests, including flies. They sprayed it on everything including their own soldiers. Everyone assumed that these pesticides were safe. The only regulation in place required that a dye be added to the pesticide to prevent its confusion with flour. The regulation was prompted by an incident in which a farmer had accidentally mixed his pesticide with flour (Wargo 1996). The Department of Agriculture was primarily responsible for the regulation of pesticides up to 1970. However, this department largely served farming interests and focused more on crop yields and pesticide potency than on safety.

⟶ Environmental Policy Regime Change

The environmental policy regime changed in 1970. The conservationist regime disintegrated and a new environmental policy regime emerged. Power arrangements shifted from industry to environmental interests. A new environmental paradigm replaced the old conservation paradigm. A new federal agency, the Environmental Protection Agency, was created, and a series of new environmental policies were enacted.

Stressors

Several enabling events or stressors impacted the old policy regime. In 1969 the Cuyahoga River in Cleveland, Ohio, burst into flames. This event stunned the nation and made the public much more aware of environmental problems. In that same year, an oil spill off the coast of California near Santa Cruz proved to be an environmental catastrophe, killing hundreds of fish and animals. These events dramatized environmental problems, captured media attention, and raised the visibility of pollution issues. Other stressors included the intellectual assault on the old industrial paradigm and the emergence of the environmental social movement.

A barrage of environmental studies bombarded the old conservationist paradigm. The single most influential study was written by **Rachel Carson**. Her book *Silent Spring,* first published in 1962, explained the pesticide problem in laymen's language. With a writing style that was easy to understand, Carson summarized the research on the toxic chemicals. She documented cases in which pesticides caused the disintegration of liver tissue, the destruction of kidneys, and the breakdown of the central nervous system, producing violent convulsions and death in people. She explained how organic chemicals bonded to carbon molecules and to plant and animal tissues and accumulated with more chemical exposure. She illustrated how these chemicals, once introduced to the environment, tended to remain there for a long time and tended to move up the food chain and poison people.

Carson demonstrated that the situation with pesticides was critical and growing worse, as the manufacturing and use of pesticides was increasing astronomically. At the end of World War II, the chemical industry produced about 100 million pounds of pesticides; by 1960 it was producing over 600 million pounds (Carson 1962/1994, 17).

The chemical industry attacked Carson's work as unscientific and invalid. President Kennedy put together a blue ribbon panel of experts to examine its conclusions. The panel supported and confirmed Carson's conclusions. They blasted the chemical industry for its disregard of the evidence and its attempt to discredit Carson (Gore 1994 xvii–xviii). Carson's book and the scholarly community that supported it dealt a critical blow to the old industrial paradigm.

Other studies continued the assault on the conservationist and industrial paradigms. For example, in 1966 Kenneth Boulding published his classic article "The Economics of the Coming Spaceship Earth." He assailed most of the assumptions of the old paradigm—that the earth had inexhaustible resources, unlimited space for waste disposal, and regenerative abilities (Boulding 1966). Like the writers of other environmental studies, Boulding concluded that the people of the earth, like people on a spaceship, must be concerned about the disposal of waste and the overuse of resources, or they would end up without any resources and buried in waste.

In 1970 Ralph Nader's study group published *Vanishing Air* (Esposito 1970) which documented the hazards of air pollution. It presented data demonstrating an association between high respiratory-related morbidity and mortality rates and high levels of air pollution. In short, air pollution makes people sick and die. The study identified the major sources of air pollution and pointed out the costs of pollution in terms of lives lost, health costs, and property damage. The study was severely critical of automobile producers, steel industries, electrical power companies, and other industries which it implicated as major producers of air pollution. *Vanishing Air* and other studies not only attacked the old paradigm, but also presented compelling evidence of a substantial environmental crisis, redefined the air pollution problem, offered alternative policy solutions, and contributed to the formation of a new environmental policy paradigm.

The Environmental Social Movement and Power Shifts

The most critical stressor was the environmental movement. This movement grew rapidly and challenged corporate power. Membership in older environmental organizations, such as the Sierra Club and the Wilderness Society, increased sharply. New, more aggressive environmental organizations were established, including the Environmental Defense Fund (1967), the Council on Economic Priorities (1969), and, a year later, the Center for Science in the Public Interest, Citizens for a Better Environment, Environmental Action, Friends of the Earth, the League of Conservative Voters, and the National Resource Defense (Switzer 1994).

This dramatic increase in the size and activities of environmental organizations signaled a social movement. This movement involved teach-ins, Earth Day celebrations, and demonstrations. It raised the visibility of environmental issues and promoted the new environmental paradigm which changed public thinking about the environment. According to Gallup polls, environmental issues were not mentioned as problems between 1967 and 1969, but in the spring of 1970, the environment was ranked as the second most critical problem (just after the Vietnam War) and was considered an important issue by well over 50 percent of respondents (Switzer 1994, 15).

Environmental groups challenged corporate interests. The Environmental Protection Agency (EPA) was created. The new environmental policy regime ushered in a series of legislative acts in several areas of environmental policy such as clean air, clean water, pesticides, and hazardous waste disposal.

Clean Air Policy

The Clean Air Act of 1970 was probably one of the most important environmental policies of the 20th century. This act identified two major sources of air pollution: mobile and stationary sources. This act set air pollution emission standards for automobiles, requiring a 90 percent reduction of the 1970 level of automobile emission of nitrogen oxide by the 1976 automobile model and a 90 percent reduction of carbon monoxide and hydrocarbons by the 1975 model. This act established national ambient air quality standards. It gave states the responsibility for establishing plans to achieve these standards. It authorized the EPA to monitor and amend these plans, to seek injunctions to stop the emissions of pollution that endangered public health, and to impose fines on those who knowingly violated clean air policy.

The *Clean Air Act of 1977* amended the 1970 act. The amended act was the result of a compromise between industry and environmental interests. The automobile industry could not make the 1975–76 deadlines on pollution standards, which were initially extended for a year by the EPA. By 1977, however, the country was experiencing a shortage of petroleum and showing signs of a recession. Public attention shifted away from environmental issues as people became concerned about jobs. The United Auto Workers sided with the automobile industry in relaxing the air pollution regulations. At the same time, environmental interests continued to dominate the environmental policy regime and supported a modest expansion of clean air policy. Overall, the 1977 act represented an incremental adjustment to the 1970 act, as some rules were loosened and others tightened.

Assault on the Clean Air Policy Regime

In the early 1980s the Reagan administration assaulted the new environmental policy regime on several fronts. First, Reagan officials attacked regulatory policies on ideological grounds. They blamed the economic problems of the late 1970s and early 1980s, particularly high inflation and unemployment rates, on what they claimed were overly aggressive government regulations.

Second, Reagan recruited top-level administrators who had a reputation for their hostility to EPA regulations. Examples of these officials include Ann Gorsuch Burford, a former Colorado state legislator who was appointed EPA director; Rita Lavell, a public relations specialists from Aerojet General; Kathleen Bennett, a lobbyist for the American Paper Institute; and Robert Perry, an attorney for Exxon Corporation (Tolchin and Tolchin 1983; Vig 1984, 87).

Third, the Reagan administration cut the EPA's research and development budget by over 45 percent from 1981 to 1984 (Vig 1984). These cuts made it difficult for the EPA to conduct its own independent tests and made the agency more dependent on industry for accurate information.

Finally, Reagan issued an executive order requiring that all proposed changes in EPA rules be submitted to the Office of Management and Budget for review and that all new regulations undergo an impact and cost-benefit analysis (Tolchin and Tolchin 1983; Vig and Kraft 1984). This new requirement had a chilling effect on new regulations. Heartened by Reagan's regulatory ideology, industry groups formed the Clean Air Working Group to coordinate their national lobbying efforts and their attack on the EPA (Bryner 1993, 86)

Reagan and the industrial interests failed to account for the environmental paradigm. They made a number of miscalculations about public opinion and environmental organizations. They assumed that public attention had shifted to economic issues, that people were no longer concerned about clean air, and that environmental organizations had flared up but burnt out. They did not consider the enduring effect of the environmental paradigm: People now believed in the necessity for environmental regulations.

Reagan's assault on environmental regulations incited public wrath and energized environmental organizations which mobilized and counterattacked. They formed the National Clean Air Coalition to lobby for stronger clean air legislation. Members of this coalition included a number of environmental organizations, medical associations such as the American Lung Association, religious organizations, and labor unions, particularly the United Steelworkers Union (Bryner 1993, 81). The result of this counterattack was that by the late 1980s, many of the antienvironmental administrators were removed, many budget cuts restored, and many environmental policies were strengthened. By the end of the decade, the EPA had issued additional automobile emissions regulations that removed lead from gasoline.

The New Politics of the Clean Air Act of 1990

The passage of the Clean Air Act of 1990 illustrated the powerful and persistent influence of the environmental paradigm and the dynamics of the conflict between environmental and industrial interests. Most studies of environmental policies suggest that policy making in this area involved an environmental issue network and a pluralist political process, characterized by a balance of power between environmental and industrial interests. However, industrial and business organizations adopted the environmental paradigm and played a much stronger role in shaping the Clean Air Act of 1990 than the pluralist or issue network models would suggest.

In the late 1980s major corporate leaders had begun expressing concerns over state environmental policies. A number of states had established strict regulations for the chemical composition of paint, for additives in gasoline, and for automobile emissions. Corporate leaders expressed concerns over the patchwork of strict state regulations. A General Motors official said that "if auto manufacturers are forced to respond to a patchwork of different emission standards throughout the nation production, distribution and sales of vehicles will become increasingly complex and costly to customers" (Gonzalez 2001, 97). This patchwork of emission standards amounted to "a legal balkanization threat" that industry could not afford to ignore. A chemical industry official said, "I'm arguing for a more assertive federal government in terms of preemption issues and having the guts to say that in certain areas it makes sense to have national environmental laws" (Gonzalez 2001, 97). Corporate leaders had learned that total opposition to environmental regulations during the environmental policy regime was simply not feasible. Many industrial organizations promoted specific provisions of the Clean Air Act of 1990. Illustrating this point is the following observation:

> The House subcommittee also drafted the final legislation's language on reformulated gasoline (Title II). The key aspects of this provision were crafted by the oil industry. It calls for the sale of so-called clean gasoline in the nine most polluted cities. . . . The legislation set gasoline emission standards for the gasoline sold in these nine areas, but the oil industry would determine how to meet these standards. (Gonzalez 2001, 107)

Environmentalists had opposed this language, as they preferred regulation of gasoline content to ensure cleaner-burning gas that would further reduce smog-creating automobile emissions. However, the petroleum industry opposed the regulation of gasoline additives and the industry-crafted regulations prevailed.

One of the most controversial provisions of the 1990 act was the trade in pollution credits, a provision written by the Environmental Defense Fund. Under this provision a polluter who reduced emissions below a specified level earned pollution credits. Firms that exceeded pollution limits could purchase credits from firms that had earned them. The pollution credit was based on a market approach to pollution control, which was favored by industry.

The Clean Air Act of 1990 set overall targets for the reduction of sulfur dioxide, nitrogen oxide, and ozone-depleting chemicals. It imposed stricter emission standards for new motor vehicles. It gradually phased out the production of ozone-depleting chemicals. Overall, the bill expanded air pollution regulations, but it did so in ways less offensive to business and industrial interests. Indeed, these interests had played a major role in crafting the bill. Gonzalez reached the following conclusions:

> The 1990 Clean Air Act benefited the business community by rationalizing environmental regulations under largely one national regulatory regime. Moreover, in responding to the business community's objections, those officials directly responsible for determining the content of the 1990 Clean Air Act prevented environmental activists from participating meaningfully in the formulation process that produced the act. The most significant environmentalist proposal to make it into the act—the permit trading system—conforms to the corporate view of a regulatory regime. . . . (2001, 111)

Gonzalez used the term *corporate liberalism* to describe the role of major corporations in forging clean air policies. Brian Tokar suggested that by the 1990s, established environmental organizations were heavily dependent on corporate contributions and were more willing to compromise with industrial interests. For example, there were direct ties between the Ford Motor Company and the Environmental Defense Fund, and major contributors to the Sierra Club included British Petroleum, PepsiCo, United Technologies, and several large banks (Tokar 1997, 19).

Environmental organizations have challenged and checked the power of major corporations, but environmental organizations are far from dominant in this policy area. Corporations still exercise considerable influence over the development of environmental policies. They have direct involvement in the policy-making process, sometimes to the exclusion of environmental interests.

A small group of executives representing coal-burning utilities broke ranks with other corporations and pressured the George W. Bush administration to roll back clean air regulations. In 1999 the EPA had pursued lawsuits against nine utilities for expanding their facilities without adding pollution controls, as required by the 1990 act. The utilities joined a group called the Electric Reliability Coordinating Council. Representatives of this group met with Vice President Dick Cheney in an effort to quash the lawsuits and relax the regulations.

Over the objections of the director of the EPA, Christine Todd Whitman, the powerful lobbyists succeeded in getting the rules relaxed and the lawsuits dropped (Drew and Oppel 2004, A10).

Impacts of Clean Air Policy

Although the use of the automobile has increased substantially since the passage of the Clean Air Act of 1970, most pollutant levels have declined. Since 1970 the emissions of five out of six major pollutants have declined measurably. The emission of lead has almost completely disappeared, from a level of over 200,000 metric tons per year in 1970 to almost zero in 1990. Since 1970 the emission of carbon monoxide and suspended particles has declined substantially while emissions of sulfur oxide and volatile organic chemicals (VOCs) have declined slightly. However, the emission of nitrogen oxide has increased since 1970 (Bryner 1993, 46, 57–60).

Ozone levels continue to be distressing. There are two problems with ozone. First, it provides a protective layer in the upper area of the atmosphere. This layer shields living organisms from the sun's ultraviolet rays. The problem is that the ozone layer has been decreasing because of the ozone hole over Antarctica which has been growing in size since the late 1970s. The prime source of ozone depletion is from the emission of chlorofluorocarbons (CFCs) which combine with ozone molecules in the atmosphere to reduce the supply of ozone. Declines in the ozone layer have been directly linked to increases in rates of skin cancer. The Clean Air Act of 1990 banned the manufacture of CFCs after the year 2000.

Second, ozone at a lower atmosphere level produces a range of health problems. In urban areas, high temperatures increase the evaporation rate of volatile organic compounds and produce ozone. In the summer, urban areas sometimes have ozone alerts, and people are urged to stay inside. A number of health and environmental organizations insist that EPA ozone emission standards are too low (Kraft 1996; Smith 2000).

Clean Water Policy

The federal government became directly involved in regulating water pollution with the passage of the *Clean Water Act of 1972*. Like the Clean Air Act, the Clean Water Act set a deadline—1985—for industry to cease discharging waste materials into major waterways. The act required industries to establish the best practicable water pollution control technology by 1979. With the establishment of the National Pollution Discharge Elimination System, it prohibited the discharge of pollutants into the water without a permit (Switzer 1994, 173). A major goal of clean water policy was to make all waterways "fishable and swimmable" by 1983. Like previous clean water acts, this bill allocated money to assist local governments in building or upgrading their wastewater treatment facilities. It authorized about $18 billion between 1973 and 1975 for local facilities (Rosenbaum 1991, 196).

There are two major sources of water pollution: point and nonpoint sources. **Point sources** of water pollution are stationary. One can see point sources because they are fixed—

a building, water treatment facility, factory, dam, or sewer system. The major producers of point source water pollution are industries and municipal governments. The Clean Water Act gave the Environmental Protection Agency authority to regulate all point sources of water pollution. It did not address nonpoint source pollution.

Nonpoint sources of water pollution are those you cannot see. They are generally hidden and difficult to identify. Examples of nonpoint source water pollution include agricultural pesticide runoff, buried hazardous waste, septic tanks, landfills, mining operations, and construction site runoffs. Farmers spray chemical herbicides and insecticides on their crops. As rain mixes with these chemicals, they run off the soil into nearby surface waterways (streams, rivers, or lakes) and they drain through the soil into underground water systems. Underground water systems often run into surface waterways. With the consolidation of poultry and pork-producing farms over the past few decades, animal feces have become a major source of nonpoint source water pollution, which affects both surface and groundwater (Rosenbaum 1991). Rosenbaum summarized this problem:

Nonpoint pollution—pollution arising from diffuse, multiple sources rather than from a pipe or other "point sources"—is estimated to be the major cause of pollution in 65 percent of the stream miles not meeting state standards for their designated use. Overall, more than one-third of the stream miles in the United States appear to be affected by nonpoint pollution. (1991, 201).

The Clean Water Act of 1972 addressed neither the issue of safe drinking water nor nonpoint source water pollution. With the passage of the *Safe Drinking Water Act of 1974,* the EPA began setting standards for safe drinking water. It identified substances that contaminated drinking water such as microorganisms, chemical agents, and turbid substances, and it set maximum limits for them. The *Safe Drinking Water Act of 1986* set maximum limits for 61 additional contaminants by 1989, to "create 25 more standards from a new list by 1991, and set standards for 25 additional chemicals every three years thereafter" (Rosenbaum 1991, 207).

Point source pollution has declined substantially. The EPA has been effective in assisting municipal governments in constructing and improving their waste treatment facilities and in reducing the direct discharge of industrial waste into the waterways. However, nonpoint water pollution was ignored until the passage in 1987 of the *Water Quality Act.* This act required states to develop nonpoint source water pollution control plans, much like the Clean Air Act required states to develop air pollution control plans. State governments were to play

A drainage pipe.

a major role in water pollution regulations; the federal government provided financial assistance to support water pollution demonstration projects (Rosenbaum 1991, 197; Switzer 1994).

Because of inadequate nonpoint source regulations, the quality of groundwater has worsened. Groundwater is important because it is a major source of fresh drinking water. "Roughly half of the U.S. population relies on groundwater for drinking water, and in some areas groundwater provides close to or all of the domestic water supply" (Smith 2000, 119).

Impact of Clean Water Policy

EPA policies have had mixed effects on water pollution. The condition of surface waterways has improved; streams, rivers, and lakes today are not as polluted as they were in the 1970s. It has been over 30 years since the Cuyahoga River caught fire. However, two persisting water pollution problems remain. First, the elements and organic chemicals poured into the waterways in the 1960s and 1970s were not biodegradable. They are still there. In the case of Lake Erie, most have settled to the muddy bottom of the lake and, when disturbed, they resurface. These elements include mercury, lead, and arsenic. The organic chemicals include DDT, polychlorinated biphenyls (PCBs), and others.

The second problem is nonpoint source water pollution. Agricultural production is too dependent on pesticides and chemical fertilizers for the EPA to make any progress in this area. Agricultural runoff is one of the major sources of groundwater contaminants. Other sources of nonpoint water pollution include septic tanks, leaching hazardous waste dumps, and underground tanks. Whereas the quality of surface waterways has improved, the quality of groundwater has deteriorated.

Pesticides and Hazardous Waste

The EPA became involved in pesticide regulation with the passage of the *Federal Environmental Pesticide Control Act of 1972*. This act amended the federal *Insecticide, Fungicide, and Rodenticide Act of 1947*, shifting responsibility for pesticide regulation from the Department of Agriculture to the EPA. It allowed the EPA to set standards for pesticide residue on raw food and required it to consider unreasonable risks to people and the environment. The EPA should balance health and safety risks with economic and social costs (Wargo 1996; Kraft 1996). This organizational change was an important aspect of the emergence of the new environmental policy regime.

The 1972 act also required the EPA to reevaluate all existing pesticides, especially after several studies raised serious health and safety questions about the pesticides already in use. Shortly after the passage of this bill, the EPA banned DDT. Eventually, the EPA banned a few other pesticides such as dieldrin, heptachlor, and toxaphene that were more lethal and dangerous than DDT.

The EPA acquired broader powers to regulate toxic chemicals with the enactment of the *Toxic Substance Control Act (TSCA) of 1976*. This law gave the EPA the authority to "identify, evaluate and regulate risks associated with the full life cycle of commercial chemicals, both those already in commerce as well as new ones in preparation" (Kraft 1996, 94). Like the Pesticide Control Act, this policy required the EPA to consider unreasonable risks to people and the environment and undue burdens to businesses and industry. EPA regulation of toxic substances involved four objectives: information gathering, screening, testing, and control. The EPA gathers information on all toxic chemicals and requires the manufacturers to test them. It does some testing of select chemicals on its own. Finally, it controls these chemicals. Congress gave the EPA a range of options. It could ban a chemical entirely and prohibit its sale, distribution, and use, or it could establish guidelines for the use of a toxic substance or set limits on its production.

Congress amended TSCA in 1986, with the *Asbestos Hazard Emergency Response Act of 1986.* This bill required the EPA to inspect schools for asbestos and to control asbestos risks. In 1992 Congress amended TSCA to include lead-based paint regulations with the goal of reducing public exposure to lead paint (Kraft 1996, 95).

The EPA became involved in the regulation of solid and hazardous waste disposal with the passage of the *Resource Conservation and Recovery Act (RCRA) of 1976.* This act required the EPA to monitor toxic substances from the cradle to the grave; that is, the EPA must keep records on toxic chemicals from the point that they were manufactured to the time they were buried. After a number of catastrophic incidents involving toxic waste dumps, Congress strengthened EPA authority in this area.

The Love Canal Catastrophe

A prime example of this type of catastrophe is the case of Love Canal. Love Canal was located in Niagara Falls, New York. William Love financed the project at the end of the 19th century to provide hydroelectric power in the area. The canal was a waterway perpendicular to the Niagara River. The project went bankrupt, leaving a pit in the ground that was 1 mile long, 15 yards wide, and 10 to 40 feet deep. Sometime before World War II, Hooker Chemical Company bought the land, began operations, and started dumping its hazardous waste in the pit. Michael Brown summarized Hooker's contribution to the Love Canal problem.

> Beginning in the late 1930s or early 1940s (no one could be sure just when), the Hooker Company, whose many processes include the manufacture of pesticides, plasticizers, and caustic soda, had used the canal as a dump for at least 21,800 tons of waste residues. . . . The chemical garbage was brought to the excavation in fifty-five gallon metal barrels staked on a small dump truck and was unloaded. . . . The drums dumped in the canal contained a veritable witch's brew of chemistry, compounds of truly remarkable toxicity. (1981, 5, 9)

Hooker Chemical Company dumped into the pit some of the most toxic chemicals known. In the 1950s Hooker covered up the pit and sold the land to the local school board for a dollar. People forgot about the pit. A school was built on the area and developers constructed homes around it.

Twenty years later, residents of the area began complaining about foul-smelling liquids seeping into their basements. State officials insisted that it was nothing. In the late 1970s an EPA study verified that the chemicals in the pit had migrated through the ground. A medical study reported serious health problems related to chemical poisoning. One study of 245 homes reported 34 miscarriages and 18 birth defects. "In house after house children were underweight or too short or with red blotched skin; bronchioles had been slammed shut by asthma, bladders were infected, lymph tubules closed with clots; there were numb limbs, brain disorders, and birth defects that ranged from the subtle (club feet) to the bizarre (three ears)" (Brown 1981, 48–49).

State officials attacked the medical study, claiming that no control group was used in the study, that households were not randomly selected, and that the study was not scientific.

Other critics of the study argued that there was no link between the alleged ailments and the chemicals and that no fatalities were associated with the chemicals. These critics insisted that Love Canal was not a problem and that people were hysterical.

In another medical study, Dr. Dante J. Picciano of the Biogenics Corporation tested 36 people and found 11 cases of unusual chromosomal damage. Later the EPA did blood tests of selected residents and found 20 different toxic chemicals and eight metals in the subjects' blood (Brown 1981, 61, 63).

A young boy who died had played at a creek near Love Canal that contained many of the chemicals found in people's basements. His parents were chemists. The boy's mother said this about her deceased son:

> Luella said, "He played in the creek all the time. . . . He died of nephrosis. Proteins were passing through his urine. Well, in reading the literature, we discovered that chemicals can trigger this. There was no evidence of infection, which there should have been, and there was damage to his thymus and brain. . . . So our feeling for now is that the chemicals probably triggered it." (Brown 1981, 46)

Love Canal was not an isolated case; there were hundreds of cases of communities affected by toxic waste dumps across the country. But the Love Canal case raised the visibility and public awareness of this type of problem and helped put the issue of hazardous waste dumps on the federal government's agenda.

Congressional Actions

Congress responded to this issue with the *Comprehensive, Environmental, Response, Compensation and Liability Act of 1980*, also known as the *Superfund* bill. This bill authorized the EPA to respond to crises precipitated by hazardous waste dumps like the one at Love Canal. It charged the EPA with the responsibility of assisting the residents and cleaning up the sites. It allocated $1.6 billion (the Superfund) for this purpose, but it also made companies liable for the cleanup costs and the damages resulting from their waste dumps.

Congress had underestimated the extent of the problem and the costs of cleaning up the hundreds of other leaching toxic dumps like Love Canal. There were far more problems than expected. Consequently, Congress amended the Superfund bill in 1986 to increase the money set aside for cleanup from $1.6 billion to $8.5 billion and to establish more stringent cleanup standards (Kraft 1996, 97).

Whereas the Superfund act dealt with cleaning up dump sites, the Resource Conservation and Recovery Act (RCRA) dealt with the management of waste sites. In response to the Love Canal catastrophe and other shocking cases and to the EPA's seeming inaction, Congress amended RCRA in 1984 to establish detailed regulations for managing hazardous waste. "The 1984 RCRA amendment ranks among the most detailed and restrictive of environmental measures ever enacted, with 76 statutory deadlines, eight of them with 'hammer' provisions that were to take effect if the EPA failed to act in time" (Kraft 1996, 93). The statute set new and more stringent standards for underground storage tanks and banned the disposal of bulk liquid in landfills (Rosenbaum 1991).

As the EPA implemented the RCRA, it had to extend some of the deadlines and negotiate with hazardous waste disposal companies over certain regulations. There have been continuing cases of companies improperly disposing waste and reported cases of toxic chemicals leaching underground. However, the EPA has claimed to take the regulations seriously and to be committed to cleaning up hazardous waste sites that threaten public health and safety. The EPA's Website offers the following statement:

> Forty high-priority hazardous waste sites across the country were cleaned up in fiscal year 2003 (Oct. 2002–Oct. 2003). . . . To date, EPA has cleaned up 886 sites on the Superfund National Priorities List (NPL). These sites are considered some of the highest health threats in the nation. (Ryan 2003, 1)

The EPA site also noted that the Superfund budget allocation for fiscal year 2004 is about $1.4 billion, with about $290 million in the trust fund available for cleaning up sites.

Recent Trends in Environmental Policies

Environmental policies continued to develop incrementally throughout the 1990s and into the early years of the 21st century. In 1990 President George H. W. Bush had found a balance between environmental and industrial interests, as he supported the Clean Air Act of 1990. He declared a moratorium on oil drilling in the **Arctic National Wildlife Refuge** in Alaska. He continued to allocate money for local water treatment.

Although President Clinton was not known for his support of environmental policies as governor of Arkansas, his vice president, Al Gore, was. Gore had a strong reputation as an environmentalist. Clinton appointed officials sympathetic to environmental causes and like his predecessor, Clinton continued to balance the interests of industry with those of environmentalists.

Rollback of Environmental Regulation

President George W. Bush began his term in 2001 with a number of issues and controversies related to environmental policy. Bush rolled back some of the environmental regulations introduced during the Clinton administration. He suspended the EPA regulation that lowered the acceptable limit of arsenic in water to 10 parts per million and restored the higher 50 parts per million limit. He proposed opening up the Arctic National Wildlife Refuge and U.S. coastal shores along the Gulf of Mexico and Pacific Ocean.

Bush's new regulatory changes had been driven by what was perceived as an energy crisis. There were two aspects of this crisis. First, gasoline prices had increased substantially. Bush assumed that a good way to reduce gasoline prices was to increase the supply of petroleum, and one way to do that was to open federal land to oil drilling. Second, there had been a shortage of electrical power in California. Bush also attributed this problem to the petroleum shortage and suggested building more nuclear energy plants.

Environmentalists were critical of Bush's proposals. They argued that the United States constitutes 5 percent of the world's population and uses 25 percent of the world's petroleum energy. They claimed that rather than drilling in the Arctic National Wildlife Refuge, where petroleum supplies are limited, we should focus on reducing our use of petroleum. A report by the Natural Resources Defense Council made this claim:

> Indeed, fuel efficiency improvements can deliver more oil, more quickly and more cheaply than the Arctic Refuge. . . . The available oil from the Arctic National Wildlife Refuge is a drop in the bucket of America's energy needs. The best U.S. Geological Survey estimate is that less than a six-month supply of oil could be economically recovered from the Arctic Refuge (about 3.2 billion barrels, spread out over a 50 year period), and that it would take

Pollution over the Bronx.

at least 10 years of exploration, drilling and pipeline construction before the oil would
reach the refineries. (2001, 2)

Environmentalists argued that we should invest in renewable sources of energy, like hydroelectric or wind-generated electricity. They argued further that we need automobiles that get
more miles per gallon of fuel, that we should get rid of the gas-guzzling sport utility vehicles
(SUVs), that we should lower the speed limit to the more fuel-efficient 55 miles per hour,
and that we need to provide incentives for automakers to create electric cars or other alternatives to the internal combustion engine. Environmentalists pointed out that nuclear energy
suffers from two problems: it is far more expensive than advocates claim and it faces the persistent problem of disposing of hazardous waste. As for California's energy crisis, environmentalists pointed out that less than 1 percent of the electricity in California is generated
from petroleum; most comes from coal-burning generators.

The Special Case of Global Warming

Global warming is a relatively new issue. The idea did not gain widespread acceptance in the
scientific community until the early 1990s. Until then, scientific reports had been contradictory. In 1896 a Swedish scientist, Svante Arrhenius, warned that the increase in carbon dioxide emitted from factories, especially coal-burning furnaces, would cause the earth's
temperature to increase. The carbon dioxide in the atmosphere would act as a glass bowl,
trapping heat underneath, and causing increases in temperature. During the 1930s scientists
documented gradual increases in the earth's temperature, but temperatures decreased in
the 1940s and 1950s. Other scientists theorized that the ocean and vegetation would absorb

increases in carbon dioxide. Congress even held hearings on the threat of global cooling in 1969, 1972, and 1974 (Davis, forthcoming). Scientists did not accept the global warming theory in the late 1970s.

Evidence of global warming began to accumulate in the 1980s as temperatures again began to rise. Advancement in weather satellites, computer technology, and scientific models contributed to the growth of a consensus in global warming among scientists. In 1989 James Hansen, director of the National Aeronautics and Space Administration (NASA) research team at the Goddard Institute, testified before Congress that "the greenhouse effect had now been detected and it is changing our climate now" (quoted in Davis, forthcoming, 15).

Environmentalists have insisted that the earth is getting warmer, evidenced by record-breaking summer temperatures, the melting of mountain glaciers, and the shrinking of the polar ice caps. Environmentalists also pointed to increases in carbon dioxide, which was documented by the EPA and the National Academy of Sciences. One reason for the increase in carbon dioxide levels is deforestation.

> Deforestation has resulted in a reduction in the carbon dioxide to oxygen conversion. It is estimated that deforestation contributes 1 billion to 2.5 billion tons of carbon dioxide emissions annually. (Smith 2000, 104)

Global warming not only will melt glaciers and the polar ice caps, but also will increase the water level of the oceans and expand deserts. Some expect the rising water levels to submerge coastal cities.

The Kyoto Protocol   By the early 1990s most scientists in the United States and around the world accepted the greenhouse theory. During the mid-1990s the United Nations sponsored conferences on global warming which culminated in the 1997 Kyoto Protocol, a series of principles designed to reduce greenhouse gases. Greenhouse gases include carbon dioxide, methane, nitrous oxide, and chlorofluorocarbons. Developed countries signing the protocol would agree to reduce their carbon dioxide emissions by 6 percent to 8 percent below their 1990 levels by 2008 to 2010. Although President Clinton supported the protocol, the U.S. Senate did not and passed a resolution rejecting any treaty reducing emissions.

There was strong opposition to the Kyoto Protocol from industry. The largest organization opposing the protocol was a coalition called the Global Climate Coalition which represented organizations such as the American Petroleum Institute, U.S. Chamber of Commerce, National Association of Manufacturers, and many multinational corporations and other corporate interests. The Edison Institute estimated that the protocol would cost the American economy between $100 billion and $200 billion. The American Petroleum Institute spent millions of dollars "to convince Americans that the Kyoto Accord was based on shaky science" (Davis, forthcoming, 10).

The Senate never ratified the Kyoto Protocol as a treaty by the time Clinton left office. George W. Bush did not support it, insisting that scientific evidence of global warming was insufficient and that the Kyoto Protocol would put too much of an economic burden on the United States and not enough on Third World countries.

Other critics of the global warming theory argued that if the earth is getting warmer, it is probably because of natural climatic changes, not any increase in carbon dioxide. Some argued further that the earth may be entering into a post-ice age, which explains the melting of the ice caps rather than any greenhouse effect.

Summary

The chapter identifies three environmental policy regimes: industrial, conservation, and environmental. The industrial policy regime lasted until about 1900. Industrial, mining, timber, and farming interests substantially dominated this policy regime. The dominant policy paradigm saw the earth as dead matter, assumed that it had unlimited and inexhaustible supplies of natural resources, encouraged the unrestrained exploitation of the earth, and discouraged the formation of any environmental policy that interfered with industrial expansion. Industry operated to keep clean air, clean water, and other environmental policies off the political agenda.

Industrialists concerned with the depletion of natural resources joined with conservationists and preservationists in creating the conservation policy regime, which lasted from 1900 to about 1970. The dominant paradigm of this regime encouraged the exploitation of the earth, but assumed that it had limited, yet replenishable, resources. It called for the managed use of land and resources. This regime produced national parks and conservation policies. Industrial, mining, timber, and farming interests worked with conservationists, but they dominated this regime and prevented the emergence of other environmental policies such as clean air and clean water.

The environmental movement of the late 1960s introduced the environmental policy regime, which lasted from 1970 to the present time. The dominant paradigm assumed that the world, limited in space and resources, was interconnected with ecosystems that were fragile and full of life. The poisoning of one part of the earth impacted other parts. This paradigm assumed that environmental regulations were absolutely necessary.

The passage of the Clean Air Act of 1970 signaled the establishment of a new environmental policy regime. Power had shifted from industry to the environmentalists, and the old industrial and conservationist policy paradigms were replaced by a new environmental paradigm which ushered in a series of laws affecting air pollution, water pollution, pesticides, hazardous waste disposal, and others. The establishment of the new environmental policy regime created the possibility for the federal government to make progress in resolving other environmental problems.

Most of the changes in environmental policies since the early 1970s have been incremental. The Clean Air Act of 1977 represented a retreat from ambitious objectives established in 1970. Despite strong efforts on the part of the Reagan administration and industry to eliminate environmental regulation, the environment policy regime endured. The EPA tightened up automobile emissions rules and phased out the use of lead in gasoline. The Clean Air Act of 1990 represented an incremental policy increase over the 1977 act. New acid rain regulations were added, although within a market model. Despite President George W. Bush's rejection of the Kyoto Protocol and his weakening of clean air and clean water regulations, there is still substantial support for environmental policies. The environmental policy regime has endured and continues to have an impact.

Review Questions

1. Discuss the development of clean air policy throughout the 20th century.
2. Identify the interest groups on both sides of the environmental protection issue.

3. Discuss the development of clean water policy throughout the 20th century.
4. Discuss the shift from the old environmental policy regime to the contemporary environmental policy regime.
5. What is the significance of the Love Canal?
6. What laws were enacted as a result of this catastrophe?
7. To what extent does the pluralist model of policy making explain the development of environmental policies?
8. To what extent does the elite model explain environmental policies?

Select Websites

This is the official Website for the U.S. Environmental Protection Agency.
http://www.epa.org

This is the Website for the Sierra Club, one of the oldest environmental interest groups.
http://www.sierraclub.org

This is the National Wildlife Federation's Website.
http://www.nwf.org

Key Terms

Arctic National Wildlife Refuge
Rachel Carson
conservationists
DDT
global warming
George Perkins Marsh

John Muir
national forests
national parks
nonpoint source
point sources
preservationists

CHAPTER 9

Labor Policy

Labor policy is typically placed in the category of a protective regulatory policy, a type of policy that protects individuals from unintended harms produced by the market. Protective regulatory policies have features similar to redistributive policies. They tend to be contentious and divided along ideological lines, and labor policy has been the most contentious and violent public policy issue throughout U.S. history, more violent than abortion policy.

Labor policy has been shaped by conflicts between organized workers and management over wages, working conditions, and workplace health and safety. The history of labor policy can be discussed in terms of four policy regimes: classical (1789–1910), Progressive (1910–1938), New Deal (1938–1970), and protective (1970–present). Under the classical regime employees had no right to organize. **Collective bargaining**—the process in which a labor union, representing employees, negotiates with employers for a contract dealing with wages and working conditions—was illegal.

The Progressive labor regime (1910–1938) introduced laws concerning child labor, minimum wages, maximum working hours, and workers' compensation. However, the courts struck down most of these laws, except workers' compensation. State and federal policies continued to undermine collective bargaining efforts. Violence was especially severe during this period.

Violence and strikes intensified during the 1930s, creating a national crisis in labor policy which led to the New Deal policy regime (1938–1970). This regime protected the rights of employees to organize and to engage in collective bargaining.

The workers' protection regime emerged out of several social movements of the late 1960s—civil rights, public service union, environmental, and consumer protection. The Occupational Safety and Health Administration (OSHA) was the hallmark of this regime.

✦ The Classical Labor Policy Regime, 1789–1910

Master craftsmen, manufacturers, merchants, and small businesses dominated the classical labor policy regime and operated to outlaw collective bargaining. Although classical economic theory emerged during this period, the dominant labor policy paradigm went beyond this theory. Classical economic theory emphasized the rights of individuals, free and open competition, and limited government interference in the market. Classical economic theorists assumed that wages, like the prices of commodities, would be subject to the law of supply and demand; that is, wages would increase when the demand for labor increased and the supply remained constant. However, while the dominant labor policy paradigm incorporated classical theory, it also assumed that collective bargaining was illegal and immoral. Labor policy during this period rejected the laissez-faire notion of no government interference in the market. Instead, it expected government to interfere and arrest union leaders attempting to engage in collective bargaining.

The case of the shoemakers illustrates this point. The shoemakers organized in 1792 primarily to prevent the reduction of wages and to set their own wage scale to which all of their members would agree. They threatened to withhold services unless they got a fair rate for their labor. Later they went on strike in several cities such as New York, Philadelphia, and Boston. The organizers were arrested for criminal conspiracy (Brooks 1971). Under common law, it was a crime for workers to organize and conspire to raise wages. Legal scholar Christopher Anglim summarized this policy:

> As "combinations" intent on raising wages and reducing hours, unions were considered
> illegal conspiracies in restraint of trade. As a result, unions were outlawed as criminal
> conspiracies, and all workers' attempts at self-protection were deemed illegal ends through
> the common law "unlawful means–unlawful ends" test. (1997, 13)

By 1806 the shoemakers' union was dead. In 1842, however, the common law doctrine against collective bargaining was overturned in Massachusetts (Brooks 1971, 21). Other states followed suit during the 1850s. Nevertheless, many states continued to outlaw collective bargaining up to the Civil War.

The outlawing of collective bargaining allowed for the effective suppression of unions during this period. Although unions were suppressed, they were not the only type of labor organization. Other types included guilds or craft organizations, benevolent societies, and associations. Guilds or craft organizations dated back to ancient times, although they were more closely associated with the medieval period. **Guilds** were organizations of people in the same craft or trade which operated to protect trade secrets, promote the trade or profession, maintain professional standards, and train new members. The guilds often set the fees and regulated those within the trade. **Benevolent societies** raised money primarily for members who were injured on the job, for the widows of deceased members, and for disabled members. **Associations** generally had political agendas: to promote laws more favorable to their trade. Unions emerged primarily for the purpose of collective bargaining.

After the Civil War, the Industrial Revolution impacted the classical labor policy regime. It contributed to the emergence of industrial labor organizations and increased efforts toward collective bargaining. Industrial and trade unions emerged in the late 19th century and pushed harder for collective bargaining. This push contributed to violent conflicts between unions and employers. Two cases illustrate this point: the Knights of Labor and the steelworkers of Homestead, Pennsylvania.

The Knights of Labor and the Haymarket Riot

Union organizing increased after the Civil War, especially with the rapid expansion of industries. In 1869 the Noble and Holy Order of the Knights of Labor emerged out of the Garment Cutters Association, a benevolent society (Brooks 1971, 56). The **Knights of Labor** began as a secret society, keeping its organizing efforts secret because organizers could be fired and blacklisted. **Blacklisted** is an old term for a list shared among employers with the names of people to bar from employment because of their union activities. The Knights of Labor was not a single union, but a federation of local unions in several craft and industrial occupations—garment workers, railroad workers, shipyard workers, farm laborers, cigar makers, steelworkers, and workers in many other areas. The number of members increased rapidly, from a little more than 9,000 in 1879 to over 100,000 by 1885, and over 700,000 by the end of 1887 (Brooks 1971, 59). The Knights grew bolder as the organization grew larger. Its affiliated unions had initiated several strikes and the national organization engaged in a campaign for the eight-hour workday.

The Knights declined after the **Haymarket riot** in Chicago in May 1886. The Haymarket riot began as a strike and demonstration for the eight-hour working day on the part of affiliates of the Knights of Labor.

> On May Day, 1886, 40,000 workers struck for the shorter day; their number doubled within the next four days. An additional 45,000, mostly packinghouse workers, were granted the shorter day without a strike.
>
> On the third day of May, striking lumber-shovers met near the McCormick reaper works to hear August Spies, a strike leader and anarchist editor of the *Arbeiter Zeitung,* and to appoint a committee to meet with lumber yard owners. During the course of the meeting, about 200 left to go to the McCormick works to harass strikebreakers, who were then leaving work. Within fifteen minutes, some 200 policemen arrived on the scene, wielding clubs to break up the crowd. Others at the Spies meeting hurried to join their fellow workers. They were met by the police, who fired upon the strikers, wounding many and killing four. (Brooks 1971, 68–69)

Angry about the death of the workers at the hands of the police, Spies called for a mass meeting on May 4 at 7:30 p.m. in Haymarket Square. About 3,000 people came. Spies and prominent leaders of the Knights of Labor spoke to the crowd, but had left by 10:00 p.m., and the crowd dissipated. Nevertheless, the police marched into the square to disperse those who remained. A bomb exploded near the police, wounding about 66, seven of whom later died (Brooks 1971, 69). The police then fired into the crowd, killing several and wounding over a hundred. The organizers and speakers were arrested, tried, and convicted, although there was no evidence connecting the speakers to the bomb. Several of those convicted were hanged, including Spies.

The Knights of Labor declined after the convictions and hangings, as assaults on unions continued. Authorities in several cities arrested leaders of the organization. In the Deep South, several members of the Knights were murdered. For example, the governor of Louisiana sent state militia to suppress a strike among sugar workers. Two Knights officials were arrested and a mob later lynched them. Local militia killed about 20 strikers (Foner 1982). By 1888 membership in the Knights of Labor had fallen to 222,000; by 1895 it was only about 20,000.

> Every strike undertaken by the Order after 1886 was lost. Employers organized strong associations to fight the Knights, making liberal use of the lockout, the blacklist, armed guards, and detectives. Agreements with the Order were broken as soon as convenient since employers considered them as contracts signed under duress and, therefore, not to be honored. (Brooks 1971, 84–85)

The Amalgamated Association of Iron and Steel Workers and the Homestead Strike

The Homestead strike of 1892 further illustrates the extent of labor violence during this period. Homestead was a small steel town located about seven miles from Pittsburgh, Pennsylvania. Most people were employed by the Carnegie Steel Company, which later became the United States Steel Corporation, and belonged to the Amalgamated Association of Iron and Steel Workers (AAISW). Until 1892 Carnegie Steel had a decent relationship with the AAISW. This relationship changed after the company hired Henry Clay Frick, who had a reputation for busting unions, as the head of operations. In February negotiations began for a new contract, but just before the contract expired in June, Frick unilaterally cut the salaries of AAISW workers. The workers responded by demonstrating and hanging Frick in effigy. Frick closed down the plant and contracted with the Pinkerton detective agency. Pinkerton sent 300 armed detectives from Pittsburgh down the river on barges where they were met by armed AAISW strikers. It is not clear who fired the first shot, but three detectives and seven strikers were killed. The governor of Pennsylvania called in the state militia. After order was restored, many of the strike leaders were arrested. Three were indicted for murder, two for rioting, and one for conspiracy. Later, 27 were indicted for treason against the State of Pennsylvania. Although everyone was acquitted, the AAISW union was dead by the end of the year (Brooks 1971, 86–92).

American Federation of Labor

The **American Federation of Labor (AFL)** was founded in 1886 by a group of union leaders dissatisfied with the Knights of Labor. Whereas the Knights favored industrial unions representing unskilled workers and aggressive tactics, the AFL favored trade unions representing skilled workers and passive tactics. In the early 20th century, the AFL engaged in a buy-union campaign to support companies that were unionized and to provide an incentive for anti-union companies to accept unions. The AFL encouraged people to **boycott** or refuse to buy the products of companies hostile to unions. Antiunion business organizations such as the National Association of Manufacturers and the short-lived Citizens Industrial Association targeted the AFL for its boycott tactics. When a hatmaking company went on strike in 1902, the AFL initiated a boycott against it. With the support of the Citizens Industrial Association, the company sued the AFL under the Sherman Antitrust Act the next year. This law prohibited individuals and groups from conspiring, organizing, or contracting for the purpose of restraining trade. The Supreme Court used the Sherman Act to uphold the right of a company to sue the union over a boycott, and to sue individual union members, as well as members of its executive board. The suit cost the AFL $420,000 and it crippled the union (Brooks 1971).

Labor Policies of the Classical Period

These cases—the Knights of Labor, the AAISW, and the AFL—illustrate this point: The classical period was not a laissez-faire era with no government interference in labor-management relations. Public policies and government actions were far from neutral. Laws favored employers and businesses over employees and unions. Common law outlawed collective bargaining up to the Civil War. The Sherman Antitrust Act of 1890 was used to destroy unions.

Throughout the early 1900s—under both the classical and Progressive labor policy regimes—employers continued to use a variety of tactics to break up unions. They used blacklists, yellow dog contracts, spies, hired guards, and company unions. A **yellow dog contract** is a contract given to an employee at the time of hiring, in which the employee agrees to refrain from joining a union, engaging in union organizing, or instigating strikes. Engaging in any of these activities would be grounds for immediate dismissal. In order to break any strike, employers would fire the strikers and hired nonunion workers. Employers hired people to follow workers into bars to spy on them and report any union activity. Employers hired private guards to deal with aggressive unions. Labor violence did not subside until the 1920s, after the destruction of the major industrial organizations.

↦ *The Progressive Labor Policy Regime, 1910–1938*

The Progressive labor policy regime emerged with the Progressive movement. This policy regime was characterized by changes in public policies, power arrangements, the organization of the national government, and the dominant policy paradigm.

Progressive Policies

The Progressive movement secured the passage of minimum wage, maximum working hours, child labor, and workers' compensation laws. The Supreme Court struck down most of the Progressive laws—child labor, minimum wage, and maximum working hours—arguing that these laws violated the contract rights of individual workers and the due process clause of the Constitution. Workers' compensation laws survived because they had broad and strong political support among the civic, business, and labor organizations that formed the political base of the Progressive policy regime. Workers' compensation, along with the Clayton Act, defined the Progressive labor policy regime.

The Clayton Act of 1914 was designed to exempt unions from antitrust prosecution. It limited antitrust suits and injunctions against labor unions. While some labor leaders considered this bill a Magna Carta for labor, the implementation of this law provided little relief for unions. In 1917, for example, three years after the passage of the Clayton Act, the Supreme Court ordered the United Mine Workers of America to cease organizing coal miners in West Virginia because the union was doing more than simply organizing: It was trying to change the behavior of the mining companies. The mineworkers had signed yellow dog contracts. The Court upheld these contracts and ordered the union to cease its organizing activities. The Court also found other unions in violation of antitrust laws, despite the Clayton Act (Robertson 2000).

Power Arrangements

Political power arrangements changed as conservative labor unions formed alliances with civic and business organizations to promote the Progressive labor policy agenda. The AFL formed alliances with many national organizations. Its president, Samuel Gompers, served on the National Civic League, an organization of business leaders, with political, religious, and labor leaders. John D. Rockefeller, Jr., contributed to the American Association of Labor Legislation (AALL) and New York Child Labor Committees (Gitelman 1988, 8). Labor and civic organizations, with the support of some industrialists, were temporarily successful in securing legislation outlawing child labor.

A number of manufacturing, business, civic, and labor organizations formed a coalition in support of workers' compensation laws. The National Association of Manufacturers, despite its strong opposition to unions, joined too. Several businesses and industries had suffered major losses from lawsuits brought by the families of workers killed on the job. They found it cheaper to get state governments to establish workers' compensation than to suffer losses in courts or to finance their own insurance (Robertson 2000, 235).

Organizational Changes in Government

There were a few organizational changes in government during the Progressive labor policy regime. Congress established the Department of Labor and Commerce in 1903 and separated it into two departments 10 years later. The Labor Department was responsible for promoting improvements in labor conditions and mediating labor-management conflicts.

Collective Bargaining and Labor Violence

During this period, labor policies undermined collective bargaining. Federal and state governments generally supported businesses in destroying the more aggressive unions. In a few cases, the Department of Labor acted as a mediator between labor and management, especially when the level of violence became so extreme that it provoked public outrage. Two cases illustrate these points: (1) the rise of the Industrial Workers of the World (Wobblies) and (2) the United Mine Workers and the Ludlow massacre.

The Industrial Workers of the World

In 1905 industrial leaders dissatisfied with the passivity of the AFL established the **Industrial Workers of the World (IWW)**. The IWW, also known as Wobblies, was a more radical industrial labor organization. The IWW advocated the eight-hour day, minimum wages, racial integration, gender equality, worker control of the workplace, and other ideas. The Wobblies opposed U.S. involvement in World War I. By the end of this war, most of the IWW leaders were dead, in jail, or exiled. The federal government used the *Espionage Act of 1917* to go after the union's leaders.

> In June 1917, the federal government indicted the whole top leadership of the IWW under the wartime espionage laws. Over 150 were jailed. The IWW, in the end, was destroyed by continual harassment by the federal authorities during the war and the prosecutions under various state criminal syndicalist statutes following the war. (Brooks 1971, 123)

The Espionage Act of 1917 was used to suppress free speech and to incarcerate the more radical labor leaders, anarchists, socialists, and Communists. The Supreme Court considered their ideas "a clear and present danger." Some labor leaders advocated the violent overthrow of the government. Others, like the socialist Eugene V. Debs, simply believed in workers having more control over production and a more equal distribution of wealth. Debs ran for president of the United States in 1912, receiving about 6 percent of the vote. He was arrested under the Espionage Act in 1917 and was sentenced to 10 years in jail. While in prison he ran for president in 1920. On December 25, 1921, President Warren G. Harding pardoned him, but Debs died shortly afterward. The espionage law was used effectively to repress radical labor unions into the mid-1930s.

Ludlow Massacre

The **Ludlow massacre** illustrates the role of the federal government in mediating a severe labor dispute. The conflict emerged in the summer of 1913, when the United Mine Workers began organizing coal miners in northern Colorado. Coal miners lived in isolated mining camps owned and controlled by mining companies. The company owned the land, the houses, the stores—everything. Miners were not paid for the hours of hard work spent digging for the coal, only for the weight of the coal they extracted. The miners demanded the right to get paid for the time they worked, whether they extracted coal or not; the right to shop at the store of their choice; the right to choose their own doctors; the right to work without armed guards watching them; and other rights. In September 1913, more than 8,000 miners went on strike.

> Any knowledgeable observer could have predicted tragedy, for armed conflict was almost certain to occur. Coal mining imposed a degree of vassalage so inconsonant with the American ideal of freedom, that the resort to arms was practically inevitable. . . . Even in peaceful times, the civil rights of the miners had been routinely ignored. Once the strike began and miners were openly cast as enemies, all restraints were dropped. The companies imported several hundred additional deputies and mine guards, among them Texas desperadoes and thugs provided by the Baldwin-Felts Detective Agency. (Gitelman 1988, 3)

The miners armed themselves and moved out of the company camps and set up tents. Violence between company hirelings and miners was pervasive and severe. The governor of Colorado sent the state militia to keep the peace. It was not clear who fired the first shot, but armed company guards entered the Ludlow camp and a gun battle ensued. Labor historian Howard Zinn described the events as follows:

> On the morning of April 20, a machine gun attack began on the tents. The miners fired back. Their leader . . . was lured up into the hills to discuss a truce, then shot to death by a company of National Guardsmen. The women and children dug pits beneath the tents to

escape the gunfire. At dusk, the Guard moved down from the hills with torches, set fire to the tents, and the families fled into the hills; thirteen people were killed by gunfire. The following day, a telephone linesman going through the ruins of the Ludlow tent colony lifted an iron cot covering a pit in one of the tents and found the charred, twisted bodies of eleven children and two women. This became known as the Ludlow Massacre. (1990, 347–348)

The largest mining company, Colorado Fuel and Iron, was partially owned by the Rockefellers. The U.S. Department of Labor attempted to contact John D. Rockefeller, Jr., and persuade him to negotiate to avoid the loss of lives. Rockefeller refused to make any concessions. He made this point clear at a congressional hearing:

CHAIRMAN: And you are willing to go on and let these killings take place . . .

ROCKEFELLER: There is just one thing . . . to settle this strike, and that is to unionize the camps; and our interest . . . demands that the camps shall be open camps . . .

CHAIRMAN: And you will do that if it costs all your property and kills all your employees?

ROCKEFELLER: It is a great principle.

CHAIRMAN: And you would do that rather than recognize the right of men to collective bargaining? Is that what I understand?

ROCKEFELLER: No sir. Rather than allow outside people to come in and interfere with employees who are thoroughly satisfied with their labor conditions—it was upon a similar principle that the War of the Revolution was carried out. It is a great national issue of the most vital kind. (cited in Gitelman 1988, 14–15)

Dualism of the Dominant Policy Paradigm

Rockefeller's perspectives reflected the dominant way of thinking during this period. On the one hand, Rockefeller joined the alliance with the AFL and supported the AALL. On the other hand, he adamantly opposed collective bargaining. This dual perspective arose from the Progressive and classical paradigms. The Progressive paradigm was subordinate; it argued for the Progressive policies of the period.

The classical paradigm, however, was dominant; it portrayed unions as illegitimate and threatening to the prerogatives and freedoms of property owners: the right of owners to hire and fire whomever they wanted, and to manage their own property and employees as they saw fit. This paradigm promoted a view of individual and constitutional rights antagonistic to any notion of the collective rights of workers. The classical paradigm operated to undermine unions and prevent collective bargaining. Unions interfered with the basic rights of workers: their contract rights and their freedom of association. This view was popular with the U.S. Supreme Court, which struck down minimum wage and maximum working hour legislation on grounds that such laws violated the contract rights of employees protected by the due process clauses of the Fifth and Fourteenth Amendments. To express this point in money terms, the Court said that a law that set the minimum wage at 50 cents an hour violated the right of a worker to accept a job making a nickel an hour. Nowhere did the classical paradigm accept the collective rights of workers to livable wages, fair treatment, decent working conditions and lives, and safe and healthy workplaces.

Finally, antiunion business and political leaders defined unions and collective bargaining as un-American, criminal, and treasonous. This perspective of Americanism reemerged during the McCarthy era of the 1950s. It legitimized violence against radical organizations and industrial labor unions throughout the early 20th century.

✧ *The New Deal Labor Policy Regime, 1938–1970*

Industrial union organizing erupted with a vengeance during the 1930s. The combination of massive labor organizing and the Great Depression strained the Progressive labor policy regime and created pressures for a policy regime change. Efforts to suppress collective bargaining were like holding the lid on a boiler that was already overheated and about to explode. Keeping the lid on tight made the explosion inevitable, and explosions occurred across the country.

Industrial Union Organizing and Labor Strife

Union organizing, labor strife, and violence intensified in the volatile decade of the 1930s. The number of strikes increased sharply, doubling in just one year from 841 in 1932 to 1,695 in 1933, increasing to 1,856 in 1934, and to 2,014 in 1935 (Piven and Cloward 1979, 133). By 1937 there were 4,740 strikes across the nation. It was like a civil war: employees against employers with epic battles. These battles involved thousands of workers fighting hired company guards, local police, and state militia. They included the Electric-Auto-Lite Company workers in Toledo, truck drivers in Minneapolis, dockworkers in San Francisco, and textile workers across the country. The International Longshoremen's Association (ILA) and the Maritime Workers Industrial Union closed down the port of San Francisco. Piven and Cloward described the strikes of the textile workers:

> The textile strike that erupted across the nation in the summer of 1934 took on the character of a crusade as "flying squadrons" of men and women marched from one southern mill town to another, calling out the workers from the mills to join the strike. By September, 375,000 textile workers were on strike. Employers imported armed guards who, together with the National Guard, kept the mills open in Alabama, Mississippi, Georgia, and the Carolinas. Before it was over, the head of the local union in Alabama had been shot, his aides beaten; Governor Talmadge of Georgia declared martial law and set up a detention camp for an estimated 2,000 strikers; fifteen strikers were killed . . . in Honea Path, South Carolina; riots broke out in Rhode Island, Connecticut. . . . (1979, 125)

The labor war gained momentum with the establishment of the **Congress of Industrial Organizations (CIO).** Initially the CIO was located inside the American Federation of Labor (AFL), but industrial labor leaders formed the new organization out of frustration with the AFL's passivity and neglect of industrial unions. The CIO broke with the AFL and began a more aggressive organizing campaign. It rejoined the AFL in the 1950s to form the AFL-CIO, as it is known today.

Organizing among Automobile Producers

In 1936 the labor war spread into the automobile industry. General Motors (GM), the largest automobile producer, was hit first. Workers initiated a sit-down strike that paralyzed the company by the end of the year. The strike spread quickly throughout the country, hitting GM plants across the nation. At the firm's plant in Flint, Michigan,

> . . . the first response of the company was to use police in an attempt to isolate the strikers in Flint and starve them out. Next, an injunction was obtained against the seizure of the plants by the strikers. Both policies failed. The sit-down strikers of the Fisher Plant number 2 in Flint not only held their own in a five-hour battle with the police but for good measure later seized a transmission plant to bolster the strike. (Widick 1989, 70)

Flint police failed to capture the Fisher Plant from the autoworkers. To restore order, the governor of Michigan sent in the National Guard, which surrounded the plant. The autoworkers called on the leader of the CIO, John L. Lewis, to intervene. Widick described the confrontation between the governor and the labor leader:

> When Governor Murphy hinted that he might use national guards to oust the sitdowners, Lewis declared: "I shall personally enter the General Motors plant, . . . I shall order the men to disregard your order and to stand fast. I shall then walk up to the largest window in the plant, open it, and divest myself of my outer raiment—remove my shirt and bear my bosom. Then, when you order your troops to fire, mine will be the first breast that its bullets will strike. (1989, 71)

With all the publicity and with the possibility of large numbers of casualties, the governor backed down. Eventually, GM settled the strike. However, sit-down strikes spread to other plants and then to Chrysler and Ford. Organizing in the auto industry continued throughout the 1930s and into the 1940s.

A Crisis in Labor Policy

The rapid organizing, the mobilization of unions, and the pervasive violence and chaos constituted a crisis in labor policy, which strained the old policy regime. Fighting the unions was too costly in terms of the loss of life, property, and productivity. By the mid-1930s business and industrial leaders were ready to strike a bargain with labor unions. Industrial leaders would recognize unions and legitimize collective bargaining; in exchange, unions would control their own members and limit their political involvement. Out of this bargain, the New Deal labor paradigm emerged to replace the old one. This paradigm accepted the rights of employees to join unions, the right to collective bargaining, and the idea of collective rights to decent wages and working conditions. It reflected the compromise between unions and management and supported the New Deal labor policy regime.

Under the new regime, with the support of business and labor leaders, the Roosevelt administration and Congress responded to the labor crisis with new labor laws. Congress passed several major labor bills.

- The *Norris-LaGuardia Act of 1932* outlawed yellow dog contracts and limited the use of injunctions against unions.
- The *Wagner Act of 1935* guaranteed the right of workers to organize and bargain collectively.
- The *Fair Labor Standards Act of 1938* established minimum wages, set overtime pay and maximum working hours, and prohibited child labor. The National Labor Relations Board was established to enforce the new law and to regulate unionizing and collective bargaining.

The Supreme Court shifted its position on labor policies when in 1937 it upheld the constitutionality of the NLRB (*NLRB v. Jones and Laughlin Steel Corp.*). Four years later the Court upheld the Fair Labor Standards Act and overturned previous cases that had invalidated child labor, minimum wages, and maximum working hours. These cases represented a profound change in the position of the Supreme Court on labor policy.

Labor Policy Changes of the 1950s

After World War II, labor policies changed incrementally, but in a conservative direction. Congress passed the Taft-Hartley Act and the Landrum-Griffin Act.

The *Taft-Hartley Act of 1947* outlawed the closed shop, but permitted the union shop and right-to-work state laws. The **closed shop** rule prohibits the hiring of an employee unless he or she joins the union. Under the **union shop,** employees have the option of paying the collective bargaining fee without paying the additional union membership fee. Employees in a **right-to-work state** can work without joining a union and without the mandatory requirement of paying fees for union services. These laws made it difficult for unions to succeed in organizing employees. The Taft-Hartley Act established several other rules. It prohibited unions from charging excessive dues, required them to file reports on union expenditures, and outlawed secondary boycotts and wildcat strikes. A secondary boycott occurs when workers in one factory refuse to purchase products to support workers in another factory or company.

The *Landrum-Griffin Act of 1959* required unions to file detailed reports on union finance, elections, and operations to the Department of Labor. It established secret ballots in union elections, free speech at union meetings, and the right to sue the union for unfair practices. It barred ex-convicts and Communists from serving as union officers, a provision that was used to purge radicals from labor unions during the McCarthy era of the 1950s. In 1965 the Supreme Court struck down the provision prohibiting Communists from serving as union officers.

The National Labor Relations Board

The **National Labor Relations Board (NLRB)** is an independent regulatory commission with five members appointed by the president and approved by the Senate. It has regulatory and quasi-judicial powers and is responsible for implementing the Wagner, Taft-Hartley, and Landrum-Griffin acts. The NLRB oversees authorization elections which are held by employees to determine by majority vote whether or not they want to be represented by a specific union in the collective bargaining process. The NLRB certifies those unions authorized to represent employees and also has the power to decertify a union—that is, denying it the legal right to represent employees.

The NLRB is responsible for protecting the rights of unions, employers, and individual employees. It adjudicates disputes of **unfair labor practice.** Unfair practice complaints can be filed by an employer against a union, by a union against an employee, or by an employee against the union.

There are many examples of unfair labor practice complaints. Typical unfair labor practice complaints filed by a union against an employer include:

- Failure to bargain in good faith.
- Deliberately trying to provoke a strike.
- Circumventing the union board and negotiating directly with employees.
- Refusing to process grievances.

Unions sometimes engage in picketing in order to attract public attention to labor issues.

Typical unfair labor practice complaints filed by employers against unions include:

- Failing to bargain in good faith.
- Deliberately inciting a strike.
- Calling a strike before the expiration of a contract.
- Filing excessive numbers of trivial or bogus grievances.

An employee has the right to file an unfair labor practice complaint against the union for failing to represent the employee in a legitimate grievance or for suppressing free speech in a union meeting.

In processing unfair labor complaints, the NLRB operates like a court. It holds hearings like a trial, and trial examiners conduct the hearings like a judge. The NLRB also investigates issues and makes rulings. It has the power to issue cease and desist orders, to seek federal court injunctions, and to issue regulations that have the force of law.

➔ *From the New Deal to the Protective Labor Policy Regime*

The New Deal labor policy regime lasted from 1938 to 1970. Several political developments of the 1960s contributed to the policy regime change. The expansion of public service unions enhanced the power of labor unions. By the end of the 1960s, labor also had alliances with civil rights, environmental, and consumer protection organizations, forming a powerful coalition. This coalition constituted the political power base of the protective labor policy regime.

The Rise of Public Sector Unions

The power base of the protective labor policy regime expanded with the rapid growth of public service unions. Public service organizations antedate the 20th century, although most were benevolent societies. Postal workers had organized in the late 19th century. Boston police officers went on strike in 1919 for higher wages and union recognition. Calvin Coolidge, the governor of Massachusetts at the time, sent the AFL president the following message: "There is no right to strike against the public safety by anybody, anywhere, anytime" (quoted in Shafritz and Russell 2000, 395).

Organizing among public service workers increased during the 1960s for two reasons. First, the acceptance of labor unions in the private sector encouraged organizing in the public sector. Second, the increase in wages among workers in the unionized private sector and the growing wage gap between the public and private sectors created pressures for union organizing among public sector workers. Federal employees began to organize after President John F. Kennedy issued an executive order permitting them to engage in collective bargaining.

The 1960s saw a dramatic increase in union organizing and strikes among public employees. There were bitter organizing battles involving sanitation workers and teachers. Several leaders of teachers unions were arrested and jailed for supporting strikes. In 1969, for example, the president of the American Federation of Teachers, David Selden, was jailed for 40 days after marching with teachers on a picket line in Newark, New Jersey. Other public employees at the local level increased their unionizing efforts. In 1968 Martin Luther King, Jr. was assassinated in Memphis, when he came to the city to support the strike of city sanitation workers.

One of the fastest-growing public service unions of the late 20th century was the **Association of Federal, State, County and Municipal Employees (AFSCME),** which emerged during the Depression and aggressively lobbied state legislatures during the 1950s and 1960s to secure the passage of laws allowing collective bargaining among public employees. AFSCME had a membership of just over 10,000 before World War II; by the mid-1980s it had grown to more than a million members. It has continued to grow since then, but at a slower pace.

In response to the unionization of the public sector, many states established special boards of labor relations. These boards are often called **public employee relations boards, or PERBs, or state employee relations boards, or SERBs.** They operate like the NLRB. States also established procedures to encourage fair bargaining, to facilitate the resolution of labor-management disputes, and to avoid strikes or work stoppages. States provide for mediation, arbitration, and binding arbitration. **Mediation** involves an intermediary who acts as a facilitator when negotiations break down. The goal of the mediator is to get both sides back to the bargaining table, to facilitate negotiations, and to encourage each side to reach a settlement. **Arbitration** involves conducting hearings with each side presenting arguments, data, and information supporting its position. Sometimes the hearings operate like a trial. After listening to both sides, the arbitrator makes a decision and presents a suggested settlement. In the case of **binding arbitration,** both sides must accept the arbitrator's decision. Most states with strong public service unions mandate binding arbitration for unions that deal with the protection of persons and property—police and firefighters unions. Binding arbitration forces the settlement of labor disputes without the risk of a strike.

In 1978 Congress passed the *Civil Service Reform Act,* which gave the president more power over the federal bureaucracy, established the Office of Personnel Management, and created the Merit System Review Board. This bill also created the **Federal Labor Relations Authority (FLRA),** which operates like the NLRB, except that it deals with federal public sector unions and collective bargaining. The *Postal Service Reorganization Act of 1970* placed postal unions under the NLRB.

The Occupational Safety and Health Administration

The passage of the *Occupational Safety and Health Act of 1970* and the establishment of OSHA signaled the emergence of the protective labor policy regime. Several factors contributed to this policy regime change. First, government studies demonstrated the severity of the problem—that before the establishment of OSHA more than 14,000 workers were killed on the job and over 2 million workers were disabled. The National Safety Council reported a 29 percent increase in work-related accidents between 1961 and 1970. Of course, the increase may be due in part to increased attention to these accidents, greater awareness of the issue, and more accuracy in reporting. For 1970 alone, the U.S. Department of Labor estimated the number of deaths due to occupation-related diseases at 100,000 (Gerston, Fraleigh, and Schwab 1988, 173). Major catastrophes such as the disaster in November 1968 at Consolidated Coal Company mines raised public attention to the issue of workplace safety. An explosion trapped 78 miners, all of whom died. Congress responded by passing the *Mine Safety Act of 1969* (Cobb and Elder 1983). A year later Congress established OSHA.

Second, a power shift occurred in favor of OSHA policies, including an increase in the political influence of unions. Unions had increased in numbers, membership, and political influence. This increase was helped in no small measure by the upsurge of public service unions and the political strength of the AFL-CIO. Major unions made occupational health and safety issues top priority. Industrial workers, construction workers, textile workers, and workers in other areas had become more sensitive to workplace hazards and put increased pressure on their unions to give safety issues a high priority.

The power shift was boosted by the emergence of other public interest organizations, which joined with labor unions to form a strong coalition for workplace health and safety regulations. Environmental groups such as the National Resource Defense Council, health groups such as the Cancer Institute, consumer interest groups such as Ralph Nader's study group, and some civil rights groups joined together in a powerful coalition to support OSHA policies.

OSHA, an agency of the Department of Labor, regulates safety and health in the workplace. Initially, it focused almost exclusively on safety, but it was overzealous in establishing safety regulations and precipitated strong criticism from both liberal and conservative groups. In its first two years of operation, OSHA established over 4,000 new standards, most copied from established sources, with some obsolete and absurd. OSHA's aggressive pursuit of trivial safety regulations exacerbated its conflict with business organizations and eroded its reputation and credibility. Businesses challenged OSHA in court. The threat of lawsuits made OSHA operate more cautiously.

Labor unions were unimpressed with the safety regulations and, along with health agencies, unhappy with the lack of health regulations, especially workers' exposure to hazardous and toxic substances such as carcinogenic agents. The **National Institute of Occupa-**

tional Safety and Health (NIOSH) produced studies alerting OSHA and the public to the possible dangers of worker exposure to asbestos, benzene, cotton dust, and other agents. NIOSH urged OSHA to regulate worker exposure to these agents.

As a result of public pressure, OSHA began to respond to union concerns for workplace health. In the mid-1970s, it began setting standards for worker exposure to these hazardous agents. Industry challenged the new standards in the courts. The courts required OSHA to prove that exposure to these agents significantly impaired the health of exposed workers. OSHA had to rescind its benzene regulations. Businesses attacked cotton dust regulations as too costly. However, the Supreme Court rejected the cost argument because it was not included in the legislation. By the early 1980s, OSHA policy was well established.

→ Labor Policy Changes from 1980 to the Present

Labor policies continued to change after 1980. However, the changes up to the present were incremental. During this period, each president entered the White House with a definite agenda, moving labor policy in either a conservative or a liberal direction, promoting either less protection or more protection for workers.

President Reagan entered the White House with an agenda that favored business over labor. A good example of his position on labor is illustrated in the case of the **Professional Air Traffic Controllers Organization (PATCO),** a public union with over 11,000 members. In August 1981, PATCO went on strike over concerns related to working conditions: the increase in air traffic, the workload of controllers, and pressure. Although PATCO had supported Reagan's campaign for president in 1980, Reagan fired all of the striking controllers and replaced them with military controllers and new civilian trainees. Eventually, PATCO was decertified and it went bankrupt.

Another illustration of Reagan's coldness toward labor is his record of appointing pro-business candidates to the NLRB and OSHA. Most of Reagan's appointments to regulatory agencies tended to favor business over labor. Criticizing Reagan's pro-business appointments to the NLRB, William Greider wrote:

> The National Labor Relations Board has been converted by business appointees into a regulatory agency that adeptly protects management by stalling and suppressing workers' grievances. In the first 150 days of the Reagan administration, the NLRB reversed eight major precedents. Its pro-business decisions in union-representation cases soared to 72 percent, compared to 46 percent in the Carter administration and 35 percent under Gerald Ford. (1993, 193)

The number of undecided cases more than doubled, "effectively nullifying the workers' complaints by postponing a remedy for years and years" (Greider 1993, 193).

Reagan and OSHA

Reagan appointed Thorne Auchter, a construction company executive, with a poor record with OSHA to head this agency. His company in Florida had been cited for 48 safety violations (Gerston, Fraleigh, and Schwab 1988, 184). Nevertheless, Auchter claimed he was committed to changing the direction of OSHA and to making it more business friendly. He wanted the agency to move away from a police style of administration to a cooperative approach. But Reagan cut OSHA's budget by 25 percent, which hurt OSHA's ability to develop new regulations and to implement existing regulations. OSHA had to reduce the number of its inspections, which made it easier for businesses to evade OSHA regulations.

Officials in the Reagan administration tended to focus on the cost of administration. For example, prior to becoming the head of Reagan's Council of Economic Advisers, Murray Weidenbaum estimated the costs of regulations for 1979 alone at $103 billion (Tolchin and Tolchin 1983, 127). Concerns about costs drove most of the regulatory changes of the Reagan administration.

Dr. Sidney Wolfe, the former director of the Public Citizen Health Research Group, insisted that the major question was not how much hazards in the workplace cost, but who should bear the costs. He argued that prior to the establishment of OSHA, the costs were borne by workers' compensation, Supplemental Security Income disability payments, public health programs, individual workers suffering from occupation-related diseases or injuries, and the families of workers who died from work-related illnesses or accidents. Lloyd McBride of the United Steel Workers added, "Even under the most adverse conditions, OSHA has uncorked a bottle of knowledge of workplace hazards and unleashed an educational process which has awakened workers to the dangers they confront on the job. It has put all employers on notice of the regulatory intent of the government" (Gerston, Fraleigh, and Schwab 1988, 195).

The Effectiveness of OSHA

There has been a great deal of debate over the effectiveness of OSHA. Both liberals and conservatives attacked this policy. Liberals attacked OSHA for being too passive and not doing enough to protect workers; conservatives criticized the agency for imposing silly and useless regulations, levying unacceptably high fines on businesses, and doing nothing for workers. Table 9.1 summarizes data on the number of deaths and disabling injuries from accidents on the job. Despite the criticism of OSHA, deaths and disabling injuries from job-related accidents have declined substantially over time.

Labor Policy since 1990

Labor policies continued to expand gradually under the administrations of George H. W. Bush and Bill Clinton. Bush's agenda was moderate compared to Reagan's conservatism. The Americans with Disabilities Act (ADA) of 1990 and the Civil Rights Act of 1991 were passed under the Bush administration. As you have read, the ADA prohibited discrimination on the basis of disabling conditions and the Civil Rights Act of 1991 forbade racial harassment on the job. The *Family Leave Act of 1993,* passed during the Clinton administration, required employers with 50 or more workers to allow employees an unpaid leave of up to 12 weeks for childbirth or the care of a spouse, parent, or close relative. The law required an employer to guarantee that employees would have their jobs back when they returned from the 12-week leave.

Ergonomics

The most recent and the most controversial development in labor policy is OSHA's ergonomic regulations. **Ergonomics** refers to occupation-related injuries resulting from repetitive motions. This issue has its roots in the Reagan and Bush administrations. In 1988

TABLE 9.1

Deaths and Disabling Injuries from Job-Related Accidents

Year	Number of Deaths (in 1,000s)	Number of Disabling Injuries (in 1,000s)
1945	16.5	13.8
1950	15.5	12.9
1955	14.2	12.2
1960	13.8	12.1
1965	14.1	12.3
1970	13.8	12.1
1975	13.0	11.4
1980	13.2	11.5
1985	11.5	10.3
1990	10.1	9.1
1995	5.0	4.3
2000	5.0	4.4

SOURCE: U.S. Census Bureau *Statistical Abstract of the United States,* 2002.

Secretary of Labor Elizabeth Dole ordered her department to study the issue and explore the prospect of developing regulations. By the end of the 1990s, OSHA had developed comprehensive ergonomic regulations covering several industries and job categories. They were the most extensive set of regulations since the early years of the agency, yet they had been developed much more cautiously than other regulations.

To illustrate the ergonomics problem from the perspective of labor, Molly Ivins and Lou Dubose described the experiences of Sherry Durst, a catfish skinner in Mississippi.

> In order to keep her job at Freshwater Farms, Durst has to skin a minimum of twelve fish a minute. At times, a white supervisor stands behind her with a stopwatch, calculating minutes and catfish. Durst never falls below fifteen, at times hits twenty, and has skinned more than twenty-five catfish a minute. (2003, 57)

Sherry Durst "skinned between 8,100 and 10,800 catfish" in a 10-hour shift (Ivins and Dubose 2003, 58). Durst was a member of the United Food and Commercial Workers Union. The old contract allowed for a 30-minute lunch and a 10- to 15-minute break. The main issue at the end of contract negotiations was bathroom breaks. Workers were not allowed to take bathroom breaks without permission from a supervisor, and supervisors were reluctant to give permission for fear of falling behind in meeting quotas for the number of fish skinned. Women complained of supervisors entering restrooms to get workers back on the assembly line. After going on strike and getting the help of celebrities like Reverend Jesse Jackson, Dick Gregory, and others, the catfish skinners got a contract that protected the right to privacy in the restroom, overtime pay, and a reasonable lunchtime policy. However, the union was unable to deal with the ergonomics issue, which was completely outside the scope of the contract. Moreover, fish companies were unwilling to risk slowing down the pace of processing fish. Consequently, there was a high rate of ergonomic-related injuries such as hand and joint problems, wrist in-juries, cysts, and arthritis among workers still in their 20s.

Dr. Ron Myers treated many of the fish workers and reported seeing young women ages 24 to 26 with the arthritic wrists of 60-year-olds (Ivins and Dubose 2003, 61). Many fish workers were physically unable to continue working because of injuries received from the intense repetitive pace of the job. Former workers who were disabled by the work were now receiving some form of disability support. The stories of the fish workers illustrate that the er-gonomics problem is real.

In response to labor unions and a genuine concern for the issue, President Clinton is-sued an executive order directing OSHA to move more quickly on the regulations. OSHA is-sued 600 pages of new regulations in January 2001, just after George W. Bush took office.

Reaction from industry was swift and furious. Business and corporate leaders stormed Congress. "[T]he National Coalition on Ergonomics and companies such as United Parcel Service . . . hired legal help of their own to fight the rule" (Skrzycki 2003, 111). Congress re-sponded to the pressure, called hearings, and acted under the *Congressional Review Act of 1996*, which allows Congress to overturn an executive order, to pass a special law killing the regulations in 2001. Commenting in support of the legislation, President Bush said:

> Today I have signed into law . . . a measure that repeals an unduly burdensome and overly broad regulation dealing with ergonomics. . . . There needs to be a balance between an understanding of the costs and benefits associated with Federal regulations. In this instance, though, in exchange for uncertain benefits, the ergonomics rule would have cost . . . employers billions of dollars and presented employers with overwhelming compliance challenges. Also, the rule would have applied to a bureaucratic one-size-fits-all solution to a broad range of employers and workers—not good government at work. (quoted in Skrzycki 2003, 47)

Consistent with Reagan's approach, George W. Bush appointed antiregulatory and pro-business officials to Labor Department positions. After Congress repealed the ergonomics reg-ulations, Secretary of Labor Elaine Chao assured concerned senators that she would consider developing comprehensive and workable ergonomic policies in the near future. Two years later, she proposed voluntary ergonomic regulations. As of 2005 there are no ergonomic regulations.

Overtime Pay

Chao provoked opposition from labor when in March 2003 her department proposed sub-stantial changes in the Fair Labor Standards Act (FLSA) overtime policy. Chao claimed that the changes would benefit both employers and employees. Under the new regulations, the bottom wage level of the workers guaranteed overtime pay was raised from about $9,000 an-nually, the level set in 1975, to about $22,000. In other words, any worker who earned less than $22,000 would be guaranteed time-and-a-half pay for every hour worked beyond 40 hours a week. A $65,000 annual salary limit was set for overtime pay. The regulations diluted the educational requirements for professional employees and expanded that group to include occupations that historically had been protected or guaranteed overtime pay.

Labor leaders and policy critics opposed the regulations for several reasons.

- The lower threshold for guaranteeing overtime pay was too low.
- If the 1975 threshold standard were indexed to the cost of living, the new threshold would be $27,000, not $22,000.

- The new regulations diluted the educational requirements for the definition of a professional status. This change increased the number of occupations classified as a profession exempt from overtime regulations to include licensed practical nurses, medical assistants, dental assistants, firefighters, and many others. In other words, the new regulations denied overtime pay to millions of workers.
- The new regulations penalized veterans because training in military service also counted as professional training. (Eisenbrey and Bernstein 2003)

Labor leaders mobilized in the summer of 2003 to derail the regulations scheduled to take effect in March 2004. They converged on Congress in the fall. They lobbied the House which passed a bill to rescind the regulations. Business counterattacked; President Bush interceded and pressured key senators to back off the legislation. By early 2004 Senate efforts to stop the new regulations had died.

Weak Unions and Public Policy

The power of U.S. labor unions peaked in the early 1970s. They are weaker politically in the United States than in other developed countries, and they continue to decline. In the early 1980s about 20 percent of the workforce belonged to a union. This figure fell to 13.5 percent by 2000 (*Statistical Abstract of the United States* 2003).

France, Germany, Great Britain, Italy, and other developed countries have strong and active labor and socialist political parties that are more directly involved in shaping the policies of those countries. The absence of a labor party in the United States tends to enhance the advantage of business and corporate interests, as labor unions tend to counterbalance these interests.

There are several reasons why there is no labor party in the United States. First, the United States has a winner take all two-party system that discourages other parties. In contrast, parliamentary systems, which award seats to candidates for the national legislative body on the basis of the proportion of votes they receive, encourage the participation of many parties. Labor parties are common in these systems and sometimes elect prime ministers as is the case of Tony Blair in Great Britain. A third-party candidate has never won a presidential election and few have won congressional races. Labor unions in the United States have the choice of supporting one or the other of the two major parties and no chance of winning a presidential election.

Second, craft or skilled trade unions and industrial unions have been divided over political candidates and racial issues. For example, skilled trade unions supported Herbert Hoover, Richard Nixon, and Ronald Reagan. The Edsalls claimed that race was a major factor in explaining the defection of skilled trade unions from the New Deal coalition and union support for Nixon and Reagan, as Nixon opposed busing and Reagan opposed affirmative action (Edsall and Edsall 1992).

Third, government action, especially during the first half of the 20th century, destroyed radical unions and crushed socialist parties. The labor unions that survived at the end of the century were committed to compromising with business.

The absence of a labor party and the weakening of labor unions have thus enhanced the advantage of business interests in the policy-making process. The issues of ergonomics and overtime policy illustrated this advantage.

Summary

Labor policy has experienced four different policy regimes: classical, Progressive, New Deal, and protective. In the classical labor policy regime, the dominant paradigm criminalized collective bargaining, first through common law and later through the Sherman Antitrust Act. Merchants, master craftsmen, landowners, and manufacturers dominated this regime. State governments arrested labor leaders who tried to strike for wage increases.

The Progressive labor policy regime supported the classical labor paradigm, which recognized individual contract rights and property rights, but denied the collective rights of workers to fair wages and safe working conditions. This paradigm defined labor leaders as anti-American, outside troublemakers who coerced happy employees into unions. Passive conservative unions acquired some influence and worked with industrial leaders. Progressives passed several laws—child labor, minimum wage, maximum working hours, and workers' compensation. Only workers' compensation survived the Supreme Court's onslaught. The Court decided that these laws violated individual contract rights protected by the due process clauses of the Constitution.

The big change in labor policy came with the New Deal labor policy regime. Business leaders understood that the classical labor policy regime was too costly in terms of the loss of life, property, and labor time. It was better to reach a bargain with labor. Corporate and business leaders would recognize unions and accept them as unequal partners or partners with substantial limits. The unions could ask for more money and better working conditions, but issues involving control of the company were not even open to discussion.

Union membership, especially public service unions, continued to grow throughout the 1960s. In the late 1960s unions joined forces with civil rights, environmental protection, and consumer rights groups to push for workplace health and safety. These changes gave rise to the protective labor policy regime and the Occupational Safety and Health Administration which protects the safety and health of workers. Despite all the criticism against OSHA, the number of fatalities in work-related accidents has declined remarkably. By the end of the century, the membership and political influence of labor unions had declined. However, developments in protective labor policy continue to evolve at a slow pace in the first decade of the 21st century.

Review Questions

1. Summarize the classical view of labor unions. How would this view explain labor-management conflict?
2. The period of labor policy before the New Deal is often called a laissez-faire period. Why? What are some problems with this view?
3. Discuss how state governments and the federal government responded to labor unions and collective bargaining prior to the New Deal. What explains this type of response?
4. What were some indications of advances in labor policy during the Progressive period?
5. How would you characterize the New Deal labor policy regime? How does it differ from the classical and Progressive labor policy regimes?
6. How did labor policy change in the late 1960s and early 1970s? What factors contributed to these changes?

7. Discuss the pros and cons of ergonomics.
8. What are some contemporary labor policy issues?
9. Discuss the types of issues likely to provoke an unfair labor practice complaint.
10. Why does the United States not have a labor party like those found in other democratic developed countries?

Select Websites

This is the official Website for the U.S. Department of Labor.
http://www.dol.gov

This is the Website for the U.S. Occupational Safety and Health Administration.
http://www.osha.gov

This is the Website for one of the oldest labor unions, the AFL-CIO.
http://www.aflcio.org

This is the Website for one of the fastest-growing labor unions, the AFSCME.
http://www.afscme.org

Key Terms

American Federation of Labor (AFL)
arbitration
Association of Federal, State, County and
    Municipal Employees (AFSCME)
associations
benevolent societies
binding arbitration
blacklist
boycott
closed shop
collective bargaining
Congress of Industrial Organizations (CIO)
ergonomics
Federal Labor Relations Authority (FLRA)
guilds
Haymarket riot

Industrial Workers of the World (IWW)
Knights of Labor
Ludlow massacre
mediation
National Institute of Occupational Safety
    and Health (NIOSH)
National Labor Relations Board (NLRB)
Professional Air Traffic Controllers
    Organization (PATCO)
public employee relations boards (PERBs)
right-to-work state
state employee relations boards (SERBs)
unfair labor practice
union shop
yellow dog contract

CHAPTER 10

Competitive Regulatory Policy

Competitive (sometimes called economic) regulatory policies entail the regulation of competition by the government. This type of policy includes regulation of prices, entry into the market, the rules of competition, standards for the quality of products or services, the quantity of goods produced, the areas of the country served, and accounting practices. Sometimes it involves the dismantling of artificial monopolies or promoting emerging technology or new industries.

Policy theory assumes that competitive regulatory policies, like distributive policies, are noncontroversial and involve iron triangles or close relationships among special interest groups, congressional subcommittees, and lower-level bureaucratic agencies. However, iron triangles have operated only so long as powerful interests have prevailed in keeping other interests out of the policy-making arena. Competitive policies have been as contentious as redistributed policies during periods of policy regime change and when the policy shifted wealth from one group to another.

There have been intense ideological disputes over competitive regulatory policies, especially between libertarians and conservatives on one side and communitarians and liberals on the other (see Chapter 1). Libertarians and conservative economists generally oppose these types of policies. They believe that regulations undermine competition, reduce efficiency, and violate the right to private property. They argue that open competition constrains firms to operate efficiently and to produce better quality products for lower prices. The market punishes inefficient firms that produce low-quality goods and charge high prices, as these firms soon lose customers to their more efficient competitors and then go out of business.

Communitarians and liberals have supported competitive regulatory policies. They argue that competitive regulations are needed to deal with some of the negative aspects of unregulated markets. Whereas unregulated open markets produce more efficient firms, sometimes these markets create unintentional problems: monopolies, unstable markets, disorganized markets, unscrupulous competitive practices, and other problems. Faced with these problems, communitarians insist that to maintain the benefits of open competitive markets, some form of competitive regulatory policy is needed. Also, they believe that competitive regulatory policies are needed when private businesses engage in activities that involve a public use, have public consequences, or impact the public interest.

→ Markets and the Development of Government Regulation

Competitive regulatory policies have been around for centuries. Early examples have included the role of government in establishing a uniform system of weights and measures, building harbors, and regulating shipping and other businesses involving public use. State governments have long regulated entry into the market by granting charters to corporations. The Industrial Revolution aggravated the negative tendencies of markets and created a greater demand for competitive regulations. A closer examination of these problems—monopolies, disorganized markets, unstable markets, and unscrupulous competitive practices—illustrates the point.

A monopoly is poisonous to a competitive market because there is no competition when one firm controls the market. Two types of monopolies emerged with the Industrial Revolution: natural and artificial. **Natural monopolies** occur when the initial costs of entering the market are extremely high and when a single firm is able to provide the goods or services more efficiently and cheaper than several competing firms. A utility company is a good example of a natural monopoly. **Artificial monopolies** arise out of predatory competition, when one firm sets out to buy out, bankrupt, or destroy other firms.

When one firm controls the market, there are fewer incentives to lower prices, to innovate, to produce better-quality products or services, or to operate more cost-effectively. Monopolies are especially troubling when consumers are harmed by high prices, poor quality products, or little opportunity to enjoy more advanced technology. Under a monopoly, a customer only has two choices: Do without the product or pay the higher price. Government regulations help to solve this problem by breaking up the monopoly or regulating it.

Disorganized markets arise when open competition prevents the development of a new technology. A prime example of a disorganized market is early radio. With several radio stations initially operating on the same frequency, no firm could successfully operate on the air. Government regulations helped to resolve this problem by issuing licenses that designate which station may operate on which frequency. You will read more about radio and television later in the chapter.

Unstable markets are characterized by extremely high numbers of business failures. A classic example is the near collapse of the banking industry during the Great Depression.

Bank customers had lost confidence in the market until the federal government guaranteed their deposits through regulations.

Examples of unscrupulous competitive practices include a butcher selling horse meat as prime beef, one business stealing the logo of a successful competitor, and other unethical practices. Left unchecked, these practices could destroy consumer confidence, undermine markets, and disadvantage reputable businesses. In the small, stable community of the preindustrial market, consumers could more easily detect and correct these problems. However, in the mass, transient society of the industrial era, it is more difficult to police these practices. Consumers and reputable business leaders looked to government to perform this function and restore consumer confidence.

Congress created several agencies in the late 19th and early 20th centuries to regulate specific industries or address specific problems. For example, Congress created the **Interstate Commerce Commission (ICC)** to regulate the railroad industry and later the trucking industry; the **Federal Communications Commission (FCC)** to regulate telephones, radios, and televisions; and the **Civil Aeronautics Board (CAB)** to regulate airplanes. Congress created the **Antitrust Division of the Justice Department** to regulate trusts and break up illegal, artificial monopolies, and the Federal Trade Commission to regulate fair competition. Each agency became the center of a separate policy regime.

The case of the ICC illustrates major shifts in competitive regulatory policy regimes, from promotional to competitive regulatory, to protective/minimal regulations. The FCC illustrates the problem of disorganized markets and the political need for diversity. The Antitrust Division of the Justice Department demonstrates the enduring problem of monopolies and consolidation.

→ Railroad Regulations and the Interstate Commerce Commission

Government regulation of railroads was a classic example of competitive regulatory policy. It involved three periods of development or policy regimes: promotional (1800–1887), competitive regulatory (1887–1987), and protective/minimal regulatory (1987–present).

The Promotional and State Regulatory Period

The promotional period was characterized by federal and state support for the emerging railroad industry. Railroads were established in the eastern part of the United States prior to the Civil War. State and federal governments supported this growth through tax breaks, land acquisitions, land grants, bonds, loans, and other methods. Railroads continued to expand throughout the 1860s, again with substantial support from government. For example, "between 1862 and 1871, the states granted 17 million acres to railroads, and the federal government granted 130 million acres" (Dempsey and Thomas 1986, 7). As railroads spread westward during the 1870s, western towns competed with each other to attract a railroad line. A railroad line made the difference between the life and death of a town. Towns sold bonds, offered grants, loaned money, gave away land, and provided other inducements. This substantial government support made the rapid expansion of railroads possible.

Railroad companies engaged in fierce, cutthroat competition to eliminate competitors and dominate the industry. They competed for major contracts and routes. They engaged in price wars, secret agreements, kickbacks, and other practices. As some companies went out of business, others consolidated and formed regional monopolies. As companies fought to dominate the market, their tactics created problems for others. For example, a railroad company would reduce its prices well below what it could afford in order to drive competitors out of business or obtain a preferred shipping contract. To make up for the losses, the company would increase prices substantially in other areas. It was common for a railroad company to charge low rates for long hauls in order to meet the competition and high rates for short hauls, where it operated as a monopoly. In response, farmers organized to protect themselves from the railroad companies and their unfair practices.

As early as 1867 farmers established the Patrons of Husbandry and the Farm Alliance, organizations that assisted farmers in pooling their resources and protecting their economic and political interests. These organizations formed the basis of the **Granger movement,** a powerful political movement of farmers successful in a number of midwestern and western states in securing the passage of state laws regulating the prices of railroad haulage and grain storage. By the 1870s, the Granger movement expanded into a larger social movement called the **Populist movement.** This movement demanded government regulations of monopolies, especially railroad monopolies.

Court Challenges to State Regulations

Two major Supreme Court cases challenged state regulations: *Munn v. Illinois* (1876) and *Wabash, St. Louis and Pacific Railway Co. v. Illinois* (1886). The *Munn* case is important because it involved a fundamental constitutional challenge to competitive regulatory policy. The State of Illinois had enacted laws to regulate railroads and grain warehouses or elevators. The law required owners of grain warehouses to obtain a license to operate and it set a maximum limit on the price of storage. Munn insisted that his warehouse was private property and that the state law violated the Fifth and Fourteenth Amendments, which prohibited states from depriving individuals of private property without due process. He refused to obtain a license and charged a rate above the maximum limit. The Supreme Court sided with Illinois and upheld the law. In writing the majority decision, Chief Justice Morrison R. Waite made a number of important points.

1. He insisted that when private property is used in ways that affect the public and impact the larger community, a public interest is created and government acquires a responsibility to regulate that property for the common good. [*Munn v. Illinois* 94 U.S. 113 (1876)]
2. He cited English common law cases of government regulation of ferries, wharves, warehouses, and other forms of private property with a public use. In the United States, Alabama regulated the licensing of tavern keepers and the price of inns.
3. The immense grain elevators in Chicago, holding up to a million bushels, were affected with a public interest because they stored grain for several farmers and served the entire region.

The *Munn v. Illinois* case was important because it provided the legal argument for the expansion of competitive regulatory policies. These policies spread to other states across the country.

The *Wabash* case was a setback. In this case the Supreme Court struck down certain aspects of state railroad regulations that involved interstate commerce. It held that the federal government had exclusive jurisdiction in this area. Although there was already strong pressure for federal regulation of the railroads and a number of bills had been introduced before the *Wabash* case, this decision created an urgency for federal action.

The Interstate Commerce Commission

In 1887 Congress passed the *Act to Regulate Commerce,* which did several things:

1. Created the Interstate Commerce Commission (ICC).
2. Required fair and just rates.
3. Mandated that all rates be published and adhered to.
4. Prohibited undue preference and higher rates for the short hauls than for the long hauls.
5. Gave the Interstate Commerce Commission responsibility for monitoring the railroads to make sure they complied with the law.

The ICC was the first national independent regulatory commission. Its creation signaled the beginning of a new competitive regulatory regime.

Most historians attribute the establishment of the ICC to the Populist movement, a social movement among farmers that expanded beyond the Granger movement. Populists demanded the creation of the ICC. However, historian Gabriel Kolko argued that merchants, industries, and railroad companies called for the establishment of the ICC. These interests were angry with railroad companies that made secret deals with preferred customers. For example, the Petroleum Association was especially angry with railroad companies that made secret deals with the Standard Oil Company for low transportation rates. Standard Oil, in turn, used the low rates to lower its prices on petroleum in order to bankrupt other petroleum companies. Outraged, other petroleum companies called for a federal regulatory agency to prevent the secret deals. Merchants, too, were upset by the extreme variations in prices. Kolko insisted that many railroad companies also supported regulations because they wanted stability and security in the industry, and an end to debilitating price wars (Kolko 1965).

The more accurate story is most likely a combination of the two views. The Populist movement certainly created strong pressures for the establishment of the ICC, but when merchants, industrial corporations, and railroad companies joined them in calling for national regulations, they formed a powerful coalition.

The Interstate Commerce Commission was initially weak. It could not impose penalties or fines on railroad companies for violating the Act to Regulate Commerce. It had to take a company to court because only a federal court could impose a fine. In the early decades of the 20th century, however, Congress strengthened the powers of the ICC. It prohibited railroad rebates, required railroads to give a 30-day notice before increasing rates, and gave the ICC the power to rescind rate increases if the ICC determined them unreasonable and unjust. In 1935 Congress passed the *Motor Carriers Act,* giving the ICC jurisdiction over trucks and buses. The law allowed the ICC to establish maximum working hours for truck drivers, maximum and minimum rates for hauling material, and quality standards for trucks and trucking equipment. Also, it gave the ICC responsibility for safety regulations. During the civil rights movement of the 1950s and 1960s, the ICC played a major role in desegregating passenger trains and buses engaged in interstate travel.

The railroad industry declined after World War II. Truck and bus companies emerged to compete with the railroad industry. With the creation of the interstate highway system in the mid-1950s and increased truck production, trucks transported an increasing number of goods that were once hauled by train. By the 1960s reliance on rail transportation had declined substantially as businesses began using trucks for rapid delivery of products. People relied more on airplanes, automobiles, and buses for travel. These changes threatened the economic solvency of railroads; major railroads went out of business. Congress gave the ICC the power to regulate the closing of railroad passenger lines.

In response to the financial crisis in passenger railroad lines, Congress passed the *Rail Passenger Service Act of 1970,* which authorized the formation of the **National Railroad Passenger Corporation.** This corporation established a special subsidized quasi-public government corporation, the American Track Corporation or **Amtrak.** Today Amtrak is the largest passenger rail company in the United States where it operates as a monopoly in many areas.

The Roots of Deregulation

The Interstate Commerce Commission was deregulated in the 1980s. It lost its powers and by the end of the century it was gone. Four factors contributed to this policy regime change: (1) economic conditions, (2) a liberal assault, (3) a conservative assault, and (4) government officials.

Economic Conditions

Major changes in economic conditions contributed to the deregulation movement. First, the railroad industry was no longer the mammoth it used to be. It had declined substantially in the face of strong competition from the trucking industry. Moreover, passenger railroads were losing customers to airplanes, buses, and automobiles. Second, the economy was in crisis. During the late 1970s, it was suffering an energy shortage and experiencing high inflation and unemployment rates. This crisis created pressures for policy change.

The Liberal Assault

Liberal political organizations assaulted the ICC. These organizations, especially consumer interest groups, were concerned about excessively high prices. A good example of a consumer interest group is the Ralph Nader Study Group. The Nader Group attacked the ICC as a "captured" agency. **Capture** means two things: (1) the agency has formed a close mutual relationship with the industry, sometimes exchanging personnel from agency to industry and back; (2) the agency regulates for the benefit of the industry instead of the public.

The Nader Study Group published *The Interstate Commerce Omission* which documented the close relationship between ICC officials and leaders of the railroad and trucking companies. It cited cases in which ICC officials attended industry-sponsored conferences and cocktail parties held on yachts owned by industry executives. It listed cases in which ICC officials were offered and accepted jobs from railroad and trucking companies or lobbying firms representing the regulated industry. It demonstrated that the regulations benefited the railroad and trucking industries, not the public interest. It also pointed out that there were few safety regulations (Fellmeth 1970).

In response to consumer pressure, Congress created three new agencies. In 1966 it established the Department of Transportation (DOT) and, within that department, the **Federal Railroad Administration (FRA).** The FRA acquired responsibility for safety regulations.

- It set licensing requirements for railroad engineers.
- It limited the maximum working hours for railroad workers.
- It set safety standards for tracks and the security of heavy and loose cargo, such as tree logs.
- It worked with state agencies to coordinate crossing regulations.

The third agency, the **National Highway Transportation Safety Administration,** was created. This organization is responsible for investigating accidents involving automobiles.

The Nader Group's campaign for consumer protection regulations and opposition to competitive regulations explain the mixed response from Congress. Congress hacked away at competitive regulations, but supported consumer protection regulations over the next two decades.

Conservative Assault

Conservative economists insisted that because the trucking industry was competitive, because trucking freight companies competed with railroad freight companies, and because consumers had a choice to travel by car, bus, train, or airplane, ICC regulations could no longer be justified on grounds of government regulation of a monopoly. They argued that ICC regulations produced inefficiency and high prices. They called for the deregulation of the ICC.

Public Officials

By the mid-1970s, ICC commissioners favored deregulation and produced a study outlining the advantages of relaxing regulations. Also, the Carter administration had given a high priority to the deregulation of competitive regulatory policies.

Regulatory Policy Regime Change

In 1980 Congress passed the *Motor Carrier Reform Act, Staggers Rail Act,* and the *Household Goods Transportation Act.* The Motor Carrier Act relaxed regulations and made it easier for trucks and trains to enter the market. The Staggers Rail Act allowed railroads for the first time, within certain bounds, to set their own rates. It made it easier for railroads to close down unprofitable lines. Together these two acts eased the regulations and opened the railroad and trucking markets.

The Household Goods Transportation Act was a consumer protection bill directed at the moving van industry. It responded to abuses in the interstate moving business. For example, consumer interest organizations accused local agents of nationwide moving companies of "lowballing"—that is, quoting a customer an extremely low price, and then adding hidden prices after the customer had signed a binding contract. The company would warehouse the customer's property, charging a daily storage rate and keeping the property until the customer paid the full price. This act prohibited lowballing and required national moving companies to honor agreements made by local agents.

The ICC was abolished in 1995, although railroad regulations did not completely disappear with it. Its powers and responsibilities were transferred to other agencies. The Federal Railroad Administration acquired the power to regulate railroad safety. In 1996 Congress created the **Surface Transportation Board (STB),** which acquired some of the ICC's competitive regulatory responsibilities. This agency regulates mergers, acquisitions, and line abandonment. It also regulates moving companies and certain trucking companies.

The old competitive regulatory policy regime died with the ICC. A new regulatory policy regime—the protective/minimal regulatory regime—emerged with three defining characteristics. First, the new policy regime protected select passenger railroad companies under the new Amtrak system, which enjoyed government support and subsidies. Second, competitive regulations were minimal and fragmented. The responsibilities of the centralized ICC were divided among several federal agencies. Finally, safety and a few consumer protection regulations continued, but under different agencies.

✦ Regulatory Policy and the Communications Industry

Another form of competitive regulatory policy involves the communications industry. This industry includes the telephone, telegraph, radio, television, cable television, Internet, satellites, wireless phones, and many more. Most communications regulations involve antimonopoly and market entry policy: breaking up huge phone monopolies and licensing broadcast stations. Recently, it has involved the promotion of new telecommunications technology.

The Telephone Industry

The telegraph was invented in 1835, Samuel Morse created the Morse code by 1844, and the telephone was patented in 1876. The telephone inventor, Alexander Graham Bell, helped form the Bell Telephone Company, which later incorporated the long-distance subsidiary American Telephone and Telegraph Corporation (AT&T). By the end of the century AT&T had became Bell's parent company. Bell initially used its patents to control the market. It franchised smaller companies to operate in local markets and lease its equipment. It operated like a monopoly until its patents expired at the end of the 19th century. At the beginning of the 20th century, hundreds of small companies emerged to compete with AT&T. However, backed by major New York banks, AT&T engaged in an aggressive strategy to drive competitors either out of business or into the Bell system. It bought out local companies, refused to allow competitors to use its long-distance service or provided them with poor connections, and barred the use of non-Bell equipment on its own telephone lines. AT&T also bought a 30 percent interest in Western Union, the telegraph company (Davies 1994).

Competitors filed complaints as they were excluded from the market. In 1912, as the result of an antitrust suit pursued by the Justice Department, AT&T agreed to allow customers to install phones made by companies other than AT&T, to allow competitors to connect to its long-distance service, to stop buying up or bankrupting competitors, and to divest Western Union.

The Justice Department went after AT&T two more times: once in the 1950s and again in the 1980s. Under the renewed threat of breaking up the company, AT&T reached another consent agreement with the Justice Department in 1956. The agreement barred AT&T from entering into unregulated markets, which included data processing facilities. It

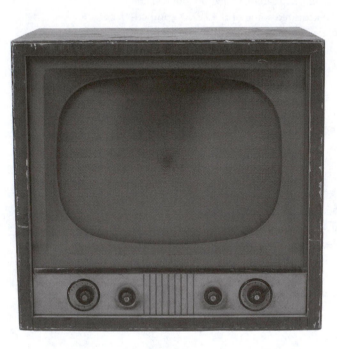

An early television set.

was allowed to keep Western Electric. By 1980 AT&T had emerged again as a giant monopoly. Through its direct ownership of 22 local Bell companies, "AT&T supplied approximately 90 percent of all domestic and international long-distance services" (Davies 1994, 157). In a consent agreement with the Justice Department, AT&T was required to divest its 22 Bell companies and form seven Regional Bell Operating Companies. The Baby Bells, as they were popularly known, were required to give customers a choice of long-distance companies. The agreement allowed the regional Bells or other companies to continue to operate local monopolies, but it opened up the long-distance phone market to competition. This competition was expected to do two things: push down prices and increase investment in new technology. Prices have not come down even with the increased number of new companies using new technologies. The new technology includes the use of microwave, fiber optics, digital transmissions, and an increased integration of phones and computers.

Radio and Television

Radios appeared in the first decade of the 20th century. There was some initial difficulty in its development because several people and companies held patents on different parts of the radio. Companies such as Westinghouse, AT&T, General Electric, and Western Electric formed a partnership to share patents: the Radio Corporation of America (RCA).

The U.S. Navy had an early interest in radio communications. As a result of its promotion of the radio, private radios emerged quickly in the shipping industry where they were used in ship-to-ship and ship-to-shore transmissions. Small commercial radio stations emerged rapidly in the early 1920s. By the mid-1920s, the major radio companies created networks, such as the National Broadcasting Company.

Radio broadcasting companies immediately faced problems with the hundreds of new radio stations filling the radio frequencies, especially in large urban areas. More than one firm could not operate on the same frequency, a problem that produced chaos on the airwaves. A voluntary agreement among several stations to operate on a designated frequency did not work because any new firm not part of the agreement could enter the airways and produce chaos again. Without rules for getting firm commitments to operate on a designated frequency and for operating on the air, and without a legitimate entity to police the airways and enforce the rules, there could be no commercial radio broadcasting. The industry understood that government regulation was necessary in order for broadcasting to take place and broadcasters called for government intervention.

The U.S. Department of Commerce took the lead in establishing ground rules for commercial broadcasting stations to obtain a fixed frequency and operate on the air. The department began licensing stations and organizing conferences of radio broadcasters. In 1927 Congress established the Federal Radio Commission (FRC), which inherited the Department of Commerce responsibilities. The FRC designated channels for broadcasting and helped bring stability to a chaotic market. In 1934 Congress established the Federal Communications Commission (FCC) to replace the FRC. The FCC acquired jurisdiction over radio, television, telephones, telegraphs, and other forms of communications.

Television appeared during the 1930s, but it did not expand rapidly until the 1950s. In 1946 there were about 10,000 television sets; by 1950 there were 10 million (Comstock 1991).

The FCC focused its resources largely on radio and television. It had responsibilities in five major areas: promotion, access to airwaves, policing the airwaves, speech, and competition within the broadcast industry. Because Congress provided little money for promotion, the FCC was unsuccessful in this area. Its other functions were chiefly the same as those established for the FRC. Commercial radio stations were confined to FM or AM. Television stations were restricted to very high frequency (VHF) until Congress passed a law in 1962 expanding the access of television broadcasting to include ultra high frequency (UHF) channels. The FCC began licensing UHF stations in the mid-1960s. It also issued rules requiring television manufacturers to include UHF receivers on the sets they manufactured.

The FCC's policing responsibilities involved the routine practice of monitoring the airways and responding to the complaints of consumers and broadcasting stations of interference with unauthorized broadcasters or pirates. The FCC had special equipment to triangulate pirates and prosecute them.

The FCC regulated speech on the air, a type of regulation that collided head-on with free speech issues. In recent times, three major free speech issues have arisen over FCC regulations: the fairness doctrine, obscenity, and diversity.

The Fairness Doctrine

The **fairness doctrine** originated with the Federal Radio Commission in 1927 and was promoted by the FCC from 1934 to 1988. Initially, the FCC required broadcast stations to allot equal time to candidates for political office. Congress and the FCC refined the fairness doctrine during the 1960s and required broadcast stations to (1) allot equal time in the coverage of candidates for public offices and (2) "operate in the public interest and to afford reasonable opportunity for the discussion of conflicting views on issues of public importance" (Section 301 of the *Communications Act of 1934,* quoted in Krasnow, Longley and Terry 1982, 20). Later the personal attack rule was added, requiring a broadcast station responsible for an attack on a person's honesty, character, or personal qualities to give that person a reasonable opportunity to respond.

Opponents of the fairness doctrine opposed it on two grounds. First, it constituted a clear violation of the First Amendment protection of free speech and free press. They pointed out that while it was unconstitutional for the government to require the licensing of newspapers and to tell them what views to print, the fairness doctrine required the licensing of broadcast news stations and the government telling broadcasting stations what views to air. The requirement that stations provide expensive airtime to opposing viewpoints constituted a de facto and unconstitutional form of prior restraint censorship. The expensive costs of requiring stations to provide free time to opposing views would have a chilling effect on speech.

Second, opponents claimed that the fairness doctrine was now obsolete. It was based on the notion of scarcity—the presence of only two or three television stations in an area meant that views excluded from those stations would be excluded from the public airways. Scarcity created a compelling reason for the fairness doctrine, but with advancements in technology—satellites, cable, microwaves, Internet—scarcity no longer existed. With hundreds of venues for thousands of views, stations no longer needed to cover them all.

Supporters disagreed for three reasons. First, they rejected the First Amendment argument, claiming that it pertained to the right of the people to free speech and to a free exchange of ideas, not to the right of a private corporation to suppress those ideas. The airways belonged to the public and should be open to the marketplace of ideas.

Second, they rejected the technology argument. Although technological advances had opened up many other venues of news and communications, the number of local broadcasting stations remained limited. Moreover, the consolidation in the ownership of broadcast and cable companies meant that control of the airways would remain in the hands of the few, not the many.

Finally, supporters insisted that the so-called chilling impact of the fairness doctrine was based on misconceptions over its implementation. For example, Ray (1965) claimed that in implementing this doctrine, the FCC required equal coverage of candidates running for public office, not equal coverage of competing views. For example, the FCC rejected the claim of atheists that the fairness doctrine required them to have equal time on stations that broadcast religious programs. The FCC also rejected the claim of a minister who demanded equal time on stations that aired beer and wine commercials to speak on the evils of alcohol. Contrary to the claims of its opponents, the fairness doctrine never required stations to air any particular view. It expanded speech; it did not suppress it.

The End of the Fairness Doctrine

The FCC administered the fairness doctrine up to 1987. Broadcast corporations and networks opposed it. Consumer, civil rights, and civil liberty groups supported it. In the early 1980s the majority of FCC commissioners produced a study concluding that the fairness doctrine was obsolete and violated the First Amendment. The study disagreed with the Supreme Court's *Red Lion* decision of 1969.

The *Red Lion Broadcasting v. FCC* case was instructive. A journalist, Fred J. Cook, had published a book titled *Goldwater: Extremist on the Right*. On a Red Lion television program, a minister accused the journalist of being a liar and a Communist. Cook asked for the opportunity to respond to the accusations. The station refused so the journalist filed a complaint with the FCC. The FCC insisted that responsible journalism and public interest required the station to allow a response from the journalist. The FCC did not require equal time, only a reasonable effort to present a fair and balanced view. The Court unanimously sided with the FCC. Eighteen years after this decision, the FCC ended the fairness rule.

Obscenity

The FCC has established standards of decency for local radio and television stations. The Supreme Court has upheld these standards, primarily because radio and television are unlike other forms of media such as art, videos, or CDs. Radio and television programs are beamed into people's living rooms in almost every home in America. Because children have easy access to these programs, the FCC applies different standards and rules than it does for other media. The Court does not accept the **obscenity rules** as a violation of First Amendment rights, and the FCC continues to enforce these rules. Moreover, the agency appears to be drifting in a more conservative direction, as evidenced by two high profile cases and by large fines imposed on radio or television stations that violate obscenity rules. One case involved the indecent exposure of entertainer Janet Jackson during the 2004 Super Bowl half-time entertainment. Ms. Jackson claimed that the incident was the result of a "wardrobe malfunction." The FCC fined CBS $550,000 for the incident. Another case involved Howard Stern, a radio talk show host with a reputation for lewd and lascivious comments. The FCC imposed steep fines on Stern and the radio company that aired his show. Clear Channel established a zero-tolerance policy in early 2004 and later fired Stern for his obscene comments made on the air. In the 2005 Superbowl CBS banned a commercial made by Mickey Rooney because he had exposed his naked rear.

Consolidation

The consolidation issue has been a central problem in FCC regulations. **Consolidation** concerns one firm buying up many other firms. Consolidation was most evident in the telephone industry, especially with the AT&T monopoly, and to a lesser extent in the television and radio industries. When a single firm owns all the telephones in an unregulated market, it can charge as much as customers are willing to pay. When a single company owns all the television and radio stations, it is well positioned to control a primary source of news information and to limit the political views expressed on television and radio.

There are three major types of consolidation in the media: (1) vertical, (2) horizontal, and (3) cross-media ownership. Vertical consolidation has to do with a nonmedia corporation owning a mass media company. A good example of vertical consolidation is General Electric's ownership of the National Broadcasting Company (NBC) through purchase of RCA. Horizontal consolidation has to do with one media company buying another or others. This can occur two ways: station-station, or network-affiliate. Cross-media consolidation is the purchase by one media (e.g., a newspaper) of another media (e.g., a television station).

For a long time, FCC regulations restricted consolidation. It explicitly prohibited one television station in a local area from owning another television station in the same area. It limited the number of radio stations a single company could own. It prohibited station-station and cross-media consolidation. In the early 1970s the FCC barred cross-media ownership in the same location; for example, a St. Louis newspaper could not own a television station in that city. The FCC has always limited the share of the market one television firm was able to control.

Various media organizations such as the National Citizens Committee for Broadcasting (NCCB) sued the FCC on grounds that these rules violated the First and Fifth Amendments. In the late 1970s, the Court rejected the free speech and property rights argument and upheld the regulations in *FCC v. NCCB* (1978).

TABLE 10.1	
The Largest Media Corporations and Their Subsidiaries and Affiliates	
Companies	**Subsidiaries/Affiliates**
General Electric	NBC, which has 13 affiliates. 25% to 50% of A&E, CNBC, Court TV (with Time Warner), History Channel (with Disney)
Walt Disney	Owns ABC, ABC Network News, ABC Radio, Disney Channel, 80% of ESPN, 50% of Lifetime, a small percent of A&E
Viacom	Owns CBS, Blockbuster Video, Paramount, Simon & Schuster, Infinity Radio, Nickelodeon, MTV, VH1, M2, TNN, FLIX, Movie Channel. Part owner of Sundance Channel, All News Channel, Comedy Central
News Corporation	20th Century Fox, *New York Post, London Times, TV Guide,* HarperCollins; Fox News, Fox Family Channel, National Geographic Channel; several sports teams
Time Warner	Turner Broadcasting, HBO, CNN, TNT, WIN, TBS, Cinemax, Cartoon Network; Warner Books

SOURCE: Bagdikan, Ben. *Media Monopoly.* Boston: Beacon Press, 2000; Digital TV Project. *Who Controls the Media?* 2003; Fallow, James. "The Age of Murdoch." *Atlantic Monthly,* September 2003.

The FCC began to relax these regulations in the late 1970s and early 1980s. It offered waivers to cross-ownership rules. It legalized the practice of local newspapers owning local television and radio stations, provided the ownership served a public interest. It allowed one company to own up to eight radio stations in a single area. It permitted more consolidation on the national level.

As the rules on consolidation were relaxed, consolidation increased. Ben Bagdikian documented this increase in his *Media Monopoly* (2000). In the early 1980s about 50 firms dominated most of the broadcast market. By the early 1990s this figure had declined to about a dozen. By 2004, five megacorporations were the parent companies of all of the television networks: General Electric, Walt Disney, Viacom, News Corporation, and Time Warner. Table 10.1 shows the extent of their holdings.

Shifting Arenas of Conflict: The Deregulation War

FCC regulations have remained relatively stable over the century. As with most competitive regulatory policies, the policy-making process involved little conflict, low visibility, and slow incremental change. The pattern of policy making followed the iron triangle—a close relationship between the television and radio industry, the FCC, and related congressional committees. The broadcast industry has clearly dominated the FCC policy-making process, often to the exclusion of other interest groups.

Cable Television Act of 1992

Policy making became somewhat contentious over the *Cable Television Act of 1992.* This bill involved a conflict between local television stations and cable companies. Consumer interests and local broadcast stations formed a temporary alliance to support this bill. Consumer groups complained of escalating cable bills and declining cable services. Local broadcast stations complained of cable companies excluding local stations. The alliance prevailed over the cable companies, and Congress passed the Cable Television Act, which set limits on the costs of cable television, restricted price increases, and required cable companies to include local broadcast stations.

Telecommunications Act of 1996

The FCC policy-making process quickly returned to normal. Industry clearly dominated the policy-making process with the passage of the *Telecommunications Act of 1996*. Nonindustry interests such as consumers were closed out of the iron triangle. Telephone, television, radio, cable, cell phone, long-distance phone companies, Internet, and other industry interest were directly involved with debates over this act.

The Telecommunications Act of 1996 was a smorgasbord of industry proposals. It repealed most of the Cable Television Act, eliminating price regulations on cable television, but continuing to require cable television to carry local stations. The act provided guidelines for broadcast television transitioning from analog to digital and high-definition television, the latest development in television technology. It promoted competition within the telephone industry and encouraged telephone companies to enter other communication markets, including cable television. The Telecommunications Act allocated money for research and development in telecommunications.

The most controversial aspect of the 1996 act was its attempt to deregulate the FCC. Beginning in 1998 the FCC was required to review all its regulations to eliminate those that were no longer necessary, and to review the remaining regulations every two years. By making provisions of the act ambiguous and giving the FCC responsibility for determining what rules should be eliminated, Congress shifted the conflict over this policy from itself to the FCC. It made the FCC the lightning rod of conflict. The FCC attracted fire the moment it began the rule-making process involved in implementing the act.

The FCC chairperson, Michael Powell, Colin Powell's son, was enthusiastic about implementing the Telecommunications Act. He argued that the old regulations were outdated, that things had changed over the past 20 years, and that there were more choices in the media today. Powell insisted that the FCC could no longer justify the old rules prohibiting a newspaper from owning a television station, forbidding one television station from owning other stations, or limiting market ownership. In the spring of 2003, after several hearings, the FCC formally proposed eliminating the rules. This proposal provoked a political war, as interest groups shifted the battleground from the FCC back to Congress. Political armies for and against the rule change organized themselves for major battles.

Having much to gain from eliminating FCC rules, the parent companies and the major networks joined the side of the FCC and supported Powell. They insisted that the scarcity and diversity issues were now irrelevant, and that more consolidation was a good thing because it was cost-efficient and would eliminate the duplication of efforts in the media. Moreover, FCC regulations infringed on their private property rights.

A wide range of diverse political interest mobilized against the FCC and its proposed rule changes. These interests included business, professional, liberal, and conservative organizations. Locally owned television stations, the affiliates of the major networks, were afraid that the elimination of the regulations would allow the big fish networks and their parent companies to gobble up the little fish—them. This change was against the public interests of local communities because a local station loses its independence when it is bought by a network. This loss of independence would mean the loss of the right to interrupt a network program to make emergency announcements about a hazardous chemical spill or to air gubernatorial debates. The local stations insisted that the FCC's mission was to promote the public interest, and this interest would be lost with the elimination of regulations.

The FCC consolidation issue split the National Association of Broadcasters (NAB). The networks supported the rule changes, but the local affiliate stations opposed them. Professional interests including journalists, television announcers, and others were concerned that further consolidation would lead to the loss of jobs, the loss of professional control, the erosion of professional standards, and the loss of diversity. They worried that the networks, through their cost-cutting efforts, would reduce the quality of broadcast journalism.

Liberal groups included the National Organization for Women, the Rainbow Coalition, the Consumer Union, and others. They were especially concerned about rules governing diversity and free speech. Further rollbacks in FCC rules would threaten the current status of diversity in broadcasting, black-owned radio and television stations would disappear, more women and minorities would lose jobs in broadcasting, and television programs sensitive to women and minority interests would diminish.

A consumer interest group, the Center for Public Integrity, found that although FCC regulations prohibit a company from owning more than 8 radio stations in a single area, there were 34 metropolitan statistical areas (MSAs) in which a single company owned and operated more than 8. It also found that the greatest concentration of radio ownership was in smaller rural communities. One company, Clear Channel, owned more than 1,200 radio stations nationwide, as many as 15 in Washington alone (Dunbar and Pilhofer 2003).

Conservative groups opposed to the FCC rule changes included the Christian Coalition and the National Rifle Association. The Christian Coalition was concerned that the demands for increased profits by the parent corporations would mean more sex and violence on television and fewer wholesome family programs. They were also concerned about the future of religious programs. The National Rifle Association was concerned about the loss of competing viewpoints on broadcast television.

These organizations converged on Congress and were successful in getting the Senate to hold special hearings. The hearings ended with the Senate voting to overturn the rules. However, the rule changes remain in place because the House had not joined the Senate in overturning them. In the summer of 2004, the United States Court of Appeals for the Third Circuit struck down the FCC regulatory changes. The federal appeals court claimed that the FCC had not provided a reasonable analysis to justify the rule change. In January 2005, the FCC decided not to appeal the decision to the Supreme Court.

The Future of the Federal Communications Commission

The FCC is likely to survive throughout the 21st century, although power arrangements supporting this agency and its policies have changed. In the past, broadcast networks dominated the FCC. Today megacorporations do so. The development of cable television, the Internet, and satellite technology has allowed the emergence of large numbers of television channels and different ways of getting television to the market. Whereas the parent corporations and the current FCC see these changes as contributing to more diversity in the media, opponents see the ownership of these media sources by megacorporations as contributing to less diversity. These opponents include an unlikely coalition of business, professional, liberal, and conservative groups. The ability of the FCC to continue to promote the public interest may depend on the ability of this tenuous coalition to mobilize.

→ *Antitrust and Antimonopoly Policy*

Whereas the Federal Communications Commission focused on competition among radio and television broadcast stations, another agency regulated competition across industries and enterprises: the Antitrust Division of the Justice Department. This agency was established in 1890, when Congress enacted the Sherman Antitrust Act of 1890, a few years after the Interstate Commerce Commission (ICC). Like the ICC, the Antitrust Division was a product of the Populist movement. The Antitrust Division became the center of a generic regulatory policy regime that has lasted for more than a century and is likely to continue throughout the 21st century.

The early years of the Antitrust Division were rocky. The Sherman Act was vague and did not clearly prohibit monopolies or spell out that most contracts restrained trade. The Antitrust Division pursued cases in civil court and lost most of the early ones. A good example of one early major loss is the *U.S. v. E.C. Knight* decision (1895). E.C. Knight was a sugar company that controlled more than 98 percent of the U.S. sugar market. Despite this obvious monopoly, the Supreme Court did not see any violation of the law, arguing that E.C. Knight constituted a monopoly only in manufacturing, not in commerce or trade. The Court pointed out that the Sherman Act prohibited restraint of commerce or trade, not monopolies in production.

In the 1900s the Sherman Act was used against labor unions. The Supreme Court ruled that union contracts restrained commerce and violated the act (see Chapter 9). The Antitrust Division was more successful in the *Standard Oil v. U.S.* case (1911). In this case, as in others, the Court insisted that the Sherman Act did not prohibit monopolies, but forbade unreasonable actions that restrained trade and produced monopolies. The Antitrust Division prevailed because it was able to identify specific actions of Standard Oil that contributed to its control of over 80 percent of the petroleum market. The illegal actions identified by the Antitrust Division included engaging in price wars, using dummy trust and holding companies, and controlling transportation of oil for the purpose of bankrupting competitors and obtaining a monopoly. The Court broke up Standard Oil into 33 different companies and established the unreasonable action rule in judging whether a monopoly was legal or not (Meier 1985). The *Standard Oil* case illustrates what Alan Stone (1977) called the contradiction of the open competitive markets. According to Stone, one of the goals of competition is to eliminate competitors and to control the market. Of course, when this goal is achieved, the market ceases to be open and competitive.

Throughout the past century, the Antitrust Division pursued an active antitrust policy. It secured the breakup of International Harvester (1918), Eastman Kodak (1920), International Business Machines (1956), United Fruit (1958), and AT&T (Meier 1985). The Antitrust Division's most recent case involved Microsoft.

Microsoft Case

Several state governments joined the Antitrust Division in a complicated and controversial suit against Microsoft in the late 1990s. Microsoft manufactured both the Windows program and the Internet Explorer Website browser. It had established a monopoly with its Windows 95 and Windows 98 programs. Most computer manufacturers installed the Windows programs. Initially, Netscape's Navigator was the top seller in the early 1990s, controlling about 80 percent of the Website browser market. Microsoft's Internet Explorer controlled only

3 percent. The coding that Microsoft installed on its Windows program made it extremely difficult to remove the Internet Explorer without damaging the Windows program. Netscape sales plummeted while Internet Explorer sales soared. The Antitrust Division and states considered Microsoft's actions as constituting an unreasonable monopoly. Microsoft considered its actions good business strategy; it argued that its market shares increased because it offered a good product for a cheap price and it provided better service than its competitors.

The federal district court ruled in favor of the Antitrust Division. Microsoft appealed and the appeals court overturned much of the lower court decision, but still found Microsoft in violation of antitrust law. Ultimately, Microsoft reached an agreement with the Antitrust Division which allowed the company to develop new Windows programs, but required it to reduce the costs of its program licensing and to allow licensees to make adjustments to its programs, including removal of the Internet Explorer program.

Regulation versus Deregulation

There has been a great deal of recent debate over antitrust policy. On one side of the debate are scholars who argue against these policies. One of the most interesting contributions to this position is Robert Bork's book *The Antitrust Paradox* (1978). According to Bork, the paradox is that antitrust laws are intended to enhance competition but have the opposite effect: they produce higher prices, obstruct innovation, and promote inefficiency. Moreover, the unscrupulous behavior that some of these antitrust regulations are supposed to prevent rarely occurs and, when it does, this behavior is best addressed by law enforcement agencies, rather than by competitive regulatory policies. Opponents of antitrust regulations insist that monopolies should not be judged inherently bad. If the monopoly is efficient, then it should be accepted as legal.

Robert Kuttner offers a good critique of Bork's work in *Everything for Sale* (1997). Kuttner argued that Bork provided little evidence to support his paradox and assumed uncritically that private markets are inherently efficient and that predatory pricing is practically nonexistent. Kuttner and other supporters of competitive regulations offered several examples to support their position. First was the collapse of the savings and loan industry. Savings and loan associations got in trouble after regulations governing their investment patterns were relaxed. Many invested in junk bonds, investments in businesses that had high returns on investments but high rates of bankruptcy. When the high-risk junk bond investments collapsed, savings and loan associations lost billions of dollars. Second, supporters of competitive regulation pointed to the Enron case.

Enron

There is no better example of the impact of unscrupulous practices than Enron. This company was established in 1985 with the merger of Houston Natural Gas, headed by Kenneth Lay, and Inter North, a Nebraska-based gas company. Enron grew rapidly, buying other companies and building power plants in other countries and purchasing energy. By 2000 it boasted revenues of $100.8 billion (Fox 2003, 221). That same year Congress passed the *Commodity Futures Modernization Act* and relaxed energy and electronic trading regulations. Enron established electronic trading in one division and began trading energy in another. At the end of 2001, it became the largest firm in history to declare bankruptcy up to that time.

The consequences of Enron's bankruptcy were devastating. Thousands of people lost their jobs and pensions, as pension funds were heavily invested in Enron stock.

It is not entirely clear why Enron went bankrupt. Some blame bad investment, the purchase of insolvent businesses, the use of Enron stock as collateral, and the trading in energy. But it is clear that Enron had followed unscrupulous practices. These practices were revealed through investigations and indictments.

Among those indicted was Arthur Andersen, one of the nation's most renowned accounting firms. Arthur Andersen helped Enron deceive its investors by grossly overstating the company's revenue. In a questionable but legal practice, the company listed the full value of a trade as revenue, rather than the net gain of the trade.

> So if Enron bought $100,000 worth of natural gas, then sold it an hour later for $101,000, Enron booked the full $101,000 as revenue rather than the $1,000 in gross profit it made on the deal. (Fox 2003, 221)

Andersen helped Enron hide revenue lost in many deals by shifting the losses to other companies in other countries. Andersen was not indicted for the practice of deceiving investors, but the firm was indicted and convicted for obstruction of justice. When the Securities and Exchange Commission began to investigate Enron, Arthur Andersen employees had begun destroying documents. A number of Enron executives were indicted, including Andrew Fastow, the former chief financial officer, Jeff Skilling, the chief executive, and Kenneth Lay, the chairperson of the board. Fastow was sentenced to 10 years. Lay and Skilling are awaiting trial.

In the aftermath of the Enron fiasco, Congress passed new laws regulating pension funds and corporate finance disclosure. It allowed employees greater discretion in investing in areas other than the company's stock. It required honesty in financial reporting. It made recommendations for professional auditing practices, especially that the firm that audits a company not be the same firm that advises it. The Enron story illustrates the consequences of deregulation and unscrupulous business practices. The behavior of Enron employees and the devastation of the bankruptcy gave policy makers reasons to reconsider competitive regulatory policies.

Summary

Several competitive regulatory policy regimes emerged in the late 19th and early 20th centuries. Most related to a specific policy area and were anchored by a specific agency. Examples include the Interstate Commerce Commission, the Federal Communications Commission, the Antitrust Division of the Justice Department, and the Civil Aeronautics Board. Most of these agencies came under attack during the deregulation era of the late 1970s and the 1980s. Some agencies were untouched, such as the Antitrust Division. Some agencies were attacked but survived, such as the FCC. Some agencies were dismantled, with their responsibilities transferred to other agencies, such as the ICC. Other agencies, such as the CAB, succumbed to the deregulation movement. Their regulations ended and they were dismantled.

The dismantling of the ICC and CAB signaled a policy regime change. The economic crisis of the late 1970s stressed the old regulatory regime. Political power shifted when liberal interest groups such as Nader's Study Group emerged in opposition to these agencies. The policy paradigm changed when government regulations appeared to do more harm than good. The elimination of regulations marked the end of the old regime and the birth of the new deregulatory regime.

Review Questions

1. Discuss the early years of the ICC and Antitrust Division. What were some similar problems in the two organizations?
2. Discuss why and how the FCC was established.
3. Discuss the pros and cons of competitive regulatory policies. What were the major objections to antitrust regulations?
4. What factors explain the demise of the ICC?
5. What is the current status of FCC regulations?

Select Websites

This is the home page of the Federal Communications Commission.
http://www.fcc.gov/

This is the Website for the U.S. Department of Justice Antitrust Division.
http://www.usdoj.gov/atr/

Key Terms

Amtrak
Antitrust Division of the Justice
   Department
artificial monopolies
capture
Civil Aeronautics Board (CAB)
consolidation
disorganized markets
fairness doctrine
Federal Communications
   Commission (FCC)

Federal Railroad Administration (FRA)
Granger movement
Interstate Commerce Commission (ICC)
National Highway Transportation Safety
   Administration
National Railroad Passenger Corporation
natural monopolies
obscenity rules
Populist movement
Surface Transportation Board (STB)
unstable markets

CHAPTER 11

Fertility Control Policy

Fertility control policy involves the regulation of abortions, contraceptives, sex education, and family planning. It falls into the category of morality policy. This type of policy is simplistic, highly visible, and extremely contentious. It involves high levels of participation. It entails debates over right and wrong, good and evil, and thus, sometimes involves religious organizations.

Abortion is one of the most intensely emotional and contentious of the fertility control policies. Opponents of abortion consider it murder, that the millions of abortions that have been carried out since 1973 are equivalent to genocide. They define themselves not as anti-abortion but as pro-life. Supporters of abortion see this as a woman's right to control her own body. Because they do not necessarily support abortion, they define themselves as pro-choice. They advocate the right of a woman to choose if and when she has a baby.

Three fertility control policy regimes can be identified: the early policy regime (up to the 1870s), the moralistic policy regime (1870–1973), and the current or *Roe v. Wade* policy regime (1973 to the present). *Roe v. Wade* is the Supreme Court decision that struck down state laws prohibiting abortions.

During the early policy regime, there were few restrictions on abortions and contraceptives. Abortions during the first trimester were generally legal and unregulated. In the moralistic policy regime, abortions were outlawed, except when necessary to save the life of the mother. Contraceptives were illegal in many states. Today contraceptives and abortions are legal.

→ A Brief History of Fertility Control

Looking at the past history of fertility control policy helps to understand contemporary policy. Most ancient societies practiced some form of fertility control. Contraceptives and abortions were common in ancient Egypt, Greece, Roman Empire, Japan, India, China, and many other societies. Most had a variety of herbs, chemicals, techniques, and devices to prevent pregnancy, some to induce miscarriage. Abortions were risky because many of the herbs and chemicals used were poisonous and the techniques dangerous.

Ancient philosophers held a variety of views on abortion. The Greek philosopher Pythagoras opposed abortion, but Aristotle and Plato supported it, especially as a method of population control. Aristotle identified three stages in the development of a fetus: vegetable, animal, and rational. This distinction among stages of fetal development had implications for the morality of abortions. Early stage abortions were easier to justify than late stage abortions.

Under Roman law, fetuses had no rights except inheritance. Abortions were legal. During the late Roman Empire, a pregnant woman was required to get her father's permission before having an abortion.

The Jewish tradition prohibited abortions, except when necessary to save the life of the mother. However, in this tradition the fetus did not become a person with a soul until birth; it was considered part of the mother and abortion was not considered murder. The killing of the fetus was regarded "as a tort rather than a homicide" (Schiff 2002, 27).

The early Christian tradition was divided over the abortion issue. Initially, there was some tolerance for early stage abortions. St. Augustine opposed abortion, yet he accepted Aristotle's notion of the stages of fetal development. St. Thomas Aquinas tolerated early stage

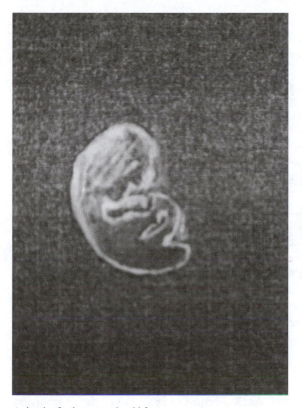

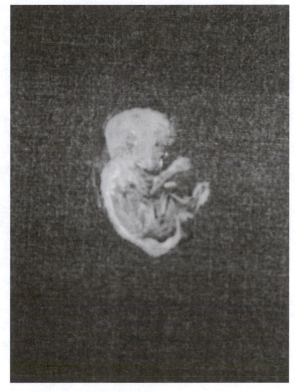

A sketch of a three-month -old fetus.   A sketch of an eight-week-old embryo.

abortions. "Aquinas's ideas influenced Pope Innocent IV, who in 1257 declared that abortion before the infusion of the soul was not homicide" (McFarlane and Meier 2001, 26). By the 16th century the abortion issue had become volatile. Pope Sixtus V declared abortion to be premeditated murder and an excommunicable offense. In 1591 Pope Gregory XIV distinguished between early stage and late stage abortions and pardoned the former. This distinction was made until 1869, "when Pope Pius IX restored the policy of Pope Sixtus V" (McFarlane and Meier 2001, 26).

Some historians insist that the witch hunts of the 16th and 17th centuries were driven by the desire to eliminate knowledge about birth control and abortions and to increase the population of northern Europe, which had been decimated by the black plague of the 14th century.

> The witch massacres were massive and widespread, and these executions were sanctioned by the church. . . . That midwives were the major target is confirmed in the *Hammer of Witches* (1487), the first comprehensive apologia for witch-hunts published by the Dominican order . . . which discussed "midwives who surpass all others in wickedness." Among their listed offenses were contraception and abortion. (McFarlane and Meier 2001, 25)

Nevertheless, by 1869 Pope Pius IX had eliminated the distinction between early stage and late stage abortion and defined abortion at any stage as murder. Henceforth, the Roman Catholic Church has opposed abortions.

U.S. Fertility Control Policy: From the Early Regime to the Moralistic Regime

Abortions were legal, with some restrictions, in the United States throughout the 18th and the first half of the 19th centuries. Most states followed English common law on abortions, which allowed abortions before **quickening,** the moment the fetus begins to move. In 1821 Connecticut became the first state to enact a law prohibiting abortions after quickening. In 1828 New York passed a law making abortions a misdemeanor if performed before quickening and a felony if performed after quickening.

A pro-life movement emerged after the Civil War as part of a larger purity or antivice movement. The antivice movement consisted of religious, civic, and women's organizations. It targeted bars, dance halls, prostitution, gambling, alcohol, obscenity, and other alleged vices, including contraceptives and abortions.

Religious leaders opposed abortions and contraceptives. They lobbied state legislatures for antiabortion and anticontraceptive laws. The Young Men's Christian Association (YMCA) formed the Committee for the Suppression of Vice, which campaigned for antiabortion and anticontraceptive laws. Religious leaders insisted that abortion was murder and they were opposed to contraceptives because they encouraged immorality and were associated with prostitution. Moreover, many ascribed to the religious belief that the main purpose of sex was procreation and that contraceptives undermined this purpose.

The American Medical Association (AMA), formed in 1847, joined the antiabortion movement for three reasons. First, the AMA opposed abortion on moral grounds. Life began at conception and abortion was murder. It made no moral distinction between quickening and before quickening; abortion was murder at any stage of fetal development.

Second, the AMA opposed abortion for professional reasons. It believed abortions were dangerous to women. The herbs and chemicals used to induce abortions were poisonous and the medical devices could induce life-threatening infections and hemorrhages. Indeed, abortion-related death rates were high in the early 19th century; for example, the rate of abortion-related deaths in New York state was 30 percent (McFarlane and Meier 2001, 35).

The third reason for medical doctors' opposition to abortion was to eliminate competition with nonphysicians. McFarlane and Meier made the following point:

> The AMA's antiabortion movement also coincided with its efforts to establish monopoly control by physicians over the practice of medicine. Midwives and other alternative practitioners were frequently the source of information on abortion. By repressing abortion, the AMA could restrict the demand for medicine practiced by nonphysicians. (2001, 36)

Even before the Civil War, medical doctors had been in competition with midwives, herbalists, and other nonphysician practitioners who were heavily involved in abortions and contraceptives. The AMA proposed laws that would make abortion illegal, unless necessary to save the life of the mother and unless approved by two reputable doctors. These laws prohibited most of the activities of midwives and nonphysician practitioners. The net effect of antiabortion laws was to shift control over abortions from women to the male-dominated medical profession (Luker 1984).

The Moralistic Regime and the Comstock Act

The passage of the Comstock Act inaugurated the moralistic regime. A few states had passed antiabortion laws at the beginning of the Civil War. New York and Massachusetts laws made abortion a felony. After the war, many more states passed antiabortion laws. In the early 1870s, Anthony Comstock introduced to Congress an Act for the Suppression of Trade in, and Circulation of, Obscene Literature and Articles of Immoral Use. This act, known as the *Comstock Act of 1873,* prohibited the interstate trading in obscene literature, materials, or "any article whatever for the prevention of conception, or for causing unlawful abortion" (McFarlane and Meier 2001, 30). The act made it a felony to mail contraceptives or any information used to prevent or abort pregnancies.

By the end of the 19th century, state laws no longer distinguished between early term and late term abortions. It was a felony in every state except Kentucky for a woman to have an abortion anytime during her pregnancy. Of course, many states allowed an abortion to save the life of the mother and when approved by a reputable physician.

Despite these laws, fertility rates declined during the late 19th century and throughout the 20th century. Antiabortion laws did not eliminate abortions; probably more abortions were performed in 1910 when they were illegal than in 1810 when they were legal. If the law did anything, it shifted control over abortions from women and midwives to medical doctors, made it more difficult for most women to obtain abortions, and made them more dangerous. Nevertheless, abortions continued under two different sets of circumstances.

First, some abortions were available to well-to-do women with connections to the medical community. The law allowed therapeutic abortions, those necessary to save the life of the woman. States gave physicians a varying amount of discretion to determine when therapeutic abortions were necessary. Of course, attitudes toward abortions varied among physicians. Some refused to perform abortions under any circumstances; others performed abortions when the pregnant woman suffered from heart disease and childbirth would certainly kill her, when the pregnant woman threatened suicide, or when the pregnancy threatened to destroy the woman's life (Luker 1984).

Second, back alley abortions, performed by nonphysicians, were available for working-class women. Although these abortions were illegal, they continued underground. The mortality rates were higher for illegal abortions than for legal ones, and most of those who died were low-income and minority women.

> In New York, for instance, during the several years preceding the decriminalization of abortions in that state, some 80 percent of the deaths caused by illegal abortions involved Black and Puerto Rican women. (Davis 1983, 204)

Generally, the police would investigate an illegal abortion only after a woman died from one.

Antiabortion and contraceptive laws precipitated the reproductive rights movement. Margaret Sanger was one of the founders and leaders of this movement in the first half of the 20th century.

Margaret Sanger and the Birth Control Movement

Margaret Sanger is responsible for coining the term *birth control.* She began her career as a nurse, driven by a genuine desire to help women, especially working-class women. She related stories of women overwhelmed from having too many children and later dying from self-induced abortions. One story involved Sadie Sachs, a 28-year-old woman on the Lower East Side of New York City. Sanger came with a medical doctor to treat Mrs. Sachs who had botched a self-induced abortion. Mrs. Sachs asked the doctor for birth control information. The doctor told her to tell her husband to sleep on the roof. Davis added:

> Three months later Sadie Sachs died from another self-induced abortion. That night, Margaret Sanger says, she vowed to devote all her energy toward the acquisition and dissemination of contraceptive measures. (1983, 212)

Mortality from self-induced abortions provoked Sanger to initiate the **reproductive rights movement.** Around 1914, she founded the magazine *The Woman Rebel,* which provided facts on birth control. A few years later she established a birth control clinic.

She was arrested twice, the first time in 1914 for violating the Comstock Act by distributing birth control information through the mail. She fled the country because she faced up to 40 years in prison. She returned two years later to campaign against the law. Under public pressure, the federal government dropped the case. Two years later she was arrested in New York for operating a clinic that distributed birth control devices and sentenced to 30 days in a workhouse.

Sanger emerged as a passionate crusader for women's reproductive rights. She argued that women have a right to control their reproduction and that this right is essential for women to participate in society as equals to men. In her 1920 book *Women and the Race,* Margaret Sanger said:

> No woman can call herself free who does not own and control her own body. No woman can call herself free until she can choose consciously whether she will or will not be a mother. (quoted in Roberts 1999, 58)

In 1921 Sanger established the American Birth Control League, which combined with other organizations to become the Birth Control Federation of America. Today her organization is known as Planned Parenthood Federation of America. As a result of Margaret Sanger's efforts, a federal court eventually struck down the Comstock Act in 1937. She is credited with paving the way for the emergence of the pro-choice movement of the 1960s.

The Dark Side of Birth Control Debate

The birth control movement had a dark side through its ties to the eugenics movement. However, critics are divided over the meaning of these ties. For example, Angela Davis pointed out that Sanger supported forced sterilization, a surgical process advocated by proponents of eugenics to reduce the numbers of African Americans, Native Americans, and other so-called undesirable groups (Davis 1983). Another critic, Dorothy Roberts, claimed that although Sanger supported some aspects of eugenics thinking, she also supported programs for African-American women to reduce infant and maternal mortality rates and improve their health and living conditions (Roberts 1999, 81).

It seems that racial prejudices common in the early part of the 20th century affected both sides of the birth control debate. Some leaders of the pro-life movement ascribed to eugenics ideas. White Anglo-Saxon Protestant (WASP) leaders expressed concerns about the relative decline in the WASP population and the increase in minority populations, especially non-Protestant immigrants from Ireland, Italy, and eastern Europe, as well as African Americans, Native Americans, and others. They opposed the use of contraceptives and abortion by WASP women because they wanted to ensure the continued superior numbers of WASPs.

✷ *Policy Change and Regime Change*

Fertility control policies changed substantially in the late 1960s and early 1970s, primarily because of Supreme Court decisions. The Court struck down anticontraceptive laws in *Griswold v. Connecticut* (1965) and liberalized abortion laws in the *Roe v. Wade* (1973) decision. These changes indicated a policy regime change.

Several factors contributed to this significant policy regime change: (1) a change in the social position of women, (2) change in the medical profession, (3) the women's liberation movement, and (4) changes in public attitudes.

The Changing Social Position of Women

Just after the Civil War, most people lived on farms and most women worked in the home. By the 1960s most people lived in urban or suburban areas and most women worked outside the home. The number of women pursuing a professional career increased. They were entering law schools and medical colleges in record-breaking numbers, and beginning to enter into other professional areas such as accounting, broadcasting, business management, and natural sciences that used to be the exclusive domain of men. The increase in the number of working and professional women meant more women who needed to control their reproduction and who supported contraceptives and abortions. Survey data indicate that professional women are more likely to identify with the pro-choice movement than women who are homemakers (Craig and O'Brien 1993).

Change in the Medical Profession

The medical profession had changed its position on abortion by the 1960s owing to two major factors. First, advancements in medical technology, antibiotics, and medical instruments made abortions safer. Mortality rates from all abortions had declined. By the 1960s physicians considered them relatively safe when performed by a medical doctor (Luker 1984). Second, physicians began to recognize different stages of fetal development. The scientific community distinguished between viability and previability. Viability has to do with the ability of the fetus to live outside the womb, independent of the mother. By the 1960s most physicians no longer considered early stage abortion murder. The emergence of more liberal views toward abortion among physicians led to the American Medical Association's acceptance of the pro-choice perspective. By 1973 the AMA supported the *Roe v. Wade* decision.

The Women's Liberation Movement

The **women's liberation movement** contributed to the substantial changes in fertility control policies in the late 1960s and early 1970s. Women have always been politically active. They fought for the right to vote, which they won in 1920, for the mothers' pension programs of the 1920s, and for the Aid for Dependent Children (ADC) program in 1935. The women's movement gained momentum during the 1960s, especially after **Betty Friedan** published *The Feminine Mystique* (1963) and cofounded the **National Organization for Women (NOW).** For Friedan, women's liberation meant creating conditions that permitted women to "gratify their basic need to grow and fulfill their potentialities as human beings." It meant removing barriers to equal opportunity for women, allowing women to pursue careers as professionals, and permitting women to choose whether and when they wished to bear children. NOW emerged as a powerful political force committed to changing fertility control laws to legalize contraceptives and abortion.

Changing Public Attitudes toward Fertility Control

The increase in women in professional careers, the liberalization of attitudes in the medical profession, the woman's liberation movement, and changes in public attitudes—these four factors contributed to the substantial policy changes of the 1960s and early 1970s. By the 1960s, a few states such as New York and California had passed laws to permit early term abortions. Two Supreme Court decisions produced the fertility control policy change of the century: *Griswold v. Connecticut* and *Roe v. Wade*.

✦ The Supreme Court and Policy Change

Griswold v. Connecticut

The *Griswold v. Connecticut* decision struck down an 1879 Connecticut law that prohibited the dissemination of information about contraceptives. The Planned Parenthood League of Connecticut had been challenging the law in court since the 1940s and had unsuccessfully lobbied the state legislature to repeal the law. Initially, the Court would not consider the case because no one had been arrested under the law. In 1961 Estelle Griswold, the executive director of the Planned Parenthood League of Connecticut, opened a birth control clinic in New Haven, which was operated by Dr. C. Lee Buxton, a licensed physician and professor of medicine at the Yale Medical School. Buxton and Griswold gave contraceptive information to married couples. Because she was the executive director, Griswold was arrested 10 days after the clinic opened (O'Brien 2003).

The U.S. Supreme Court decided that the Connecticut anticontraceptive law violated the right to privacy, a right not specifically stated in the Constitution. Justice William O. Douglas, the author of the majority decision, insisted that it was implied in the Fourth Amendment, which protects against unreasonable search and seizure, the Fifth Amendment regarding self-incrimination, and the Ninth Amendment, which can be interpreted that the listing of specific rights in the Constitution does not preclude the existence of a right to privacy. Furthermore, Douglas argued that the right to privacy is older than the Constitution and is found in the sanctity of the institution of marriage.

The reaction to the *Griswold* case was one of widespread acceptance. By 1965 most couples practiced some form of birth control and most people accepted this practice as a right.

Contraceptives and Birth Control Policy

Today contraceptive use among adults is not an issue. *Griswold* invalidated state laws prohibiting the sale and distribution of contraceptives. Public attitudes and sexual mores have become more liberal. Nevertheless, the sensitive issue today is the exposure of teenagers to sex education and contraceptives. This issue emerged when organizations like Planned Parenthood proposed exposing teenagers to sex education and birth control. Religious and moral groups opposed these proposals, contending that they encourage premarital sex.

The sex education and contraceptive issue was complicated by the human immunodeficiency virus (HIV) epidemic of the late 1980s. HIV causes AIDS, the acquired immunodeficiency syndrome, a disease that almost always ends in death. The virus is transmitted through either blood or the exchange of body fluids during unprotected sexual intercourse. The U.S. Surgeon Generals, whether liberal or conservative, Democrat or Republican, have recommended sex education and condoms as effective methods of preventing or reducing the spread of the HIV virus and other sexually transmitted diseases. These recommendations have placed the Surgeon General in the middle of the sex education and contraceptive issue. For example, Surgeon General Dr. Everett Koop, a conservative Republican who served under the Reagan administration, recommended condoms for reducing the spread of the HIV virus. Dr. Jacelyn Elders, a liberal Democrat who served under the Clinton administration, infuriated religious and moral conservative groups for promoting sex education and condoms among young teenagers to reduce teen pregnancy and the transmission of sexually transmitted diseases. In 2001 Surgeon General Dr. David Satcher provoked the wrath of religious and moral conservative groups with a report that recommended a sex education program for teenagers that emphasizes both abstinence and safe sex. Opponents, including President George W. Bush, criticized the report for not recommending abstinence-only programs, despite studies indicating that abstinence-only programs were not as effective in preventing teen pregnancy and sexually transmitted diseases as programs that emphasized both abstinence and safe sex. Safe sex requires the use of condoms.

Roe v. Wade

In *Roe v. Wade,* the Supreme Court struck down a Texas law that prohibited abortions unless necessary to save the life of the mother. This was one of the most contentious Court decisions of the 20th century.

The *Roe v. Wade* suit was initiated by Norma McCorvey, a pregnant low-income, high school dropout, with a five-year-old daughter. She sought an abortion, but could not get one because state law prohibited it. She arranged to have her baby adopted. Her attorney introduced her to two recent University of Texas law school graduates, Sara Weddington and Linda Coffee, who agreed to challenge the state antiabortion law on constitutional grounds. To protect McCorvey's privacy, they used the name of Jane Roe. The lawsuit originated in Dallas against Henry Wade, the Dallas County District Attorney.

The Constitutional Debate

Weddington and Coffee argued that the antiabortion law violated both the right to liberty and the right to privacy and harmed women in other ways. They maintained that liberty meant "liberty from being forced to continue the unwanted pregnancy" (quoted in O'Brien 2003, 1226). They also argued that the law violated women's right to privacy. The decision to have a baby is a personal and private one. Thus, the government is interfering with women's right to privacy when it forces them to have babies against their will. Weddington and Coffee further argued that the law harmed women in other ways: it caused distressful lives and futures, it imposed the stigma of unwed motherhood, and it inflicted psychological damage.

Henry Wade, the district attorney for Dallas County, Texas, defended the antiabortion law, noting that the state had a compelling interest in protecting human life. He insisted that human life begins at conception and that abortion kills the unborn child and threatens the life of the mother. The law had been enacted to protect the lives of both mother and unborn child. He countered Weddington and Coffee's arguments. There is no right to privacy and women do not have a right to an abortion. Women had a right to choose if and when they had a baby, but they make that choice at the time of conception.

The *Roe* case dealt with critical questions. Is there a constitutional right to an abortion? When does human life begin, at conception or birth? If it begins at conception, is abortion murder? Does a fetus have rights under the Constitution? Does the state have a compelling interest in restricting or prohibiting abortions?

Justice Blackmun wrote the majority opinion which responded to the critical questions. The *Roe* decision established the following:

- There is a constitutional right to privacy and it covers a woman's decision to end her pregnancy.
- The life and rights guaranteed by the Constitution begin at birth. Life does not begin at conception.
- Fetuses have no rights under the Constitution.
- For the first trimester (first three months of pregnancy), states cannot regulate or prohibit abortions apart from their being performed by licensed physicians.
- For the second trimester, states are permitted to regulate abortion procedures in ways that are reasonably related to the health of the mother.
- For the last trimester, states may prohibit abortions.

Reaction to the *Roe* Decision

Roe v. Wade did not settle the abortion issue. Instead it ignited a firestorm of reaction. Senator Orin Hatch compared it to the *Dred Scott* decision, the pre–Civil War case that declared that African Americans were not citizens of the United States. The decision provoked a political war that continues to this day. Armies of pro-life and pro-choice organizations and supporters have fought over the abortion issue in state legislatures, Congress, and the Supreme Court.

State Government Reaction

The reaction of state governments to the *Roe v. Wade* decision was mixed. Most state governments complied with the decision; some ignored it. "Ten state legislatures passed laws or resolutions pledging to ban abortion or restrict it severely in anticipation of Roe's eventually being overturned. Fifteen others kept their pre-Roe antiabortion laws on the books" (Craig and O'Brien 1993, 79).

Other states passed new laws to restrict access to abortions. They passed laws to:

- Prohibit the use of state funds or personnel for abortions.
- Bar any advertisement on abortion or the location of abortion clinics.
- Forbid abortions performed in places other than hospitals. Since many hospitals in some states did not approve of abortions, the hospital-only laws had the impact of banning abortions.

TABLE 11.1

Status of Restrictive State Abortion Laws

State Laws	Current Status
Prohibit the use of state funds for abortions.	Still on the books in most states.
Prohibit advertisement for abortions.	Struck down by the Court.
Prohibit abortions in places other than hospitals.	Struck down by the Court.
Require pregnant women to obtain the permission of the father before aborting the fetus.	Struck down by the Court.
Require antiabortion counseling before allowing abortions.	Struck down by the Court but brought back later.
Require a 24- or 48-hour waiting period before allowing an abortion.	On the books in most states.
Require parental permission for pregnant teens.	Still on the books in most states, with the proviso that it allows court intervention under special circumstances.

States established other restrictions on abortions.

- A requirement that pregnant women get the permission of the baby's father before getting an abortion.
- A requirement that women who consent to an abortion wait 24 or 48 hours or submit to counseling on the harmful effects of abortions before having one.

The Supreme Court struck down some of these new state restrictions, but allowed others. Table 11.1 summarizes the status of restrictive state abortion laws.

The states passed new laws prohibiting partial-birth abortions in the 1990s. These laws were eventually struck down in 2001.

Federal Laws

Congress and the president became involved in the political wars over abortion. Congress passed a number of antiabortion laws in the 1970s and early 1980s. Several pro-life constitutional amendments were introduced during the 1970s, but all failed.

In 1977 Congress passed the *Public Health Service Act* and the *Hyde Amendment* to the Medicaid Act. The Public Health Service Act prohibited discrimination against persons who oppose abortion in programs that receive federal money. It was directed at medical schools that deny admission to or discriminate against applicants because they oppose abortion. According to this law, medical schools that receive federal money cannot deny admissions to or discipline a student because, for moral or religious reasons, the student refuses to participate in performing or assisting with an abortion.

The Hyde Amendment, introduced by Representative Henry Hyde, prohibited the use of federal funds to perform an abortion, unless one is clearly necessary to save the life of the mother. Supporters argued that many Americans considered abortion murder and were opposed to using their tax dollars to murder unborn children. The Hyde Amendment effectively banned the use of Medicaid for abortions. The amendment was modified under the Clinton administration to allow abortions in cases of rape, incest, or life-threatening conditions.

Most states supported the Hyde Amendment by passing laws prohibiting the use of state funds or personnel for abortions. Some 32 states have such laws. No state allows the use of public funds for abortions on demand.

In the 1980s President Reagan supported a number of pro-life initiatives, including a pro-life constitutional amendment, which died early in his administration. He supported the *Defense Appropriation Act of 1982,* which barred abortions from military bases or institutions and prohibited the use of defense money for abortions. Reagan's secretary of Health and Human Services issued a gag rule that prohibited agencies receiving federal funds for family planning from engaging in abortion counseling.

In 2003 Congress passed the *Partial Birth Abortion Ban Act,* a law banning partial-birth abortions—a law that earlier had been vetoed by President Clinton. It is likely to be challenged in court.

Supreme Court Reaction: Abortion Decisions after Roe

State laws that obstructed the *Roe v. Wade* decision precipitated more lawsuits and additional Supreme Court decisions. In the decade after *Roe,* the Court struck down state laws requiring antiabortion counseling, hospital-only abortions, permission from the father, and advertisement for abortions (see Table 11.1). From 1973 to 1989, the Court struck down regulations prohibiting abortions during the first trimester, with two exceptions: the Court allowed states to require licensed doctors to perform abortions and to prohibit the use of state funds for abortions.

Two cases marked a significant departure from the *Roe* decision: *Webster v. Reproductive Services* (1989) and *Planned Parenthood of Southeastern Pennsylvania v. Casey* (1992). Although these cases upheld *Roe v. Wade,* they chipped away at the right to unregulated abortions. A third case, *Stenberg v. Carhart,* reaffirmed that right.

Webster v. Reproductive Services   This decision arose from a challenge to a Missouri law of 1986, which stated that life begins at conception. It required medical doctors to test the gestation age, weight, lung capacity, and other signs of fetal viability before performing an abortion. It prohibited the use of public facilities, funds, or employees to either perform an abortion or encourage a woman to have one. The Supreme Court upheld the Missouri state law, but refused to overturn *Roe v. Wade.* However, in *Webster* the Court departed from a few *Roe* principles.

1. The Court accepted the notion that human life begins at conception.
2. States could require physicians to test the viability of a fetus before aborting it.
3. The Court prohibited the use of public employees or money for abortions, implying that abortion was not a right to which Medicaid recipients were entitled.

Planned Parenthood of Southeastern Pennsylvania v. Casey Decision   This decision in 1992 allowed for additional abortion regulations. The Court upheld the following provisions of Pennsylvania law:

- Require doctors to counsel women on the harms caused by abortions.
- Require women to wait 24 hours after consenting to an abortion.
- Require physicians to report each abortion to state authorities.
- Require unmarried, underaged women to obtain parental consent before obtaining an abortion, providing that the state allowed for the court to act as a surrogate parent.

Again, the Court upheld the *Roe* decision and struck down the Pennsylvania provision requiring a woman to get permission from her husband before getting an abortion.

Stenberg v. Carhart Decision   The *Stenberg v. Carhart* (2000) decision related to a Nebraska law of 1997 which prohibited partial-birth abortion, making it a felony punishable by up to 20 years of prison. Similar laws were enacted in about 30 other states.

Partial-birth abortion is a politically charged term generally used by pro-life advocates to refer to a procedure in which a medical doctor partially delivers a fetus by inserting a suction catheter into the head, removing brain tissue, and allowing the fetus to pass through the birth canal.

Justice Stephen Breyer wrote the majority opinion for the *Stenberg v. Carhart* decision. He reaffirmed *Roe v. Wade* and struck down the Nebraska law banning partial-birth abortions on the grounds that it violated *Roe v. Wade* and was so vague that other abortion procedures could also be banned. He noted the intense conflict over the abortion issue, with millions of people on one side believing that life begins at conception—that in this case partial-birth abortion was especially offensive—and millions of people on the other side fearful that outlawing abortion would deny dignity and opportunity to women. Breyer added:

taking account these virtually irreconcilable points of view, aware that constitutional law must govern a society whose different members sincerely hold directly opposing views, and considering the matter in light of the constitutional guarantees of fundamental individual liberty, this Court, in the course of a generation has determined and then redetermined that the Constitution offers basic protection to the woman's right to choose. (*Stenberg v. Carhart* 2000)

A pro-choice demonstration.

The Supreme Court has consistently upheld one basic principle of *Roe v. Wade:* that the government cannot prohibit a woman from having an abortion before the third trimester of her pregnancy. However, in the past 10 years, only five of the nine Supreme Court justices have supported this principle. A change in one of these five justices could spell the end of *Roe v. Wade* and of legal abortions. Because of the critical role of the Court, the retirement of a *Roe* supporter is likely to precipitate an epic battle between pro-choice and pro-life forces.

Interest Group Reaction: Pro-Life

Mainstream conservative, well-established religious organizations have long been pro-life. Many conservative religious leaders were shocked by the *Roe v. Wade* decision, and some reacted immediately. The National Council of Catholic Bishops called on Catholics to support pro-life issues. The U.S. Catholic Conference supported the formation of a new organization, the National Committee for a Human Life Amendment (NCHLA), which lobbied Congress for a pro-life constitutional amendment that would nullify the *Roe v. Wade* decision.

Some pro-life groups emerged in reaction to the women's liberation movement and to the proposed Equal Rights Amendment (ERA). This amendment, proposed in 1972, stated, "Equality of rights under the law shall not be denied or abridged by the United States or any state on account of sex." The ERA provoked Phyllis Shafley to establish Stop ERA, an organization committed to defeating this amendment. Shafley argued for traditional family values and the traditional role of women as mothers and homemakers. She fought against the National Organization for Women (NOW) and most of the issues it stood for, including abortion.

An organization similar to Shafley's, Concerned Women of America (CWA), was formed in 1978 by Beverly LaHaye in reaction to what she referred to as anti-God and antifamily feminists. CWA has fought against abortions since its establishment and it continues today with its pro-life crusade.

Pro-life organizations planned marches on Washington to protest the *Roe v. Wade* decision and to promote a pro-life constitutional amendment. In January 1974 over 6,000 antiabortion demonstrators went to the nation's capital and, around the same time, pro-life demonstrations took place across the country (Craig and O'Brien 1993). The number of pro-life demonstrators in Washington peaked at 70,000 in 1978.

The pro-life movement gained momentum in the 1980s. New organizations were formed: Reverend Jerry Falwell's Moral Majority, the Religious Roundtable, Christian Voice, National Christian Action Coalition, and Pat Robertson's Christian Coalition. These organizations developed a number of political strategies:

- Supporting pro-life political candidates for local and national offices, and defeating pro-choice candidates.
- Promoting a pro-life political agenda in state and federal governments.
- Securing the appointment of pro-life officials to key positions, especially the U.S. Supreme Court.
- Lobbying state legislatures to preserve old antiabortion laws or to pass new laws restricting access to abortions.
- Lobbying Congress on behalf of pro-life laws.

In the 1980 election pro-life groups and conservative evangelical organizations supported Ronald Reagan for president.

A strong pro-life coalition emerged by the end of the 1990s, consisting of religious, professional, women's, single-issue, and traditional conservative organizations. Feminists for Life, a self-proclaimed feminist organization, joined the pro-life movement. Professional groups included the American Academy of Medical Ethics, the American Association of Pro-Life Obstetricians, and Doctors for Life. Table 11.2 provides a select list of pro-life and pro-choice organizations in three categories: medical, religious, and traditional.

TABLE 11.2		
Select Pro-Life and Pro-Choice Organizations		
Type of Organization	**Pro-Life**	**Pro-Choice**
Medical	American Academy of Medical Ethics	American Academy of Pediatrics
	American Association of Pro-Life Obstetricians	American Medical Association
	American Association of Pro-Life Pediatricians	American Medical Women's Association
	Doctors for Life	American Nurses Associations
	Missouri Doctors for Life	American Public Health Association
Religious	Baptists for Life	Catholics for a Free Choice
	Catholics United for Life	Episcopal Diocese of Massachusetts
	Christian Advocates Serving Evangelism	Episcopal Women's Caucus
	Lutheran Church–Missouri Synod	Unitarian Universalist Association
	Lutherans for Life	United Church of Christ Coordinating Center for Women
	Southern Baptists for Life	New Jewish Agenda
	United States Catholic Conference	
Traditional	Feminists for Life	Feminists Institute
	Focus on the Family	National Organization for Women
	International Right to Life Federation	National Abortion Rights Action League
	National Right to Life Committee	League of Women Voters of the U.S.
		National Black Women's Health Project
		National Education Association
		National Family Planning and Reproductive Health Association
		National Urban League
		Planned Parenthood of Atlanta Area
		Women for Racial and Economic Equality

Pro-Choice Reaction and Abortion Political Conflict

A strong pro-choice coalition had emerged by the time of the *Roe v. Wade* decision. It included reproduction rights and women's rights groups such as Planned Parenthood and the

National Organization for Women (NOW); traditional civil rights groups such as the American Civil Liberties Union and the Urban League; and many religious and traditional medical organizations. New organizations were formed to support choice such as the National Abortion Rights Action League (see Table 11.2). A powerful pro-choice coalition was well in place by the 1990s.

During the 1980s, the nomination of pro-life justices to the Supreme Court and the perceived threat to abortion rights reinvigorated the pro-choice movement. President Reagan's nomination of pro-lifer Robert Bork to the Supreme Court provoked an intense and successful pro-choice campaign to derail his candidacy. When the Court rendered the *Webster* decision, over 300,000 pro-choice supporters came to Washington, D.C., from all over the country to demonstrate in support of abortion rights.

→ *Violence and the Abortion Issue*

Most of the conflict over abortion occurred within political institutions. It involved political battles, most of which were fought in state legislatures, Congress, and the Supreme Court. However, some of the conflict involved more extreme groups.

The Development of Extremism

One extreme pro-life group is Operation Rescue, organized by Randall Terry in 1986. **Operation Rescue** adopted strategies of nonviolent passive resistance similar to those used by the civil rights movement. It targeted abortion clinics. For example, in 1988 over 1,200 Operation Rescue members obstructed the entrances to all of the abortion clinics in Atlanta. Several members, including Terry, were arrested. Operation Rescue also blockaded abortion clinics in several other cities, which precipitated confrontations and violence between pro-life and pro-choice groups. Nevertheless, Randall Terry expressed a commitment to nonviolence. In 1989 he told a journalist:

> I believe in the use of force. But, I think to destroy abortion facilities at this time is counterproductive because the American public has an adverse reaction to what it sees as violence. (quoted in Craig and O'Brien 1993, 58)

Some of the pro-life rhetoric encouraged more extreme measures against abortion. For example, pro-life groups defined fetuses as unborn children, abortion as murder, and abortion doctors as murderers. Some have depicted abortion clinics as sites of mass murder. This rhetoric brought about more drastic action against abortions and even more extreme groups emerged.

Violence against abortion clinics escalated in the 1990s. Since 1991 pro-life extremists have shot and killed 7 abortion clinic doctors and staff members and attempted to murder 17. For example, in 1994 an extremist went on a shooting rampage firing a rifle into two abortion clinics in Brookline, Massachusetts, and one in Norfolk, Virginia, killing two clinic receptionists and wounding five other people. The violence has continued into the 21st century, with hundreds of cases of bomb threats, harassing calls, death threats, vandalism, and disruptions. There have also been cases of bombings, arsons, and assaults.

Reaction to the Violence

Pro-choice groups have reacted to the violence in several ways. They have lobbied the federal and state governments to use existing laws to protect abortion clinics or to pass new laws providing greater protections. They persuaded Congress to pass the *Freedom of Access to Clinic Entrances Act (FACE) of 1996,* which made aggressive blockades of abortion clinics a federal offense. Pro-choice groups had attempted to use existing federal laws against pro-life extremists. Attempts to use provisions of the *Racketeer Influenced and Corruption Organizations Act (RICO)* to sue pro-life groups were overturned by the Supreme Court in 2003.

Recently, pro-choice groups won a multi-million-dollar settlement against 12 individuals and 2 pro-life groups—Advocates for Life Ministries and the American Coalition of Life Activists—that set up a "Nuremberg Files" Website with a list of the names and addresses of abortion clinics and physicians. The site claimed that the clinics were operating death camps like those of the Nazis. One of the doctors listed on the Website was murdered; shortly afterward, the site noted his elimination. The pro-choice groups were awarded a settlement of more than $100 million against the individuals and organizations responsible for the Website. The pro-choice tactics have been somewhat successful, as the extreme violence has subsided.

The Continuing Debate over Abortion

The abortion debate is likely to continue throughout the 21st century. Pro-life and pro-choice proponents operate within different paradigms, with entirely different perspectives. A great deal of the abortion debate rests on three issues: fetal development, choice, and the image of women.

Pro-life proponents see different stages of fetal development as unimportant. They insist that human life begins at conception and that a fertilized egg is a human being, worthy of the protection of government. Many consider the fertilized egg as a stage in human development, much like old age, adulthood, childhood. Once the premise is accepted that human life begins at conception, then all pro-choice arguments fail. If the fetus is human life, then all arguments for abortion become rationalizations for murder. The choice argument becomes irrelevant. Pro-life groups believe that women made their choice when they decided to have sex and risk pregnancy; the only choice left is whether to keep the child or to put the child up for adoption. Pro-lifers find it appalling that a woman would kill her unborn child to further her career or to improve her financial status.

Pro-choice proponents operate in an entirely different paradigm. They distinguish stages of fetal development. For example, Mary Gordon pointed out that we react differently to the involuntary loss of a fetus, depending on its age—that is, if a women who is a few days pregnant loses the fetus, we say she had a miscarriage. If she is seven months pregnant and loses the fetus, we say the baby was stillborn.

> Our ritual and religious practices underscore the fact that we make distinctions among fetuses. If a woman took the bloody matter—indistinguishable from a heavy period—of an early miscarriage and insisted upon putting it in a tiny coffin and marking its grave, we would have serious concerns about her mental health. (2003, 223–224)

Pro-choice proponents argue that redefining a fertilized egg as a human being does not make it a human being any more than redefining a brain-dead accident victim as alive makes the victim come alive. If there is no brain life, there is no human life. While pro-choice proponents might concede that moral problems arise over late term abortions, the overwhelming majority of abortions are early term abortions.

Radical feminists offer a different perspective on the issue of choice. They see antiabortion laws as inherently repressive and symptomatic of a male-dominated society that has little regard for the humanity of women and would force them to bear children against their will.

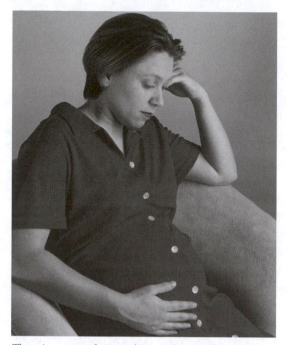

The quiet, contemplative, and private decision of a woman to become a mother or not is often overshadowed by the boisterous and tumultuous politics of abortion.

Too many women live in a social context in which they do not have access to comprehensive medical care, which includes effective contraceptives and sex education. Feminists believe that women should have the constitutional right to choose if and when they bear children.

→ *The Impact of Abortion Policy*

Today abortion is legal, with some restrictions. State and federal governments prohibit the use of public funds or employees in the performance of abortions. The Defense Department has banned abortions on military bases and military hospitals. Most states require women who have given consent to have an abortion to wait 24 or 48 hours before having one. Several states mandate that doctors perform viability tests before doing an abortion. Physicians are required to report all abortions performed. Most states require parental consent before allowing abortions for pregnant unmarried teenagers under the age of 18.

Abortion rates declined in the late 1990s (see Table 11.3). The number of abortions peaked in 1990 at about 1.6 million. By 1997, the number had declined to about 1.3 million. Three factors have contributed to this decline:

1. The HIV epidemic and the Surgeon General's campaigns for condoms have reduced the rate of the expansion of the virus and of unplanned pregnancies.
2. Advances in medical birth control technology, such as the Norplant implant, have contributed to reductions in the number of unplanned pregnancies.
3. Violence against abortion clinics has contributed to several closings and a reduction in the accessibility of abortions.

TABLE 11.3

Number of Abortions

Year	Number (1,000)	Year	Number (1,000)	Year	Number (1,000)
1975	1,034	1992	1,529	1997	1,335
1980	1,554	1993	1,495	1998	1,319
1985	1,589	1994	1,423	1999	1,315
1990	1,609	1995	1,359	2000	1,313
1991	1,557	1996	1,360		

SOURCE: U.S. Census Bureau, *Statistical Abstract of the United States*, 2005.

TABLE 11.4

Birth Rates

Year	Rate (per 1,000 people)	Year	Rate (per 1,000 people)
1950	24.1	1980	15.9
1955	25.0	1985	15.8
1960	23.7	1990	16.7
1965	19.4	1995	14.8
1970	18.4	2000	14.4
1975	14.6	2002	13.9

SOURCE: U.S. Census Bureau, *Statistical Abstract of the United States*, 2004.

Changes in abortion rates have not been even. Whereas upper- and middle-income women experienced significant declines in abortion rates, the rates for low-income women have increased. From 1994 to 2000, two factors contributed to increases in the number of low-income women having abortions. First, welfare reforms encouraged abortions. They required women to work. They limited the duration of benefits and provided no additional funds if a woman had additional children. Thus, having another child became a substantial financial liability.

Second, low-income women were less likely to have access to comprehensive health care or insurance, which includes contraceptives. The lack of access to birth control contributed to higher rates of unplanned pregnancies and, therefore, higher abortion rates.

Birth rates have been up and down during the last half of the 20th century (see Table 11.4). These rates peaked in 1955 at 25 per 1,000, hit a record low in 1975 at 14.6, climbed to 16.7 in 1990—the highest rate of the last quarter of the century—and then declined to 14.7 by 2000.

Abortion and birth rates are associated with each other, but in unexpected ways. Between 1975 and 1980 abortion rates and birth rates increased. Between 1990 and 2000 abortion rates and birth rates declined, very likely because of increases in access to contraceptives.

→ *Fertility Control in World Perspective*

Abortion is legal, with some restrictions, in most developed countries of the world. About two-thirds of the countries of Europe allow abortion during the first trimester (12 weeks), some during the first 16 weeks of pregnancy. A few countries allow abortion on demand, with no restriction. Many countries have restrictions similar to those found in the United States. Turkey requires a woman to obtain permission from the baby's father before getting an abortion. Ireland prohibits abortions.

Recorded abortion rates vary among countries that have legalized the procedure. Table 11.5 examines the percentages of pregnancies terminated by abortions in 12 select countries. With 22.9 percent of pregnancies terminated, the United States has the highest rate, followed by Sweden, Denmark, and Canada. The Netherlands has the lowest rate in this group.

Two points emerge from an examination of abortion policies among the world's nations. First, outlawing abortion does not eliminate the practice. It drives this practice underground and contributes to high rates of maternal deaths. For example, abortion is illegal in Nigeria, yet each year about 610,000 unsafe abortions are performed and about 20,000 women die from complications resulting from illegal abortions (Raufu 2002). Abortions are illegal in Argentina, yet about 500,000 women have them each year, with botched abortions accounting for 80 percent of the 625 cases of maternal deaths each year (Valente 2003). When Romania outlawed abortion in 1961, "the number of abortion-related deaths increased sharply," but declined after the country legalized abortion in December 1989 (World Health Organization 2004, 3).

The second point is that countries with comprehensive health care and birth control policies for women also have low abortion rates and low death rates attributable to botched abortions. The availability of birth control reduces the demand for abortion.

TABLE 11.5

Abortion Rates by Country in 1996

Country	Pregnancies Aborted (%)	Country	Pregnancies Aborted (%)
Sweden	18.7	Italy	11.4
United States	22.9	Finland	10.0
Canada	16.4	Germany	7.6
England and Wales	15.6	Switzerland	8.4
Norway	15.6	Netherlands	6.5
Denmark	16.5	Belgium	6.8

SOURCE: Stanley K. Henshaw, Susheela Singh, and Taylor Haas. "Recent Trends in Abortion Rates Worldwide." *Perspectives on Sexuality and Reproductive Health* Vol. 25, Number 1, NY: Guttmacher Institute, 1999.

Summary

There were three major fertility control policy regimes: the early regime (up to the 1870s), the moralistic regime (1870 to 1973), and the current or *Roe v. Wade* regime (1973 to present). The early policy regime allowed early term abortions and tolerated birth control. This regime dissolved when the American Medical Association joined forces with moralistic religious organizations and the antivice movement to form a powerful pro-life coalition. This movement promoted the ideas that abortion and contraceptives were associated with vice and that abortion was dangerous and even murderous. Antiabortion and anticontraceptive laws spread across the country like wildfire. The passage of the Comstock Act marked the beginning of this moralistic policy regime. Fertility control policies prohibited contraceptives up to 1965 and abortions up to 1973.

Fertility control policies changed in the late 1960s and early 1970s. The women's movement was at its peak. The American Medical Association and several other medical organizations shifted sides and joined with the National Organization for Women, traditional civil rights organizations, and others to form a powerful pro-choice coalition. The notion emerged that women had a right to decide if and when they became mothers. The idea of stages in fetal development had reemerged and legitimized early term abortions. Power shifts and changes in ideas contributed to the emergence of a pro-choice fertility control policy regime. Like most morality policies, these policies have been and will continue to be volatile.

Pro-life groups emerged in the 1980s with a vengeance and have fought pro-choice forces to a stalemate. The only factor likely to upset the current policy regime is a shift in the Supreme Court in favor of pro-life justices.

Review Questions

1. What were some of the policies that characterized the early fertility control regime?
2. What factors contributed to the emergence of the moralistic regime?
3. What role did Margaret Sanger play in the development of fertility control policy?
4. What was the dark side of the early birth control movement?
5. What factors contributed to the demise of the moralistic regime?
6. How did state governments respond to *Roe v. Wade?*
7. Explain the violence surrounding abortion policy. What can be done to reduce the violence?
8. Discuss the controversy surrounding partial-birth abortion. What is the Supreme Court's decision on this form of abortion?
9. The *Roe v. Wade* regime has come under severe assault but it has endured. Why? What factors contribute to the endurance of this policy regime?
10. What are some other ways of reducing abortion rates, other than arresting abortion doctors? How effective is this approach likely to be?
11. Why are abortion rates higher in the United States than in the Netherlands, France, Denmark, and other countries?

Select Websites

This is the official Website for the Planned Parenthood Federation of America.
http://www.plannedparenthood.org

This is the Website for Operation Rescue.
http://www.operationrescue.org

Key Terms

Betty Friedan   partial-birth abortion
Margaret Sanger   quickening
National Organization for Women (NOW)   reproductive rights movement
Operation Rescue   women's liberation movement

CHAPTER 12

❦

Criminal Justice Policy

Criminal justice policies are designed to protect society from crime. Crime has to do with forms of behavior that threaten or harm people; that involve the loss or damage of property; that disrupt the safety and well-being of communities; or that threaten community values and morals. Crimes that threaten or harm people include murder, battery, assault, and rape. Crimes that entail the loss or damage of property include robbery, theft, embezzlement, fraud, arson, and vandalism. Crimes that disrupt the safety and well-being of communities include riots, disorderly conduct, reckless driving, and drunk driving. Crimes that threaten community values and morals consist of prostitution, child pornography, gambling, and drug abuse.

The definition of crime is not absolute. It varies from time to time and from place to place, as society and political leaders change. Forms of behavior considered crimes today may not be considered crimes tomorrow. For example, during the Prohibition period of the 1920s, it was a crime to sell, distribute, or possess alcoholic beverages. Today the sale, distribution, or possession of alcoholic beverages is legal, so long as the seller has a license, complies with state regulations, and the user is over 21. For another example, 100 years ago cocaine and opiates were legal and available at the corner store and through mail-order houses. Cocaine was used in a popular soft drink, Coca-Cola (Bollinger 1990). Today cocaine and heroin are illegal. Of course, some forms of behavior like murder, rape, or theft have been illegal throughout time.

Crimes are often classified as felonies or misdemeanors. **Felonies** are the more serious crimes and are punishable by long prison sentences. They include murder, assault, rape, arson, and armed robbery. **Misdemeanors** are less serious crimes such as petty theft (stealing candy), minor vandalism, disorderly conduct, and minor traffic violations.

Criminal justice is a form of morality policy. This type of policy is uncomplicated, highly visible, pervasive, and contentious. It occasionally involves religious beliefs or organizations. It entails clear and simplistic distinctions between right and wrong, good and evil, and the legal and the illegal. It is pervasive because it is frequently in the news and most people have strong feelings on the subject. It is contentious; debates often arise over what forms of behavior to outlaw, how severe penalties should be for crimes, or whether drugs should be legal.

Criminal justice policies involve an intricate system of governmental institutions: police departments, district attorneys, coroners, criminal courts, prisons, jails, parole boards, and probation officers. The policies and procedures of each institution change from time to time and vary from state to state. Moreover, each institution operates within an intergovernmental system, which entails local, state, and national governments.

Criminal justice policies have historically involved state and local governments—that is, most criminal law is state law. Until the 1920s the federal government had been only marginally involved in fighting crime, dealing with smuggling, counterfeiting, piracy, kidnapping, and a few others. Then the federal government became involved in Prohibition. It became more involved in local law enforcement during the 1960s. Its involvement has increased even more in the early 21st century.

Although there is a great deal of consistency in criminal laws in the 50 states, there are some significant differences. For example, some states allow the use of marijuana for medical purposes; others do not. Penalties for crimes vary among the states. Some states have capital punishment; others do not.

Criminal justice policies have changed profoundly over time. Several criminal justice policy regimes can be identified: the colonial regime (1610–1790), the preindustrial regime (1791–1870), the industrial regime (1870–1960), the rights regime (1960–1994), and the incarceration regime (1994–present). These regimes vary in terms of the dominant ideas about the causes and prevention of crime, the nature of punishment, and the organizational response to crime. The colonial regime applied a moral definition of crime and relied on physical punishment. The preindustrial regime gave rise to the penal system. The industrial regime emphasized professional approaches to the treatment of felons. The rights regime emphasized the rights of people accused of crimes. The incarceration regime of the present is characterized by extremely high rates of imprisonment.

→ The Colonial Criminal Justice Regime, 1610–1790

The colonial criminal justice regime, modeled after the English criminal justice system, lasted from colonial times to about 1790. It ended with the construction of the first prison (1790) and the ratification of the Bill of Rights (1791). This regime was characterized by physical punishment. Sheriffs enforced law in the counties. Constables maintained law in the towns and cities. The dominant view was that moral deficiency or evil people caused crime.

Imprisonment as a penalty for crime was rare. Towns and cities had jails, but jails were used to keep people arrested for crimes before they went to trial. A few workhouses were used as prisons. Because the Quakers opposed physical punishment and dominated the colony, Pennsylvania became the first colony to establish a prison system. Nevertheless, the colonial justice system relied heavily on physical punishment.

Social philosopher Michel Foucault argued that punishment during the colonial era was largely a public spectacle. That is, punishment was visible, public, and physical. Forms of punishment included banishment, branding, whipping, the stocks, mutilation, quartering, and hanging. It was not uncommon for law enforcement officials to deal with convicted criminals by forcing them to leave town; branding them with a hot iron; whipping them; cutting off a limb, ear, or nose; or hanging them. Punishment was commonly administered in the public square in the center of town.

Physical punishment was sometimes extreme. The purpose of the punishment was to inflict extreme pain, to punish the convict beyond death, to make a public spectacle of the punishment, and to terrorize the public into obedience to the law. These extreme practices explain the Eighth Amendment's prohibition against cruel and unusual punishment in the Constitution.

The ideas of the colonial justice system were often rooted in religious fundamentalism—a belief in the literal interpretation of the Bible, with an emphasis on eternal damnation for nonbelievers or sinners. This system relied on physical punishment rather than imprisonment and sometimes imposed the death penalty for heresy, adultery, or blasphemy.

Moral Panics

Political reaction to crime is not always based on real threats. Sometimes this reaction arises from moral panics. The colonial justice system was subjected to **moral panics**—violent political reactions to imagined or exaggerated offenses. The Salem witch trials in Massachusetts illustrate this point. The trials arose from a moral panic that began in 1692 after a few girls had seizures. The cause of the seizures is unknown; historians speculate they were caused by bad food or perhaps the girls were hysterical. At that time, however, people believed the seizures were caused by witchcraft, a practice that violated state law. In an atmosphere of pervasive fear, public officials targeted imagined witches.

There were no witches or devil worshipers in Salem. Nevertheless, over 20 people were convicted of witchcraft and subsequently hanged. Almost all were women. All were innocent. Most of the women arrested did not fit the ideal image of the obedient, submissive, married

Puritan woman. They threatened the status quo. The few men who attempted to defend the women were executed.

Moral panics are sometimes triggered by economic crises, international threats, or perceived threats to people's way of life, social status, or values. Although there are no more hunts for witches and no more delusions about witches, moral panics and witch hunts flare up from time to time and influence the shape of criminal justice policies.

→ The Preindustrial Criminal Justice Regime, 1791–1870

Three primary factors changed the colonial justice system: The American Revolution, the Bill of Rights, and the Enlightenment. The American Revolution generated strong ideas about limiting police powers and opposing physical punishment, especially as this form of punishment was used against revolutionaries.

Ideas about crime and justice changed after the American Revolution. Enlightenment philosophers such as Locke, Montesquieu, Rousseau, and Voltaire influenced this change. The criminal was no longer thought to be inherently and irretrievably evil. People were believed to be basically rational and criminals redeemable, if taken out of their environment and given the opportunity to change. These ideas supported the rise of prisons.

Beccaria and Reform of Criminal Punishment

In 1764 **Cesare Beccaria** published *On Crimes and Punishment,* in which he attacked physical punishment as barbaric and argued for the construction of workhouses and prisons to incarcerate convicted felons. He believed that prisons would force criminals to think about their crimes and find penitence—the prison would be a penitentiary. Beccaria insisted punishment should be proportionate to the crime; that is, the length of the imprisonment should be related to the seriousness of the crime.

Beccaria's ideas were popular among leaders of the American Revolution and no doubt influenced Thomas Jefferson and James Madison who introduced the Bill of Rights, the first 10 amendments to the Constitution.

Prison Expansion

Beccaria's advocacy of penal reform encouraged prison construction in the United States.

The Quakers of Pennsylvania led the prison reform movement and built the first prison in 1790, the Walnut Street Jail. It was a small jail and workhouse that isolated serious offenders in small cells and kept less serious offenders in the workhouse. In the early nineteenth century, two prison models emerged: the Philadelphia and the Auburn models. The Philadelphia model was designed like a wagon wheel. Most cells contained a private, walled-off courtyard. Each prisoner stayed in his or her own cell in isolation for the entire duration of the sentence. The goal of this arrangement was to guard against moral contamination through evil association and to encourage self-reflection and remorse. This prison type soon disappeared.

The Auburn facility was built like a factory, with many stories. It could hold more prisoners than the Philadelphia model. Although prisoners lived in their own cells, they were not totally isolated. They slept in the cells at night, but they ate in a common dining room and exercised in a common gym or courtyard. The Auburn model replaced the Philadelphia one.

Prison construction proliferated in the early part of the 19th century. By midcentury prisons were common in almost every state (Inciardi 2005).

→ The Industrial Criminal Justice Regime, 1870–1960

Two major historic trends of the late 19th century impacted the criminal justice system: the rise of segregation in the South and the Progressive reform movement in the North. Southern states segregated their prisons and established prison and convict lease systems. Progressive reformers advocated the establishment of indeterminate sentences, the probation system, and professional police organizations.

Racial Segregation in Prisons

Racial segregation emerged in the southern criminal justice system at the end of the 19th century. During the era of slavery, state laws in the South gave plantation owners authority to deal with crime among slaves. Civil rights laws during the Reconstruction period delayed the emergence of segregation, but after the 1896 *Plessy v. Ferguson* decision established the separate but equal principle, racial segregation spread across the South like a plague, infecting every institution, including the criminal justice system. Courtrooms, jails, and prisons were segregated. Criminal laws were administered in a racially discriminatory manner. African-American males often received harsher sentences than white males for similar forms of criminal behavior. For example, if a black man committed the crime of raping a white woman, he was likely to be hanged, whereas a white man would more likely be incarcerated. By the 1960s segregated prisons had disappeared.

The Convict Lease System

The **convict lease system** emerged in the South and West. There were three forms of leases: prison lease, external convict lease, and internal convict lease.

Under the prison lease system, a private firm or business leader would lease and run the prison for the state. This type of lease was popular because it was believed that private businesses were more efficient than government. A prime example of this type of lease is San Quentin, a large prison built in the San Francisco area before the Civil War. It was constructed on the land of a rich and powerful landowner, Mariano Guadalupe Vallejo, with the help of an influential state legislator, James Estell. Estell obtained a state contract to run the prison as a private business. Because the state had financial troubles, contracting with a private firm or individual was attractive. However, there were problems; one was the sale of early releases and pardons. Also, to save money, the firm spent little on food, clothing, or repairs, leaving inmates ill clothed and ill fed and the prison in ill repair. The problems became so bad that the state sued to recover the prison. Although it lost the suit, the state paid off the contract and took back the prison.

> In 1860 a final settlement was achieved between California and the lessee, who received $275,000 compensation, a substantial amount of money at that time, and the prison was returned to state management. Governor John Downey stated after the settlement: "I would most seriously object ever again to allow the prison or its management to pass out of the exclusive control of the State." (Shichor 1995)

In the external convict lease a private firm would lease the convicts, pay the prison a fixed amount, obtain custody of the prisoners, and assume responsibility for guarding, housing, clothing, and feeding the prisoners. The advantage to the firm was cheap prison labor. This system was popular in the South where the freeing of the slaves increased the demand for prison labor. Former plantation owners, mine owners, and other types of employers would bid on state contracts for prisoners (Comejo 1976, 203).

The convict lease system had two problems. First, firms often overworked prisoners, leading to a high death rate. For example, the death rate for convicts leased by railroad construction firms in South Carolina, the harshest system, was 45 percent from 1877 to 1879; in other words, in two years almost half the convicts were dead. Around the same time, the death rate in Arkansas was 25 percent, and 16 percent in Mississippi (Shichor 1995, 36).

The second problem with the convict lease system was that it took jobs from hard-working, law-abiding citizens. Opposition to this system increased in the early part of the 20th century, especially from labor unions.

The internal convict lease system involved companies contracting with the state or directly with the prison administration to employ prisoners while they were inside the prison, generally under direct state supervision. Like the external lease system, the advantage of the internal lease system was cheap labor.

The privately managed prison died out at the end of the 19th century but has recently returned. The convict lease system continued up to the 1930s when Congress passed laws banning prison-made goods from interstate commerce (*Hawes-Cooper Act of 1929* and the *Ashurst-Sumners Act of 1935*). States then limited prison-made goods to prison uniforms and state license plates—products that would not enter the private market.

Reform Movements

The Progressive reform movement of the late 19th and early 20th centuries produced two spin-off movements that impacted the criminal justice system. The first spin-off was the penal reform movement, which opposed chain gangs and convict lease systems, and produced a number of changes in the penal systems. This movement emerged from the National Conference on Penitentiary and Reformatory Discipline, which proposed rehabilitation, indeterminate sentences, and parole.

The idea that convicts could be rehabilitated encouraged the adoption of indeterminate sentences and the parole system. **Indeterminate sentences** entailed a time range such as 2 to 10 years. This range gave discretion to both judges and prison administrators. During sentencing, judges could take into consideration the character of the accused and his or her prospect for rehabilitation. This range in sentences also gave prison administrators power over inmates. The prison administrator could recommend shortening a sentence depending on the inmate's behavior. Indeterminate sentences also provide a system of rewards and punishment that could be used in the process of rehabilitating inmates, as sentences could be reduced for good behavior.

Another spin-off of the Progressive movement was the municipal reform movement. This movement introduced civil service systems and scientific management into city governments. Its contribution to the criminal justice system was the creation of professionalized city police departments in which police are selected by merit, trained in police administration, and making a career out of enforcement.

Alcatraz, a former federal prison in San Francisco Bay.

→ *The Rights Criminal Justice Regime, 1960–1994*

The next big change in criminal justice policy occurred during the 1960s, primarily as a result of the impact of the civil rights movement and the expansion of federal powers. Two major changes occurred during this period: (1) the end of racial segregation in the South and the expansion of civil rights and the rights of the accused; and (2) the expansion of the federal role in local law enforcement.

The Supreme Court and Expansion of the Rights of the Accused

The civil rights movement attacked blatant racial bias in the justice system. Civil rights policies ended racial segregation in prisons. Blatant forms of racial discrimination in the system all but disappeared. The civil rights movement encouraged the expansion of other rights, notably the rights of those accused of crimes.

The rights of people accused of crimes expanded during the 1960s. The groundwork for this expansion had already been established through the Bill of Rights and the Fourteenth Amendment. Four of the amendments in the Bill of Rights address criminal justice issues.

The Fourth Amendment protects against unreasonable search and seizure.
The Fifth Amendment guards against self-incrimination and double jeopardy.
The Sixth Amendment guarantees the right to an attorney, a speedy trial, and a jury of
    one's peers.
The Eighth Amendment protects against cruel and unusual punishment.

From the ratification of the Bill of Rights in 1791 to the *Mapp v. Ohio* decision in 1961, the Supreme Court was reluctant to apply the full force of the Bill of Rights to the states. In an 1833 decision, the Court ruled that the Bill of Rights applied only to the federal government, not the state governments. However, the Fourteenth Amendment (adopted in 1868) was intended to remedy this problem.

> The Fourteenth Amendment forbids the states to abridge by law any privilege or immunity of U.S. citizens. But what are these "privileges and immunities"? Representative John A. Bingham, an Ohio Republican who authored the amendment, believed that the "privilege and immunities" of citizens of the United States . . . are chiefly defined in the first eight amendments to the Constitution. . . . These eight articles were never limitations upon the power of the States, until made so by the Fourteenth Amendment. (Barker et al. 1999, 15)

Despite the Fourteenth Amendment, the Supreme Court did nothing until the 1960s.

The Supreme Court had a double standard for its use of the Bill of Rights in limiting federal police powers but not those of the states. A good example is the Court's use of the **exclusionary rule,** the principle derived from the Fourth Amendment protection against unreasonable search and seizure, which requires criminal courts to exclude evidence obtained illegally by the police. The Supreme Court applied this rule to lower federal courts, but refused to apply it to state courts until 1961. The Court made strong statements emphasizing the importance to a free society of "the security of one's privacy against arbitrary police intrusion . . ." but it refused to exclude evidence obtained illegally by the police (*Wolf v. Colorado* 1949).

Another example of the Court's double standard is the *Palko v. Connecticut* decision of 1942. Palko was found guilty of murder and sentenced to life imprisonment. The prosecutor, who was seeking the death penalty, appealed the case, arguing that the judge did not follow state law in explaining the meaning of first degree murder and the conditions that allowed the death penalty. The state supreme court agreed with the prosecutor and ordered a retrial. Palko was tried again for the same crime and sentenced to death. He appealed to the U.S. Supreme Court on grounds that the state had violated the Fifth Amendment prohibition against double jeopardy. The Court, however, did not find the double jeopardy violation severe enough to invalidate the second trial.

The Court ruled against state governments in a few extreme cases; for example, it threw out confessions obtained through torture. In *Skinner v. Oklahoma* (1942) the Court also struck down a state law requiring the sterilization of prisoners found guilty of three or more moral crimes such as stealing a chicken or robbery. The Court struck down the state law because it applied to certain forms of robbery, but not to others; it targeted black males; and it destroyed a man's ability to procreate. In the famous **Scottsboro case** nine young African-American males from Scottsboro, Alabama, were convicted and sentenced to death in 1931 for raping two young white females with whom they had been stowaways on a train. In *Powell v. Alabama* (1932), the Court ordered a retrial. It was troubled by the state court's sentencing the poor, illiterate boys to death after a hasty, racially charged trial. The Court established the rule that defendants in death penalty cases were entitled to a competent attorney, even if they could not afford one. These cases provided the basis for the expansion of rights during the 1960s.

In the 1960s the Court began to apply the Bill of Rights to restrain police powers and local governments and to protect the rights of the accused. Although there are several cases that defined the rights regime, the main cases are as follows: *Mapp v. Ohio* (1961), *Gideon v. Wainwright* (1963), and *Miranda v. Arizona* (1966).

Mapp v. Ohio

In the *Mapp v. Ohio* case, the Supreme Court established the exclusionary rule for state courts. In 1957 three Cleveland, Ohio, police officers looking for a suspect knocked on the door of Dollree Mapp. Ms. Mapp called her attorney who informed her that she did not have to open her door unless the police produced a warrant. She asked for a warrant and refused to open the door. The police left, but returned with more officers, broke down the door, and entered the home. Again Mapp, while inside her home, asked for a warrant. An officer showed her a piece of paper and said it was a warrant. She snatched the paper and a police officer wrestled it from her. The officers continued to search the home, but found only obscene material for which Dollree Mapp was arrested and convicted. Her attorney appealed the conviction, arguing that the evidence against Mapp was obtained illegally; there was no evidence that the police ever had a warrant to search her home. The State of Ohio insisted that even if the evidence used against Mapp was obtained illegally and violated the Fourth Amendment, the Supreme Court had long established a precedent to allow such evidence in court. Justice Tom Clark, writing the majority opinion in this case, explained that the exclusionary rule was created and applied in federal cases for several reasons. Without this rule the Fourth Amendment would be nothing but words and there would be no way to deter police from violating the amendment. The use of evidence obtained illegally violated the Constitution and the rights of the accused. Clark noted that the Supreme Court had refused in the past to apply the exclusionary rule to states, but the situation had changed by 1961: Most states applied the exclusionary rule and it had become part of effective and professional police administration. Clark simply extended the rule to other states.

Gideon v. Wainwright

The *Gideon v. Wainwright* decision (1963) required courts to appoint an attorney for defendants who could not afford one. This case began in Panama City, Florida, when Earl Gideon was arrested for breaking into a pool hall, smashing a vending machine, and stealing the change. When he appeared in court, he asked the judge for an attorney because he could not afford one. The judge told him that the court could only assign attorneys in capital punishment cases. Gideon was convicted. While in jail he studied law and handwrote his appeal to the Supreme Court, arguing that the trial court denied his Sixth Amendment right to counsel by not appointing an attorney for him. The Supreme Court agreed with him. In earlier cases the Court had decided that a defendant did not need an attorney except in capital cases. However, in *Mapp v. Ohio* (1961) the court changed its position: A poor man could not get a fair trial unless the court appoints an attorney for him.

Miranda v. Arizona

The *Miranda* case (1966) established the Miranda rule, which requires police officers to inform suspects of their rights at the time of arrest. Miranda was actually the lead case of several. Ernesto Miranda was arrested in Phoenix, Arizona, on charges of kidnapping and rape. The police interrogated him for two hours before obtaining a written confession from him. He was informed of neither his right to an attorney nor his right to remain silent before the police secured the confession.

The intent behind the Miranda rule was to prevent coerced confessions, which violate the Fifth and Sixth Amendments. Supporters of this rule insist that it improves police administration; opponents claim that it hamstrings the police and helps criminals avoid prosecution.

Reaction to the Supreme Court Cases

In these cases the Supreme Court applied the Bill of Rights to the states. The Court acknowledged principles that were already in practice in most states. By the time of the *Mapp* decision about two-third of the states were already applying the exclusionary rule and most states acknowledged Fifth Amendment protections. Nevertheless, these decisions ignited a firestorm of reaction. Police organizations and conservative political leaders across the country protested. In 1968 presidential candidate Richard Nixon denounced the decisions as coddling criminals and endangering the public. Some public officials defined the problem of crime in terms of a criminal justice system that was too lenient.

Moratorium on Capital Punishment

The Supreme Court continued to expand rights in the 1970s. In 1973 it declared a moratorium on the death penalty (*Furman v. Georgia*), principally because this penalty was administered in an arbitrary and capricious manner. For example, in one city a man convicted of rape could be sentenced to death, whereas in another city a man convicted of multiple murders could be sentenced to prison, with the chance of parole. The Court declared that this arbitrary administration of capital punishment violated the Eight Amendment prohibition against cruel and unusual punishment. State legislatures had to revise their laws and develop more uniform procedures for capital punishment. States did two things to respond to the problem.

1. They limited the application of capital punishment only to cases involving aggravated murder: multiple murders, serial murders, or murder in the commission of another felony.
2. They established a two-part court procedure in death penalty cases. In the first part, a jury determined the defendant's guilt or innocence. In the second part, the jury determined whether to recommend to the judge the death penalty or not. This process required the evaluation of both aggravating and mitigating circumstances.

By the end of the 1970s the Court had accepted these changes and allowed states to resume administering capital punishment. Today capital punishment has been reestablished in several states.

Expansion of the Federal Role in Law Enforcement

In the late 1960s the role of the federal government expanded in local law enforcement. In 1965 President Johnson established a special task force, the National Commission on Law Enforcement and Criminal Justice. The commission produced one of the most comprehensive studies of crime and criminal justice ever. It recommended increasing federal spending on local law enforcement and the creation of metropolitan law enforcement task forces. In response to the commission's report, Congress passed the *Safe Streets and Community Act of 1968*, which provided grants for local law enforcement and incentives for cooperation in law enforcement across metropolitan areas. In 1970 Congress passed the *Law Enforcement Assistance Act*, which established the Law Enforcement Assistance Administration (LEAA) within the Justice Department to facilitate metropolitan cooperation among law enforcement agencies. The idea was that crime, especially drug trafficking and organized crime, crossed city borders to become a problem best addressed through metropolitan task forces.

Although the LEAA was abolished in 1978 due to lack of funds, efforts to improve coordination among metropolitan agencies continued, especially in drug enforcement and organized crime. In 1970 Congress passed the Racketeer Influenced and Corruption Organization Act (RICO) to target organized crime. Three years later Congress established the Drug Enforcement Administration (DEA) to centralize drug enforcement and cooperate with other federal agencies—Federal Bureau of Investigation (FBI) and Alcohol, Tobacco, Firearms, and Explosives (ATF)—and local law enforcement.

Even with the elimination of the LEAA, federal involvement in local drug enforcement increased during the 1980s. With the passage of the *Anti-Drug Abuse Act,* Congress established the Office of National Drug Control Policy, the chief of which is known popularly as the drug czar. The drug czar is responsible for coordinating drug enforcement among federal and local agencies.

Retreat from Rights in the 1980s

During the 1980s conservative political leaders continued to attack the rights regime as too lenient and overly committed to protecting the rights of the criminal, and uncommitted to protecting the public from crime. Some conservative leaders blamed the increase in crime on the rights granted to the accused during the 1960s. They told stories about courts letting hardened criminals free on minor legal technicalities. The Supreme Court began to roll back rights, making the system less lenient and more difficult for defendants to be released on technicalities. It established many exceptions to the rights and principles established during the 1960s, especially the exclusionary and Miranda rules. Some of the most notable exceptions include the following:

Good faith
In plain view
In hot pursuit
Inevitable discovery
Public safety

Good Faith   In the **good faith** exception, the Court allows evidence even if there is a technical error on a warrant. The case that created this exception involved an arrest for drugs. The police had obtained a search warrant, searched the house, and found the drugs. The defense attorney asked the judge to throw out the evidence because the search warrant had an error: The address on the warrant was incorrect. The judge allowed the evidence because the police had operated in good faith. Judges will no longer refuse to admit evidence because of technical errors in a warrant (*U.S. v. Leon* 1984).

Plain View   The **plain view** exception arose from a case in which police, while investigating a robbery, knocked on the suspect's door. The suspect's mother answered the door and invited the police into the home. There the police saw the stolen goods. Because the stolen goods were in plain view, the judge allowed them to be used as evidence in court, even though the police did not have a search warrant.

Hot Pursuit   The **hot pursuit** exception allows police to pursue a fleeing felon into buildings, even though the police may not have a search warrant. Legally, without a warrant, police cannot go into buildings looking for suspects. However, they are allowed to chase a suspect who they know just committed a felony into a building.

Inevitable Discovery   Police detectives had a mass murder suspect in custody. The patrol officers were in the process of searching a wooded area for the body of the suspect's last victim. It was a matter of time before they would make the **inevitable discovery** of the body. The suspect's attorney told the police not to talk to his client until he was brought into the police station. While in the police car en route to the station and while passing the wooded area, a detective asked the suspect were he had buried the body so they could put the minds of the victim's family to rest. The suspect told the police where the body was buried. The attorney wanted evidence of the body excluded from the trial, but the Court refused to exclude the evidence because its discovery was inevitable (*Nix v. Williams* 1984).

Public Safety   The **public safety exception** arose from a case in which two police officers pursued a suspected rapist into a supermarket. The officers apprehended the suspect, who did not have a gun although he had used one to commit the crime. Before reading the suspect his Miranda rights, the officers asked where he had hidden the gun. The suspect nodded in the direction of some empty boxes, saying the gun was there. The officer found the gun. The suspect's attorney motioned the court to throw out the evidence of the conversation and gun, because they were obtained before the police had read the Miranda rights. The Supreme Court allowed the use of the gun and statement, on the grounds that the safety of the police officer and the public was more important. The Court had established the public safety exception to the Miranda rule (*New York v. Quarles* 1984).

Several cases decided throughout the 1980s and 1990s further weakened the rules and principles established during the 1960s. Although substantially weakened, these rules remained in place.

→ *The Incarceration Criminal Justice Regime, 1994–Present*

Criminal justice policies continued to change during the 1990s. As rights principles were eroded, new, more punitive laws were passed which contributed to a substantial increase in incarceration rates. (See Figure 12.1.) These rates indicate the number of adults in prison or jail for every 100,000 people.

FIGURE 12.1

Incarceration Rates per 100,000 People from 1925–2000
SOURCE: U.S. Department of Justice, Bureau of Justice Statistics, *Sourcebook of Criminal Justice Statistics,* 2004.

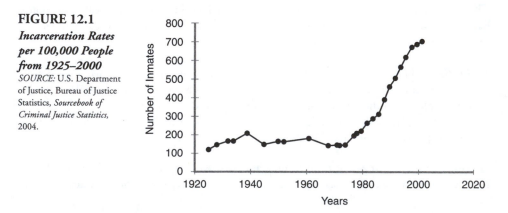

By 1994 the rights regime was gone. It was replaced by a new **incarceration regime,** characterized by extremely large numbers of people in local jails or state prisons. Incarceration had been the primary method of punishment for over 200 years. The incarceration rates had remained stable throughout most of the 20th century. Beginning in the 1980s, however, incarceration rates increased sharply. In 1990, at a rate of 292 per 100,000, the rights regime was clearly disappearing. The high rates contradicted the idea of a rights regime or a lenient criminal justice system. The rates almost doubled over the next five years, reaching the staggering level of 403 per 100,000 by 1995. Then they climbed even higher, setting world and historic records at 681 per 100,000 in 2000, and continued to increase in the 21st century to 718 per 100,000 by 2003.

The number of people incarcerated in state prisons or local jails is staggering. In 1980 a half million people were incarcerated. By the end of the 1980s, over a million were incarcerated. Today, more than 2 million people are incarcerated, a little less than 1 percent of the population.

The total number of people within the justice system has also reached record high levels. In 1980, 1.8 million people were in the justice system, either in jail, in prison, on probation, or on parole. By 2001 this figure had exceeded 6.5 million, almost 2.5 percent of the U.S. population. (See Tables 12.1 and 12.2.)

The dramatic growth in the number of people incarcerated has been matched by a dramatic

Police headquarters in downtown Detroit.

TABLE 12.1						
Number of People in Jails or Prisons, 1980–2002						
Year	**Number**	**Year**	**Number**	**Year**	**Number**	
1980	501,886	1988	949,659	1995	1,577,842	
1982	555,114	1989	1,076,670	1996	1,637,928	
1983	645,713	1990	1,146,401	1997	1,734,538	
1984	681,282	1991	1,216,664	1998	1,806,808	
1985	742,939	1992	1,292,347	2000	1,933,503	
1986	799,171	1993	1,364,881	2001	1,962,220	
1987	856,906	1994	1,469,947	2002	2,021,223	

SOURCE: U.S. Department of Justice, Bureau of Justice Statistics, *Sourcebook of Criminal Justice Statistics,* 2004.

FIGURE 12.2
Number of Inmates on Death Row, 1968–2003
SOURCE: Reprinted from *Criminal Justice Statistics: A Practical Approach* by Arthur J. Lurigio, 1997, p.1, with permission from Elsevier.

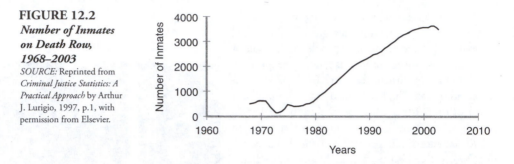

TABLE 12.2					
Population of Offenders in the Criminal Justice System					
Select Year	**Estimated Total**	**Probation**	**Jail**	**Prison**	**Parole**
1980	1,840,400	1,118,097	182,288	319,598	220,438
1985	3,011,500	1,968,712	254,986	487,593	300,203
1990	4,350,300	2,670,234	405,320	743,382	531,407
1995	5,342,900	3,077,861	507,044	1,078,542	679,421
2000	6,445,600	3,826,209	621,149	1,316,333	724,486
2001	6,581,700	3,931,731	631,240	1,330,007	732,333
2002	6,759,100	4,024,067	665,475	1,367,856	750,934
2003	6,889,800	4,073,987	691,301	1,387,269	774,588

SOURCE: U.S. Department of Justice, Bureau of Justice Statistics, *Sourcebook of Criminal Justice Statistics,* 2004.

growth in the number of people executed each year and the number of people on death row. The number of annual executions peaked in the late 1930s at close to 200. This number declined to zero by the time of the *Furman* decision (1973), which suspended executions. The number of executions has increased since the Supreme Court reinstated capital punishment in the late 1970s. Today there are around 60 or 70 executions a year.

The number of people on death row has increased dramatically since the late 1970s. In 1973 there were only 134 people on death row, a figure that increased to 691 by 1980. By 1990 it had increased by a factor of three, exceeding 2,300. In 2003 there were 3,525 people on death row. Figure 12.2 illustrates the sharp increase in the number of death row inmates since 1968.

By the end of the 20th century the rights regime was gone and replaced by a more punitive incarceration regime. The United States had the highest incarceration rates in its history and among the highest rates in the world. The new incarceration policy regime, which was characterized by more severe penalties for crime and extremely high incarceration rates, was preceded by major shifts in power and ideas.

Increase in Crime Rates and Incarceration

It was the more punitive criminal justice policies, not an increase in crime, that produced the dramatic increase in incarceration rates. Crime rates had been up and down throughout the past 40 years, and down over the past 10.

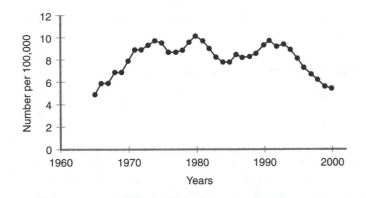

FIGURE 12.3
Murder Rates, per 100,000, 1965–2000
SOURCE: U.S. Census Bureau, *Statistical Abstract of the United States,* 2003.

TABLE 12.3

Crime Rates per 100,000 Population

Year	Total Violent Crime*	Total Property Crime†
1980	596.6	5,353.3
1985	558.1	4,666.4
1990	729.6	5,073.1
1995	684.5	4,590.5
2000	506.1	3,618.3
2001	504.5	3,658.1
2002	494.6	3,624.1

*Murder, robbery, forcible rape, aggravated assault.

†Burglary, larceny/thief, motor vehicle thief.

SOURCE: U.S. Census Bureau, *Statistical Abstract of the United States,* 2004.

Murder rates are fairly accurate indicators of violent crime. These rates have been relatively stable over the past 40 years. In the early 1960s murder rates were around 5 murders per 100,000 people. These rates climbed to close to 10 by the late 1970s and hovered between 8 and 10 from 1975 to 1995. By 2000 they were back to around 5.5 murders per 100,000, the lowest rate since the late 1960s.

Figure 12.3 illustrates the ups and downs of the murder rate between 1965 and 2000. The recent decline in murder rates cannot, however, explain the sharp rise in the incarceration rates.

Other measures of violence followed the same pattern as the murder rate. The first column in Table 12.3 lists changes in total violent crime rates in select years from 1980 to 2002. Violent crimes include murder, robbery, forcible rape, and aggravated assault. These rates peaked at 729.6 per 100,000 people in 1990, and have now declined throughout the 1990s and the first few years of the 21st century.

The second column in Table 12.3 lists property crime rates. Property crime rates were up and down during the same time period. These rates have now declined to 3,618.3 per 100,000 people by 2000. They increased and decreased marginally the next two years. In no way can property crime rates, like declining murder rates, explain the substantial rise in incarceration rates. The decline in all types of crime during the late 1990s does not explain the increase in incarceration rates. Instead, new, more punitive criminal justice policies produced the increased incarceration rates.

Policy Changes: Sentencing and the War on Drugs

The new policies that produced the high incarceration rates include mandatory sentencing, truth in sentencing, three strikes you're out laws, and targeted drug enforcement. Each one of these new policies increased incarceration rates different ways.

Mandatory Sentencing, Truth in Sentencing, and Three Strikes

Mandatory sentencing laws increased incarceration rates by replacing indeterminate sentences that had a range of, say, 2 to 10 years with a higher and fixed prison term such as 10 years. This new policy eliminated the discretion judges had to impose lighter prison terms. New York was one of the first states to pass mandatory sentencing laws. Most of these laws pertain to drug- or firearm-related offenses. Many states added a mandatory two additional years onto felony convicts involving handguns. The state of Michigan mandates life without parole for possession of more than 650 grams of heroin or cocaine for a first-time offender (Wright 1998, 17). Both the federal government and most state governments impose a mandatory five-year prison term for the possession of more than 5 grams of crack cocaine.

Critics claim that because mandatory sentencing takes away the discretion of judges, they produce unreasonably long prison terms. Illustrating this point, the National Criminal Justice Commission Report (1996) cited several cases of unreasonably long prison terms imposed by these laws.

> In Mobile, Alabama, Nicole Richardson fell in love at age twenty with a small-time drug dealer who worked out of a local bar. One day, an undercover agent asked her where he could buy some drugs. She told him to talk to her boyfriend. For that degree of involvement, she was sentenced to ten years in prison with no possibility of parole. Her boyfriend had information on other drug dealers to trade. After cooperating with authorities, he received a prison sentence of five years.
>
> Michael Irish was a carpenter from Portland, Oregon, whose life savings had been wiped out to pay for the medical bills of his cancer-stricken wife. Irish, who had no criminal history, was caught and convicted of unloading boxes of hashish from a boat. Under the mandatory minimum law, he was sentenced to twelve years in prison with no possibility of parole—an incarceration that will cost [the state] at least $250,000. (Donziger 1996, 25–27)

Another type of law similar to mandatory sentencing is the **truth in sentencing** laws. These laws increased sentences by eliminating early releases or early paroles for good behavior.

Another new policy contributing to the high incarceration rate is the **three strikes you're out** law. These laws impose long prison sentences for a third felony conviction, generally 25 years or life. Both the federal and the state governments have passed these laws. An early example of this type of law is the *Armed Career Criminal Act of 1988,* a federal law that mandates a 25-year sentence with no chance of parole for any third-time felon who possessed, not necessarily used, a firearm in the commission of a crime. The most recent trend in three-strikes laws is the imposition of life sentences for commission of a third felony. In 1993 Washington became the first state to establish a three strikes you're out policy mandating a life sentence for third-time felons, followed by California. The 1994 federal crime bill has a similar three-strikes provision. At the end of 2003, most states had some form of a three-strikes law (Wright 1998).

Recently, the Supreme Court upheld the constitutionality of the three-strikes law in California, after a man named Ewing was sentenced to life imprisonment for stealing three golf clubs. The law was challenged on grounds of violating the Eighth Amendment prohibition against cruel and unusual punishment. In *Ewing v. California* (2003) the Court rejected the challenge because the law did not impose a life sentence for a misdemeanor and because the purpose of the law was to target violent and career criminals. Ewing had several prior convictions; in one conviction he had broken into a home and terrorized the inhabitants.

Like other mandatory sentencing laws, the three-strikes law restricts the discretion of the judge. However, in some states the judge has the option of reducing the charge from a felony to a misdemeanor. Nevertheless, a University of California study found that about 85 percent of those sentenced to life under the three-strikes law were convicted of nonviolent offenses (Wisely 1998). Willie Wisely suggested that whereas the system was reacting to a fear of violent predatory offenders, it ended up locking up "the Three Stooges." The following are three examples:

> Larry Fisher, 35, was convicted of his third strike in Snohomish County superior court in Washington. He is in prison and will stay there for the rest of his life. Fisher was convicted of putting his finger in his pocket, pretending it was a gun, and robbing a sandwich shop of $151 dollars. An hour later police arrested him at a bar a block away while he was drinking a beer. Fisher's two prior strikes involved stealing $360 from his grandfather in 1986 and robbing a pizza parlor of $100.
>
> In March 1995, Jerry Dewayne Williams of Los Angeles got 25 years to life for stealing a slice of pizza from a group of children on a pier. . . .
>
> In Monterey County, Joel Murillo faced a term of 35 years to life for stealing television sets. But, Judge Robert Moody exercised his discretion and disregarded a prior felony conviction, sentencing Murillo to an 18-year term. (1998, 16, 21–22)

The War on Drugs

The **war on drugs** is another public policy that directly contributed to the sharp increase in incarceration rates, not because more people were abusing drugs, but because the federal government concentrated more resources and power on apprehending drug offenders.

In the early 1980s President Reagan initiated the war on drugs primarily in reaction to the rise of crack cocaine in inner cities and the violence associated with the crack trade. Crack cocaine is a cheaper form of cocaine, made from cooking powdered cocaine, baking soda, and water. It costs a few dollars a dose and spread quickly to a number of large cities. The Reagan administration fought this drug epidemic by targeting cocaine-producing countries and the inner cities. The targeting of inner cities increased drug arrests and produced higher incarceration rates.

According to Mark Mauer of the Sentencing Project, drug abuse had declined since 1979. He cited surveys conducted by the U.S. Department of Health and Human Services indicating that in 1979, 14.1 percent of the population reported using illegal drugs in the past month and that by 1995 this was down to 6.1 percent (Mauer 1999, 145). Of course, during the 1980s, as drug use was declining among the general population, there was an increase in drug overdosage, as more people abuse drugs more intensely, but this intense drug abuse and overdoses also declined during the 1990s. Mauer insisted that although drug abuse was declining, local and federal police continued to aggressively target inner-city drug users, which also dramatically increased the incarceration rate of African-American males.

Explaining Policy Regime Change

Several factors contributed to the demise of the rights regime, the formation of the incarceration regime, and the establishment of new criminal justice policies. First, political power shifted from liberal pro-rights groups to conservative pro-incarceration groups. Second, new ideas encouraged the emergence of the incarceration regime. Third, political leaders and the mass media exploited the fear of crime and exaggerated the crime problem.

Political Power Shifts

Political power shifted during the 1980s and 1990s. Organizations supporting the rights of the accused and prisoners declined. New organizations emerged supporting more severe penalties. Prisoner rights organizations that were active during the 1970s were gone by the 1980s. Civil rights organizations that were involved with issues of racism and criminal justice had shifted their attention to other issues. Of course, civil rights groups had recently become involved with the racial profiling issue.

A new power block emerged to promote tougher anticrime laws: National Rifle Association (NRA), anticrime civic organizations, business interests, and the prison-industrial complex (i.e., prison guards and private prison corporations). The NRA is a large national organization with over 3 million members. It was established in 1871 to promote marksmanship and the safe use and enjoyment of firearms. It has been a strong supporter of the Second Amendment and has actively lobbied against federal gun-control laws. The NRA funded the Institute for Legislative Action, which was involved with statewide campaigns for mandatory sentences and three-strikes you're out laws. Critics claimed that the NRA shifted its focus to anticrime legislation to divert public attention away from the link between handgun availability and gun-related violence (Wright 1998, 7).

Paul Wright studied the politics behind the passage of the State of Washington's three-strikes law. Three types of organizations supported this law: civic, business, and law enforcement. There was no mention of organized opposition (Wright 1998).

Other studies identified the role of a prison-industrial complex in promoting prison expansion and more punitive laws. This complex encompasses construction companies that build prisons, organization of prison guards whose jobs depend on prisons, and private corporations that run prisons for profit. They played a key role in promoting three-strikes legislation. For example, the California Correctional Peace Officers Association (CCPOA), a labor union of prison guards with a membership of 23,000 by 1996, made substantial contributions to the campaign to pass California's three-strikes law (Pens 1998).

> The crowning glory of the CCPOA's political action campaign is without a doubt the passage of Proposition 184, the "Three Strikes" Initiative. The CCPOA contributed $101,000 to get Prop 184 on the ballot. The CCPOA donation was clearly a key factor in getting the initiative on the ballot and on getting it passed. (Pens 1998, 137)

Total spending in support of this proposition has been estimated as high as $1.2 million (Davis 1996, 75).

Private prisons are also part of this complex. The number of private prison corporations and the level of investment in them have increased recently. "Private prison companies have also begun to push, even if discreetly, for the type of get tough policies needed to ensure their continued growth. All the major firms in the field have hired big time lobbyists" testifying before Congress in favor of tougher anticrime legislation (Silverstein 1998, 159). Ken Silverstein has also documented increased investments in private businesses by well-established corporations.

> American Express has invested millions of dollars in private prison construction in Oklahoma and General Electric has helped finance construction in Tennessee. Goldman Sachs & Co., Merrill Lynch, Smith Barney, among other Wall Street firms, have made huge sums by underwriting prison construction with the sale of tax-exempt bonds, now a thriving $2.3 billion industry. Weapons manufacturers see both public and private prisons as a new outlet for "defense" technology, such as electronic bracelets and stun guns. (1998, 162)

Because new prisons create new jobs, local communities have competed with each other to attract state money for prison construction. The prison-industrial complex, together with the NRA and other civic organizations, constitutes a major power block in the incarceration regime.

Crime Literature

The conservative social science literature provided support for more punitive criminal justice laws. There are four major strands in this literature: neoconservatism, underclass, career criminal, and victim rights studies.

The neoconservative strand maintains that crime has increased because government has been too lenient on criminals. A good example of the neoconservative view is found in Charles Murray's *Losing Ground.* Murray argued that the liberal policies of the 1960s changed social rules. They reduced the penalty for crime and contributed to a substantial increase in the crime rate. Between 1963 and 1980 the murder rate increased by 122 percent, the robbery rate by 215 percent, the burglary rate by 189 percent, the larceny rate by 159 percent, and the auto theft rate by 128 percent. To Murray, crime rates increased precisely because the new rights of the 1960s reduced the chances of going to prison and therefore reduced the cost of crime. Crime increased because it became more profitable. The logical solution is to increase penalties for crime, make the justice system more punitive, and substantially increase prison terms.

The underclass strand emphasizes the violence of the urban poor. It depicts the urban poor as pathological and dangerous, contributing to dramatic increases in random violence that threatens the middle class. Many underclass scholars defined this class to consist of the long-term welfare dependents, drug addicts, permanently unemployed, and street criminals who live in high poverty areas of inner cities. A good example of this view is found in Ken Auletta's *The Underclass.*

> Although individuals often defy categories, in general members of the underclass seem to fall into four distinct groups. First are the hostile street and career criminals who openly reject society's dominant values, a surprisingly small number of whom are responsible for the majority of crimes in most cities. The second group consists of the hustlers, those who out of choice or necessity operate in the underground economy, peddling hot goods, reefers, or hard drugs, gambling, and pimping. (1983, 43)

Auletta includes the long-term welfare dependents and drug addicts in his description of the underclass. He attributed a great deal of violent crime to the underclass. "For the average person, the most worrisome group are the violent criminals. Crime in America is now both more violent and more random" (Auletta 1983, 44).

Auletta was not alone in the way he depicted the urban underclass. William J. Wilson, a liberal sociologist, also defined the underclass as people engaged in street crime, gangs, drug dealing, and other forms of aberrant behavior (Wilson 1987). This view of the urban under-class has contributed to the public's growing fear of crime and to tougher anticrime legislation.

The career criminal strand focuses on a small group of habitual criminals allegedly re-sponsible for a substantial percentage of all crimes. In 1970 Marvin Wolfang, Robert Figlio, and Thorsten Selling examined the arrest record of all people born in Philadelphia in the year 1945. They found that about 6 percent of them committed over half of all the crime for this age group. The 6 percent group were identified as career criminals. During the 1980s studies of career criminals proliferated, supporting the enactment of mandatory sentences and three-strikes laws (Wolfang et al. 1972).

The last trend is the victim rights and retribution studies. A good example of this trend is *Victims Rights, Restitution and Retribution* (1996) by Williamson Evers of the Hoover In-stitution. Evers argued that the rehabilitation programs of the past were failures and that criminal justice policies would be more effective if they shifted from protecting the interest of the state to promoting the rights and interests of the victims. The idea of victim's rights is used to justify capital punishment.

In sum, the social science literature has promoted ideas or a dominant policy paradigm that supported more punitive criminal justice policies. Its advocates blamed increases in crime, especially violent crime, on government policies that were too lenient on criminals; defined the urban poor as a dangerous class prone to random acts of violence; created the concept of a small group of career criminals responsible for most crimes; and emphasized the need for the justice system to incorporate the feelings and needs of victims for retribution. They supported mandatory sentencing, longer prison terms, three-strikes laws, and capital punishment.

Public Officials

Political leaders have played a key role in promoting more punitive criminal justice policies. With rising levels of public anxiety over random violent crime, political leaders have found much to gain by promoting a get-tough-on-crime political agenda. Few people support crim-inals and most favor harsher anticrime policies. Political leaders—regardless of political party—have exploited the fear of crime for political gain. In the 1988 presidential election, for example, Republican candidate George H. W. Bush used television commercials to attack his Democratic opponent, Michael Dukakis. One commercial related the story of Willie Horton, a black male who was released from prison on a furlough program and, shortly afterward, raped a middle-class white woman. Although Bush pulled this commercial from the air, it had effectively exploited people's worst fears of crime and depicted Dukakis and the criminal justice system as too soft on violent criminals. Also, Bill Clinton stopped his presi-dential campaign in 1992 to go back to Arkansas to oversee an execution in his home state. Another example is George W. Bush's 1994 campaign for governor of Texas against the in-cumbent Ann Richards. Bush attacked Richards for being soft on crime and his campaign ran a commercial with actors dramatizing an abduction and murder in a parking lot. The com-mercial concluded with the announcement that Richards had released over 7,000 offenders from prison before they completed their term. "Exit polls revealed that Richards lost the elec-tion partly because of the Bush ads on crime" (Donziger 1996, 80).

The political strategy of depicting opponents as soft on crime and promoting more punitive criminal justice laws has contributed to an exaggerated public perception of crime and an almost insatiable public appetite for tougher crime laws. Quite apart from the effectiveness of promoting the tough-on-crime image, some political leaders saw anticrime policies as a religious crusade. They called for a battle against evil. In initiating his war on drugs, Ronald Reagan said, "In this crusade, let us not forget who we are. Drug abuse is a repudiation of everything America is . . . (quoted in Kappeler, Blumberg, and Potter 1996, 166). These political leaders see drugs as destroying families, taking human lives, and tearing apart communities. For them, this crusade justifies extreme measures.

The Media

The media has played a key role in creating an exaggerated image of crime. Both television and print media are culprits. Television contributes to this image through news and regular programs. Murder constitutes only 0.2 percent of all crime reported, but it occupies 25.0 percent of news reports about crime (Kappeler, Blumberg, and Potter 1996, 48). Most local six o'clock news programs feature the latest violent crime and crime coverage in the news tripled in the top three networks "from 571 stories in 1991 to 1,632 stories in 1993—despite the fact that crime declined slightly over that period" (Donziger 1996, 69). Moreover, regular television has a disproportionate number of programs that feature exaggerated violence: *NYPD, Law and Order,* and others. Reality television features night patrols with local police. Although few police calls involve violence, the program focuses almost exclusively on street crime and violence. Like television, print media often focuses on violence. Steven Donziger cited a front-page headline: "Teenage Crime Wave in S.F.—Homicide Arrests Up 87%" (Donziger 1996, 72). The article compared the number of San Francisco homicide referrals to the juvenile department with the number of attempted homicides, two different and unrelated figures. The actual increase in juvenile homicides was zero percent.

Both television and print media tend to focus attention on violent crimes and exaggerate the crime problem. Their role encourages a more punitive approach to crime and supports the new incarceration policies.

Public Debates and Opposition

All of these factors contributed to the destruction of the rights regime and the emergence of the incarceration regime: the disappearance of prisoner rights organizations, advocates for prisoners, and antipoverty organizations; the shift in the focus of civil rights groups from the rights of inmates; the rise of pro-incarceration power groups such as the NRA, prison guard unions, and conservative think tanks.

Today few people defend the rights of persons accused or convicted of crimes. Most Americans assent to the beliefs of the dominant policy paradigm—that is, they tend to believe the following:

1. The expansion of rights during the 1960s encouraged the rise of violent crime in the 1980s and 1990s.
2. The United States has a high violent crime rate because the criminal justice system is too lenient on criminals.
3. The best way to solve the crime problem is through more aggressive police policies, not through wasteful and costly rehabilitation or antipoverty programs that never worked.

4. The best way to solve the violent crime problem is through more punitive laws such as mandatory sentencing and three-strikes laws, which target violent habitual offenders.

5. The primary reason crime rates may be going down is because of the positive impact of the three-strikes laws.

Most Americans also favor capital punishment. Supporters argue for the death penalty because they accept the following beliefs:

1. The death penalty brings emotional closure to the pain and suffering of the families of murder victims.

2. It prevents murderers from ever murdering again.

3. It sends a powerful message to would-be murderers and thus acts as a deterrent.

4. It is consistent with the biblical tradition of an eye for an eye.

Despite the popularity of tough-on-crime campaigns, there has been sporadic opposition. Opponents claim that the incarceration regime is racially biased, costly, irrational, and barbaric. The Congressional Black Caucus and the Sentencing Project, a think tank that focuses on the incarceration issue, claim that the crack cocaine policy is racially biased because it imposes a mandatory five-year prison sentence on those caught with over 5 grams of crack cocaine, but only probation for those with up to 500 grams of pure cocaine. Poor blacks are more likely to use the cheap crack, whereas well-to-do whites are more likely to use the more expensive pure cocaine. Moreover, drug enforcement policy routinely targets inner-city drug users, who are more likely to be African American.

Drug enforcement policy has resulted in an extremely high incarceration rate for African-American and Hispanic males.

- Almost 1 of 3 (32.2 percent) African-American men in the age group 20–29 is either in prison, in jail, on probation, or on parole on any given day.
- More than 1 of every 10 Hispanic men (12.3 percent) in the same age group is either in prison, in jail, on probation, or on parole on any given day.
- African Americans and Hispanics constitute almost 90 percent of offenders sentenced to state prison for drug possession. (Irwin and Austin 1997, 4)

Critics have pointed out not only that the United States has the highest incarceration rates in the world, but also that these rates are a drain on state budgets. A number of state teachers unions have made this claim. The Justice Policy Institute claimed that the three-strikes laws have added more than $8 billion to California's prison expenditures from March 1994 to September 2003. Moreover, violent crime rates have declined more substantially in states without the three-strikes policy (Ehlers, Schiraldi, and Ziedenberg 2004). Furthermore, the incarceration rate for third strikes among African Americans (143 per 100,000 African-American residents) is 12 times higher than the rate for whites (12 per 100,000 white residents). Social scientist Elloit Currie argued that contrary to the popular press, properly administered rehabilitation programs are more effective in reducing crime than locking people up (Currie 1985).

The strongest opposition to the incarceration regime has come from several groups opposed to the death penalty. In Illinois, a conservative Republican governor, who formerly favored capital punishment, suspended the death penalty after the *Chicago Tribune* published a series of articles in the late 1990s on the problems connected to this form of punishment and the many ways innocent people ended up on death row: overzealous police officers, overly ambitious prosecutors, perjured witnesses, erroneous testimony, mistaken identity, errors in judgment, incompetent defense attorneys, unscrupulous jailhouse informants, inadequate resources for defense investigations, racial prejudices, and many others.

A number of other groups have joined the movement against capital punishment, including the Catholic Bishops, the American Bar Association, the ACLU, and Amnesty International. Other human rights groups also have joined the movement. They pointed out that the United States is the only industrialized country, with the exception of Russia, to have the death penalty. All countries that abolished capital punishment have lower homicide rates. Russia has a substantially higher homicide rate. Opponents of the death penalty also claim that it has no deterrent effect and may contribute to a rise in murder rates, as the act of the state executing people diminishes respect for human life.

Summary

Four major criminal justice policy regimes have been identified, characterized by distinct sets of policies. The colonial regime (1610–1790) was characterized by public and physical punishment. Public floggings and hangings were common. The American Revolution destroyed this regime and ushered in the preindustrial regime during which public punishment and most forms of physical punishment disappeared. The big policy change came with the ratification of the Bill of Rights in 1791. The preindustrial regime (1791–1870) was characterized by the use of prisons and by the ideal that the length of prison sentences should be proportional to the severity of the crime. The social movements of the late 19th and early 20th century produced a new regime, the industrial regime (1870–1960). Prisons continued as before; however, in the South the criminal justice regime was marred by segregation, racial bias, and a harsh convict lease system. The positive features included indeterminate sentences, paroles, and an increase in professionalism.

The civil rights movement produced the criminal justice policy changes of the 1960s and contributed to the formation of the short-lived rights regime (1960–1994). Prisons continued, but new policies underscored the rights of the accused and those imprisoned. Rights began to be eroded by policy changes in the 1980s. The emergence of new anticrime organizations, the shifting of old but powerful organizations to the criminal justice policy area, the popularity of the new anticrime politics, and a new anticrime literature destroyed the rights regime. Moreover, prisoner rights organizations had disappeared and civil rights organizations lost interest in the civil rights of criminals. What emerged next was the incarceration regime, which was characterized by extremely high incarceration rates and exceptionally punitive laws, including the death penalty. Today, the United States has the highest incarceration rate among the world's industrialized countries.

Review Questions

1. What is crime?
2. How has the definition of crime changed from time to time?
3. What were some of the differences in criminal punishment between the colonial, the industrial, and the rights regimes?

4. What is a moral panic and how does this panic affect criminal justice policy?
5. Discuss the similarities and differences between the industrial and the incarceration policy regimes.
6. Why are incarceration rates so high in the United States?

Select Websites

The FBI Website provides up-to-date crime statistics.
http://www.fbi.org

This is the Website of the U.S. Department of Justice.
http://www.usdoj.gov

Key Terms

Cesare Beccaria
convict lease system
exclusionary rule
felonies
good faith
hot pursuit
incarceration regime
indeterminate sentences
inevitable discovery

mandatory sentencing
misdemeanors
moral panic
plain view
public safety exception
Scottsboro case
three strikes you're out law
truth in sentencing
war on drugs

PART V

Distributive Policy

CHAPTER 13

Education Policy

Public education is generally considered a distributive policy. It benefits the entire community. It is a public good, a necessity for the survival of individuals and communities in a technologically advanced society, an instrument for social advancement, and a precondition for a democratic society. It rarely involves conflict and generally enjoys broad political support. Occasionally, educational policy issues have had redistributive characteristics, such as desegregation of public schools, Head Start, school vouchers, and others.

Four education policy regimes can be identified: the preindustrial, industrial, rights, and choice. In the preindustrial education regime there were no grades, few students attended beyond one or two years, and schools emphasized the classics. It lasted from colonial times to the end of the 19th century. The industrial education regime emphasized mass education, vocational education, and hierarchical education—ranking students from the first to the last and tracking students in high-performing, middle-performing, and low-performing tracks. This regime lasted to the end of the 1960s. Desegregation and compensatory education programs characterized the rights education regime, which lasted up to the mid-1990s. The choice or contemporary education regime in operation today emphasizes charter schools and choice in education.

✦ *The Preindustrial Educational Policy Regime, 1700–1900*

The preindustrial educational policy regime had several distinguishing characteristics. First, most public schools were authorized by the state government and received some state support. Local governments and individual families were expected to make up the differences. In the early years, parents paid tuition. Free schools did not emerge until the early 19th century.

Second, in the North, public schools were universally supported and had broad-based support. The Boston public school system provides a good illustration of this point. A free public school system was established by a petition drive presented to the Boston Town Meeting in 1817. The Boston residents who signed the petition represented all classes. An analysis of their background determined that about one-fifth were from the working class, with the remainder from the middle and upper classes (Bowles and Gintis 1977). There was little opposition over the establishment of public schools in Boston, but there was a dispute over whether the schools should be racially integrated or segregated. Initially, the schools were segregated but in 1855 Massachusetts inaugurated school integration, the first state in the country to do so (Kousser 2000, 35).

Third, attendance in the preindustrial school was noncompulsory. Before the Civil War, most school-aged children went to school for a few years and dropped out. Until 1890 less than 4 percent of children aged 14 to 17 attended high school (Bowles and Gintis 1977, 181). **Compulsory attendance** laws did not appear in Massachusetts until 1852. By the mid-1880s about 16 states had laws that required elementary aged children to attend school, although these laws were rarely enforced. Up to the 1930s, it was not uncommon for children to drop out of grade school and go to work.

Fourth, the curriculum of the preindustrial school emphasized the basics at the lower level and the classics at the upper level, although school quality varied widely from region to region. Sometimes rural schools remained in session for only a few months during the winter, as school-aged children worked on farms the other three seasons—spring, summer, and fall. It was not uncommon for urban schools to remain in session all year, with a two- or three-week break between seasons.

The type of grade system that exists in public schools today did not exist at the beginning of the 19th century. Few schools arranged students into grades like first, second, and third. This developed slowly throughout the century. Also, there were no high schools or kindergartens. The first high school, Boston English Classical School, was established in 1821. Kindergartens were not established until the 1870s (Spring 2005).

Finally, there was a strong tradition of local control over public schools. State governments authorized the establishment of public schools and provided some financial support. However, local educational leaders developed and carried out policies in the local schools. They hired the teachers, instituted the curriculum, and managed the schools. There was strong opposition to a centralizing state role and little state oversight.

⇒ The Industrial Educational Policy Regime, 1900–1970

Public schools changed dramatically at the turn of the century. With the Industrial Revolution and the Progressive movement, the preindustrial educational policy regime gave way to the industrial educational policy regime. The number of schools increased and enrollment skyrocketed in both elementary and high schools. For example, between 1890 and 1930, "the percentage of all fourteen to sixteen year olds attending public high schools rose from 4 percent to 47 percent" (Bowles and Gintis 1977, 181).

Political Pressures for School Expansion and Reorganization

There was almost universal support for the expansion of public schools, although different groups supported this expansion for different reasons. Middle-class and working-class parents supported it because they believed education opened avenues to social and economic advancement. Industrialists supported it, believing that education added value to the workforce. Many conservatives saw the public school as a stabilizing institution that would reduce labor unrest and violent strikes and teach immigrants American values. Many Social Progressives supported the expansion of public schools because they believed schooling raised the level of civil culture, made democracy possible, and equalized opportunities for social and economic advancement. The Social Progressive writer Robert Green Ingersoll expressed this view eloquently in a short article published in 1890.

> I BELIEVE that education is the only level capable of raising mankind. If we wish to make the future of the Republic glorious we must educate the children of the present. The greatest blessing conferred by our Government is the free school. In importance it rises above everything else that the Government does. . . . We need far more schoolhouses than we have. . . . It is far cheaper to build schoolhouses than prisons, and it is much better to have scholars than convicts.

Progressives believed that an investment in the education of children was an investment in the future and a better world.

Few groups opposed the expansion of public education. Nevertheless, two contentious issues emerged: vocational education and testing.

Vocational Education

Vocational education was one of the more controversial educational issues of the industrial educational regime. A number of powerful groups, most notably corporate interests, advocated **vocational education,** the teaching of skilled trades such as auto mechanics, electrical repair, plumbing, metalworking, woodworking, carpentry, cooking, and so forth. Bowles and Gintis summarized the political struggle for vocational education:

> Building on the quite distinct manual training movement of the 1880s, the vocational education movement during the 1890s gathered the political support of major educators and the financial backing of a number of leading capitalists—J. P. Morgan and John D. Rockefeller among them. With the founding of the National Association of Manufacturers in 1896, the movement gained what would become its most important advocates and acquired a strong antiunion orientation. From the late 1890s until World War I virtually every national N.A.M. conference passed resolutions advocating vocational education. (1977, 192)

The National Association of Manufacturers (NAM) played a major role in promoting vocational education. This organization published a series of reports on vocational education beginning in 1905. The 1912 report insisted that the failure to develop vocational programs led to a waste in human capital and put U.S. industrial firms at a competitive disadvantage compared to firms in other industrialized countries. The report concluded that vocational education was a national issue (Spring 2005).

Congress responded by creating its own Committee on National Aid to Vocational Education. The committee report provided many reasons why vocational education was a national issue. It would:

- Improve the competitiveness of U.S. firms.
- Reduce labor unrest.
- Respond to diverse educational needs.
- Give students who would ordinarily drop out of high school a reason to continue in school.
- Provide equal opportunities for all students.

In 1917 Congress enacted the *Smith-Hughes Act,* which set aside federal money for vocational education in local schools.

A few Progressive scholars joined industrial leaders in advocating vocational education, but for different reasons. They argued that educational programs should be flexible and tailored to the needs of students. They favored a diverse educational curriculum for a diverse public school population. They argued for the creation of several tracks such as college preparation, vocational skills, business education, and home economics.

Opposition to vocational education came from two primary sources: skilled trade unions and professional teacher organizations. Labor leaders in the skilled trade unions controlled the process of training new skilled workers. These leaders worried that the creation of vocational education in the public schools would take this control from the unions. They feared that as the number of skilled workers increased, wages would decline.

Professional educational associations opposed vocational education on philosophical grounds. They believed that it would diminish the quality of education. One major professional organization was the **National Education Association (NEA),** which saw vocational education replacing the classics and traditional college preparatory programs.

State and National Educational Policies

Although support for local control of schools remained strong throughout this period (1900–1970), the state role had increased. State governments developed state superintendent offices and created state boards of education. They provided standards for accrediting schools, teacher certification, and high school graduation. This role was important in improving the quality of public schools.

The federal government played a miniscule role in local public schools during this era. As noted earlier, the Smith-Hughes Act of 1917 set aside federal money for local public schools to create vocational educational programs. The federal government did play a role in higher educational policies. Through the *Morrill Land Grant Act of 1862*, it provided land to states for the construction of colleges. Nearly a century later, prompted by the Soviet Union sending up a satellite (*Sputnik*) to orbit the earth, the federal government became involved again. Congress passed the *National Defense Education Act of 1958*, which allocated $1 billion to support education and research in the sciences at public universities.

Although the industrial education regime was successful in terms of raising high school graduation rates and increasing college enrollment, racial segregation and gender biases remained problems. The rights policy regime addressed these areas.

Public school student reading.

→ *The Rights Educational Policy Regime, 1970–1995*

The rights educational policy regime has focused on desegregation and compensatory education. The desegregation of public schools was a main goal of the civil rights movement and compensatory educational programs emerged out of the war on poverty during the 1960s. By the mid-1990s, efforts to continue to desegregate public schools came to an end. Compensatory education programs continued and were expanded throughout the 1990s and into the 21st century.

Desegregation

Most public schools had been racially segregated up to the 1970s. Southern states had laws that prohibited blacks from going to white schools. In the *Plessy v. Ferguson* (1896) decision the Supreme Court gave constitutional legitimacy to racially segregated schools based on the separate but equal doctrine. This doctrine held that so long as racially segregated public schools were equal, segregation did not violate the Constitution. This doctrine remained in effect until the *Brown v. Board of Education* decision of 1954. In this case the Court decided that racially segregated schools harmed black children by destroying their self-image and self-esteem, based on the premise that black children were inferior and undesirable. The reaction to *Brown* was violent; many southern political leaders refused to comply. Ten years later, there still was little compliance in the South. The Court began to take more aggressive measures in the early 1970s.

The Supreme Court began ordering busing to integrate school districts in 1971 (*Swan v. Charlotte-Mecklenburg*). The Court initially targeted southern school districts for busing because of their past record of deliberately segregating schools. A few years later the court began to target northern school districts (*Keyes v. Denver School District Number One* 1973). Large cities like Boston, Cleveland, and Detroit were required to bus students to integrate the schools (see Chapter 7). Both white and black parents opposed busing because they supported neighborhood schools and resented the transporting of their children across the city.

By the mid-1990s the desegregation movement had ended. The Supreme Court had succeeded in ending deliberate racial segregation and in integrating many southern schools. However, it had not been as successful in desegregating northern school districts. Cities like Detroit are more segregated today than in 1954. A large number of white families left Detroit just after the riot of 1967, an exodus that continued through the 1970s and 1980s. There are too few white students in Detroit to make integration meaningful.

Compensatory Education

Compensatory educational programs were a distinguishing feature of the rights educational policy regime. **Compensatory education** was based on the presumption that children—regardless of socioeconomic, racial, or ethnic background—have the potential to succeed academically; that children from low-income families were disadvantaged because of fewer educational resources in their homes compared to middle-class families; and that additional educational resources can compensate for these disadvantages. Two compensatory educational programs arose in the 1960s: Head Start and the Elementary and Secondary Education Act (ESEA). They both emerged as part of President Lyndon Johnson's War on Poverty. They were expected to reduce poverty by providing equal opportunities for the poor and disadvantaged.

Head Start
Head Start targets preschool children from low-income families. Its goals are to enhance the nutritional, social, and educational experiences of low-income preschool children. Also, it encourages parent participation.

Head Start was controversial because initial evaluations were negative, indicating that the program was ineffective. A study conducted by the Westinghouse research group concluded that Head Start was only marginally effective with participants compared to nonparticipants and that the test scores of participants were well below the national norm. The negative studies were used by the Nixon and Ford administrations to reduce funding for the program. Later studies, however, were more positive, showing "that Head Start is very successful in cutting down the rate of school failure, in improving IQ scores and reading achievement, and in helping children gain self-confidence" (Rodgers 1979, 235). Other studies indicated that Head Start participants were more likely to stay in school and graduate than comparable nonparticipants. These positive studies contributed to increased spending for Head Start under the Clinton administration and continuing in the Bush administration (Fischer 1995).

The Elementary and Secondary Education Act (ESEA)

The Elementary and Secondary Education Act (ESEA) was established in 1965. **Title I,** the major program, set aside $1 billion to enhance the educational experience of grade school children from low-income families. Initially, like Head Start, the program was a complete failure. It had little impact on the test scores of low-income participants, which remained well below the national norm. In 1969 the NAACP Legal Defense Fund published an evaluation report indicating that Title I money had been misappropriated. Local education agencies took the money, mixed it with their local budget, and did nothing to provide educational programs for low-income, low-achieving students.

Congress responded to the report by amending the law to require the creation of supplemental academic programs, specifically in reading and math. Local education agencies hired Title I specialists and aides, and created math and reading laboratories where low-achieving students from low-income families were removed from nonacademic classes and placed. Subsequent studies indicated that when properly administered, these programs were modestly successful in raising the math and reading achievement scores of the Title I participants.

Major changes occurred in the Title I program under the Reagan administration in the 1980s. First, funding for the program was cut significantly. Second, state governments acquired more control over the program as ESEA money that once flowed directly from Washington, D.C., to local educational agencies was redirected through state governments.

The Title I program changed twice under the Clinton administration, first with the *Reauthorization Act of 1994,* which allowed a select few schools to experiment with schoolwide programs. That is, rather than targeting low-income, low-achieving students, school administrators worked with parents and teachers to develop programs for the entire school. These programs included math and science enrichment courses, after-school tutorial programs, and special test preparation classes.

The Clinton administration expanded the Title I program again with the passage of the *Education Excellence for All Children Act of 1999,* which increased spending for Title I to more than $8 billion, allowed for greater expansion of schoolwide programs, and encouraged the use of "research-based strategies for reforming the entire school." It required all schools to establish goals based on a specific percentage increase in test scores.

No Child Left Behind

The George W. Bush administration built upon the educational policy initiatives of the Clinton administration. Congress passed President Bush's *No Child Left Behind Bill of 2002,* reauthorizing ESEA and increasing its funding. The **No Child Left Behind** program emphasized accountability, flexibility, and choice. The accountability provision mandated states to establish performance standards and to test all children in grades 3 through 8 in the subjects of math and reading. It required states to make available to parents and the public annual report cards indicating whether the school was doing a good, fair, or failing job of educating the children.

Public school teacher reading to students in the school library and holding their interest.

Another aspect of the accountability provision targeted low-performing schools that had not exhibited progress. These schools were to be identified for school improvement and given technical assistance to develop a two-year improvement plan. Schools that failed to show progress in subsequent years would eventually lose federal money and be forced to shut down. The flexibility provision gave states and local school districts greater discretion over ESEA programs. It consolidated several ESEA programs and allowed school districts to transfer up to 50 percent of the funds from one program or title to another. The choice provision allowed parents with children in failing schools to immediately transfer them to better-performing schools.

The No Child Left Behind program is unprecedented with regard to the level of federal involvement in public education. Historically, the federal government deferred to the states and respected local control of schools. Mandating the testing of every student in every public school in grades 3 to 8, targeting schools for closure, and changing transfer policies to allow parents greater choice collectively constituted an unprecedented level of federal involvement.

Critics of the No Child Left Behind program contended that it was unworkable. They claimed that it provided no money for the expanded testing and not enough money to finance necessary school improvement programs. They insisted that there were too few better-performing central city schools to accommodate students from the many failing schools.

Special Education
The federal government became involved with special education programs with the passage of **Title VI** of the 1965 ESEA Act. This program allocated funds to local school districts to

assist them in providing special educational program. In 1975 Congress passed the *Education for All Handicapped Children Act (EAHCA)*. This law gave federal protection to children with disabilities and protected their rights to an education. In 1997 Congress amended EAHCA and changed its title to the *Individuals with Disabilities Education Act (IDEA)*. This amendment required school districts to educate children with disabilities "to the maximum extent appropriate."

A Nation At Risk

Many new policy initiatives at the turn of the century arose from a report on education, *A Nation At Risk*, published in 1983. Under the Reagan administration, the Secretary of Education established the National Commission on Excellence in Education to investigate the quality of education in the United States. Some of the highlights of the report follow:

- Some 23 million American adults are functionally illiterate by the simplest tests of everyday reading, writing, and comprehension.
- About 13 percent of all 17-year-olds in the United States are functionally illiterate. Functional illiteracy among minority youth may run as high as 40 percent.
- Average achievement of high school students on most standardized tests is now lower than 26 years ago when *Sputnik* was launched.
- The College Board's Scholastic Aptitude Tests (SATs) demonstrate a virtually unbroken decline from 1963 to 1980. Average verbal scores fell over 50 points and average mathematics scores dropped nearly 40 points.
- College Board achievement tests also reveal consistent declines in subjects such as physics and English.
- A steady decline in science achievement scores of 17-year-olds was measured by national assessments of science in 1969, 1973, and 1977.
- Between 1975 and 1980, remedial mathematics courses in public four-year colleges increased by 72 percent and now constitute one-quarter of all mathematics courses taught in those institutions. (National Commission on Excellence in Education 1983, 7–8)

Overall, the study lamented the decline of the quality of education in the United States. The report concluded that the U.S. educational system is now mediocre, inferior to the systems of its major rivals. The survival of technologically advanced societies depends on the quality of their educational systems. The report made several recommendations including more standardized testing to monitor student progress, more math and science in high school curricula, and more parental involvement.

❖ The Choice Educational Policy Regime

A Nation At Risk prompted other studies that attempted to explain why schools are failing and what should be done about them. Terry Moe and John Chub (1990) argued in *Politics, Markets and America's Schools* that the major problem with public schools is the central city school bureaucracy, which operates as a monopoly. In competitive markets, firms are compelled by competition to provide higher-quality products at cheaper prices than their competitors or they will lose customers and go out of business. With a monopoly, there is only one firm and no competition, and there are no incentives for the monopoly to innovate, improve the quality of services, or reduce costs. Its customers have no choice. Moe and Chub insisted that public schools, especially in central cities, continuously provide poor-quality education at high costs precisely because they operate as monopolies, with captured customers. Unlike some middle-class parents who can afford to move or send their children to high-quality private schools, low-income, central city parents have no choice but to continue to send their children to the same poor-quality public schools. They can neither afford to move nor afford private schools. The solution to the problem of the public school monopoly is to introduce competitive market conditions into the system. This means giving parents **school choice**—alternatives to public schools and opening up the monopoly public school to competition with alternative schools (Moe and Chub 1990).

Proponents of school choice compared public schools with private schools and found that private schools outperformed public schools. The main reason for the higher performance of private schools is that they operate under competitive market conditions while public schools do not.

The idea of school choice did not originate with Moe and Chub. As early as 1962 in *Capitalism and Freedom,* economist Milton Friedman advocated vouchers as a solution to segregated schools. In 1981 he advocated vouchers as a solution to poor-quality central city schools (Friedman and Friedman 1981).

There are several policy options designed to introduce competitive market conditions into central city public schools: magnet schools, districtwide and areawide choice, vouchers, and charter schools.

Magnet Schools, Districtwide Choice, and Areawide Choice

Magnet schools, districtwide choice, and areawide choice are the least controversial of the choice options. **Magnet schools** are the most popular and have been around the longest. Most magnet schools are located in large central city school districts and have the dual goal of providing a high-quality academic program and an integrated school. They attract students, like a magnet, from all parts of the school district. Some magnet schools emerged in the 1970s as experimental schools, testing new teaching methods, such as open classrooms or ungraded schools (that is, students must master skills such as multiplying or converting fractions to decimals, but are not graded on an A–F scale). Burton International in Detroit is an elementary school specializing in foreign languages. It is open to students from across the city. Cass Technical is a Detroit high school with a curriculum specializing in science and technology.

Schoolwide choice involves a school district eliminating attendance boundaries and allowing parents to send their children to the school of their choice. Most students go to neighborhood schools; however, a number of school districts in large cities have established waiver policies that allow parents to transfer their children from a neighborhood school to another school in a different area of the city. Many school districts adopted this policy to encourage school integration. This option has stirred little opposition because it involved few transfers. A few pilot schoolwide choice programs have recently been established in Florida.

Areawide choice allows parents within the central city to send their children to schools within a suburban district of their choice. In 1996 Ohio passed special legislation allowing parents of elementary schoolchildren, in the city of Cleveland only, to send their children to an adjacent suburban school district of their choice. For unknown reasons, very few parents have used this option.

Vouchers

Vouchers are the most controversial of the choice options. A voucher is like a certificate or check, with a specific dollar value, that can be used to purchase a product or service and that can be exchanged for money. Food stamps are vouchers that can be used to purchase food; grocers who receive food stamps can exchange them for their cash value. School vouchers can be used to cover all or part of the costs of tuition for a private or parochial school. The school can exchange the voucher for money.

Vouchers create competitive markets directly by giving low-income central city parents the option of taking their children out of public schools and placing them in private or parochial schools. The possibility of public schools losing large numbers of students and the state money attached to them creates marketlike conditions, as public schools compete with private schools. Supporters argue that this possibility creates a powerful incentive for public schools to improve. The case of the Cleveland school district illustrates the voucher issue.

In 1995 a federal district court declared that the entire Cleveland Public School District was suffering a "crisis of magnitude" and placed the entire school district under state control. Shortly afterward, the Ohio Auditor's Office declared that the Cleveland school district was experiencing a "crisis that is perhaps unprecedented in the history of American education" (quoted in *Zelman v. Simmons-Harris* 2002). The school district had failed to meet any of the state of Ohio Department of Education's 18 minimal performance standards. Only 10 percent of the district's ninth graders passed the state's ninth-grade proficiency test. Student performance on other proficiency tests was equally dismal and well below that of most other districts in Ohio. The *Zelman* case added the following description of the Cleveland school district:

> More than two-thirds of high school students either dropped or failed out before graduation. Of those students who managed to reach their senior year, one of every four still failed to graduate. Of those students who did graduate, few could read, write or compute at levels comparable to their counterparts in other cities. (*Zelman v. Simmons-Harris* 2002)

In response to the crisis of Cleveland's public schools, the state of Ohio created a special voucher program exclusively for Cleveland called the Pilot Project Scholarship Program. It provided financial assistance to select families living within the Cleveland school district, with priority given to low-income families—the lower the income, the higher the priority. It paid up to $2,250 for the cost of tuition. The families that received this voucher or tuition scholarship could choose to send their children to any private or parochial school within Cleveland. The voucher was available not only for parochial schools, but for adjacent public schools as well. Nevertheless, 96 percent of the vouchers went to religious schools, most of which were Catholic.

A group of parents sued the Ohio Department of Education on grounds that the voucher system funneled public money—Ohio taxpayer dollars—to religious institutions. They argued that the voucher program violated the First Amendment which has been interpreted to mean that the government cannot finance religious institutions or religious education. Most of the schools receiving vouchers required that students take classes in religion.

In a hotly divided *Zelman v. Simmons-Harris* decision rendered in the summer of 2002, the majority of Supreme Court justices ruled that the vouchers did not violate the Constitution and the separation of church and state. Writing for the majority, Chief Justice William H. Rehnquist set forth several arguments why they did not.

1. In the past the Court had allowed federal money to go to religious schools to purchase books, to finance math and reading programs, to assist with transportation costs, and to teach sign language to deaf children.
2. The money did not go directly to the religious schools; it went to the parents. It gave parents a wide range of choices: adjacent public schools, private nonreligious schools, and parochial schools. Parents made the choice to use the money to send their children to religious schools, not the government.
3. The program was part of a larger state effort to respond to the Cleveland public school crisis.

Justices Breyer, Ginsburg, Souter, and Stevens dissented. Although they agreed with Rehnquist that in the past the Court had allowed federal money to go to parochial schools for nonreligious instructions, the Court had never allowed money to finance religious instruction under any circumstances. They maintained that using public money to finance religious education, whether directly or indirectly, violated the Constitution. They rejected the argument that an exception should be made because the program was a response to a crisis and the money did not go directly to the religious schools. Justice John P. Stevens added the following:

> The fact that the vast majority of the voucher recipients who have entirely rejected public education receive religious indoctrination at state expense does, however, support the claim that the law is one "respecting an establishment of religion." The State may choose to divide up its public schools into a dozen different options and label them magnet schools, community schools, or whatever else it decides to call them, but the State is still required to provide a public education and it is the State's decision to fund private school education over and above its traditional obligation that is at issue in these cases. . . . (*Zelman v. Simmons-Harris* 2002)

Cleveland, Ohio, is not the only district with vouchers. Vouchers have been established in other cities and states including Milwaukee, Wisconsin; Vermont; and New York City.

Charter Schools

Another controversial choice option is the charter school. **Charter schools** are community schools sponsored by state, local, or county boards of education or state universities which give the community group, private nonprofit group, or private for-profit organization a contract, or charter, to provide the school. Charter schools have their own independent governing boards. They hire their own teachers and staff, and develop their own curriculum. They are generally chartered because they offer something innovative, something unique, or something not done by an established public school. For example, some charter schools offer year-round instruction, some specialize in the performing arts, some target juvenile delinquents, and some specialize in business education, vocational education, or math and science.

Charter schools are much more pervasive than school vouchers. These schools emerged out of statewide political movements that have swept across the country. Today, 39 states have passed charter school legislation and established charter schools in several central cities. (See Table 13.1.)

The Voucher and Charter School Wars

Political wars are being fought over vouchers and charter schools. Powerful political coalitions have lined up on both sides of the issues, and arguments have been intense. Vouchers are the more controversial, have drawn the most fire, and have gained the least ground. The fighting over charter schools has abated; today most states have them and they enjoy bipartisan support.

Voucher Supporters

Political support for school vouchers comes from two sources: religious organizations and conservative think tanks. Organizations such as the Christian Coalition and the Traditional Values Coalition have campaigned for vouchers at both the national and state levels. Conservative think tanks such as the Cato Institute, the Heritage Foundation, and the Hoover Institution have sponsored studies supporting vouchers. A few business leaders supported vouchers, but as part of their general support for school choice. Republican Party leaders have supported vouchers, although with less enthusiasm than they have supported charter schools.

TABLE 13.1

Dates of State Charter School Legislation

State	Date	State	Date	State	Date
Alabama	NC	Louisiana	1995	Ohio	1997
Alaska	1995	Maine	NC	Oklahoma	1999
Arkansas	1995	Maryland	2003	Oregon	1999
Arizona	1994	Massachusetts	1993	Pennsylvania	1997
California	1992	Michigan	1993	Rhode Island	1995
Colorado	1993	Minnesota	1991	South Carolina	1996
Connecticut	1996	Mississipp	1997	South Dakota	NC
Delaware	1995	Missouri	1998	Tennessee	2002
Florida	1996	Montana	NC	Texas	1995
Georgia	1993	Nebraska	NC	Utah	1998
Hawaii	1994	Nevada	1997	Vermont	NC
Idaho	1998	New Hampshire	1995	Virginia	1998
Indiana	2001	New Jersey	1996	West Virginia	NC
Illinois	1996	New Mexico	1993	Washington	2004
Iowa	2002	New York	1998	Wisconsin	1993
Kansas	1994	North Carolina	1996	Wyoming	1995
Kentucky	NC	North Dakota	NC		

NC = no change.

SOURCE: U.S. Charter Schools Website, http://www.uscharterschools.org/, 2005.

Supporters of vouchers use several arguments to promote this program. This choice option gives low-income parents a viable alternative to the failed public school monopolies; parochial schools provide a more successful, higher-quality educational product for a cheaper cost than public schools; and the competition between private and public schools would constrain public schools to improve the quality of their instruction and to be more sensitive to the needs and interests of parents.

Charter School Supporters

Charter schools enjoy stronger political support than vouchers. The same religious organizations and conservative think tanks that support vouchers also support charter schools. Charter schools also have support from powerful business organizations like the Chamber of Commerce. For example, the Ohio Chamber of Commerce set forth the following position on the school choice issue:

> The debate over reforming public education continues to rage in our state. Many believe reform begins with a substantial infusion of state money. They include the teachers' unions and school superintendents who challenge the way Ohio funds schools and presumably, a majority on the Ohio Supreme Court.
>
> On the other hand, the Ohio Chamber believes the debate is about accountability and results, not dollars. Our message . . . has been clear: Systemic reform and direct competition to the status quo are critical to ensuring higher quality and innovation in public education. That's why we continue to support unique ideas like charter or community schools and periodic assessments of academic progress. (Education and School Finance 2002)

Supporters of charter schools believe that this choice option should be supported for four reasons. First, charter schools provide powerful market incentives for public schools to innovate and produce a higher-quality product. The threat of losing students and money is calculated to shake up the public school monopoly. Charter school supporters claim that those public schools that have lost students to charter schools are already changing: They are borrowing ideas from charter schools and doing more to boost test scores, and they are exhibiting a much higher level of interest in and sensitivity to parents.

Second, supporters argue that charter schools by definition offer innovative programs. Many state governments require charter schools to offer something new before they obtain a contract.

Third, supporters maintain that the emergence of charter schools empowers parents. When parents have the choice of pulling their children out of a school, they can command greater respect and attention from public school administrators.

Finally, academic supporters of charter schools see this option as a way to solve the problems of central city schools without having to throw excessive amounts of money at the problem. Charter schools constrain public schools to provide a higher-quality product at lower costs.

School Choice and Money Matters

Proponents of both vouchers and charter schools insist that money is not the problem. They have argued that public schools have not improved even when they get more money. Paul Ciotti of the Cato Institute made this point in his study of a magnet school in Kansas City, Missouri:

Kansas City spent as much as $11,700 per pupil—more money per pupil, on a cost of living adjusted basis, than any other of the 280 largest districts in the country. The money bought higher teachers' salaries, 15 new schools, and such amenities as an Olympic-size swimming pool with an underwater viewing room, television and animation studios, a robotics lab, a 25-acre wildlife sanctuary, a zoo, a model United Nations with simultaneous translation capability, and field trips to Mexico and Senegal. The student-teacher ratio was 12–13 to 1, the lowest of any major school district in the country.

The results were dismal. Test scores did not rise; the black-white gap did not diminish; and there was less, not greater, integration. (1998, 1)

Rather than giving more money to a bad system, proponents of vouchers and charter schools argue for overhauling the system by opening up public schools to competition with charter schools and private schools through vouchers.

Opposition to Vouchers

The strongest opposition to school choice proposals is against school vouchers. Traditional supporters of public schools oppose vouchers. These opponents include public school super-intendents, teachers unions, public school boards, most Democrats, and a number of organizations including the American Civil Liberties Union (ACLU), the National Education Association (NEA), and the National Association for the Advancement of Colored People (NAACP). For example, the ACLU and the NAACP challenged vouchers in Milwaukee, where, they believed, religious schools had discriminated in the selection of students on the basis of religious affiliation.

Opponents have five major arguments against vouchers:

1. They do not produce the academic benefits supporters claim.
2. They use public funds to support religious institutions and religious education.
3. They depress teachers' salaries.
4. They skim the best students from public schools, leaving public schools with a higher concentration of troubled students.
5. They divert attention from the problem of inadequately funded schools in poor districts.

Opponents point to studies demonstrating that voucher users exhibit few gains in academic performance after they leave public schools and attend private schools. For example, Alex Molnar (2000) of the University of Wisconsin–Milwaukee found that reducing the size of public school classes is more effective in improving the academic performance of low-income students than giving them vouchers and sending them to parochial schools. Cecilia Rouse (1998) of Princeton University found that Milwaukee's experimental student achievement program was more successful than private schools in raising low-income student test scores.

Despite the *Zelman* decision, opponents see vouchers as state governments using tax-payer money to support religious institutions. They agree with Justice Stevens' dissent that the parents' choice to send their children to a religious school is irrelevant to use of public money to support that school. They argue further that support of parochial schools has the potential for all sorts of mischief: religious schools discriminating against students of another faith and greater government regulation of religious schools.

Opponents argue that vouchers have the potential to depress teacher salaries. They base this argument on the assumption that teacher salaries are low in central city school districts and even lower in central city parochial schools. As public schools lose students and money, they will also lose the ability to increase teacher salaries. Moreover, vouchers that average less than $2,500 will be insufficient for parochial schools to increase teacher salaries.

Opponents insist that vouchers will skim the better students off public schools and leave central city schools with a higher concentration of troubled students. They argue that the skimming will occur in two ways. First, parochial schools are free to expel troubled students, whereas public schools are constrained by law to accept them. This process alone will leave problem children concentrated in central city schools. Second, the voucher grant itself discriminates in favor of the better-off central city families and against the more impoverished families. For example, if tuition costs $5,000 a year and the voucher is only $2,500, a family will have to come up with $2,500 to cover the difference.

Opponents claim that vouchers divert attention from the problem of inadequate funding of central city schools and shift funds from financially strained central cities to the private schools. This same argument is applied to charter schools.

Vouchers have come under much heavier attack and have taken more casualties than charter schools. For example, Florida recently passed a statewide voucher program, but the state supreme court found it in violation of the state constitution. When he campaigned for president in 2000, President George W. Bush advocated the establishment of a pilot federal voucher program that would provide a $1,500 grant for qualifying families. In the wake of strong opposition, he dropped the proposal and did not mention it in the 2004 presidential election.

Opposition to Charter Schools

Charter schools have less opposition than school vouchers and have gained more ground, as 39 states now have them. There is little opposition from civil rights groups and both George W. Bush and John Kerry supported them in the 2004 presidential race. State governments have reduced opposition to charter schools from central city public school boards by allowing boards to sponsor charter schools and by giving boards extra money to monitor and supervise them.

The strongest opposition has come from teachers unions. The NEA has opposed unregulated charter schools; that is, charter schools not subjected to the same state assessment criteria, auditing, and teacher certification requirements as public schools. They have opposed charter schools run by for-profit organizations and laws that prohibit teachers unions from organizing in charter schools. Aside from these objections, the NEA supports charter schools.

Although the **American Federation of Teachers (AFT)** is opposed to charter schools, it supported the original idea. The AFT has complained that instead of parents and teachers, the for-profit organizations and management companies are running charter schools. The AFT has established six criteria for an acceptable charter school:

1. Charter schools must be based on high academic standards.
2. Students in charter schools should take the same tests as other students in the state and district.
3. Charter schools should hire certified teachers.
4. Charter school employees should be covered by the collective bargaining agreement.
5. Charter schools should have the approval of local districts.

6. Charter schools should be required to make information available to the public.

The AFT claimed that no state meets all of these criteria for acceptable charter schools. In some states the AFT and state teachers unions have joined with other groups to challenge the legality of charter schools on state constitutional grounds. Since the U.S. Supreme Court has upheld vouchers, it is unlikely that it will rule charter schools unconstitutional.

Opponents have three general problems with charter schools:

1. They don't work.
2. They create unforeseen problems.
3. They divert attention from the inequality issue.

Policy analyst Gregory Shafer claimed that charter schools in Baltimore were failures.

> Educational Alternatives Incorporated, a private company that took over the Baltimore, Maryland, public schools [claimed] they could cut costs, be more efficient, and raise test scores. After only a few years, EAI was asked to leave Baltimore so the city could return its students to the public schools. This, after test scores went down, class sizes rose, and EAI was accused of lying about its enrollment and test score averages. (2001, 2)

Opponents of charter schools have maintained that one of the most common problems is the for-profit school. To make a profit, the charter school must reduce teacher salaries and overcrowd classes. This process creates profits, but shortchanges the children and cheats them out of a quality education.

Opponents also identified the tendency of charter schools, as well as vouchers, to maintain patterns of segregation. Salvatore Saporito and Annette Lareau, professors at Temple University, surveyed over 2,000 eighth-graders making the choice of high school. They found that white families tended to avoid black schools regardless of how successful these schools were in maintaining high test scores and few social or discipline problems.

> The view that racial bias is unimportant in school choice is not supported by our data. Instead, the racial motivations of families are a clear and powerful force in shaping school selection for whites, but not for blacks. White families avoid "black" schools. They do so even when these "black" schools have substantial numbers of affluent, academically able students. Instead, white families prefer "white" schools, which, in many cases, have poorer children with lower test scores. (1999, 419)

They also maintained that school choice literature "made the error of presuming a relatively standardized school selection process for families of different race and class background (1999, 419).

Finally opponents claimed that charter schools, like vouchers, divert attention from the real problem of central city schools: inadequate funding. To fully understand this problem, the money issue must be examined separately.

The Money Issue Again: Inadequate and Unequal Funding

In his book *Savage Inequalities: Children in America's Schools,* Jonathan Kozol argued that inadequate funding has savage impacts on poor central city schools. He provided examples of schools with the roofs falling in; schools located in abandoned skating rinks; schools surrounded by broken glass and litter, with no playgrounds; schools that use pictures of keyboards because they cannot afford real ones; and schools with textbooks over 15 years old.

Kozol took strong issue with those who argue that money is not the problem. He cited the problem of the scarcity of substitute teachers in Chicago public schools. "As spring comes to Chicago, the scarcity of substitutes grows more acute. On Mondays and Fridays in early May, nearly 18,000 children are assigned to classes with no teacher" (Kozol 1991, 53). To dramatize the differences between rich and poor schools, he compared New Trier, a suburban high school, with Du Sable, a central city Chicago school.

> Every freshman at New Trier is assigned a faculty adviser who remains assigned to him or her through graduation. Each of the faculty advisers—they are given a reduced class schedule to allow them time for this—gives counseling to about two dozen children. At Du Sable, where the lack of staff prohibits such reduction in class schedules, each of the guidance counselors advises 420 children. (1991, 66)

Whereas Du Sable is located on a crowded dilapidated block, New Trier is surrounded by 27 acres of land. Almost all of New Trier students are in college preparatory programs, whereas 63 percent of Du Sable students are in vocational programs, 20 percent in general education programs, and only 17 percent in college preparatory programs. Kozol suggested that poor school districts have greater needs, but fewer resources. They need more money for counselors, social workers, security officers, maintenance, science labs, and textbooks.

In *The Manufactured Crisis: Myths, Fraud and the Attack on America's Public Schools* (1995), David Berliner and Bruce Biddle insisted that the choice movement is based on several myths about public schools: the myth that private schools outperform public schools, the myth that money does not matter, and the myth that we have given too much money to public schools. They argue that private schools should do substantially better than public schools because most private schools have selective admissions; that is, many admit only students with high test scores. However, a careful analysis of the results of the National Assessment of Education Progress (NAEP) test indicates that private schools do not necessarily outperform public schools. The NAEP tests indicate that private school students did slightly better in lower-level math tests, but public school students did better in higher-level math tests. The authors concluded that "public high schools had a slight edge for students who had taken higher-level courses, while private high schools generated slightly greater scores for students who had taken only lower-level courses." They add:

> [I]t seems to make little difference whether the student attends a public or private school. What matters in mathematics achievement is whether or not the student takes advanced courses in mathematics. Thus, the biggest factor determining mathematics achievement is opportunity to learn, and it matters little whether students have the opportunity in a public or private school. (1995, 122, 124)

Berliner and Biddle also claimed that it is a myth that money doesn't matter. They argue that most studies that claim that money does not matter fail to look at what the money is used for. The implications of their position is that money spent on an Olympic swimming pool, a 25-acre wild life sanctuary, and a new building, as described in the Kansas City study, is not related to academic programs and should not be expected to improve test scores. Berliner and Biddle concluded that money spent on factors related to academic outcomes is what affects test scores. They cited several studies that indicated that an increase in spending per pupil for academic-related factors can increase scores significantly on school achievement tests (Berliner and Biddle 1995, 74). They concluded that money spent on factors known to affect academic performance—class size, tutors, time on academic tasks, teacher experience, and teacher education—tends to make a measurable difference in academic outcomes.

Berliner and Biddle pointed out that while teacher salaries increased measurably from 1960 to 1972, the increase from 1972 to the present has been small and U.S. teachers' salaries are low. Most of the recent increase in spending for education can be attributed to the cost of living and to greater spending for special education. Compared to most technologically advanced countries, spending for elementary education in the United States is low. The United States ranks 9th out of 16 nations in terms of per pupil expenditures, and 14th out of 16 in terms of per pupil expenditures for education as a percentage of per capita income (Berliner and Biddle 1995).

Along with Kozol, Berliner and Biddle have argued that the financial problems of central city school districts arise from their reliance on property taxes for most of their funding. Unfortunately, the property tax base of cities has been declining because, while some businesses and industries have been leaving the central cities, city governments have been granting tax breaks to try to keep them there and to attract new businesses. The school choice movement thus detracts attention from the real problem of central city schools: inequality in school funding.

Summary

Four educational policy regimes have been identified: preindustrial, industrial, rights, and choice. The preindustrial regime emerged slowly over several decades. Its development follows the model of innovation and diffusion mentioned in Chapter 3. A free public school was established in Boston in 1817, followed gradually by other cities. In the 1850s Massachusetts made school attendance compulsory. Other schools followed the Massachusetts example throughout the century. The first high school was established in the 1820s, the first kindergarten in the 1870s.

The type of mass education system in place today was established at the end of the 19th century. The Industrial Revolution, mass production, and the Progressive movement contributed to the shift from the preindustrial to the industrial educational policy regime. Industrial and Progressive leaders promoted mass education, vocational education, standardized testing, and other features of this policy regime.

The industrial educational policy regime emerged rapidly at the beginning of the 20th century. Vocational education programs, a major feature of the industrial policy regime, were established with the strong support of major industries.

The rights educational policy regime emerged abruptly on the crest of two social movements: the civil rights movement and the antipoverty movement. These movements ended government-mandated racially segregated schools, promoted compensatory educational policies, and encouraged the protection of the rights of students with special needs. The emergence of desegregation, compensatory education, and special education programs marked a shift from the industrial educational policy regime to the rights regime. These programs were well in place at the end of the 1960s.

In the 1995 *Missouri v. Jenkins* decision, Chief Justice Rehnquist indicated that federal courts should disengage from desegregation efforts. This decision signaled an end to the rights education policy regime. School choice marked a shift from the rights educational policy regime to the choice educational policy regime. Although this change was initiated at the state level, like the innovation and diffusion model of policy change, it spread rapidly. The change was accompanied by new arrangements of power and new ideas in education. A conservative movement consisting of religious organizations, conservative think tanks, Republican party leaders, and some business organizations challenged the power of traditional educational associations and traditional public schools. The shift in ideas occurred with the emergence of market models to increase the choices of parents, to break up the public school monopoly, and to prompt schools to operate more efficiently. Today, new education policy proposals place more emphasis on school choice. Charter schools have been established in most states. Vouchers continue to face strong opposition, although they are not likely to disappear.

Review Questions

1. What were some of the major features of the preindustrial school?
2. Why was vocational education so controversial? What concerns did unions have?
3. What is the controversy over standardized tests?
4. Discuss the educational policy changes of the 1960s and 1970s. What changed and why?
5. Why are vouchers so controversial? What is the major constitutional issue involving vouchers?
6. Which political organizations support vouchers and why? Which political organizations oppose vouchers and why?
7. What is the position of the American Federation of Teachers and the National Education Association on charter schools?
8. Discuss the controversy over school funding?

Select Websites

This is the official Website for the U.S. Department of Education.
http://www.ed.gov/index.jhtml?src=a

This is the Website for the American Federation of Teachers.
http://www.aft.org

This is the homepage for the National Education Association.
http://www.nea.org

Key Terms

American Federation of Teachers (AFT)
areawide choice
charter schools
compensatory education
compulsory attendance
Head Start
magnet schools
National Education Association (NEA)

No Child Left Behind
school choice
schoolwide choice
Title I
Title VI
vocational education
vouchers

CHAPTER 14

Economic Policy

E conomic policies deal with growing, sustaining, and managing the economy. Insofar as they benefit the general population and develop quietly without controversy, they fall into the category of distributive policies. When they shift wealth downward (or upward) and involve high levels of conflict and ideological disputes, they are redistributive policies. Historically, economic policies have shifted resources from one region to another, from one sector of the economy to another, and from one social class to another.

There are many sets of economic policies, which have been used to develop, manage, or sustain the economy. The specific set of policies used to achieve these goals has varied from period to period, depending on three factors: the dominant economic philosophy, the dominant mode of production, and the dominant economic coalition. With respect to American economic policy, there have been two dominant economic philosophies, classical and Keynesian; two dominant modes of production, preindustrial and industrial; and several forms of economic coalitions. The interaction among these factors has given rise to four major economic policy regimes: two from the classical period and two from the Keynesian period. The four policy regimes are shown in Table 14.1.

TABLE 14.1

Four Major Economic Policy Regimes

Classical Period (1789–1932)	Keynesian Period (1932–Present)
1. Pre-Civil War (1789–1860)	3. Keynesian (1932–1980)
2. Industrial (1860–1932)	4. Post-Keynesian (1980–present)

Classical economic theory dominated economic thinking from about the end of the American Revolution to the beginning of the Great Depression. Contributors to classical economic theory include Adam Smith, J. B. Say, David Ricardo, John Stuart Mill, and many others. These theorists emphasized individualism, open competition, and limited government. Most classical economic theorists placed a premium on the values of growth and efficiency.

The economic growth during the classical period was attributed largely to private activities associated with the Industrial Revolution, such as the emergence of new inventions, new energy sources, new machines, and mass production. Nevertheless, within the parameters of classical economic theory, the federal and state governments supported economic growth through various means. The federal government stimulated economic growth by acquiring new land and territory, especially land with fertile soil and natural resources; by protecting northern industries with tariffs; and by subsidizing the expansion of railroad companies. State governments supported economic growth by building roads, bridges, ports, canals, and other instruments of commerce. The federal government briefly experimented with a national bank in the early 19th century. Classical theory played a direct role in constraining government policies up until the early years of the Great Depression.

The Keynesian period can be divided into two parts: 1932 to 1980, and 1980 to the present. **Capital-intensive industries** (those that relied more on machines and less on workers), investment banks, and transnational business (those with significant investments and markets abroad) formed the major economic and political bloc supporting Keynesian economic policies. This bloc was so strong and stable that both parties adhered to the Keynesian approach.

John Mayard Keynes's ideas developed during the 1920s and 1930s, primarily in reaction to the inability of classical theory to deal with the problems of economic depressions. Whereas classical theorists saw economic downturns—periods of slow growth and high unemployment—as temporary self-correcting periods of the market, Keynes saw the Great Depression as a crisis of inadequate consumer demand that could not correct itself in the short run without government intervention; and to paraphrase Keynes, in the long run most people would be dead. Keynes's ideas provided powerful intellectual support for the many public programs introduced during the 1930s.

Keynesian economic theory called for a more activist national government. It encouraged the enactment of public works projects, unemployment insurance, social security, and many other programs. This theory included two primary approaches to contemporary economic policies: fiscal and monetary. **Fiscal policy** involves the national budget: using federal spending, purchasing, and taxing, as well as special social programs and jobs projects.

Monetary policy involves the management of the circulation of money, primarily through the Federal Reserve System.

Keynesian theory guided economic policies from the 1930s to the end of the 1970s and provided the intellectual basis for the growth of federal programs. However, the economic crisis of the late 1970s created problems for Keynesian theory. The 1970s crisis was characterized by high unemployment and inflation rates. The **unemployment rate** measures the percentage of people within the labor force who are out of work and are actively looking for a job. The **inflation rate** measures changes in consumer prices. Keynesian theorists postulate a trade-off between unemployment and inflation; that is, if inflation rises, unemployment should decline. However, both unemployment and inflation rates had increased during the late 1970s, a trend which contradicted the expectations of Keynesian theory and exposed the theory to attack.

In the late 1970s, two forms of neoconservative economic theory—supply side and monetary—emerged, attacking Keynesian theory and offering alternatives. Supply-side theory focused on the supply side of the economy—producers, businesses, and industries. Monetary theory focused on the circulation of money or monetary policy. Both versions of neoconservative theory called for less government, reductions in taxes, cuts in social programs, and rollbacks in government regulations.

Keynesian economic theory reemerged in the 1990s and dominated the decade, particularly under the Clinton administration. Today, the Keynesian and the supply-side views continue to clash. Democrats tend to favor the Keynesian approach, whereas Republicans lean more toward a supply-side approach. Both rely heavily on monetary policy. This contemporary period of conflict between neoconservative and Keynesian theories is called the post-Keynesian era.

→ *Classical Economic Period, 1789–1932*

Classical economic thought emphasized individualism, individual initiative, private property, minimum government, and open and competitive markets. Classical theorists of the 18th and 19th centuries saw open and competitive markets as the key to the growth and expansion of the national economy. These philosophers included David Hume, Adam Smith, Thomas Malthus, J. B. Say, David Ricardo, and John Stuart Mill, along with Arthur Pigou of the 20th century.

Classical Economic Theorists

David Hume

David Hume, a prolific Enlightenment philosopher, devoted only a small part of his writings to economic theory, especially his ideas about money. Hume saw an association between the amount of money in circulation and prices and profits. For Hume, increasing the money supply would increase prices and profits. These ideas foreshadowed contemporary monetarists. Hume saw the expansion of the wealth of a nation generally benefiting the entire population. Nevertheless, he opposed policies that hurt poor people simply to expand wealth. Moreover, he opposed extreme inequality. Specifically, he wrote:

> A too great disproportion among the citizens weakens any state. . . . No one can doubt, but such an equality is most suitable to human nature and diminishes much less from the happiness of the rich than it adds to that of the poor. (quoted in Lekachman 1976, 66–67)

Adam Smith

In the same year the Declaration of Independence was signed, **Adam Smith,** one of the most renowned economists then and since, published *Wealth of Nations*. He attacked mercantilism, advocated open competitive markets, and supported a modest role for government in the market. Mercantilism concerned, in part, Great Britain's restraint of trade by requiring British subjects to purchase only British goods.

Smith insisted that mercantilism retarded economic growth. While its intent was to protect the interest of British producers, its effect was to harm the interest of consumers and to block the expansion of the economy. He argued against direct trade restrictions, against rules prohibiting the sale of goods not transported on British ships, and against bounties paid for colonial goods.

Smith valued individualism and argued that when individuals pursue their own self-interest in an open, competitive market, the economy will grow. He used the metaphor of an invisible hand operating to promote the public interest; an individual

> . . . is in this, as in many other cases, led by an invisible hand to promote an end which was no part of his intention. Nor is it always the worse for society that it was no part of it. By pursuing his own interest he frequently promotes that of the society more effectually than when he really intends to promote it. (1776/1952, 194)

Smith recognized a modest role for government which had three major duties: to promote the national interest, to build public works, and to maintain a system of justice. Government had a responsibility to build roads, bridges, ports, and other public works; he supported the imposition of taxes to pay for these responsibilities and accepted a role for government in supporting markets and ensuring fair and equitable practices. Smith deplored permanent monopolies as injurious to the people.

Smith seemed to favor minimum wage laws and other policies that benefited workers: "When the regulation, therefore, is in favour of the workmen, it is always just and equitable; but it is sometimes otherwise when in favour of the masters" (Smith 1776/1952, 61). He added, "Where wages are high, accordingly, we shall always find the workmen more active, diligent, and expeditious than where they are low . . ." (Smith 1776/1952, 34).

Adam Smith opposed extremes in wealth and poverty. No society could flourish if the greater part were poor and miserable. He believed that improving the conditions of the lower ranks of people was advantageous to the entire society.

> Is this improvement in the circumstances of the lower ranks of the people to be regarded as an advantage or as an inconveniency to the society? The answer seems at first sight abundantly plain. Servants, labourers, and workmen of different kinds, make up the far greater part of every great political society. But what improves the circumstances of the greater part can never be regarded as an inconveniency to the whole. No society can surely be flourishing and happy, of which the far greater part of the members are poor and miserable. It is but equity, besides, that they who feed, clothe, and lodge the whole body of the people, should have such a share of the produce of their own labour as to be themselves tolerably well fed, clothed, and lodged. (1776/1952, 33)

In the United States, Adam Smith's ideas appeared at a time of violent opposition to British rule, the symbol of centralized, concentrated, and oppressive governmental powers. Smith was not an unqualified promoter of laissez-faire capitalism—leave the market alone— as some contemporary free market economists claim. He opposed the mercantile system and its high level of government control primarily because this system favored producers, ignored consumers, and oppressed the poor. The Nobel Prize–winning economist James Tobin summarized Smith's contributions:

> Adam Smith is not responsible for excesses committed in his name. His main purpose was to oppose protectionism and other regulations favoring special interests at the expense of the general public. (1996, 14)

J. B. Say

The French economist **J. B. Say** is most noted for his belief that supply creates its own demand. Economists see two sides of an economy: the supply side and the demand side. The **supply side** consists of producers, those who produce goods and services sold in the market. The **demand side** consists of the consumers who purchase those goods and services. Classical economic theory set forth the **law of supply and demand** and prices. The law works like this: If the supply of a good remains the same and the demand for it increases, then the price will increase, because producers can now get more money as more consumers want the good. If the supply of a good remains the same and demand declines, producers have to reduce the price to keep sales at the same level. If supply increases and demand remains the same, then the price declines. If supply declines and demand remains the same, then the price increases.

Say was a pure market economist in the sense that he perceived the economy as a place of trade; that is, when producers produced goods, they took their products to the marketplace and exchanged them for other goods. Producers produced goods others wanted in order to exchange them for goods they wanted. Money disguised the nature of the exchange. Summing up Say's theory, economist Dudley Dillard wrote:

> Say assumed that the only reason people work and produce is in order to enjoy the satisfaction of consuming. In an exchange economy, therefore, whatever is produced represents the demand for another product. Additional supply is additional demand. (1949, 18)

This notion that supply creates its own demand is known as **Say's law.**

Thomas Malthus

Thomas Malthus was a pessimistic classical economist. He believed that poverty was inevitable and that it is likely to increase automatically as populations increase. His theory gave economics its reputation as the "dismal science." Malthus insisted that populations will increase geometrically and create a crisis of severe poverty, and there was little that governments could or should do about the crisis because it would take care of itself. Increasing the minimum wage would only encourage families to have more children and thus hasten the poverty crisis.

David Ricardo

David Ricardo expanded upon Adam Smith's theory of wages, value, and the division of labor. Ricardo distinguished between natural and market wages. Natural wages were those needed for subsistence and market wages were those that workers could obtain in the labor market. Ricardo's theory of value assumed that labor created value, and a part of that value was equal to the costs needed for the subsistence of the worker. Another part, surplus value, was realized as profits. Ricardo, like Smith, recognized the value of machinery and the division of labor in creating wealth. Ricardo saw the expansion in the use of machinery as contributing to the expansion of the wealth of the entire society. Ricardo, like Say, expected expansion in production to generate expansion in consumption.

John Stuart Mill

John Stuart Mill expanded on the ideas of the earlier classical economists, Smith, Ricardo, and others. Mill believed in open and competitive markets, a central theme in his classic work on economics, *Principles of Political Economy* (1894). He called for minimal government interference with the market: "Laissez-faire . . . should be the general practice: every departure from it, unless required by some great good, is a certain evil" (quoted in Lekachman 1976, 195). This principle explicitly acknowledges that some governmental involvement is necessary and permissible. Mill supported eminent domain—government taking land and providing fair compensation for public use.

> The claim of the landowners to the land is altogether subordinate to the general policy of the state. The principle of property gives them no right to the land, but only a right to compensation for whatever portion of their interest in the land it may be the policy of the state to deprive them of. (quoted in Lekachman 1976, 196)

Mill supported taxes, particularly estate or inheritance taxes, but opposed taxing the rich at a substantially higher rate than workers. Mill opposed government interference in business cycles, which he saw as natural mechanisms that operated to correct market inefficiencies. Mill harbored a number of liberal views; for example, he believed that producers should share their profits with workers, because these profits would act as powerful work incentives.

Arthur C. Pigou

Arthur Pigou, the early 20th century economist, opposed government tinkering with the economy. He applied the law of supply and demand to labor markets. He reasoned that if the demand for labor declined and the supply remained the same, then the price of labor or wages would also decline. If the demand for labor increased and the supply remained the same, then wages would increase. Pigou believed that as long as wages were flexible and labor markets followed the law of supply and demand, there could be no involuntary unemployment. Minimum wage legislation and labor unions interfered with labor markets and upset the balance between labor supply, demand, and wages. Pigou insisted that government and unions contributed to artificially high levels of unemployment. His ideas thus supported the laissez-faire policies of the first third of the 20th century.

Summary of Classical Economic Thought

Smith, Ricardo, Say, Mill, Pigou, and many others contributed to the classical school of economic thought. They did not always agree. The dominant theme of this school was that markets do best when they are open and competitive, when there is limited government interference, and when a premium is placed on individualism. The underlying assumption was that open competition with little government interference was the best way to expand the economy.

While they advocated free markets, they were not always opposed to government regulations. Hume and Smith opposed extreme inequality. Smith supported minimum wage laws. Mill supported producers sharing wealth with laborers. All the classical theorists supported some kind of tax, although they differed on the type. Mill was likely to support a flat tax, Smith a progressive tax. All were likely to support public works that supported commerce and trade.

→ Economic Policy Regimes of the Classical Period

Classical economic theory set the parameters for two major periods of economic policies: the pre-Civil War, 1789–1860; and the industrial, 1860–1932. The theory allowed for minimum government tinkering with the economy. The government would support economic expansion through the acquisition of new territory; the seizing of land for the railroads; the building of roads, ports, and canals; the imposition of tariffs to protect northern industries; managing the money supply; and experimenting with a national bank.

The Pre-Civil War Period, 1789–1860

Two sets of economic interests competed for control over economic policies during the period before the Civil War. On one side of the political divide stood the southern interests: planters who owned slaves and large plantations, small farmers, mine owners, and others who tended to support first the Democratic-Republican Party, and then the Democratic Party. On the other side of the political divide stood northern interests: bankers, merchants, manufacturers, and others who tended to support the Federalist Party and later the Whig and Republican parties.

The Federalist Party dominated the period from the founding of the United States under the Constitution in 1789 to 1800. This party levied excise taxes, imposed tariffs, and raised money to honor revolutionary war bonds and to support the national currency. It also established a national bank, the Bank of the United States. These policies favored northern interests.

The Democratic-Republican Party opposed the national bank and initially decided not to renew its charter when it expired in 1811. However, they renewed when the War of 1812 created pressures for wartime spending. In 1832 Democrat Andrew Jackson vetoed a bill to recharter the bank. He claimed northern elites and foreign investors dominated the bank.

Pre-Civil War economic policies also focused on land expansion, a policy move that favored southern plantation owners. Thomas Jefferson greatly expanded American territory through the purchase of the Louisiana Territory from France in 1803. Jackson opened a large amount of land to settlers in the 1830s by forcibly removing Native Americans from territory east of the Mississippi River. The territory of the United States was increased again in the 1840s after the Mexican War during the Democratic administration of James Polk.

Most pre-Civil War economic policies were state policies. For example, New York State contributed to an enormous expansion of trade by building the Erie Canal, which opened the floodgates of trade, connecting the eastern United States to the West. Also, northeastern states assisted in the expansion of railroads.

The Industrial Period, 1860–1932

Two sets of economic interests competed for control over economic policies during the period from 1860 to 1932. On one side stood northern economic interests: banking, manufacturing, railroads, and others, generally supporting the Republican Party. On the other side stood farming, plantations, and mining interests, generally supporting the Democratic Party. The conflict between these two sets of interests split the country and, with the election of Abraham Lincoln in 1860, precipitated the Civil War.

To pay for the war, Lincoln engaged in deficit spending and introduced the first income tax and increased it twice before the end of the war. In 1895 the U.S. Supreme Court struck down a reestablished income tax as a violation of the Constitution, but in 1913 the Sixteenth Amendment was ratified, giving the federal government the constitutional power to impose an income tax.

The federal government became more actively involved in the economy after the Civil War. It played a key role in the expansion of the railroads across the continent. In 1865 the federal government based its currency on the gold standard and began reducing the supply of money. Former adviser to Richard Nixon and political analyst Kevin Phillips summarized the economic policies of this period as follows:

> Most important was the decision to strengthen the dollar and eventually redeem it in gold. The effect was to shrink the amount of currency in circulation between 1865 and the mid-1870s. Agricultural and mineral commodity prices fell; bond prices rose; and investors redirected money in new and profitable directions—out of agriculture and into railroads and manufacturing. (1991, 104)

The gold standard, however, hurt farmers, reduced the money supply, and made it more difficult to pull the country out of depressions. Farmers organized to pressure the government to switch from the gold standard to the silver standard. In response, Congress passed the *Sherman Silver Purchase Act of 1890,* which required the federal government to purchase 4.5 million ounces of silver a month. Summarizing the impact of this law, James Lindeen said:

> The 1890 Sherman Silver Purchase Bill called for the Treasury to buy virtually all the annual production of silver and to pay for it by issuing legal tender Treasury notes redeemable in either gold or silver. Prosilver forces . . . were able to pass the bill by threatening to oppose the protectionist McKinley tariff. The new law did increase the amount of currency in circulation but not enough to satisfy the Populist party, which led the campaign for more and cheaper money. (1994, 45)

In 1895 the Sherman Silver Purchase Act was repealed. In 1900 Congress passed the *Currency Act,* which reestablished the gold standard, a move that reduced the money supply and later made it more difficult to pull the economy out of the Great Depression of the 1930s.

The **Federal Reserve Board,** created in 1913, is an independent agency consisting of seven governors appointed by the president and approved by the Senate. It regulates the money supply by varying the interest rates of member banks and the percentage of deposits they must keep in their vaults.

By the 1920s the federal government was committed to a laissez-faire policy. In the past there had been several **business cycles,** periods of upswings and downturns in the economy. An **upswing** is a period of economic growth and low unemployment; a **downturn** is a period of slow growth and high unemployment. The general policy of the federal government during an economic downturn in this period was to do little. This philosophy was best captured by Andrew Mellon, the secretary of the treasury under Herbert Hoover: "Liquidate labor, liquidate stocks, liquidate real estate . . . values will be adjusted, and enterprising people will pick up the wreck from less-competent people" (quoted in Phillips 1991, 106). This public philosophy was consistent with the dominant economic ideas of the period.

→ *The Keynesian Economic Era, 1932–Present*

The 1929 crash and the Great Depression stressed the industrial economic policy regime and facilitated a policy regime change. The Great Depression discredited classical economic theory, contributed to the popularity of Keynesian economic theory, produced a power shift, and encouraged the emergence of the Keynesian policy regime.

Keynesian Economic Theory

Several years before the Great Depression, the British economist **John Maynard Keynes** had challenged classical economic theory on two grounds: theoretical and practical. He argued that the laissez-faire policy prescription of the classical view was theoretically unsound and would have disastrous consequences in practice. He warned policy makers about the instability of capitalism and the need for governments to assume a more active role in regulating the economy through fiscal and monetary policies. Keynes, like other economists, believed in free enterprise. However, for free enterprise and competitive markets to survive, he warned, government intervention was necessary. The only questions involved the nature, scope, and limit of the intervention.

Keynes traced the historical development of the concept of laissez-faire and attributed part of its popularity to incompetent governments, to the chance performance of markets, and to its philosophical appeal to groups such as Social Darwinists. He insisted that Adam Smith's use of the metaphor "the invisible hand" had more to do with Smith's optimism and moral philosophy and less to do with the reality of contemporary markets. Keynes said it was a false claim that "enlightened self-interest always operates in the public interests." He added, "Many of the greatest economic evils of our times are the fruits of risk, uncertainty, and ignorance" (Keynes 1927, 39, 47). For Keynes, policy makers who leave the performance of the economy up to chance are flirting with catastrophe.

Earlier, Keynes had argued for government regulation of the money supply. He claimed that principles like the law of supply and demand were limited by the supply of money. Increasing the money supply would increase demand and inflate prices. Decreasing the money supply would decrease demand and deflate prices.

He debunked Say's law that supply creates its own demand. He suggested that the law ignored the possibility of inadequate demand and overproduction, which produced involuntary unemployment—a phenomenon that could not exist within Say's framework.

Keynes suggested that high levels of inflation were unjust, but high levels of unemployment were worse: "inflation is unjust and deflation is . . . worse; because it is worse, in an impoverished world, to provoke unemployment than to disappoint the rentier" (quoted in Lekachman 1966, 64).

In his 1933 book *Means to Prosperity,* Keynes introduced the **multiplier effect,** an impact of an activity on the economy by a factor greater than one. Explaining this effect, he said, "If the new expenditure is additional and not merely in substitution for other expenditure, the increase of employment does not stop there. The additional wages and other incomes paid out are spent on additional purchases, which in turn lead to further employment . . ."

(quoted in Lekachman 1966, 73). For example, a government job takes an unemployed person with no money and turns that person into a consumer. That consumer purchases food, clothes, household products, and other commodities. These purchases increase demand, stimulate the economy, and encourage businesses to increase production and hire more people who also become consumers. Keynes insisted that creating government jobs had a more powerful impact, or multiplier, on the economy than tax cuts.

A national **budget deficit** occurs when federal spending exceeds revenue. Whereas classical and conservative economists had concerns about budget deficits, Keynes saw them as largely irrelevant. Keynes postulated that deficit spending was necessary and beneficial during depressions or recessions. Although deficit spending would increase the deficit, it should stimulate economic growth. The government revenue should increase as the economy expands, reducing the deficit. Overall, Keynes favored both fiscal and monetary policy, although his discussion of the multiplier effect suggested a preference for the fiscal approach. A summary of Keynesian economic theory—especially Keynes's ideas on demand, investment, and employment—can be found in his major work, *The General Theory of Employment, Interest, and Money* (1936).

The Great Depression and Policy Regime Change, 1929–1945

The Great Depression impacted economic theory and political power arrangements. The stock market crash of 1929 was followed by a plummeting gross national product, the measure of the total value of goods and services produced and sold domestically and abroad, which declined from about $103 billion in 1929 to $56 billion by 1933. The crash was followed by massive business failure, home foreclosures, falling prices, and massive unemployment. By the 1932 election, unemployment had reached about 25 percent. Banks were going out of business at a record-breaking pace. In 1929, 659 banks failed; by 1931, another 2,294 banks closed (Blum et al. 1968, 663–664). The per capita net income of farmers declined from $162 in 1929 to $48 in 1932. A severe drought further aggravated the situation of farmers.

The severity and persistence of the Great Depression strained the credulity of classical economic theory. Cities with over half the working age population desperately looking for jobs of any kind for any pay belied the theory that involuntary unemployment did not exist. The notion of a self-correcting market was contradicted by increases in farm and home foreclosures, business failures, and bank closings. A more effective approach to the Depression required a more active government role in regulating the economy.

The Great Depression impacted power arrangements as well as economic theory. A number of political groups shifted political alliances to support Roosevelt and to form the New Deal coalition. These groups included the south, large cities, farmers, organized labor, racial and ethnic minorities, and the economic alliance. This economic alliance formed the power base for the Keynesian economic policy regime.

This economic alliance consisted primarily of leaders from capital-intensive industries and international businesses that supported the New Deal. Thomas Ferguson provides a detailed analysis of this new coalition in *Golden Rule: The Investment Theory of Party Competition and the Logic of Money-Driven Political Systems*. He notes that corporate leaders from capital-intensive and international businesses became strong supporters of the new Keynesian economic philosophy, including Standard Oil, General Electric, R. J. Reynolds, and many others. John D. Rockefeller of Standard Oil and Gerard Swope of General Electric became strong supporters of Roosevelt and his Keynesian policies. The banking industry divided over the New Deal. J.P. Morgan was a strong opponent of the New Deal, but most investment banks joined the New Deal Coalition. Ferguson added the following:

> With workers, farmers, and many industrialists up in arms against finance in general and its most famous symbol, the House of Morgan, in particular, virtually all the major non-Morgan investment banks in America lined up behind Roosevelt. And, in perhaps the least appreciated aspect of the New Deal, so did the now Rockefeller-controlled Chase National Bank. (1995, 147)

Labor-intensive and domestic businesses emerged as the most vociferous opponents of the New Deal. They had a strong voice in the National Association of Manufacturers. However, the Keynesian economic approach had strong support within a powerful and stable economic coalition consisting of capital-intensive industries, international businesses, and investment banks. Despite opposition, the powerful economic coalition behind the Keynesian economic policy regime contributed to the long-term stability of Keynesian economic policies.

The Keynesian Economic Policy Regime, 1932–1980

The Keynesian economic policy regime emerged with the election of Franklin D. Roosevelt, lasted from 1932 to 1980, and was characterized by the federal government taking a greater role in regulating the economy.

The 1932 presidential election marked a critical change in national economic policies. The contrast between the two candidates was sharp. President Hoover expected the Depression to be temporary, requiring little government interference. His campaign was largely a reaction against Franklin D. Roosevelt's promises. At a campaign address in New York in October 1932, Hoover said:

> The proposals of our opponent will endanger or destroy our system. . . . At first I could not believe that anyone would be so cruel as to hold out a hope so absolutely impossible of realization to these 10,000,000 who are unemployed . . . it would cost upwards of $9 billion. (Blum et al. 1968, 674)

President Hoover, constrained by classical economic theory, was reluctant to tinker with the economy and opposed any form of federal relief. He allocated some money to the Federal Home Loan Bank to assist the banks and he supported the creation of the Reconstruction Finance Corporation to lend money to banks and insurance corporations. He tried to deal with the Depression through modest monetary policies. These policies failed and the economy worsened. Hoover lost the election to Roosevelt.

New Deal Policies, 1933–1945

President Roosevelt attacked the economic crisis with several policy initiatives. (See Chapters 3 and 5.) Table 14.2 reviews the many New Deal acts and programs Roosevelt inaugurated to attack the Depression.

Although the New Deal programs contributed to marginal declines in unemployment rates, it was World War II that took the nation out of the Great Depression. During this time the federal government pumped billions of dollars into war production and the federal

TABLE 14.2

Roosevelt's New Deal Programs of the 1930s

Federal Deposit Insurance Corporation (FDIC) 1933	Insured bank deposits; part of Glass-Steagall Act
Agricultural Adjustment Act (AAA) 1933	Farmers received payments to reduce crops
Federal Emergency Relief Act (FERA) 1933	Funding for state and local relief
Civilian Conservation Corps (CCC) 1933	Employed young men on flood control, road, and reforestation projects
Tennessee Valley Authority (TVA) 1933	Development of dams and electric power projects in a 7-state area
Public Works Administration (PWA) 1933	Increased employment through construction projects
National Industrial Recovery Act (NIRA) 1933	Aimed at business recovery through fair-employment codes
National Labor Relations Act 1935	Created NLRB; recognized employees' rights to join unions
Social Security Act 1935	Created system of social insurance including unemployment compensation and old-age insurance; created public assistance, Aid for Dependent Children, and Aid for the Blind
Works Progress Administration 1935	Provided jobs on major federal construction projects
Federal Housing Administration 1934	Guaranteed the repayment of bank loans to families purchasing a home
Public Housing Administration 1937	Allocated money to local agencies to build and manage low income housing

budget increased by a factor of about 10. Unemployment rates fell below 2 percent, the lowest rates of the century, and a labor shortage arose, as the draft absorbed large numbers of young men. The work programs lost their usefulness and were dismantled.

By the end of World War II, the Roosevelt administration had established a tradition of government regulation of the economy through fiscal and monetary policies. The Federal Reserve Board emerged as a major player in regulating the money supply and economic performance. Social welfare and social insurance programs, such as unemployment benefits and Social Security, became a major feature of federal fiscal polices.

Postwar Growth and Prosperity, 1945–1979

The postwar era was an age of Keynesian economics. Unemployment rates remained low, but in 1946 Congress passed the *Full Employment Act,* which committed the federal government to engage in economic policies designed to keep unemployment rates below a prescribed minimum level, such as 6 percent. Congress also established the Council of Economic Advisers to assist the president in developing economic policies. The number of government programs continued to increase throughout the 1950s and 1960s. By the 1970s both Democratic and Republic policy makers ascribed to Keynesian theory.

For the most part, the postwar years were characterized by prosperity. The economy grew and the few periods of recession were followed by recovery. The Korean War contributed to the economic expansion of 1952–1953. With the end of that war, two recessions occurred in the 1950s; President Eisenhower used tax cuts and monetary adjustments to take the country out of them, but there were also some major public works projects during this administration, most notably the multi-billion-dollar federal interstate highway program.

The 1960s was a decade of growth in which the economy expanded. Unemployment rates remained low, well below 4 percent. The Kennedy and Johnson administrations cut taxes in 1964, but raised them again in 1968. The federal budget doubled between 1960 and 1970, as federal programs expanded rapidly and the Vietnam War escalated.

Nixon, who defined himself as a Keynesian, continued many of the Kennedy and Johnson programs with a few changes. Nixon favored block grants over categorical grants and he distributed federal moneys more broadly and with fewer restrictions on state and local governments.

⇒ *The Post-Keynesian Economic Policy Regime, 1980–Present*

Political leaders remained confident about Keynesian economic theory until the economic crisis of the 1970s created a crisis of confidence in Keynesian theory and inaugurated the post-Keynesian period.

Two Crises: Economic and Keynesian

By the end of the 1970s two crises had become evident: an economic crisis and a theoretical crisis. The economic crisis was characterized by high unemployment rates, slow growth, and high inflation. A new term was coined to define this economic crisis: stagflation.

Unemployment rates reached record highs for the post–World War II era (see Table 14.3). From 1944 through 1974, unemployment rates had remained below 7 percent. By 1975 it reached 8.5 percent. Although it declined to 5.8 percent in 1979, it again rose to 7.1 percent by 1980.

Stagflation—slow growth, high unemployment, and high inflation—produced the theoretical crisis because these trends contradicted the expectations of Keynesian economic theory. Keynesian economists posited a trade-off between unemployment and inflation; that is, they expected unemployment rates to decline if inflation rates increased. Stagflation thus precipitated a crisis in Keynesian economic theory and made it vulnerable to attack.

Neoconservatives, Monetarists, and Supply-Siders

New or neoconservative opponents of Keynesian economics attacked with a vengeance. They blamed the economic crisis on government policies arising from Keynesian theory. They specifically pointed to high taxes, excessive regulations, and expensive social programs. They

TABLE 14.3

Unemployment Rates by Year, 1929–2003

Year	Unemployment Rates (%)	Year	Unemployment Rates (%)	Year	Unemployment Rates (%)
1929	3.2	1954	5.6	1979	5.8
1930	8.7	1955	4.4	1980	7.1
1931	15.9	1956	4.2	1981	7.6
1932	23.6	1957	4.3	1982	9.7
1933	24.9	1958	6.8	1983	9.6
1934	21.7	1959	5.5	1984	7.5
1935	20.1	1960	6.1	1985	7.2
1936	16.9	1961	5.6	1986	7.0
1937	14.3	1962	5.5	1987	6.2
1938	19.0	1963	5.7	1988	5.5
1939	17.2	1964	5.2	1989	5.3
1940	14.6	1965	4.5	1990	5.6
1941	9.9	1966	3.8	1991	6.8
1942	4.7	1967	3.8	1992	7.5
1943	1.9	1968	3.6	1993	6.9
1944	1.2	1969	3.5	1994	6.1
1945	1.9	1970	4.9	1995	5.6
1946	3.9	1971	5.9	1996	5.4
1947	3.9	1972	5.6	1997	4.9
1948	3.8	1973	4.9	1998	4.5
1949	5.9	1974	5.6	1999	4.2
1950	5.3	1975	8.5	2000	4.0
1951	3.3	1976	7.7	2001	4.7
1952	3.1	1977	7.0	2002	5.8
1953	2.9	1978	6.1	2003	6.0

SOURCE: U.S. Census Bureau, *Statistical Abstract of the United States,* 2004/05.

blamed Keynesian theory for focusing on consumers and ignoring producers. For example, Martin Feldstein, the chair of the Council of Economic Advisors under President Reagan, insisted that high taxes created disincentives to work and to invest. Tax cuts would provide greater incentives to work, increase productivity, and free up money for investment. Overall, critics argued that tax cuts would directly stimulate economic expansion. During the 1980s, advocates of two major schools of neoconservative thought emerged in opposition to the Keynesian paradigm: monetarists and supply-siders.

The Nobel Prize-winning economist **Milton Friedman** blamed most economic problems on government policies arising from Keynesian theory. Friedman argued for tight controls over the circulation of money, regulating the flow of money like a thermostat, gradually decreasing the flow during periods of high inflation, and increasing the flow during periods of recession. Friedman identified high taxes, social programs, and government regulations as the most serious problems with the economy. Government regulations inevitably generate increased costs and social programs "weaken the family; reduce the incentive to work, save, and innovate; reduce the accumulation of capital; and limit our freedom" (Friedman 1981, 118). He advocated the elimination of the corporate tax and the establishment of a flat-rate tax.

Many of the supply-siders rejected Milton Friedman's monetarist approach, but agreed on the need for cuts in taxes and social programs and for deregulation. Most rediscovered classical economic theory. A good example of a contemporary supply-side economic theorist is **George Gilder.** In his popular book *Wealth and Poverty,* Gilder rediscovered Say's law. Restating the law, Gilder said:

> The sum of money paid to the factors of production, chiefly in rents, wages, salaries, and profits, for the making and marketing of an automobile, for example, is precisely enough to purchase it. Therefore, across an entire system, purchasing power and producing power can always balance: there will always be enough wealth in an economy to buy its products. (1981, 47)

Just as Keynes focused on getting more money in the hands of consumers, Gilder focused on getting more money in the hands of producers.

The United States Treasury Department is the heart of fiscal policy.

Supply-siders promised substantial economic growth. They were not directly concerned with equity because they believed that economic expansion benefited everyone—the rising tide that lifts all boats.

Economic Policies of the Reagan and Bush Administrations

President Reagan adopted the supply-side economic approach. He promised to reduce the size of government, cut taxes, reduce welfare spending, increase defense spending, and roll back regulations. He slowed the growth of social programs by changing eligibility standards, for example, making it more difficult for people to get AFDC benefits. He made changes in Social Security that slowed the rate of increase of spending in this program.

George H. W. Bush promised to continue Reagan's policies and not create any new taxes. However, the escalating budget deficits convinced him to rescind some of the Reagan tax cuts. Conservatives claimed that he broke his campaign promise by increasing taxes.

Aftermath of Reagan and Bush

Just as there were strong differences over the policy proposals of the Reagan administration, there were strong disagreements in the assessments of the impacts of these policies. The major points of contention were growth, equity, and deficits. Reagan supporters considered the

1980s a decade of growth, which they attributed to the success of supply-side economic policies. Reagan critics considered the 1980s a decade of huge deficits, economic decline, and inequality.

Deficit   Federal budget deficits increased substantially during the 1980s (see Table 14.4). Reagan supporters denied that Reagan's economic policy was responsible and blamed the deficit on Congress and the Democrats. Reagan opponents pointed directly to Reagan's tax cuts and increased defense spending for the budget deficits. Federal spending over the five-year period of 1980 to 1985 increased from $591 billion to $946 billion (see Table 14.5), and defense spending doubled from about $150 billion to $300 billion. With the government spending more money than it was taking in, the deficit almost tripled, from $74 billion in 1980 to $212 billion by 1985.

Growth   Reagan supporters insisted that his economic policy produced high levels of growth. For example, Robert Bartley compared the Reagan years, 1982 to 1990, to the Carter years, 1976 to 1982. He concluded that the economic growth rate averaged only 1.8 percent during the Carter years, but 3.5 percent during the Reagan years (Bartley 1992, 6). Supporters also insist that the Reagan years were a period of prosperity that contributed to increases in family income and a middle-class boom.

Critics disputed these assessments. For example, Paul Krugman insisted that although the median family income rose 11 percent, most of this increase went to families in the top 5 or 10 percent income group (Krugman 1995). He added that economic growth was more robust and median income had risen much faster in previous decades. He noted that the overall growth rate was 2.1 for the 1980 to 1992 period, compared to 3.4 percent from 1947 to 1973. "By no stretch can the growth performance of the 1980s be called exceptional or even satisfactory" (Krugman 1995, 111, 117). Bluestone and Harrison made the point more forcefully: "Over a period of more than three decades, the nation's growth rate moved inexorably down-

TABLE 14.4

Budget Deficit or Surplus, 1920–2003

Year	Surplus or Deficit (In $ millions)	Year	Surplus or Deficit (In $ millions)	Year	Surplus or Deficit (In $ millions)
1920	291	1950	−3,119	1995	−163,972
1925	717	1955	−2,993	1996	−107,473
1930	738	1960	301	1997	−21,958
1935	−2,803	1965	−1,411	1998	69,213
1936	−4,304	1970	−2,842	1999	125,563
1940	−2,920	1975	−53,242	2000	236,445
1945	−47,553	1980	−73,830	2001	127,299
1946	−15,936	1985	−212,308	2002	−157,802
1947	4,018	1990	−221,195	2003	−304,159

SOURCE: United States Office of Management and Budget: Historical Tables, http://www.whitehouse.gov/omb/, 2004.

ward, from 4.4 percent in the 1960s and 3.2 percent in the 1970s to 2.7 percent in the 1980s, and finally only 1.9 percent in the early 1990s" (Bluestone and Harrison 2000, 1).

A number of economists, including Krugman and Tobin, insisted that the Federal Reserve Board's monetary policies were largely responsible for the economic trends of the 1980s. First, the Federal Reserve Board reduced the money supply in response to the high inflation rate of the 1970s and thus generated the severe recession of the early 1980s with the highest unemployment rates since 1941 (see Table 14.2). Then the board pumped more money into the economy in response to the recession and contributed to the economic expansion from 1984 to 1988. In their view, the expansion was not a result of any supply-side economic policies, but an increase in the money supply (Tobin 1996 and Krugman 1995).

Inequality   Reagan supporters claimed that economic expansion lifts all boats or helps all families. They argued that median income increased during the 1980s, indicating a boom for the middle class. Supporters also insisted there was a high degree of social class mobility during this period.

TABLE 14.5

Total Federal Outlays, 1920–2002

Year	Actual Outlays (In $ millions)	Outlays in Current Dollars (In $ billions)	Outlays as Percentage of GDP
1920	6,358	NA	NA
1925	2,924	NA	NA
1930	3,320	NA	NA
1935	6,412	NA	NA
1940	9,468	9.5	9.8
1945	92,712	92.7	41.9
1946	55,323	55.2	24.8
1947	34,496	34.5	14.7
1950	42,562	42.6	15.6
1955	68,444	68.4	17.3
1960	92,191	92.2	17.8
1965	118,228	118.2	17.2
1970	195,649	195.6	19.3
1975	332,332	332.3	21.3
1980	590,941	590.9	21.6
1985	946,396	946.4	22.9
1990	1,253,165	1,253.2	21.8
1995	1,515,802	1,515.8	20.7
2000	1,788,773	1,788.8	18.4
2001	1,863,895	1,863.9	18.6
2002	2,010,975	2,011.0	19.5

SOURCE: United States Office of Management and Budget: Historical Tables, http://www.whitehouse.gov/omb/, 2004.

Krugman argued that although the 1950s and 1960s were periods of income growth for most income groups, the 1970s and 1980s was a period of unequal growth. Lower-income groups suffered losses, whereas upper-income groups enjoyed substantial gains.

Economist Lynn Karoly looked at several measures of inequality. She noted that the number of families in both the top and the bottom income groups increased. She concluded, "While a definition of the middle class is somewhat arbitrary, these trends in relative income percentiles indicate that lower and upper classes have been increasing in the 1980s, implying a corresponding decline in the middle class" (Karoly 1994, 76).

Policy analyst Thomas Dye examined average hourly earnings in real dollars—that is, controlling for inflation—from 1970 to about 2000. He found that average hourly earnings peaked around 1973 at about $8.60, but declined to about $7.60 by 1980 and $7.45 by 1990. It stabilized in the 1990s and increased to about $7.80 per hour by about 2000. Median family income increased during the 1980s and 1990s, primarily because more people within the family entered the job market (Dye 2001, 25–26).

Most economists attributed these increases in inequality to economic trends rather than public policy. Krugman attributed only a small part of the increase in inequality to supply-side policies. An elaborate mathematical model determined that the growth in income inequality from 1980 to 1990 was 84 percent attributable to economic trends, while 16 percent was due to public policy changes (Gramlich, Kasten, Sammartino 1994, 239).

The Center for Popular Economics published a study that focused on the impact of Reagan policy changes on the rich and the poor. The study found that the Reagan tax cuts reduced the tax burdens of upper-income earners, but increased the burden on lower-income earners. For example, an individual earning less than $10,000 enjoyed a $145 tax cut, but paid an additional $437 in Social Security tax—an overall increase of $292. An individual making between $10,000 and $15,000 enjoyed a $692 tax cut, but a $1,058 increase in Social Security taxes—a $366 increase in taxes. An individual making over $200,000 got a $73,000 tax cut, but a $13,000 increase in the Social Security tax; overall, the taxes declined by $59,000 (Center for Popular Economics 1986, 146).

The shift in the tax burden from corporations to individuals had been occurring long before Reagan took office, although his administration accelerated the shift (see Table 14.6). In 1945, for example, 35.4 percent of government revenue came from corporate taxes. This figure declined steadily over the years to 12.5 percent in 1980. Reagan simply accelerated the trend. By 1983 only about 6.2 percent of revenue came from corporate taxes as shown in Table 14.6. Today the figure is close to 8 percent.

Other critics claimed that the high level of deficit spending redistributed government resources to upper-income groups, as this group received a greater share of the interest the federal government paid on its loans.

> Not only were upper-quintile Americans collecting 80 percent of the federal interest payments made to persons, but the top tax rate applicable to these receipts was falling steadily . . . so that less of the money spent on interest would come back to the U.S. Treasury as revenues. (Phillips 1991, 90)

Economic Coalitions and Winning Elections

The most striking feature of the post-Keynesian era is the role of presidents and political parties in putting together a set of winning economic policies, that is, policy proposals designed

TABLE 14.6

Percentage Composition of Receipts by Source, 1945–2003

Fiscal Year	Individual Taxes	Corporation Taxes	Excise Taxes	Fiscal Year	Individual Taxes	Corporation Taxes	Excise Taxes
1945	40.7	35.4	13.9	1983	48.1	6.2	5.9
1950	39.9	26.5	19.1	1984	44.8	8.5	5.6
1955	43.9	27.3	14.0	1985	45.6	8.4	4.9
1960	44.0	23.2	12.6	1986	45.4	8.2	4.3
1965	41.8	21.8	12.5	1987	45.9	9.8	3.8
1966	42.4	23.0	10.0	1988	44.1	10.4	3.9
1967	41.3	22.8	9.2	1989	45.0	10.4	3.5
1968	44.9	18.7	9.2	1990	45.2	9.1	3.4
1969	46.7	19.6	8.1	1991	44.3	9.3	4.0
1970	46.9	17.0	8.1	1992	43.6	9.2	4.2
1971	46.1	14.3	8.9	1993	44.2	10.2	4.2
1972	45.7	15.5	7.5	1994	43.1	11.2	4.4
1973	44.7	15.7	7.0	1995	43.7	11.6	4.3
1974	45.2	14.7	6.4	1996	45.2	11.8	3.7
1975	43.9	14.6	5.9	1997	46.7	11.5	3.6
1976	44.2	13.9	5.7	1998	48.1	11.0	3.3
1977	44.3	15.4	4.9	1999	48.1	10.1	3.9
1978	45.3	15.0	4.6	2000	49.6	10.2	3.4
1979	47.0	14.2	4.0	2001	49.9	7.6	3.3
1980	47.2	12.5	4.7	2002	46.3	8.0	3.6
1981	47.7	10.2	6.8	2003	46.2	7.8	3.7
1982	48.2	8.0	5.9				

SOURCE: U.S. Census Bureau, *Statistical Abstract of the United States,* 2004.

to forge an economic coalition capable of winning the presidential election. This feature makes for more unstable policies and more aggressive actions on the part of presidents to win economic support through economic policies. This was a noticeable feature of the Clinton administration and that of his successor George W. Bush.

Ferguson examined specific economic interests that earlier shifted their support from George H. W. Bush to Bill Clinton, because the Clinton proposals were more attractive. For example, Clinton's decision to support the North Atlantic Free Trade Agreement (NAFTA) and to engage in aggressive efforts to open up foreign markets appealed to transnational businesses. These businesses shifted their support from Bush to Clinton. Clinton's health care proposal appealed to the insurance industry, although it was torpedoed by small businesses. In sum, Clinton's proposals appealed more to capital-intensive industries, transnational industries, high-tech industries, and government-dependent businesses. These businesses allowed him to promote a stronger set of Keynesian policies.

Clinton and Bush Policies Compared: Hybrid versus Supply-Side Keynesian Economics

The past 10 years saw shifts between two different sets of economic policies: Bill Clinton's hybrid Keynesian and George W. Bush's supply-side approaches. Seven aspects of Clinton's economic policies can be identified:

Minimum wage
Equitable tax structure
Monetary strategy
Transfer payments
Modest defense spending
Modest regulations
Deficit control

There was an increase in the minimum wage, which pulled up the incomes of the lowest income group. Clinton obtained a slight increase in the percentage of federal revenue coming from the corporate sector: 11.8 percent in 1996, but down to 10.2 percent by 2000. Clinton's monetary strategy involved letting the Federal Reserve System pump more money into the economy as unemployment rates increased, but raise interest rates if unemployment declined too rapidly. Clinton supported increases in unemployment benefits and public works projects to ameliorate unemployment.

The most significant achievement of the Clinton administration was the elimination of the deficit. In 1990 the budget deficit was $221 billion. By 1997 it had declined to about $22 billion. In 1998 there was a budget surplus of $69 billion, which peaked at about $236 billion in 2000.

George W. Bush has promoted economic policies more like those of Reagan than of his father.

However, George W. Bush did follow a strategy similar to Clinton's of putting together economic policy proposals to appeal to specific economic interests. The prescription drug policy appealed to the pharmaceutical industry and the health insurance companies. His energy deregulation proposals appealed to energy companies—oil, utilities, coal, and gas. The corporate tax cuts, the deregulation efforts, and the increase in defense spending pushed Bush into the Reagan camp of supply-side policies that produced a record-high deficit of $304 billion in 2003.

Summary

To some extent, economic policies change in ways consistent with policy regime theory. Substantial changes in economic policies followed changes in the dominant policy paradigm and in the dominant relations of power. The power arrangements and the paradigm operated to maintain stability in the policy. The dominant policy paradigm or economic theory set parameters for acceptable and unacceptable economic policies. The result has been distinct eras of economic policies: the pre-Civil War, the industrial, the Keynesian, and post-Keynesian periods.

There have been a few deviations from the theory but a number of big policy changes took place within the same era. For example, during the pre-Civil War era, a rapid establishment and then elimination of the national bank took place without any shift in a policy paradigm. However, this anomaly can be explained by a power change from the Federalists, a party dominated by northern banking and manufacturing interests, to the sudden emergence of the Democratic Party and a powerful economic coalition dominated by southern plantation and farming interests. This type of shift in economic coalitions explains most of the other major changes in economic policies within the same era.

The establishment of the Keynesian era was most consistent with policy regime theory. Until 1980 Keynesian economic philosophy had a profound influence on policy makers and presidents regardless of political party. The Keynesian policy paradigm contributed to the remarkable stability of economic policies during this era.

The economic crisis of the late 1970s destabilized the Keynesian policy regime and allowed for the emergence of neoconservative, monetarist, and supply-side economic theories and policies. The election of Ronald Reagan legitimized these theories and introduced tax breaks, deregulation, cuts in social programs, and other supply-side policy proposals. Keynesian theory did not die, but it had to compete with the neoconservative theories.

The post-Keynesian era has several major characteristics. Neoconservative and Keynesian theory now compete and set the parameters for acceptable and unacceptable economic policies. There is less emphasis on demand-side approaches, and more emphasis on monetary policies to regulate the economy. Both presidents Clinton and Bush have relied more heavily on a monetary approach than previous presidents.

Review Questions

1. Summarize the main aspects of classical economic theory. List some of the theorists. Where do they agree and disagree?
2. Discuss the pre-Civil War economic policies.
3. What were some of Herbert Hoover's policy responses to the Great Depression? To what extent was he constrained by classical economic theory?
4. What were some of Franklin D. Roosevelt's policy responses to the Great Depression?
5. What is meant by Keynesian economic theory?
6. Discuss the stagflation of the 1970s and its impact on economic theory.
7. What were the pros and cons of Ronald Reagan's economic policies?
8. Discuss the differences and similarities of the economic policies of Clinton and George W. Bush.

Select Websites

This is the Website for the Office of Management and Budget.
http://www.omb.gov

Key Terms

Adam Smith
Arthur Pigou
budget deficit
business cycle
capital-intensive industries
David Hume
David Ricardo
demand side
downturn
Federal Reserve Board
fiscal policy
George Gilder
inflation rate

J. B. Say
John Maynard Keynes
John Stuart Mill
law of supply and demand
Milton Friedman
monetary policy
multiplier effect
Say's law
stagflation
supply side
Thomas Malthus
unemployment rate
upswing

CHAPTER 15

Continuity and Change in Public Policy

Most changes in public policies are incremental, involving small adjustments in existing policies. These changes are best explained within the context of state centered or incremental decision-making theories. Substantial changes occur episodically, after long periods of incremental change. Baumgartener and Jones referred to this pattern of change as punctuated equilibrium. The policy regime theory, which focuses on policy paradigms and power arrangements, has been useful in explaining this pattern of punctuated equilibrium. Almost every policy examined in the text was supported by a policy paradigm and by a definite power arrangement. Most major policy changes were preceded by stressors and later accompanied by changes in power arrangements and the policy paradigm. Although the text focused mainly on policy regime theory, many of the other policy theories were useful in explaining political behavior surrounding the policies. Most of the theories were useful in analyzing continuity and change in public policy.

This chapter reexamines public policy theories within the context of the policies examined in the text. First, it comments on the policy types and policy change. Second, it reexamines group, state centered, and elite theories of policy change. Third, it reexamines policy regime theory. Fourth, it looks at policy spillover, the impact of changes in one policy area on other policy areas. Finally, it comments on the future of public policy.

✦ *Policy Types and Policy Change*

The text identified several different types of policies, most notably, distributive, redistributive, protective regulatory, competitive regulatory, and morality policies. These policies were distinguishable by the level of visibility, degree of conflict, and patterns of policy making. Table 15.1 summarizes the expected differences among the several types of policies.

Theoretically, distributive policies disperse benefits broadly, attract broad-based support, generate little conflict, and operate within iron triangles. These policies tend to be non-ideological; that is, they rarely involve conflicts between liberals and conservatives. Redistributive policies presumably shift value from advantaged to disadvantaged groups, generate high levels of conflict, provoke ideological disputes—battles between liberals and conservatives—and operate within issue networks. Competitive regulatory policies regulate prices and entry into the market, facilitate competition, and operate like distributive policies. Protective regulatory policies protect citizens from unintended harms and operate like redistributive policies. Morality policies are intensely contentious, often involve religious groups with strong beliefs about right and wrong, and operate within political cauldrons in which political views seethe and occasionally erupt in violence.

Although most of the policies examined conform to the expectations of policy typology theory, there have been exceptions. Most of these exceptions can be explained by two factors. First, public policies sometimes have elements of both distributive and redistributive policies. For example, the school voucher is a redistributive program nested within education, a distributive policy. Vouchers shift resources from public schools to private schools, shift public attention from the issue of inequality in school funding, and threaten the influence of teachers unions and public school administrators. Vouchers are highly visible and provoke conflict along ideological lines, a redistributive policy nested in education, a distributive policy.

Second, public policies are sometimes fluid, moving from the redistributive policy arena to the distributive arena and back again. A good example of this type of movement is the Federal Communications Commission (FCC) rule changes of 2003. The FCC regulations have been competitive regulatory policies, but they behaved like distributive policies, involving little conflict, little visibility, and iron triangles. The rule changes provoked substantial conflict and moved the policy from the competitive regulatory/distributive arena to the protective regulatory/redistributive arena. The changes threatened the existence of the independent local broadcasting stations and the access to the airways of civil rights groups, religious organizations, and other grassroots organizations.

If policy theorists Ripley and Franklin (1991) are correct, public policies tend to move in a distributive direction. That is, they move away from contentious policy-making situations toward bargaining and compromise. This tendency arises from two factors. First, it arises out of the nature of the American political system to resolve conflicts through compromise and bargaining. Policy initiatives that incited violence in the 1960s operate as distributive policies today. For example, policies to desegregate public facilities generated severe conflict in the 1960s, but are well established and widely accepted today. For another example, Head Start and Title I programs of the Elementary and Secondary Education Act were once divided along ideological lines and hotly contested. Today, liberals and conservatives support these programs. Although there is a tendency for conflicts to wane over time, some policy issues are likely to remain contentious for some time, such as abortion, capital punishment, and vouchers.

TABLE 15.1				
Policy Type and Pattern of Policy Making				
Policy Type	**Level of Conflict/Visibility**	**Patterns of Policy Making**	**Role of Ideology**	**Examples**
Distributive	Low conflict and visibility	Iron triangles	Nonideological	Education
Redistributive	High conflict and visibility	Issue networks	Ideological	Social welfare
Competitive regulatory	Low conflict and visibility	Iron triangles	Nonideological	FCC—TV/radio
Protective regulatory	Medium conflict and visibility	Issue networks	Ideological	Environmental
Morality	Very high conflict and visibility	Policy cauldron	Ideological	Abortion

Second, the short life span of grassroots organizations pushes policies from the redistributive to the distributive arena. The death of an antipoverty grassroots organization often means the end of conflict over the policy. A good example of this is welfare, a redistributive policy that has involved little conflict because most grassroots antipoverty and welfare rights organizations were gone by 1996. The low level of conflict surrounding the 1996 welfare reform bill was attributable to weak opposition, the absence of an antipoverty coalition, the disappearance of pro-welfare organizations, and divisions among middle-class women's organizations. Opposition groups had died and others were weak and disorganized.

The policy regime theory with its focus on policy paradigms and power arrangements can offer some explanation for some of the exceptions and for the conflict. Conflict can be explained by competing policy paradigms and power arrangements. Vouchers generate conflict because the policy paradigms supporting public schools are still strong and because teachers unions, public school administrators, and other political interests threatened by vouchers still have political influence. Abortion will remain contentious because of mutually exclusive policy paradigms—one defining the issue in terms of a woman's right to choose and the other in terms of the fetus's right to life at any stage of development. Policy regime theory suggests that the conflict arises not from the policy type, but from the competing political paradigms and power blocs.

◈ *Theories of Policy Change*

Group Theory

Group theory is useful in explaining some of the dynamics of the policy changes examined in the text. Many of the recent changes in public policies have involved organized interest groups initially engaged in conflict, but later working through negotiation toward compromise. Examples of group conflict included fights between logging companies and environmental interests over deforestation policies, battles between labor unions and businesses over ergonomic regulations, and skirmishes between teachers unions and state chambers of commerce over charter schools. Examples of compromise include the Social Security Act of 1983 and the Medicare Act of 2003, which brought Democrats and Republicans together to formulate bipartisan bills. These bills also involved compromises between organizations like the AARP and the U.S. Chamber of Commerce and the pharmaceutical industry.

Organized interest groups have been involved in raising issues, presenting them to the public, and influencing the public agenda. They have also worked in getting issues on the government's agenda and pushing issues through Congress.

State Centered Theory

The state centered perspective focuses on the role of government officials as central players in the process of changing public policies. Indeed, government officials make public policies. In most cases, key officials operate as policy entrepreneurs, promoting policy proposals and mobilizing political resources to get the proposal enacted. These officials can be senators, representatives, or bureaucratic administrators. Presidents often play a major role in introducing and promoting new policy agendas. For example, Roosevelt was a policy entrepreneur advocating the New Deal, Johnson delivering the Great Society, Reagan promoting Social Security changes, and George W. Bush pushing the No Left Child Behind program and drug insurance for Medicare recipients. In a few cases, public officials solicit interest group support.

Government actors generally play a stronger role in making public policies when political forces outside government are stalemated, nonexistent, or substantially take one side of an issue. This point was evident in abortion policy. When pro-life and pro-choice political groups were deadlocked over the issue of partial-birth abortion, the Supreme Court determined the policy outcome. Of course, groups losing battles at one venue tend to shift the conflict to another. As pro-life groups lost ground in the judicial arena, they took their issue back to Congress. In the fall of 2003 they were able to secure the passage of a federal law prohibiting partial-birth abortions. Of course, this law is also likely to be presented to the Supreme Court.

Some of the quiet, less visible, and less controversial policy changes best fit the state centered model. A good example is the dismantling of the Interstate Commerce Commission and the Civil Aeronautics Board, which was supported by both conservative and liberal groups.

The innovation and diffusion model, discussed in Chapter 4, is a type of state centered perspective on policy change, particularly as state governments in the United States play a major role. This model assumes that new policies begin as an experiment within one state and spread to other states if the experiment is successful. Recent examples of this process of policy change include the spread of charter schools and welfare reform.

Nevertheless, state centered policy initiatives generally do not occur in a vacuum. Changes outside government set the stage for changes inside government. For example, the rise of the trucking industry and the economic decline of railroads preceded the elimination of the ICC.

Elite Theory

Elite theory is useful in looking at policy change. This theory assumes that business leaders or corporate interests dominate the policy-making process. Indeed, corporate leaders and business interests played a more substantial role in the policy changes examined in this text than the group or state centered models suggest. Corporate interests were involved with the formation of early 20th-century policies: vocational training, railroad regulations, fair trade policies, and conservation policies. Corporate leaders also played a direct role in forging New Deal policies.

There are two perspectives on corporate leaders and contemporary policies. David Vogel (1989) presented one perspective. In his book *Fluctuating Fortunes,* Vogel insisted that corporations lost power during the 1960s and 1970s, but began to reassert themselves beginning in the 1980s. William Hudson (2001), William Domhoff (1996), and Thomas Dye (2001) presented another perspective. They insist that corporations have always dominated the policy-making process, even during the 1960s and 1970s, and the only thing that has changed is the method of corporate dominance. They note three major changes since the 1970s.

First, the number of **political action committees (PACs)** increased substantially from the mid-1970s to the late 1990s, and the number of PACs representing corporations increased every year, from 89 in 1974 to 1,836 by 1998. The number of organized labor PACs increased as well, but at a much slower pace, from 201 in 1974 to 358 by 1998 (Dye 2001, 95). The number of trade association and ideological PACs also increased substantially. The total number of PACs increased primarily because of the *Federal Election Campaign Act of 1974,* which placed limits on the amount of money organizations could contribute to candidates and political parties for elections. Federal laws had already prohibited labor unions and corporations from making direct contributions to campaigns (see Table 15.2).

Second, direct business lobbying in Washington increased. Hudson identified three different types of lobbying organizations representing business: broad interest businesses, trade associations, and direct businesses. The broad interests include organizations such as the U.S. Chamber of Commerce, the Business Roundtable, the National Association of Manufacturers, and others. The trade associations include organizations such as the American Bankers Association and the National Association of Wheat Growers. The direct businesses include lobbyists for specific corporations such as General Motors.

Third, corporate interests are involved in agenda setting and policy formulation through policy-making networks of foundations and think tanks. Older foundations like the Carnegie, Rockefeller, or Ford foundations gave to charities, demonstration projects, or

TABLE 15.2

PACs Representing Corporate, Labor, Trade, and Ideological Organizations

PAC Represented	1974	1980	1988	1998
Corporate	14.6%	47.3%	42.5%	40.5%
Labor	33.1%	11.6%	8.3%	7.9%
Trade/professional	52.3%	22.6%	18.4%	19.8%
Ideological	—	14.7%	26.1%	27.8%
All others	—	3.8%	4.6%	4.0%
Total PACs	608	2,551	4,268	4,528

SOURCE: From *Top Down Policymaking* by Thomas R. Dye. Copyright © 2001 CQ Press, a division of Congressional Quarterly Inc. Orginally published by Chatham House. Reprinted by permission.

broad-based research: local libraries, museums, youth athletic projects, or cancer research. Now there has been a dramatic increase in the funneling of money by corporations and foundations into conservative think tanks, such as the CATO Institute, the Heritage Foundation, the American Enterprise Institute, the Hoover Institute, and the Hudson Institute, devoted to the policy interests of the corporate sector.

A number of trade institutes represent specific industries and conduct research with policy implications. Examples include the American Petroleum Institute, the Chemical Industry Institute of Toxicology, and the Tobacco Institute. For a long time the Tobacco Institute published studies challenging the belief that cigarettes cause cancer. These institutes focus on research that promotes the policy agendas of their respective industries.

Corporate and business interests have been directly involved in many ways with almost every policy area, except fertility control. A new organization representing a coalition of businesses impacted by clean air policies organized the Clean Air Working Group (CAWG), which was a major player in the formation of the Clean Air Act of 1990. Corporate interests have played a major role in shaping energy policy. The pharmaceutical and health insurance industries played important roles in the development of the Medicare drug policy. Although businesses were not initially involved in criminal justice policies, more businesses have become involved with the growing privatization of prisons.

Corporations and businesses are not always united. Major policy battles have erupted over divisions among business and corporate interests. Classic examples include fights over New Deal policy, Great Society programs, and recent battles over FCC rules. Nevertheless, elite theory maintains that business and corporate interests dominate the policy-making process.

✦ Policy Regime Theory

Most of the major changes in public policies can be explained within the context of the policy regime model, which is a mix of many policy theories: group, elite, state centered. Policy regime theory incorporates the punctuated equilibrium theory and it relies on policy paradigms and power arrangements to explain both long-term stability and major policy changes. A major feature of this theory borrows the notion of policy stressors from agenda theory to explain the initial process of policy change. The theory explains substantial changes in public policies in terms of stressors and shifts in power blocs and policy paradigms. A policy regime changes when power arrangements and policy paradigms shift.

Stressors

With few exceptions, stressors initiate the big policy changes. Stressors are major blows to the policy regime. They are like earthquakes or bombardments that destroy the foundations of the old policy regime. Stressors are followed by shifts in political power and policy paradigms. They included demographic shifts, mode of production changes, economic dislocation, catastrophic events, social movements, new technology, and international events. With few exceptions, at least one stressor has preceded every substantial change in public policy. The biggest and multiple policy changes involved the interaction of one or more stressors.

Demographic changes have to do with population movements, generally from one region to another or from one sector of the job market to another. Demographic changes impacted social welfare, health care, fertility control, civil rights, and education policies. For example, urbanization—the movement of large populations from rural areas to urban areas—is a demographic shift which has impacted several different policy regimes. Urbanization impacted the old social welfare regime by contributing to large numbers of poor and unemployed people living among strangers in large cities. The movement of African Americans from rural agricultural areas to urban industrial areas is a demographic shift that created more favorable conditions for the civil rights movement. The increase of people living past age 65 is a demographic shift that has impacted Social Security policy. In many cases demographic changes interact with other stressors, such as social movements in the case of the civil rights and women's rights movements.

Mode of production has to do with the way goods are produced, the instruments used in production, and the organization of production. Changes in the dominant mode of production impacted social welfare, civil rights, criminal justice, education, and competitive regulatory policies. Industrialization was a mode of production change, which stressed several policy regimes and created a need for new types of educational experiences, vocational training, and mass education. Industrialization generated pressures for a new type of criminal justice institution, the prison system. Industrialization facilitated the emergence of monopolies and created new pressures for antitrust and monopoly regulation policies.

Economic dislocation has to do with massive job losses. The Great Depression, with extremely high unemployment rates, is an example of economic dislocation, which impacted social welfare and economic policies. The high inflation and unemployment rates during the late 1970s, which impacted economic policies and contributed to the decline of the Keynesian era, is another example.

New technology has to do with new inventions, machines, electronic devices, drugs, medical procedures, and ways to manipulate nature or use the natural sciences. Advancement in medical technology transformed the single-practice doctor into the medical complex doctor and created pressures for the rise of private insurance and Medicare and Medicaid policies. Recently, the Internet has created new policy issues. One is the copyright protection of the film and music industries from pirates who make movies, DVDs, and CDs available for anyone to download off the Internet. Another Internet issue concerns child pornography. The development of cloning and stem cell technology has generated new medical ethics issues that have policy implications.

Catastrophic events are man-made or natural phenomena that destroy property and harm people. The destruction caused by hurricanes led to the creation of the Federal Emergence Management Agency (FEMA). The 9/11 catastrophe contributed to the passage of the USA PATRIOT Act and the creation of the Department of Homeland Security.

Social movements have to do with four factors: (1) the rapid increase in membership in established grassroots organizations, (2) the creation of new and more radical organizations, (3) the spread of these organizations nationwide, and (4) the passionate articulation of a social problem with proposed policy solutions. Social movements are implicated in periods of punctuated equilibrium and episodes of massive policy change. You have read in the text about several periods of social movements and massive policy change: the Progressive movement, the civil rights movement, and the environmental movement.

Every policy area we have discussed experienced stressors before major periods of policy change. Table 15.3 summarizes the policies and their stressors.

Stressors create conditions favorable for change; in themselves, they do not change public policy. Every major policy change is accompanied by changes in policy paradigms and

TABLE 15.3	
Public Policies and Stressors	
Policy Area	**Stressors**
Social welfare	Social movement, demographic changes, mode of production, and economic dislocation
Health care	Social movement, new technology, and demographic change
Civil rights	Social movement, mode of production, and demographic change
Environmental protection	Social movement and catastrophic event
Competitive regulatory	New technology, social movement, and mode of production change
Education	Mode of production and demographic change
Economic	Economic dislocation and social movement
Fertility control	Women's movement and demographic change
Criminal justice	Mode of production change and catastrophic event

power arrangements. It is the change in ideas and power arrangements, along with the role of policy entrepreneurs inside government, that produces the big changes. The New Deal, Great Society, civil rights, environmental protection, and many other major policy changes of the 20th century were all accompanied by shifts in the dominant policy paradigm and political power arrangements.

Policy Paradigm Change

Stressors facilitate changes in policy regimes by producing conditions conducive to policy paradigm changes and power shifts. A good example of a stressor facilitating a policy paradigm change is the Great Depression. This economic depression produced conditions that made the classical economic paradigm untenable and encouraged the emergence of the Keynesian economic paradigm.

Sometimes paradigm shifts can operate as stressors or catalysts for policy changes. A good example is the case of the state of Illinois and death penalty policy, which was discussed in Chapter 12. Ten years ago the overwhelming majority of the people in the state supported the death penalty—that is, they accepted the dominant death penalty paradigm. After the *Chicago Tribune* published a series of articles demonstrating the many ways that innocent people ended up on death row, public opinion and the views of the governor began to change. As a result of the power of the articles and formation of a policy paradigm against the death penalty, the governor declared a moratorium on the death penalty and commuted the sentences of the death row inmates. The large number of innocent people found on death row stressed the incarceration regime, but only in Illinois.

Almost every major change in a public policy was undergirded by a major policy paradigm shift. The recent changes in welfare, education, and criminal justice policies illustrate the point. The passage of the welfare reform bill of 1996 was moved along by changes in ideas about the problem of poverty and images of the poor. In the 1960s poverty was defined in terms of the need for government to assist women with children. The problem of the 1990s was defined in terms of the government fostering unhealthy and long-term dependency on welfare. The education problem of the 1960s was defined in terms of inadequate funding for schools, especially schools in low-income and minority areas. The education problem of the 1990s was defined in terms of excessively large governments and powerful teachers unions operating schools like a monopoly that denied parents the choices they would have in a private market. The criminal justice problem of the 1960s was defined in terms of the need to protect the rights of the accused from excessive and potentially abusive state power. The criminal justice problem of the 1990s was defined as a need to protect the public from predatory criminals. The manner in which the policy paradigm defines the policy problem shapes the public policy solution.

Power Shifts

Almost every major policy change was preceded by a shift in power arrangements. The easy passage of the welfare reform bill was made possible by the disintegration of the coalition of civil rights and antipoverty groups, followed by the emergence of a new and powerful conservative coalition of corporate and traditional conservative interests. This profound power shift helped to usher in the policy change. Inside Congress, the Republican leadership and conservative Democrats played key roles.

The passage of charter school and voucher bills illustrates a moderate power shift. Corporate and conservative alliance pushed for the new choice proposals, but they met opposition from teachers unions, school administrators, and school boards. The opposition was more successful in preventing the spread of vouchers than it was in opposing charter schools, which were regarded as less threatening to public schools. In most states, charter school proposals emerged as compromises between the two opposing forces (see Chapter 13).

The passage of mandatory sentencing, truth in sentencing, and three-strikes laws was also undergirded by a shift in power. In the 1960s civil rights, civil liberties, and prisoner rights organizations promoted policies protecting the rights of the accused. By the late 1990s, however, the rights organizations had declined and other groups—the National Rifle Association, prison guards, and private prison businesses—had emerged demanding stiffer penalties for crimes.

→ *Conflict and Stability in Public Policy*

Policy paradigms and power arrangements explain not only major policy changes, but also conflict and stability in public policies. As noted, the persistent conflict over abortion policy is explained by mutually exclusive policy paradigms and by the balance of power between pro-life and pro-choice coalitions. The absence of conflict over some aspects of criminal justice policies is explained by the dominance of a single policy paradigm and the political weakness of opposition groups.

Stability in most aspects of civil rights policy over the past 30 years is explained by the dominance of the civil rights paradigm, a general acceptance of current policies, and consistency among civil rights organizations.

The University of Michigan decisions (*Gratz v. Bollinger* and *Grutter v. Bollinger*) illustrate the role of policy paradigm and power arrangements in maintaining policy stability. The type of affirmative action policy used by Michigan's law school was well established in the *Bakke* decision of 1978, which operated as a policy paradigm. This paradigm provided stability to the policy and was the basis of the Michigan decision. Of course, power relations played a role; powerful interests, such as major corporations and the old civil rights coalition, supported the affirmative action program of Michigan's law school.

The Spillover Effect

Many of the most profound changes in specific policy areas occurred during the same time period—the Progressive, New Deal, and Great Society eras—as if policy change in one area spilled over into other policy areas. This **spillover effect** is produced several ways.

Multi-Issue Coalitions Crossing Party Lines

First, they occur when broad-based **multi-issue coalitions** cut across policy lines. A good example of a broad-based multi-issue coalition is the New Deal. The New Deal coalition consisted of labor unions, liberal religious groups, large cities, farmers, liberal industrial leaders, and the Deep South. This was one of the broadest coalitions in the 20th century and it supported a wide range of public policies: social welfare, labor, and economic. It was associated with the Democratic Party and was responsible for this party dominating Congress and the presidency for many years.

Interest Groups Crossing Policy Areas

Second, spillover occurs when groups in one policy area form alliances with interest groups in other policy areas. A good example of a cross-policy alliance is that of consumer interests, like Ralph Nader's Study Group, teaming up with environmental and labor organizations to protect the health and workplace safety of workers and to promote OSHA policies. Also, civil rights groups had formed alliances with antipoverty groups and labor organizations during the 1960s to promote social welfare and job-training policies. It is not uncommon for social movements to spread to many different policy areas.

Social Movements Crossing Policy Areas

A third form of cross-policy spillover arises when social movements in one policy area such as labor spill over into another policy area such as civil rights. In some cases social movements inspire action in another movement. For example, the civil rights movement of the 1960s inspired organizing among farm laborers.

Political Parties Crossing Policy Areas

Fourth, party realignments have played a role in producing the spillover effect. Political parties function to develop platforms of multiple policy proposals, cultivate alliances, and build broad-based coalitions of political interests in order to win elections. Consequently, political parties have played a key role in producing changes across policy areas, although these changes have been much smaller than expected and somewhat sporadic. Political parties have produced the greatest policy changes during periods of party realignments.

    Party realignments are characterized by major shifts in the alliances of social groups and political interests from one political party to another, by the emergence of a new dominant political party, and by the promotion of new sets of policy ideas and policy proposals by the new dominant party. A good example of party realignments is the election of Franklin D. Roosevelt in 1932. In this **realigning election,** social groups such as big city, labor, racial and ethnic minority, and low-income voters shifted their allegiance from the Republican Party to the Democratic Party. The Democratic Party emerged as the new dominant party. It forged the New Deal alliance and promoted New Deal policy proposals that represented a substantial break with the past. Other realigning elections include the election of Andrew Jackson in 1828, Abraham Lincoln in 1860, and William McKinley in 1896.

Realigning elections have occurred periodically, generally every 30 or 40 years and around the same time as a major social and economic upheaval. The realigning election of Lincoln brought the Civil War, the election of McKinley accompanied the Progressive movement, and the election of Roosevelt came with the Great Depression and the New Deal. These realignments brought massive policy changes in multiple policy areas.

The 1964 election in which Lyndon Johnson defeated Barry Goldwater was expected to be a realigning election. Others claimed that the realignment was expected but a dealignment occurred instead. **Party dealignments** are characterized by declines in voter turnout, increases in split-ticket voting (e.g., Democrats voting for Republican candidates), a rise in voter alienation (feeling that their votes don't count), and the appearance of no clear majority party. Of course, the 2004 presidential election pointed to an electorate more polarized, more intense, and more active than in past elections.

Nevertheless, today, political parties continue to promote multiple policy initiatives. Although each party appeals to a different coalition, several factors operate to limit the magnitude of the differences in the policy packages. These factors explain the remarkable stability in the policy-making process:

1. The tendency of the political system and public policy making to move away from conflict and toward bargaining and compromise.
2. The winner-take-all, two-party system that requires presidential candidates to appeal to the center and avoid extreme positions in order to maintain winning coalitions and to maximize their votes.

Programs established during the Roosevelt and the Johnson administrations still exist today. Nixon eliminated some of the War on Poverty programs established by President Johnson, but continued many of Johnson's job-training and community service programs. Carter continued the block grants established by Nixon, except that he targeted the *Comprehensive Employment and Training Act* and the Community Development Block Grant on cities with high rates of poverty and unemployment. Reagan promised to substantially reduce the size of government and eliminate many of the programs of the 1960s, yet they survived, sometimes in a different form.

Over time, the policy proposals of Democratic presidents seemed more like those proposed by Republican presidents. For example, Democratic President Bill Clinton's welfare policy proposals of 1996 were similar to those of Republican President Ronald Reagan in 1981, except that Clinton's were more conservative. Both proposals called for giving states more discretion over welfare money. Both Democratic President Bill Clinton and Republican President George W. Bush promoted charter schools. Both Republican President George H. W. Bush and Democratic President Bill Clinton opposed opening up the Arctic National Wildlife Refuge to oil exploration and drilling, although Republican George W. Bush supports this proposal. George W. Bush's Medicare pharmaceutical drug program increased federal spending at rates more characteristic of a liberal Democratic proposal. The point is that political parties offer different sets of public policy proposals, but the differences are not always substantial.

→ The Future of Public Policies

The bottom line is that public policies are not likely to change much in the future, absent a realigning election, a major social movement, an economic crisis or catastrophe. Public policy will continue to change incrementally and its direction may change from conservative to liberal and back again.

The policy issues and conflicts of today are likely to continue for the next decade. A number of issues are summarized in Table 15.4. Social welfare policies such as Social Security and child welfare will remain on the political agenda for some time. Social Security is a hot topic as post-World War II baby boomers approach retirement age, life expectancy and individual benefits increase, and some political leaders talk about a growing crisis in this popular program. President George W. Bush's proposal to allow taxpayers to use a small portion of their Social Security tax to invest in the private market has already generated political conflict. Because of the substantial political support for this program, any effort to make major changes is likely to provoke fierce political battles.

As single women with children are pushed out of welfare and into the job market, the need for low-cost and reliable child care will increase. Hence, day care, minimum wage, and child poverty could remain issues into the next decade. High health care costs will remain an important issue, especially as these costs continue to rise. These costs impact the old as well as the young, as Medicare Part B premiums increased by about 17 percent in the fall of 2004.

The growing number of families without any health care insurance is already a major political issue. In education policy, charter schools are well established and more states are likely to establish experimental voucher programs since the Supreme Court settled the con-

TABLE 15.4

Public Policy Issues of the 21st Century

Policy Area	Select Issues
Social welfare	Social Security, day care, minimum wage, child poverty
Health care	Health care costs, uninsured and underinsured families
Education	Inequality in funding, vouchers
Economic	National deficit and debt
Civil rights	Sexual orientation protection and gay/lesbian marriages
Environment	Global warming
Labor	Jobs exported overseas, ergonomics
Competitive regulatory	Antitrust, media consolidation, and access to the airwaves
Fertility control	Abortion
Criminal justice	Death penalty, incarceration

stitutional issue. Inequality in public education is likely to emerge periodically as an issue. In the controversial subject of morality policy, the issues likely to dog political leaders in the near future include partial-birth abortion, stem cell research, gay and lesbian marriage, and the death penalty. Same-sex marriage is already a hot political issue. It appears unlikely that any constitutional amendment banning these marriages would obtain the necessary two-thirds majority vote to pass Congress. However, the Supreme Court has just recently extended civil rights protection to people identifiable on the basis of sexual orientation.

Review Questions

1. Discuss the strengths and weaknesses of policy typology theory.
2. Explain why distributive policies have behaved like redistributive policies and vice versa. Provide examples to illustrate your point.
3. Discuss the role of stressors in explaining the major changes in public policies.
4. Discuss the role of decision theory and state centered theory in explaining policy change.
5. Use specific elite theorists to explain changes in public policies over the past 20 to 30 years.
6. Discuss the scope and limit of policy regime theory in explaining policy change.
7. What factors contribute to the spillover effect of policy change?
8. Why don't changes in political parties produce profound changes in public policies?

Select Websites

This is the Website for the Center for American Politics and Public Policy.
http://depts.washington.edu/ampol/vavbios/jonesbio.shtml

Key Terms

multi-issue coalition
party dealignment
party realignment

political action committees (PACs)
realigning election
spillover effect

References

Introduction

Baumgartner, Frank, and Bryan Jones. 1993. *Agendas and instability in American politics*. Chicago: University of Chicago Press.

Harris, Richard, and Sidney Milkis. 1996. *The politics of regulatory change: A tale of two agencies*. New York: Oxford University Press.

Lowi, Theodore. 1979. *The end of liberalism: The second republic of the United States*. New York: W.W. Norton.

Ripley, Randall B., and Grace A. Franklin. 1991. *Congress, the bureaucracy, and public policy*. Belmont, CA: Wadsworth.

Wilson, Carter. 2000. Policy regimes and policy change. *Journal of Public Policy* 20 (3): 247–74.

Chapter 1

Anderson, James. 1994. *Public policymaking: An introduction*. Boston: Houghton Mifflin.

Dye, Thomas. 1998. *Understanding public policy*. Upper Saddle River, NJ: Prentice Hall.

Easton, David. 1965. *A systems analysis of political life*. New York: Wiley.

Gerston, Larry, Cynthia Fraleigh, and Robert Schwab. 1988. *The regulated society*. Pacific Grove, CA: Brooks/Cole.

Janda, Kenneth, Jeffrey Berry, and Jerry Goldman. 2002. *The challenge of democracy*. Boston: Houghton Mifflin.

Johnson, Haynes. 1992. *Sleepwalking through history: America in the Reagan years*. New York: Doubleday.

Lester, James, and Joseph Stewart. 1996. *Public policy: An evolutionary approach*. New York: West Publishing.

Locke, John. 1690/1952. *The second treatise of government*. New York: Bobbs-Merrill.

Lowi, Theodore. 1979. *The end of liberalism: The second republic of the United States*. New York: W.W. Norton.

Mooney, Christopher, ed. 2001. *The public clash of private values: The politics of morality policy*. New York: Chatham House.

The National Election Studies Center for Political Studies, University of Michigan. *The NES Guide to Public Opinion and Electoral Behavior*. Graph 5A.5, 16SEO03. http://www.umich.edu

Nozick, Robert. 1974. *Anarchy, state and utopia*. New York: Basis Books.

O'Connor, Karen, and Larry Sabato. 2001. *American government: Continuity and change*. New York: Longman.

Patterson, Thomas. 2001. *The American democracy*. New York: McGraw-Hill.

Reagan, Ronald. 1989. Farewell address to the nation. *The Public Papers of President Ronald W. Reagan*. http://www.reagan.utexas.edu/resource/speeches/rrpubpap.asp

Rodgers, Harrell, and Michael Harrington. 1985. *Unfinished democracy: The American political system*. Glenview, IL: Scott, Foresman.

Tolchin, Susan. 1996. *The angry American: How voter rage is changing the nation*. Boulder, CO: Westview Press.

Chapter 2

Baumgartner, Frank, and Bryan Jones. 1993. *Agendas and Instability in American Politics*. Chicago: University of Chicago Press.

Bloom, Jack. 1987. *Class, race and the civil rights movement*. Bloomington: Indiana University Press.

Campbell, John. 1988. *Collapse of an industry: Nuclear power and the contradictions of U.S. policy*. Ithaca, NY: Cornell University Press.

Cobb, Roger, and Charles Elder. 1983. *Participation in American politics: The dynamics of agenda building*. Baltimore: Johns Hopkins University Press.

Dahl, Robert. 1970. *Who governs? Democracy and power in an American city*. New Haven: Yale University Press.

Domhoff, William. 1996. *State autonomy or class domination?* New York: Aldine de Gruyter.

———. 1998. *Who rules America: Power and politics in the year 2000*. Mountain View, CA: Mayfield Publishing Company.

Gusfield, Joseph. 1981. *The culture of public problems: Drinking, driving and symbolic order.* Chicago: University of Chicago Press.

Harris, Richard, and Sidney Milkis. 1996. *The politics of regulatory change: A tale of two agencies.* New York: Oxford University Press.

Hayes, Michael. 1992. *Incrementalism and public policy.* New York: Longman.

Hudson, William. 2004. *American democracy in peril: Eight challenges to America's future.* Washington DC: Congressional Quarterly Press.

Katznelson, Ira, and Mark Kesselman. 1975. *The politics of power: A critical introduction to American government.* New York: Harcourt Brace Jovanovich.

Kingdon, John. 1984. *Agendas, alternatives and public policies.* Boston: Little, Brown.

Lindblom, Charles. 1959. The science of muddling through. *Public Administration Review* 19, Spring.
———. 1978. *Politics and markets: The world's political-economic systems.* New York: Basic Books.

Mazmanian, Daniel, and Paul Sabatier. 1989. *Implementation and public policy.* Lanham, MD: University Press of America.

Mills, C. Wright. 1973. *The power elite.* London: Oxford University Press.

Piven, Frances, and Richard Cloward. 1979. *Poor people's movements: Why they succeed, how they fail.* New York: Vintage Books.

Rochefort, David, and Roger Cobb. 1994. *The politics of problem definition.* Lawrence: University of Kansas Press.

Schatschneider, E. E. 1975. *The semisovereign people: A realist's view of democracy in America.* Hinsdale, IL: Dryden Press.

Stone, Deborah. 1997. *Policy paradox and political reason.* Glenview, IL: Scott, Foresman/Little, Brown College Division.

Truman, David. 1993. *The governmental process: Political interests and public opinion.* Berkeley, CA: Institute of Governmental Studies.

Wilson, Carter. 2000. Policy regimes and policy change. *Journal of Public Policy,* 20(3): 247–74.

Wilson, James. 1989. *Bureaucracy: What government agencies do and why they do it.* New York: Basic Books.

Chapter 3

Blum, John, Bruce Catton, Edmond Morgan, Arthur Schlesinger, Kenneth Stampp, and C. Vann Woodward. 1968. *The national experience: A history of the United States.* New York: Harcourt, Brace.

Epstein, Lee, and Thomas Walker. 2000. *Constitutional law for a changing America: A short course.* Washington, DC: Congressional Quarterly Press.

Fried, Barbara. 1998. *The progressive assault on laissez faire: Robert Hale and the first law and economics movement.* Cambridge: Harvard University Press.

Jezer, Marty. 1982. *The dark ages: Life in the United States, 1945–1960.* Boston: South End Press.

Keynes, John. 1936. *The general theory of employment, interest, and money.* London: Macmillan.

Kolko, Gabriel. 1963. *The triumph of conservatism: A re-interpretation of American history, 1900–1916.* New York: Free Press.

Moss, David. 1996. *Socializing security: Progressive-era economists and the origins of American social policy.* Cambridge: Harvard University Press.

Pressman, Jeffrey, and Aaron Wildavsky. 1973. *Implementation: How great expectations in Washington are dashed in Oakland; Or why it's amazing that federal programs work at all.* Berkeley: University of California Press.

Schlesinger, Arthur. 1959. *The coming of the New Deal.* Boston: Houghton Mifflin.

Smith, Adam. 1776/1952. *An inquiry into the nature and causes of the wealth of nations.* Chicago: University of Chicago Press.

Tolchin, Susan, and Martin Tolchin. 1983. *Dismantling America: The rush to deregulate.* New York: Oxford University Press.

Vig, Norman, and Michael Kraft. 1984. *Environmental policy in the 1980s: Reagan's new agenda.* Washington, DC: Congressional Quarterly Press.

Chapter 4

Derthick, Martha. 1972. *New towns in towns: Why a federal program failed.* Washington, DC: Urban Institute Press.

Heclo, Hugh. 1992. Issue networks and the executive establishment. In *Public administration: Concepts and cases,* edited by Richard Stillman II (pages 441–450). Boston: Houghton Mifflin.

Janda, Kenneth, Jeffrey Berry, and Jerry Goldman. 2002. *The challenge of democracy.* Boston: Houghton Mifflin.

Krutz, Glen. 2001. *Hitching a ride: Omnibus legislating in the U.S. Congress.* Columbus: Ohio State University Press.

Light, Paul. 1995. *Still artful work: The continuing politics of Social Security reform.* New York: McGraw-Hill.

Neustadt, Richard. 1986. *Presidential powers: The politics of leadership from FDR to Carter.* New York: Macmillan.

O'Brien, David. 1993. *Storm center: The Supreme Court in American politics.* New York: W.W. Norton.

Ripley, Randall, and Grace A. Franklin. 1984. *Congress, the bureaucracy, and public policy.* Homewood, IL: Dorsey Press.

Sharkansky, Ira. 1978. *The maligned states: Policy accomplishments, problems and opportunities.* New York: McGraw-Hill.

Sinclair, Barbara. 2000. *Unorthodox lawmaking: New legislative processes in the U.S. Congress.* Washington, DC: Congressional Quarterly Press.

Wildavsky, Aaron. 1995. The two presidents. In *Public policy: The essential readings,* edited by Stella Theodoulou and Matthew Cahn. Upper Saddle River, NJ: Prentice Hall.

Chapter 5

Anderson, Martin. 1978. *Welfare: The political economy of welfare reform in the United States.* Stanford, CA: Hoover Institution Press.

Banfield, Edward. 1974. *The unheavenly city.* Boston: Little, Brown.

DiNitto, Diana, and Thomas Dye. 1987. *Social welfare: Politics and public policy.* Englewood Cliffs, NJ: Prentice Hall.

Domhoff, William. 1996. *State autonomy or class dominance? Case studies on policy making in America.* New York: Aldine De Gruyter.

Federickson, George. 1971. *Black image in the white mind: The debate on Afro-American character and destiny, 1817–1914.* New York: Harper & Row.

George, Henry. 1973. *Progress and poverty: An inquiry into the cause of industrial depressions and of increase of want with increase of wealth.* Garden City, NY: Doubleday.

Gilder, George. 1981. *Wealth and poverty.* New York: Basic Books.

Gilens, Martin. 1999. *Why Americans hate welfare: Race, media and the politics of antipoverty programs.* Chicago: University of Chicago Press.

Gordon, Linda. 1994. *Pitied but not entitled: Single mothers and the history of welfare 1890–1935.* New York: Free Press.

Harrington, Michael. 1962. *The other America: Poverty in the United States.* New York: Macmillan.

Heclo, Hugh. 1992. Issue networks and the executive establishment. In *Public administration: Concepts and cases,* edited by Richard Stillman II. Boston: Houghton Mifflin.

Hernstein, Richard, and Charles Murray. 1994. *The bell curve: Intelligence and class structure in American life.* New York: Free Press.

Klebanow, Diana, Franklin Jonas, and Ira Leonard. 1997. *Urban legacy: The story of America's cities.* New York: The New American Library Inc.

Lewis, Oscar. 1961. *The children of Sanchez.* New York: Random House.

Liebow, Elliot. 1967. *Tally's corner: A study of Negro streetcorner men.* Boston: Little, Brown.

Light, Paul. 1995. *Still artful work: The continuing politics of Social Security reform.* New York: McGraw-Hill.

Moynihan, Daniel. 1973. *The politics of a guaranteed income: The Nixon administration and the family assistance plan.* New York: Vintage Books.

Moynihan, Patrick. 1987. *Family and nation.* San Diego, CA: Harcourt Brace Jovanovich.

Murray, Charles. 1984. *Losing ground: American social policy, 1950–1980.* New York: Basic Books.

Myrdal, Gunnar. 1948/1975. *An American dilemma: The Negro problem and modern democracy.* New York: Harper & Brothers.

Patterson, James. 1994. *America's struggle against poverty: 1900–1990.* Cambridge: Harvard University Press.

Piven, Frances, and Richard Cloward. 1979. *Poor people's movements: Why they succeed, how they fail.* New York: Vintage Books.

———. 2001. Forward. In *Workfare states,* edited by Jamie Peck. New York: The Guilford Press.

Randall, Ronald. 1979. Presidential power versus bureaucratic intransigence: The influence of the Nixon administration on welfare policy. *The American Political Science Review,* 73(3).

Rodgers, Harrell. 1979. *Poverty amid plenty: A political and economic analysis.* Reading, MA Addison-Wesley.

Rose, Nancy. 1995. *Work fair or fair work: Women, welfare and government work programs.* New Brunswick, NJ: Rutgers University Press.

Sidel, Ruth. 1996. *Keeping women and children last: America's war on the poor.* New York: Penguin Books.

Skocpol, Theda. 1992. *Protecting soldiers and mothers: The political origins of social policy in the United States.* Cambridge, MA: Belknap Press of Harvard University Press.

Trattner, Walter. 1999. *From poor law to welfare state: A history of social welfare in America.* New York: Free Press.

U.S. Census Bureau. 2003. *Statistical abstract of the United States.* http://www.census.gov/prod/www/statistical-abstract-us.html

Wilson, William J. 1987. *The truly disadvantaged: The inner city, the underclass, and public policy.* Chicago: University of Chicago Press.

Chapter 6

Anderson, Gerald, and Jean-Pierre Poullier. 1999. Health spending, access, and outcomes: Trends in industrialized countries. *Health Affairs, 18*(3).

Bonser, Charles, Eugene McGregor, and Clinton Oster. 1996. *Policy choices and public action.* Upper Saddle River, NJ: Prentice Hall.

Burwell, Brian, Steve Eiken, and Date Sredl. 2002. *Medicaid long term care expenditures for FY 2001.* Research Memo for Medstat, May 10. Cambridge, MA. http://www.hcbs.org/

Calkins, David, Rushika Fernandopulle, and Bradley Marino. 1995. *Health care policy.* Cambridge, MA: Blackwell Science.

Centers for Disease Control and Prevention. 2002. *Racial and ethnic disparities in infant mortality rates—60 largest U.S. cities.* http://www.cdc.gov/ (accessed January 27, 2005).

Coughlin, Teresa, Leighton Ku, and John Holahan. 1994. *Medicaid since 1980: Costs, coverage, and the shifting alliance between the federal government and the states.* Washington, DC: Urban Institute Press.

Executive Summary of the Health Security Act. 1993. *Health care that's always there.* http://www.ibiblio.org/nhs/executive/X-summary-toc.html

Freund, Peter, and Meredith McGuire. 1999. *Health, illness, and the social body: A critical sociology.* Upper Saddle River, NJ: Prentice Hall.

Graig, Laurene. 1993. *Health of nations: An international perspective on U.S. health care reform.* Washington, DC: Congressional Quarterly Press.

Kart, Cary S. 2001. *The realities of aging.* Boston: Allyn and Bacon.

Klebanow, Diana, Franklin Jonas, and Ira Leonard. 1997. *Urban legacy: The story of America's cities.* New York: The New American Library Inc.

LeBow, Robert. 2003. *Health care meltdown: Confronting the myths and fixing our failing system.* Chambersburg, PA: Alan C. Hood.

McKenna, George. 1998. *The drama of democracy.* New York: McGraw-Hill.

Navarro, Vicente. 1993. *Dangerous to your health: Capitalism in health care.* New York: Monthly Review Press.

Patel, Kant, and Mark Rushefsky. 1995. *Health care politics and policy in America.* Armonk, NY: M. E. Sharpe.

Peterson, Mark. 1998. The politics of health care policy: Overreaching in the age of polarization. In *The social divide: Political parties and the future of activist government,* edited by Margaret Weir. Washington, DC: Brookings Institution Press.

United States Census Bureau, Statistical Abstracts of the United States. 2004/05.

United States Congressional Budget Office Historical Budget Data. 2004. http://www.cbo.gov/ (accessed January 27, 2005).

Chapter 7

Adorno, Theodore et al. 1950. *The authoritarian personality.* New York: Harper.

Allport, Gordon. 1979. *The nature of prejudice.* Reading, MA: Addison-Wesley Publishing Company.

Baldwin, James. 1953/1969. *Go tell it on the mountain.* New York: A Dell Book.

Bloom, Jack. 1987. *Class, race, and the civil rights movement.* Bloomington, IN: Indiana University Press.

Bullock, Charles, and Charles Lamb. 1984. *Implementation of civil rights policy.* Monterey, CA: Brooks/Cole.

Clark, Kenneth. 1965. *Dark ghetto.* New York: Harper & Row.

Du Bois W.E.B. 1946/1976. *The world and Africa.* New York: International Publishers.

Ellison, Ralph. 1952/1972. *Invisible man.* New York: Vintage Books.

Foster, James, and Susan Leeson. 1998. *Constitutional law cases in context: Civil rights and civil liberties.* Upper Saddle River, NJ: Prentice Hall.

Fromm, Eric. 1970. *Escape from freedom.* New York: Avon.

Genovesse, Eugene. 1965. *Economy of slavery: Studies in the economy and society of the slave South.* New York: Pantheon Books.

Hurston, Zora Neale. 1937/1978. *Their eyes were watching God.* Urbana: University of Illinois Press.

Kousser, J. Morgan. 1974. *The shaping of southern politics: Suffrage restriction and the establishment of the one-party South, 1880–1910.* New Haven: Yale University Press.

Myrdal, Gunnar. 1944. *An American dilemma: The Negro problem and modern democracy.* New York: Harper & Brothers.

O'Brien, David. 2003. *Constitutional law and politics: Civil rights and civil liberties.* New York: W.W. Norton.

Smedley, Audrey. 1993. *Race in North America: Origin and evolution of a world view.* Boulder, CO: Westview Press.

Snowden, Frank. 1991. *Before color prejudice: The ancient view of blacks.* Cambridge, MA: Harvard University Press.

Stampp, Kenneth. 1956. *The peculiar institution: Slavery in the ante-bellum South.* New York: Alfred Knopf.

U.S. Civil Rights Commission. 2001. *Voting irregularities in Florida during the 2000 presidential election.* Washington, DC: U.S. Government Printing Office.

Wright, Richard. 1940/1989. *Native son.* New York: Perennial Library.

Chapter 8

Boulding, Kenneth. 1966. The economics of the coming spaceship earth. In *Environmental quality in a growing economy,* edited by Henry Jarret. Baltimore: Johns Hopkins University Press.

Brown, Michael. 1981. *Laying waste: The poisoning of America by toxic chemicals.* New York: Washington Square Press.

Bryner, Gary. 1993. *Blue skies, green politics: The Clean Air Act of 1990.* Washington, DC: Congressional Quarterly Press.

Carson, Rachel. 1962/1994. *Silent spring.* New York: Houghton Mifflin.

Clarke, Jeane, and Hanna Cortner. 2002. *The state and nature: Voices heard, voices unheard in America's environmental dialogue.* Upper Saddle River, NJ: Prentice Hall.

Crenson, Matthew. 1971. *The un-politics of air pollution: A study of non-decisionmaking in the cities.* Baltimore: Johns Hopkins University Press.

Davis, Angela Y. 1983. *Women, race, and class.* New York: Random House Inc.

Davis, David. Unpublished manuscript. *Planning for the apocalypse.*

Dowie, Mark. 1996. *Losing ground: American environmentalism at the close of the twentieth century.* Cambridge, MA: MIT Press.

Drew, Christopher, and Richard Oppel Jr. 2004. How industry won the battle of pollution control at EPA. *New York Times,* March 6.

Esposito, John. 1970. *Vanishing air.* New York: Grossman.

Gonzalez, George. 2001. *Corporate power and the environment: The political economy of U.S. environmental policy.* New York: Rowman and Littlefield.

Gore, Al. 1994. Introduction. In *Silent Spring,* edited by Rachel Carson. New York: Houghton Mifflin.

Jones, Charles. 1976. Speculative augmentation in federal air pollution policy-making. In *Cases in Public Policy-Making,* edited by James Anderson. New York: Holt, Rinehart and Winston.

Kraft, Michael. 1996. *Environmental policy and politics.* New York: HarperCollins.

Marsh, George Perkins. 1864. *Man and nature: Or physical geography as modified by human action.* London: Sampson Low, Son and Marston.

Muir, John. 1912. *The yosemite.* New York: The Century Company.

National Resource Defense Council. 2001. *Bush seeks to open Arctic National Wildlife Refuge to oil development.* January 20.

National Resource Defense Council. 2003. *Superfund cleanups lag for third straight year.* November 4.

Rosenbaum, Walter. 1991. *Environmental politics and policy.* Washington, DC: Congressional Quarterly Press.

Ryan, Dave. 2003. *Forty high-priority superfund sites cleaned up.* EPA News Release, November 4. http://www.epa.gov/superfund/news/pr-110403.htm

Smith, Zachary. 2000. *The environmental policy paradox.* Upper Saddle River, NJ: Prentice Hall.

Switzer, Jacqueline. 1994. *Environmental politics: Domestic and global dimensions.* New York: St. Martin's Press.

Tokar, Brian. 1997. *Earth for sale: Reclaiming ecology in the age of corporate greenwash.* Boston: South End Press.

Tolchin, Susan, and Martin Tolchin. 1983. *Dismantling America: The rush to deregulate.* New York: Oxford University Press

Vig, Norman. 1984. The President and the environment. Revolution or retreat? In *Environmental policy in the 1980s: Reagan's new agenda,* edited by Norman Vig and Michael Kraft. Washington DC: Congressional Quarterly Inc.

Vig, Norman and Michael Kraft, Eds. 1984. *Environmental policy in the 1980s: Reagan's new agenda.* Washington DC: Congressional Quarterly Inc.

Vogel, David. 1989. *Fluctuating fortunes: The political power of business in America.* New York: Basic Books.

Wargo, John. 1996. *Our children's toxic legacy: How science and law fail to protect us from pesticides.* New Haven: Yale University Press.

Chapter 9

Anglim, Christopher. 1997. *Contemporary legal issues: Labor, employment, and the law.* Santa Barbara, CA: ABC-CLIO.

Brooks, Thomas R. 1971. *Toil and trouble.* New York: Dell Publishing.

Cobb, Roger, and Charles Elder. 1983. *Participation in American politics: The dynamics of agenda building.* Baltimore: Johns Hopkins University Press.

Edsall, Thomas B. 1992. *Chain reaction: The impact of race, rights, and taxes on American politics.* With Mary Edsall. New York: W.W. Norton.

Eisenbrey, Ross, and Jared Bernstein. 2003. *Eliminating the right to overtime pay: Department of Labor proposal means lower pay, longer hours for millions of workers.* Briefing paper, Economic Policy Institute.

Foner, Philip. 1982. *Organized labor and the black worker 1619–1981.* New York: International Publishers.

Gerston, Larry, Cynthia Fraleigh, and Robert Schwab. 1988. *The deregulated society.* Pacific Grove, CA: Brooks/Cole.

Gitelman, H. M. 1988. *Legacy of the Ludlow massacre: A chapter in American industrial relations.* Philadelphia: University of Pennsylvania Press.

Greider, William. 1993. *Who will tell the people: The betrayal of American democracy.* New York: Simon & Schuster.

Ivins, Molly, and Lou Dubose. 2003. *Bushwhacked: Life in George W. Bush's America.* New York: Random House.

Johnson, Haynes. 1991. *Sleepwalking through history: America in the Reagan years.* New York: Doubleday.

Meier, Kenneth. 1985. *Regulation: Politics, bureaucracy, and economics.* New York: St. Martin's Press.

Meiers, August, and Elliott Rudwick. 1973. *CORE: A study in the civil rights movement, 1942–1968.* New York: Oxford University Press.

Piven, Frances, and Richard Cloward. 1979. *Poor people's movements: Why they succeed, how they fail.* New York: Vintage Books.

Robertson, David. 2000. *Capital, labor, and state: The battle for American labor markets from the Civil War to the New Deal.* New York: Rowman and Littlefield.

Shafritz, Jay M., and E. W. Russell. 2000. *Introducing public administration.* New York: Longman.

Skrzycki, Cindy. 2003. *The regulators: Anonymous power brokers in American politics.* New York: Rowman and Littlefield.

Statistical Abstract of the United States. 2002. Washington D.C.: The United States Department of Commerce, U.S. Census Bureau.

Tolchin, Susan, and Martin Tolchin. 1983. *Dismantling America: The rush to deregulate.* New York: Oxford University Press.

U.S. Census Bureau. 2003. *Statistical abstract of the United States.* http://www.census.gov/prod/www/statistical-abstract-us.html

Widick, B. J. 1989. *Detroit: City of race and class violence.* Detroit, MI: Wayne State University Press.

Zinn, Howard. 1990. *A people's history of the United States.* New York: Harper Perennial.

Chapter 10

Bagdikian, Ben. 2000. *Media monopoly.* Boston: Beacon Press.

Bork, Robert. 1978. *The antitrust paradox.* New York: Basic Books.

Brock, Gerald. 1994. *Telecommunications policy for the information age: From monopoly to competition.* Cambridge: Harvard University Press.

Comstock, George. 1991. *Television in America.* Newbury Park, CA: Sage.

Davies, Andrew. 1994. *Telecommunications and politics: The decentralized alternative.* New York: St. Martin's Press.

Dempsey, Paul, and William Thoms. 1986. *Law and economic regulation in transportation.* Westport, CT: Quorum Books.

Digital TV Project. 2003. Who controls the media. http://www.nowfoundation.org/

Dooley, Frank, and William Thoms. 1994. *Railroad law: A decade after deregulation.* Westport, CT: Quorum Books.

Dunbar, John, and Aron Pilhofer. 2003. Big radio rules in small market: A few behemoths dominate medium-sized cities throughout the U.S. The Center for Public Integrity. http://www.openairwaves.org/telecom/ (accessed January 27, 2003).

Fallow, James. 2003. The age of Murdoch. *Atlantic Monthly* (82–98), September.

Fellmeth, Robert. 1970. *The Interstate Commerce Commission: The public interest and the ICC.* New York: Grossman.

Fox, Loren. 2003. *Enron: The rise and fall.* Wiley.

Kolko, Gabriel. 1965. *Railroads and regulations, 1877–1916.* Princeton, NJ: Princeton University Press.

Krasnow, Erwin, Lawrence Longley, and Herbert Terry. 1982. *The politics of broadcast regulations.* New York: St. Martin's Press.

Kuttner, Robert. 1997. *Everything for sale: The virtues and limits of markets.* New York: Alfred Knopf.

Lowi, Theodore. 1979. *The end of liberalism: The second republic of the United States.* New York: W.W. Norton & Company, Inc.

Meier, Kenneth. 1985. *Regulation: Politics, bureaucracy, and economics.* New York: St. Martin's Press, Inc.

Nader, Ralph. 1965. *Unsafe at any speed: The designed-in dangers of the American automobile.* New York: Grossman.

Piven, Frances Fox, and Richard A. Cloward. 1979. *Poor people's movements: Why they succeed, how they fail.* New York: Vintage Books.

Ray, William. 1965. *FCC: The ups and downs of radio-TV regulations.* Ames: Iowa State University Press.

Shaw, James. 1998. *Telecommunications deregulation.* Boston: Artech House.

Stone, Alan. 1977. *Economic regulation and the public interest: The Federal Trade Commission in theory and practice.* Ithaca, NY: Cornell University Press.

Stone, Richard D. 1991. *The Interstate Commerce Commission and the railroad industry: A history of regulatory policy.* New York: Praeger.

Thomas, William E. 1986. *Law and economic regulation in transportation.* New York: Quorum Books.

U.S. Census Bureau. 2003/04, 2004/05. *Statistical abstract of the United States.* http://www.census.gov/prod/www/statistical-abstract-us.html

Chapter 11

Bork, Robert. 1999. Inconvenient lives. In *Taking sides: Clashing views on controversial political issues,* edited by George McKenna and Stanley Feingold. New York: McGraw-Hill; Guilford, CT: Dushkin.

Craig, Barbara Hinkson, and David M. O'Brien. 1993. *Abortion and American politics.* Chatham, NJ: Chatham House.

Davis, Angela. 1981. *Women, race and class.* New York: Random House.

———. 1983. *Women, race and class.* New York: Vintage Books.

Friedan, Betty. 1963. *The feminine mystique.* New York: Norton.

Gordon, Mary. 2003. A moral choice. In *Taking sides: Clashing views on controversial political issues,* edited by George McKenna and Stanley Feingold. New York: McGraw-Hill; Guilford, CT: Dushkin.

Jones, Rachel, Jacqueline Darroch, and Stanley Henshaw. 2002. Patterns in the socioeconomic characteristics of women obtaining abortions in 2000–2001. *Perspectives on Sexual and Reproductive Health* 34(5), September–October.

Luker, Kristin. 1984. *Abortion and the politics of motherhood.* Berkeley: University of California Press.

———. 1997. *Dubious conceptions: The politics of teenage pregnancy.* Cambridge: Harvard University Press.

McFarlane, Deborah R., and Kenneth J. Meier. 2001. *The politics of fertility control: Family planning and abortion policies in the American states.* New York: Chatham House.

O'Brien, David. 2003. *Constitutional law and politics: Civil rights and civil liberties.* New York: W.W. Norton.

Raufu, Abiodun. 2002. *Unsafe abortions cause 20,000 deaths a year in Nigeria.* BMJ Publishing Group Ltd. http://www.bmj.bmjjournals.com.

Roberts, Dorothy. 1999. *Killing the black body: Race, reproduction, and the meaning of liberty.* New York: Vintage Books.

Schiff, David. 2002. *Abortion in Judaism.* Cambridge, UK: Cambridge University Press.

U.S. Census Bureau. 2004/05. *Statistical abstract of the United States.* http://www.census.gov/prod/www/statistical-abstract-us.html

Valente, Marcela. 2002. *Argentina: Leap in unsafe abortions.* Inter press Service. http://www.corpwatch.org.

World Health Organization. 2004. *Unsafe abortion: Global and regional estimates of the incidence of unsafe abortion and associated mortality.* Geneva, Switzerland: World Health Organization.

Chapter 12

Auletta, Ken. 1983. *The underclass.* New York: Vintage Books.

Barker, Lucius, Twiley Barker, Michael Combs, Kevin Lyles, and H. W. Perry Jr. 1999. *Civil liberties and the Constitution: Cases and commentaries.* Upper Saddle River, NJ: Prentice Hall.

Beccaria, Cesare. 1764/1963. *On crimes and punishments.* Indianapolis: Bobbs-Merrill.

Bollinger, Winfield. 1990. Federal drug abuse policy: The evolving role of the national government in the criminal justice system. *Ohio Journal of Economics and Politics,* 4(2).

Burton-Rose, Daniel, Dan Pens, and Paul Wright, Ed. 1998. *The celling of America: An inside look at the U.S. prison industry.* Monroe, ME: Common Courage Press.

Camejo, Peter. 1976. *Racism, revolution, reaction 1861–1877.* New York: Monad.

Currie, Elliot. 1985. *Confronting crime: An American challenge.* New York: Pantheon Books.

Davis, Mike. 1996. The politics of super incarceration. In *Criminal injustice: Confronting the prison crisis,* edited by Elihu Rosenblatt. Boston: South End Press.

Donziger, Steven, Ed. 1996. *The real war on crime: The report of the National Criminal Justice Commission.* New York: Harper Perennial.

Ehlers, Scott, Vincent Schiraldi, and Jason Ziedenberg. 2004. Still striking out: Ten years of California's three strikes. Policy report, Justice Policy Institute.

Evers, Williamson. 1996. *Victims rights, restitution and retribution.* Oakland, CA: An Independent Institute.

Foucault, Michel. 1979. *Discipline and punishment.* New York: Vintage Press.

Inciardi, James. 2005. *Criminal justice.* New York: Harcourt Brace Jovanovich.

Irwin, Hohn, and James Austin. 1997. *It's about time: America's imprisonment binge.* Belmont, CA: Wadsworth.

Kappeler, Victor, Mark Blumberg, and Gary Potter. 1996. *The mythology of crime and criminal justice.* Prospect Heights, IL: Waveland Press.

Mauer, Marc. 1999. *Race to incarcerate.* New York: The New Press.

Murray, Charles. 1984. *Losing ground: American social policy, 1950–1980.* New York: Basic Books.

Pens, Dan. 1998. The California prison guards' union: A potent political interest group. In *The celling of America: An inside look at the U.S. prison industry,* edited by Daniel Burton-Rose with Dan Pens and Paul Wright. Monroe, ME: Common Courage Press.

Robertson, David. 2000. *Capital, labor, and state: The battle for American labor markets from the Civil War to the New Deal.* New York: Rowman & Littlefield Publishers, Inc.

Shichor, David. 1995. *Punishment for profit: Private/public concerns.* Thousand Oaks, CA: Sage.

Silverstein, Ken. 1998. America's private gulag. In *The celling of America: An inside look at the U.S. prison industry,* edited by Daniel Burton-Rose with Dan Pens and Paul Wright. Monroe, ME: Common Courage Press.

Smit, Dirk van Zyle, and Frieder Dunkel. 1999. *Prison labour: Salvation or slavery?: International perspectives.* Aldershot, UK: Ashgate.

U.S. Census Bureau. 2004/05. *Statistical abstract of the United States.* http://www.census.gov/prod/www/statistical-abstract-us.html

U.S. Department of Justice, Bureau of Justice Statistics. 2004. *Sourcebook of criminal justice statistics.*

Wilson, William Julius. 1987. *The truly disadvantaged: The inner city, the underclass, and public policy.* Chicago: University of Chicago Press.

Wisely, Willie. 1998. Who goes to prison? In *The celling of America: An inside look at the U.S. prison industry,* edited by Daniel Burton-Rose with Dan Pens and Paul Wright. Monroe, ME: Common Courage Press.

Wolfgang, Marvin, Robert Figlio, and Thorsten Selling. 1972. *Delinquency in a birth cohort.* Chicago: University of Chicago Press.

Wright, Paul. 1998. Three strikes racks 'em up. In *The celling of America: An inside look at the U.S. prison industry,* edited by Daniel Burton-Rose with Dan Pens and Paul Wright. Monroe, ME: Common Courage Press.

Chapter 13

Berliner, David, and Bruce Biddle. 1995. *The manufactured crisis: Myths, fraud, and the attack on America's public schools.* Reading, MA: Perseus Books.

Bowles, Samuel, and Herbert Gintis. 1977. *Schooling in capitalist America: Educational reform and the contradictions of economic life.* New York: Basic Books.

Ciotti, Paul. 1998. Money and school performance: Lessons from the Kansas City desegregation experiment. *Policy Analysis* 298, March.

Education and School Finance. 2002. Ohio Chamber of Commerce. http://www.ohiochamber.com

Fischer, Frank. 1995. *Evaluating public policy.* Chicago: Nelson-Hall.

Friedman, Milton. 1962. *Capitalism and freedom.* Chicago: University of Chicago Press.

Friedman, Milton, and Rose Friedman. 1981. *Free to choose: A personal statement.* New York: Avon Books.

Gould, Steven. 1981. *The mismeasure of man.* New York: W.W. Norton.

Green, Philip. 1981. *The pursuit of inequality.* New York: Pantheon Books.

Herrnstein, Richard, and Charles Murray. 1994. *The bell curve: Intelligence and class structure in American life.* New York: Free Press.

Ingersoll, Robert. 1890/2003. Our school. Speech given in New York, September 7. http://www.infidels.org/library/historical/robert_ingersoll/

Kamin, Leon. 1995. Lies, damned lies, and statistics. In *The bell curve debate: History, documents, opinions,* edited by R. Jacoby and N. Glauberman. New York: Times Books.

Kousser, J. Morgan. 2000. What light does the Civil Rights Act of 1875 shed on the Civil Rights Act of 1964? In *Legacies of the 1964 Civil Rights Act,* edited by Bernard Gofman. Charlottesville: University Press of Virginia.

Kozol, Jonathan. 1991. *Savage inequalities: Children in America's schools.* New York: Harper Perennial.

Moe, Terry, and John Chub. 1990. *Politics, markets and America's schools.* Washington, DC: Brookings Institution.

Molnar, Alex. 2000. *Vouchers, class size reduction and student achievement: Considering the evidence.* Bloomington, IN: Phi Delta Kappa.

National Commission on Excellence in Education. 1983. *A nation at risk: Imperative for educational reform.* Washington, DC: Author.

Rodgers, Harrell. 1979. *Poverty amid plenty: A political and economic analysis.* Reading, MA: Addison-Wesley Pub. Co.

Rouse, Cecilia. 1998. Private school vouchers and student achievement: An evaluation of the Milwaukee parental choice program. *The Quarterly Journal of Economics,* 113(2).

Saporito, Salvatore, and Annette Lareau. 1999. School selection as a process: The multiple dimensions of race in framing educational choice. *Social Problems* 46(3): 418–39.

Schafer, G. 2001. [Conference paper].

Spring, Joel. 2005. *The American school 1642–2004.* New York: McGraw-Hill.

Chapter 14

Bartley, Robert. 1992. *The seven fat years: And how to do it again.* New York: Free Press.

Bluestone, Barry, and Bennett Harrison. 2000. *Growing prosperity: The battle for growth with equity in the twenty-first century.* Boston: Houghton Mifflin.

Blum, John, Bruce Catton, Edmond Morgan, Arthur Schlesinger, Kenneth Stampp, and C. Vann Woodward. 1968. *The national experience: A history of the United States.* New York: Harcourt, Brace.

Center for Popular Economics. 1986. *Economic report of the people.* Boston: South End Press.

Dillard, John. 1949. *Caste and class in a southern town.* New York: Doubleday.

Dye, Thomas. 2001. *Top down policymaking.* New York: Chatham House.

Ferguson, Thomas. 1995. *Golden rule: The investment theory of party competition and the logic of money-driven political systems.* Chicago: University of Chicago Press.

Friedman, Milton, and Rose Friedman. 1981. *Free to choose.* New York: Avon.

Gilder, George. 1981. *Wealth and poverty.* New York: Bantam Books.

Gramlich, Edward, Richard Kasten, and Frank Sammartino. 1994. In *Uneven tides: Rising inequality in America,* edited by Sheldon Danziger and Peter Gottschalk. New York: Russell Sage Foundation.

Hume, David. 1970. *Writings on economics,* edited by Eugene Rotwein. Madison: University of Wisconsin Press.

Karoly, Lynn. 1994. The trend in inequality among families, individuals, and workers in the United States: A twenty-five year perspective. In *Uneven tides: Rising inequality in America,* edited by Sheldon Danziger and Peter Gottschalk. New York: Russell Sage Foundation.

Keynes, John Maynard. 1923. *A tract on monetary reform.* London: Macmillan and Co., Ltd.

———. 1927. *The end of laissez-faire.* London: L. & Virginia Woolf; Dubuque, Iowa: Brown Reprint.

———. 1933. *The means to prosperity.* New York: Harcourt, Brace.

———. 1936. *The general theory of employment, interest and money.* London: Macmillan and Co.

Krugman, Paul. 1995. *Peddling prosperity.* New York: W.W. Norton.

Lekachman, Robert. 1966. *The age of Keynes.* New York: Random House.

———. 1976. *A history of economic ideas.* New York: McGraw-Hill.

Lindeen, James. 1994. *Governing America's economy.* Upper Saddle River, NJ: Prentice Hall.

Mill, John Stuart. 1897. *Principles of political economy.* London: D. Appleton and Company.

Phillips, Kevin. 1991. *The politics of rich and poor: Wealth and the American electorate in the Reagan aftermath.* New York: Harper Perennial.

Smith, Adam. 1776/1952. *An inquiry into the nature and causes of the wealth of nations.* Chicago: The University of Chicago, The Great Books Series.

Tobin, James. 1996. *Full employment and growth: Further Keynesian essays on policy.* Cheltenham, UK: Edward Elgar.

United States Office of Management and Budget. 2004. *Historical tables.* http://www.whitehouse.gov/omb/

U.S. Census Bureau. 2004/05. *Statistical abstract of the United States.* http://www.census.gov/prod/www/statistical-abstract-us.html

Weidenbaum, Murray. 1980. *The future of business regulations.* New York: AMACOM.

Chapter 15

Domhoff, William. 1996. *State autonomy or class dominance?: Case studies on policy making in America.* New York: Aldine de Gruyter.

Dye, Thomas. 2001. *Top down policymaking.* New York: Chatham House Publishers.

Hudson, William. 2001. *American democracy in peril: Seven challenges to America's future.* Chatham, NJ: Chatham House.

Ripley, Randall, and Grace Franklin. 1991. *Congress, the bureaucracy, and public policy.* Belmont, CA: Wadsworth.

Vogel, David. 1989. *Fluctuating fortunes: Political power of business in America.* New York: Basic Books.

Index

Page references with an *f* or a *t* indicate a figure and/or table on the designated page.